The City Book
The politics and planning of Canada's cities

The City Book
The politics and planning of Canada's cities

edited by James Lorimer and Evelyn Ross
with the editors of City Magazine

James Lorimer & Company, Publishers
Toronto 1976

ISBN 0-88862-102-7 paper
   0-88862-103-5 cloth

Design: Robert MacDonald
Cover photo: Ted Grant,
            Information Canada Photothèque

80 79 78 77 76 1 2 3 4 5

James Lorimer & Company, Publishers
35 Britain Street
Toronto

Printed and bound in Canada

Acknowledgements

The work of assembling this book has been modest, thanks to the original effort of the other editors of *City Magazine* in seeking out this material and carrying it through the inevitable revisions and changes to publication. They are Katherine Bladen, Ron Clark, Roda Contractor, Kent Gerecke, Donald Gutstein and Audrey Stewart.

The authors were commendably prompt in providing up-dates on their material, and we greatly appreciate their willingness to contribute to what has been a co-operative effort on the part of everyone involved.

J.L.
E.R.

Canadian Cataloguing in Publication Data

Main entry under title:

The City book

Contains a selection of articles which originally appeared in City magazine.
Bibilography: p.
ISBN 0-88862-103-5 bd. ISBN 0-88862-102-7 pa.

1. Cities and towns — Planning — Canada — Addresses, essays, lectures. I. Lorimer, James, 1942-   II. Ross, Evelyn, 1946-   III. City magazine.

HT169.C3C58   711',4'0971   C76-017013-4

Contents

Introduction

James Lorimer

This book offers a group of snapshots of urban Canada in the mid-seventies, case studies of specific projects, specific politicians, particular cities, representative urban experts. It is intended as a casebook which illustrates what is going on now in Canadian cities, a range of real-life examples of the processes and political forces which operate everywhere in this country.

The range the book covers is broad. There are chapters dealing with small, one-industry towns (for instance Timmins), small cities faced with considerable growth pressures (St. Catharines, Lucerne), medium-sized cities with a range of politics and problems (Halifax, Edmonton, Calgary, Winnipeg, Saskatoon), and the three largest cities (Vancouver, Toronto and Montreal) where the most intense pressures for growth have also produced the most vigorous politics and citizen opposition in the country.

The book also deals with virtually every major area of urban studies. Along with a discussion of land ownership and the urban property industry, there are studies of several different kinds of city politics — the traditional developer-oriented politics of Timmins and Nanaimo, an account of an unsuccessful attempt to mount a citizen-oriented reform group in Winnipeg, and descriptions of the background and politics of city politics in Toronto and Vancouver where moderate "reform" politicians have replaced the "old-guard" friends of the developers. There is a discussion of the role of experts in policy-making and implementation, critical examinations of the work of four important architects and planners, and a highly-critical discussion of the Canadian planning profession. The book includes three case studies of urban development projects, including downtown urban renewal, residential high-rise redevelopment, and a civic works project. And the final section is devoted to policy issues and analysis.

The breadth of coverage in this book, and the detailed knowledge of local situations which each of the chapters reflects, is possible only because the authors are in every case residents of the cities they are writing about, involved in urban matters through their work, critics of the civic status quo rather than apologists, and often — though not always — involved themselves in citizen groups and in opposing the development industry's program and politicians where they live.

Bringing together this material to produce a casebook on urban Canada results in a book with one obvious limitation. This book records what is happening in urban Canada. But it offers only a very limited response to the obvious question: why? Why, for example, are the few large land-banking developers in every city so successful in getting planning policies which push development their way? Why has the land development industry generally played such an important role in local politics? Why are powerful urban planners so often able to override citizen objections to their schemes? Why are downtowns being steadily demolished? Why does federal urban policy pay so little heed to local interests?

For an analysis of the basic forces at work in Canada's cities, for an explanation of why things happen as they do, readers of this casebook will have to turn elsewhere. The first place to go would be to the work of analysts who share the background of most of the contributors to this book, who have also been involved in citizen groups and "reform" politics, and who have attempted to work out the forces which lie behind this situation.

The best available book of this kind is Donald Gutstein's *Vancouver Ltd.* Published in 1975, this book takes apart the business establishment which is at the heart of Vancouver's economic life, and works out the stake in local political issues of the multinational corporations, the banks and other major national concentrations of economic power, and the local business establishments. It then shows how this business establishment, through the intermediary of first one political party and then a second, managed to capture and hold power at city hall and to obtain the policies and decisions which best suited its interests from sympathetic bureaucrats and planners. *Vancouver Ltd.* records some of the long history of citizen opposition to many of these policies and decisions and describes several issues where citizens confronted the established powers and won. Residents of Vancouver of course have a special interest in *Vancouver Ltd.* because it is describing their city, their history, their problems, their politicians and their business establishment. But the book is of much broader interest than this, because the structure and patterns which it describes apply to every Canadian city. Understanding why things happen as they do in Vancouver makes it far easier to understand why parallel things are going on everywhere else.

A second book which belongs to the same school of thought, and which offers an analytic framework for understanding city planning and politics, is my *Citizen's Guide to City Politics*. This book focuses on the key link between the land development industry and city government. The first part of the book is a comprehensive account of the urban property industry in Canada. It identifies all the various businesses, industries and professions which are involved in making money out of urban real estate, discusses in some detail the operation and profitability of the land development business, and sets out the basic common interests of the industry and the policies which it seeks from government at every level. The second major section of the book uses the examples of Toronto, Winnipeg and Vancouver to show how the industry usually can control city government and explains how this control determines the content of planning, transportation, housing and development policies found in Canada. City politics and policy-making have changed since 1972 when this book was published, particularly in those cities where the pressure from citizen groups has been most intense. The *Citizen's Guide* should be read along with material which updates its cases (the Gutstein chapter on TEAM in this book, the chapter on Winnipeg city politics, and the discussion of Toronto's recent housing policy) but its framework for understanding urban policies and politics has been verified and strengthened by the investigations and case studies of the last several years.

There is in fact a school of thought which has developed since the late 1960s in Canada to which this book, *Vancouver Ltd.* and the *Citizen's Guide* all belong. It is an empirical, informal and quite non-academic approach whose roots lie in the citizen organizations and "reform" groups which starting in the mid-sixties sprang up to oppose the most brutal and crude policies of city halls in a number of Canadian cities. There was nowhere for people involved in these groups and issues to turn where they could find their experiences of city politicians and city policies reflected and explained in print. The existing books on urban Canada had nothing to offer, and the literature on the United States, Britain and other countries did not speak directly to their experiences. Under considerable pressure to explain themselves and their political point of view, trying to make sense of their experiences and of the apparently inexplicable and irrational desire of city planners and city politicians to do things which hurt many ordinary people and did nothing obviously good for the city as a whole, the citizen opposition produced an analysis of urban Canada which made sense of their circumstances and experience.

This began with case studies recording, often incredulously, the real workings of city government. This included *The Real World of City Politics* (on Toronto city hall), *The Bad Trip* (an analysis of the Spadina Expressway), *Marlborough Marathon* (the story of a middle-class neighbourhood fighting against a developer), *Up Against City Hall* (the political autobiography of Toronto community organizer turned city politician John Sewell), *Toronto: For Sale?* (accounts of several controversial Toronto development projects), and — the best by far of all of these — *Fight Back*, a detailed and carefully-told account of the long struggle of residents in Toronto's Trefann Court area against the urban renewal project planned for them.

The case studies were followed by analytic works which identified the forces which lie behind the decisions and policies of city government. Two remarkably similar magazine-style books were published in Toronto and Vancouver in 1972, Vancouver's being *Forever Deceiving You*, Toronto's being *Rules of the Game*. The *Citizen's Guide* belongs to this group, as does *Highrise and Superprofits* published in 1973.

More recently, there have been further case studies published which build on the background of previous work and which are therefore considerably more sophisticated than the earlier work. The most interesting of these are *The Kitchener Market Fight*, *The Tiny Perfect Mayor* (an account of Toronto politics in the transitional 1972-74 years), and the previously mentioned *Vancouver Ltd.*

The growing number of books, articles and other publications which belong to this informal, empirical, reform-oriented approach to urban studies are of particular interest because they developed directly from the realities of Canadian politics and economics. Together they offer an analytic framework which is quite different from work in this area which has been done in other countries. On the whole, too, this work has been done outside the universities and has not involved the scholars who are doing research in urban studies. Because so many of the people teaching in this area have been educated abroad where this material is of course largely unknown, and because they come to Canada with their minds schooled in different approaches to urban studies, this Canadian literature is not so well-known and widely-used as it might be. Perhaps this book, with its obvious usefulness as a casebook in introductory courses in urban studies, will encourage the exploration of other material which takes a parallel approach to this subject area. A fuller listing of this material is provided in the bibliography which concludes the book.

There are, besides this empirical, reform-oriented literature, two other competing schools of thought in Canadian urban studies which offer quite different answers to the question posed by these case studies about why things happen as they do in Canadian cities. One of these is liberal-functionalist, taking its inspiration from American social science. It asserts the view that the urban world is made up of a diverse set of interest groups including businessmen, the media, professionals of various kinds, voluntary organizations, and political parties who interact with each other to produce political decisions. Some U.S. writers in this school have claimed that one interest group, identified as "business", dominates city government; others have suggested that a number of interests share influence. The classic example of an application of this theoretical framework to Canadian urban studies is Harold Kaplan's study of metropolitan government in Toronto, *Urban Political Systems.*

The other school of thought in Canadian urban studies is British and Tory in its intellectual roots, and arises out of the study of the legal framework of local government. Writers such as Crawford, Plunkett and Rowat pay particular attention to the institutional structure of government, and to the possibilities of change by means of structural reform. Some of these writers have themselves been instrumental in the design of legislation regarding municipal governments and in structural reforms like second-tier metropolitan government in Toronto and Winnipeg and the "unicity" structure developed for Winnipeg by the NDP government in 1971.

Whatever analysis one favours, however, there can be little quarrel with the value of detailed accounts of Canadian urban realities. This is what *The City Book* has to offer.

The chapters of this book are organized into five major sections. The first deals with land, because real property, its servicing, regulation, use and profitability is at the heart of every urban issue. The section begins with extracts from the most comprehensive study prepared on urban land in Canada, entitled "The Land Problem's Problem" and written by Peter Spurr for Central Mortgage

and Housing Corp. CMHC has been unwilling to publish Spurr's study or to permit its publication in full; what is included here are extracts of Spurr's discussion of the ownership of urban property and the developing trend towards concentration of ownership of land, particularly land suitable for development on the suburban fringe. Spurr's general analysis is followed by accounts of land ownership in a number of specific cities, and a documentation of the way in which planning policies are often tailored to the needs of local development corporations.

Land and suburban planning leads naturally to the subject of the second section of the book, which deals with city politics and politicians. There are case studies of traditional developer-dominated city governments, the new liberal approach represented by Vancouver's mayor Art Phillips and Toronto's David Crombie in the early 1970s, and of citizen-oriented reform politicians. Included is a detailed account of exactly how one such politician ran a successful campaign for office in 1974.

The third section of the book deals with the urban experts, the professionals who work for the property industry, city hall or (occasionally) citizen groups and who turn ideas and interests into projects, policies and programs. Along with a general article on the political content of the expertise of planners, architects and city bureaucrats, there are chapters on Waterloo super-planner Bill Thomson, corporate architect Arthur Erickson and reform architects Jack Diamond and Barton Myers. The section also includes a critical analysis of the politics of the Canadian planning profession.

The fourth section contains a number of case studies of representative public and private development projects. Montreal is dealt with in an article on demolition and redevelopment. Projects in Halifax, Saskatoon and Edmonton are also examined.

The fifth section contains three case studies of urban policies. The much-touted policy of urban land banking is examined in a case study of Saskatoon's highly-publicized land bank which concludes that the land bank has increased rather than decreased the profits of local developers and has been managed so that it has no significant downward effect on land and house prices in Saskatoon. An article on the Ontario Municipal Board, often regarded as the best friend of citizen groups in that province, analyses its decision-making record and concludes that this supposedly impartial tribunal is in fact much more favourable to local councils and developers than to citizens, and is a positive instrument for the implementation of the development-oriented urban policies of Ontario's provincial government. The section concludes with an analysis of the federal government's Neighbourhood Improvement Program with case studies of its operation in Vancouver, Calgary and Toronto, and concludes that there is an enormous gap between rhetoric and reality in this latest version of federally-supported urban renewal.

The book concludes with a selected bibliography by *City Magazine* editor Kent Gerecke which lists with brief annotations the Canadian reform-oriented literature on urban studies.

How this book came about is a good example of the way in which the reform, citizen-oriented school of urban analysis itself has developed in this country. The chapters of this book all appeared originally in the pages of *City Magazine*, a periodical which began publication in summer 1974. It originated from a chance meeting in 1974 among half a dozen people who had quite different backgrounds but who shared an interest in developing a critical perspective on the work of urban professionals in Canada and on the urban policies and programs of government. Budgetted to operate on a shoestring, the magazine's first few issues were supported by a start-up grant from the Canadian Council of Urban and Regional Research. The funds were sufficient just to cover printing and mailing costs, contributors received no payment for their work, and the editors worked for nothing.

Since the magazine was launched, the editorial group has been enlarged both in terms of geographical background and in interests to better represent the audience which the magazine aims at. The editors live in Ottawa, Toronto, Winnipeg, Regina and Vancouver. Amongst them are practicing city planners, teachers of city planning, architects, and analysts and participants in city politics. They write for the magazine themselves and they look for ideas for articles and for contributors across the country.

After almost two years of publication, the magazine has almost reached the point of being financially self-sustaining (though it still relies solely on unpaid writers and editors). The bulk of its income comes from subscriptions, though as a regular medium of communication among people interested in urban matters in Canada it is attracting a certain amount of advertising from book publishers, conference organizers, and employers with jobs vacant. It has survived the first year or two, when the health of any new periodical is always the most precarious, and is now sufficiently well established that it operates on a firm basis. The publication of this book will be a further benefit to the magazine, because royalties are being divided 50-50 between the contributors and the magazine.

City Magazine was only possible because earlier books and writings had developed an audience for critical, reform-oriented publications on urban issues in Canada. It also depended to some extent on the encouragement and participation of the authors of those books, and on others who found their common ground in terms of outlook and analysis through those books. Now the magazine itself is taking the work of these writers a major step forward, bringing together material from a wide range of cities (whereas the books have been Toronto-centred in their orientation), permitting the updating and revision of analysis as events change (like the discussion of the new wave in city politics since 1972 represented by Mayors Crombie and Phillips), and expanding the range of interest from its original focus on city politics and neighbourhood planning to a broader analysis of the property industry, regional planning and architecture.

Publishing these articles from *City Magazine* in book form makes this wider, more up-to-date material much more accessible for people interested in urban studies in Canada. It will also introduce *City Magazine* to a wider audience, and speed the process of developing this medium so that it reaches more of the people whose interests or whose work involves them with this subject.

Those of us who have been involved in developing an independent, critical analysis of urban Canada see the effort as being much like a barn-raising. It is a communal effort, leading to something which no one individual could accomplish on his own. Each of us builds on what others have done, and depend on that previous work. Indeed how much we can do individually is very much a consequence of how much other people are doing. And we are all able to learn from mistakes, both those we ourselves make and those that others have made. More people are always welcome to join in the work, and indeed are badly needed. There are no mysteries for newcomers to be initiated in. People become part of the effort by pitching in and beginning to do their own work.

Quite a lot is known about how Canadian cities work, and what is being done to them by developers, property owners, planners and governments. But there is much more to find out, and much more to learn about how the role of established property interests can be reduced and that of ordinary citizens increased. This book should give you a good picture of what is happening across the country; hopefully it will encourage you to help in completing that picture, and in finding ways to change it.

I Land

The urban land monopoly

Peter Spurr

What follows are extracts from an unpublished research paper titled "The Land Problem's Problem" prepared by Peter Spurr for Central Mortgage and Housing Corp.

The report was delivered to CMHC in August 1974. Numbered copies were circulated to outside researchers and academics for their comments, but the report has not been officially released by CMHC. The first public word of its existence came in late September 1975 in an article in the *Globe and Mail* by Graham Fraser. Interviewed later by Fraser, Spurr said that the report was not secret and that copies are on deposit in CMHC office libraries across the country.

Though it is written in dry, often technical language and though the analysis of the report is not always easy to follow, this document is a blockbuster. It presents a vast array of data never before available to outside investigators. Spurr offers a goldmine of detailed reliable information on land, development, developers, financing, public land and housing programmes, profits, prices and many other subjects.

For readers who are not thoroughly conversant with the technical language and approach used by Spurr, the major difficulty about his work is the way in which the facts are hardly let to speak for themselves. Many of his most startling finds are understated and underplayed — as for instance his statistics demonstrating that in 1972-3 more than half the cost of house lots in Toronto and Vancouver were pure profit accruing to developers and speculators. Or that the average tenant in a privately-owned rent row house pays *72 per cent more rent* than the average tenant in a non-profit row house. This list could go on and on.

In the excerpts printed here, the structure of the land development industry is spelled out in enormous detail. There is comprehensive information on corporate ownership (including foreign ownership), land assemblies, and the monopoly of new land for development which a few large firms have assembled in most large cities. There is also a discussion of the housing rental business, and of developer land banks.

Spurr's report contains much more useful information, and will be invaluable to the many people across Canada interested in one way or another in the development industry and in urban planning. One way or another, copies of this report should be available soon to people who weren't on the select list receiving numbered copies from CMHC. If you'd like a copy, write to *City Magazine* and we'll let you know as soon as it becomes available. —J.L.

This overview of private development focuses on about sixty firms which produce most of the new residential land in metropolitan Canada. It examines their position in the development industry, their characteristics and activities, a survey of their assets, and a sample of their operations. It shows private development corporations are well organized, diversified, vertically and horizontally integrated, long-term producers who have and can hold a major share of the land markets in metropolitan areas.

It is estimated that the land development industry in Canada now comprises 1300 firms, about 400 of which operate in metropolitan areas. The Housing and Urban Development Association of Canada, which consists primarily of builders, had 1305 members in metropolitan Canada in 1973, from a total of 4000 member firms and individuals.[1] If this membership parallels the structure found in an earlier sample,[2] about 400 HUDAC members, including 120 large firms, develop land in metropolitan areas. The Urban Development Institute includes only developers, and has 140 member firms, all of which are located in metropolitan areas, and one-half of which have head offices in

"Headway Corporation has 1252 acres in seven cities. This includes 190 acres in Thunder Bay . . . 'giving it a virtual monopoly on land sales'."

Toronto.[3] The association of the largest developers, the Canadian Institute of Public Real Estate Companies is also metropolitan based and has 23 members. It appears, then, that about 30 per cent of the total land development industry operates in metropolitan areas, including nearly all of the large firms. There are probably 120 to 140 of these large firms active in metropolitan Canada, and while they comprise about 30 per cent of metropolitan producers, they probably account for over three-quarters of metropolitan lot production.

This examination is focused on about sixty of the largest metropolitan developers. The size and composition of this sample primarily reflect the availability of data — although it is likely that it includes all of the major developers in Canada. Data was obtained from a variety of sources — the firms themselves, their annual reports and investment prospectuses, trade magazines, planning studies, and newspaper reports. Most of the data was assembled as part of the Development Corporation Survey, an assemblage of information concerning the assets, operating locales, and ownerships of sixty firms. The survey is not exclusive — it reports those assets described in the sources listed, but the completeness of this coverage varies from firm to firm. This section describes the assets, and particularly the land held by the firms, comments on their significance, then integrates this data into an overview of the metropolitan private development industry.

Table 1 lists the major assets found in the survey, owned by sixty development firms in twenty-four different metropolitan areas. Forty-seven firms hold 119,192 acres (186 square miles) of land, including 34 firms which each own more than one square mile. Forty-five firms own 50 per cent or more of 272 subsidiary companies, and 21 of them have lesser proportions of ownership of 103 affiliated firms. Forty-two firms hold 95,174 apartment units, including 13 firms with 123 apartment buildings. Twenty-nine firms have 223 office and other commercial buildings, while 23 firms have nearly 26,000,000 square feet of commercial space. While these commercial and apartment figures may appear large, the survey is particularly incomplete in these areas.[4] Finally, twenty-seven firms have 185 shopping centres and sixteen firms own 38 hotels. Despite its incompleteness, this summary demonstrates that Canada's largest develop-

ers have immense holdings of real property, with considerable diversity in the largest firm's portfolios and marked specialization in the assets of a few firms.

A few examples provide perspective on the significance of these holdings, as their relevance is easily lost in a numerical aggregation like Table 1. In the "Acreage Held" column, Headway Corporation has 1252 acres in seven cities. This includes 1190 acres in Thunder Bay, a holding which, according to the Canadian Council on Social Development, is ". . . giving it a virtual monopoly on land sales."[5] Minto Construction owns about 8000 apartment units, most of which are located in suburban Nepean Township, which had a total of 5775 occupied rental dwellings in 1971.[6] The data on commercial buildings and space underscores the giant towers with which firms like Campeau, Trizec, Olympia and York, Marathon and Cemp have catalyzed the rebuilding of the cores of first Montreal and Toronto, then Vancouver, Calgary, Edmonton, Winnipeg, Ottawa and Halifax, during the last decade. Finally, the 185 shopping centres surveyed include most of the huge suburban regional centres which drastically changed Canadian shopping patterns during the last generation. The real impact of the large developers' operations on urban life, from city form to living, shopping, working and recreational activities is not quantifiable but lies below the surface of the large numbers in Table 1.

Table 2 gives some perspective on the size and operations of these major developers. It is a summary of the total value of assets, gross revenue and source of profit, of thirty of Canada's largest developers. Twenty-six of these firms are included in the Development Corporations Survey, and, as all the firms in this table have assets valued in excess of $18-million, all are members of the top 0.8 per cent category of real estate operators and developers in Canada. The firms have a total asset holding which is valued, conservatively, at $2.3-billion, and generate gross annual revenues exceeding one-half billion dollars. The source of these revenues varies among firms, between two main operating functions — property sales and income property. In general, the firms having the largest gross revenues and the most valuable asset inventories are income property operators like Trizec, Campeau, Bramalea, Allarco and Cadillac. A few of these operators, Trizec, MEPC, Y & R, Halifax and Canadian Allied, have specialized to the exclusion of sales, but most of them, and developers generally, operate in both revenue property and sales functions. The selling firms are also the suburban land developers, and the largest of these, Western, McLaughlin, and Markborough have assets and multiple operations at a scale slightly smaller than the larger income operators. The medium-sized selling firms — Costain, Headway, Nu-West,

Table 1 Development Corporations Survey 1973
Summary of Real Property Holdings

NAME OF FIRM (ABBREVIATED)	NUMBER OF CITIES AFFECTED	ACREAGE HELD	APARTMENTS HELD		COMMERCIAL SPACE HELD		HOTELS	SHOPPING CENTRES	SUBSIDIARIES (FIRM OWNS OVER 50%)	AFFILIATES (FIRM OWNS UNDER 50%)
			BLDGS.	UNITS	BLDGS.	SQ. FEET				
BLOCK	2	UK	UK	2,030	UK	175,400	UK	UK	14	UK
CEMP/FAIRVIEW	9	UK	UK	UK	14	UK	UK	16	2	4
CITY PARKING	7	UK	UK	UK	UK	UK	1	UK	1	UK
CONCORDIA	2	UK	UK	4,000	1	UK	2	UK	9	UK
CORPORATE	4	UK	UK	309	3	40,000	UK	5	11	UK
GREENWIN	1	UK	UK	10,000	UK	UK	UK	UK	7	UK
HALIFAX	1	UK	UK	306	5	154,000	1	UK	2	0
MANUFACTURERS	9	UK	11	3,205	6	UK	UK	UK	UK	UK
MORENISH	1	UK	3	590	45	UK	UK	UK	2	3
OLYMPIA & YORK	2	UK	UK	UK	8	UK	UK	UK	3	UK
TRIZEC	12	UK	7	1,666	38	9,448,855	7	14	9	UK
Y & F	2	UK	UK	UK	4	UK	UK	UK	5	2
MCLAUGHLIN	1	9,265	UK	1,800	1	UK	UK	1	10	UK
ALLARCO	4	8,803	UK	3,000	UK	286,000	10	3	6	8
REVENUE	3	7,724	UK	1,635	UK	882,000	UK	UK	4	UK
CAMPEAU	13	7,000	13	3,091	14	6,677,608	2	12	22	UK
CANADIAN EQUITY	3	6,908	UK	454	2	398,000	UK	5	3	UK
WESTERN	5	6,130	11	3,368	10	482,092	5	12	6	16
BRAMALEA	12	5,955	6	774	5	253,000	UK	4	5	12
GREAT NORTHERN	9	5,294	4	623	2	239,000	1	4	5	0
MARKBOROUGH	2	4,898	UK	2,210	9	934,000	1	UK	2	UK
CARMA	2	4,590	UK	UK	UK	UK	UK	UK	1	UK
RUNNYMEDE	1	4,100	UK	UK	UK	UK	UK	UK	UK	UK
QUALICO	3	4,000	UK	300	UK	UK	UK	UK	UK	3
BACM	2	3,532	UK	UK	UK	UK	UK	UK	14	0
MELTON	2	3,258	UK	459	UK	192,108	UK	UK	UK	1
BRITISH	1	2,800	UK	UK	UK	UK	UK	UK	UK	UK
NU-WEST	3	2,691	UK	718	UK	UK	UK	UK	4	5
MAJOR	1	2,600	UK	544	4	270,900	UK	3	UK	UK
MONARCH	5	2,535	UK	528	5	264,875	1	2	7	1
DAWSON	3	2,300	UK	700	2	335,000	UK	UK	11	1
ALLIANCE	4	2,256	UK	1,185	3	UK	UK	3	3	16
COSTAIN	5	2,218	3	353	UK	UK	UK	UK	2	2
CALEDON MT. ESTATES	1	2,100	0	0	0	0	0	0	0	0
GEORGE WIMPEY	4	1,897	UK	3,750	UK	UK	UK	UK	UK	UK
WALL & REDEKOP	1	1,694	UK	1,600	UK	UK	UK	UK	11	
PINETREE	2	1,564	UK	1,423	UK	405,850	UK	UK	UK	UK
ST. LAWRENCE	2	1,435	UK	UK	UK	UK	UK	1	8	UK
LADCO	1	1,426	UK	UK	UK	UK	UK	UK	5	2
HEADWAY	7	1,252	11	2,076	UK	UK	1	5	12	2
SIFTON	3	1,120	UK	800	UK	UK	UK	2	UK	UK
GRT. YORK GP.	5	1,000	UK	UK	2	UK	1	18	4	UK
CLAYTON	1	970	UK	1,100	UK	UK	UK	UK	UK	UK
MACLAB	1	900	UK	2,623	4	UK	UK	6	UK	5
MINTO	1	758	UK	8,000	UK	UK	0	1	UK	UK
BUILDEVCO	1	700	UK	UK	UK	UK	UK	1	UK	UK
NORTH AMERICAN	12	550	9	1,955	4	UK	1	3	2	UK
GROSVENOR - LAING	2	500	UK	UK	2	UK	UK	2	6	1
TRANS-NATION	2	477	UK	UK	UK	UK	UK	UK	3	UK
CADILLAC	5	325	42	15,168	4	561,500	UK	12	11	UK
CAMBRIDGE	8	301	UK	UK	UK	UK	UK	20	3	UK
METRO STRUCTURES	1	300	BLDGS.	4,000	5	200,000	1	UK	UK	UK
CONSOLIDATED	1	220	UK	2,552	UK	UK	UK	UK	4	3
MARATHON	6	217	UK	1,027	8	1,400,000	1	21	11	9
ASSALY	1	214	UK	UK	UK	UK	UK	UK	UK	UK
HAMBROS	2	107	UK	1,268	UK	UK	UK	3	5	3
ORLANDO	5	100	1	374	15	2,945,000	1	5	2	1
CONCORD GROUP	1	96	UK	30	UK	16,000	1	UK	5	UK
KAUFMAN & BROAD	1	82	UK	1,080	1	25,000	UK	UK	4	UK
PARAGON	2	30	2	2,500	1	37,000	UK	1	6	3
ALL HOLDINGS - 60		119,192	123	95,174	223	26,623,188	38	185	272	103
ACREAGE - 47		119,192								
APT. BLDGS. - 13			123							
APT. UNITS - 42				95,174						
COMM. BLDG. - 29					223					
COMM. UNITS - 23						26,623,188				
HOTELS - 16							38			
SHOPPING CENTRES - 27								185		
SUBSIDIARIES - 45									272	
AFFILIATES - 21										103

SOURCE: Development Corporations Survey - 1973. See Table A-9.

NOTE: UK indicates unknown.

Table 2 Selected Statistics, 30 Canadian Real Estate Developers, 1970, 1971

FIRM NAME (ABBREVIATED)	ASSETS IN MILLIONS OF DOLLARS 1971	1970	GROSS REVENUE IN MILLIONS OF DOLLARS 1971	1970	RANK ORDER 1971	1970	AS % OF ASSETS % 1971	1970	RANK ORDER 1971	1970	SOURCE OF OPERATING PROFIT — PROPERTY RENTAL 1971	(1970)	SALES 1971	(1970)	OTHER 1971	(1970)
TRIZEC*	$516.	$480.	$77.5	$94.0	2	1	15.0	19.6	21	17	98%	(80%)		26	2%	(20%)
CAMPEAU*	298	272	78.1	61.9	1	2	26.2	22.7	14	15	35	42	24	25	41	32
CADILLAC*	272	237	34.7	30.0	6	4	12.8	13.2	25	20	73	72	15	1	12	3
MEPC	95	80	10.7	7.9	19	17	11.3	9.8	26	25	100	99				16
BRAMALEA*	93	81	44.6	27.6	3	6	48.0	34.1	8	10	8	2	69	82	23	16
WESTERN*	88	67	17.1	15.7	12	7	19.4	23.4	18	14	16	22	57	55	27	23
McLAUGHLIN*	87	65	21.4	2.0	8	27	24.6	3.1	15	30			95	77	5	23
MARKBOROUGH*	76	59	8.6	9.0	21	16	11.3	15.2	27	19	57	42	37	46	6	12
ALLARCO*	66	62	38.9	38.2	4	3	58.9	61.6	6	4	68	37	8	23	24	40
BLOCK*	63	55	17.7	13.6	10	10	28.1	24.7	13	13	26	13	15	22	59	65
CAN. EQUITY*	57	42	7.7	4.2	22	23	13.5	10.0	23	24	47	54	49	37	4	9
Y & R*	54	44	12.1	9.3	16	15	22.4	21.1	17	16	94	90	6	6		4
NU-WEST*	48	28	38.1	28.2	5	5	79.4	100.7	3	1	15	15	81	81	4	4
ORLANDO*	43	28	15.1	11.7	13	13	35.1	41.7	11	8	46	27	19	39	35	34
CAN.GOLDALE*	41	54	6.8	6.5	23	19	16.6	12.0	19	22	34	13	31	40	35	47
HALIFAX*	37	36	3.3	2.2	28	26	8.9	6.1	28	29	100	98		2		
PEEL-ELDER	36	28	5.9	5.3	25	22	16.4	18.9	20	18	58	61	34		8	11
CAMBRIDGE*	35	31	4.6	3.9	26	24	13.1	12.6	24	21	74	92	12		14	8
DAWSON*	35	25	26.1	15.3	7	8	74.6	61.2	4	5	14	7	74		12	80
WALL & REDEKOP*	30	25	12.3	13.5	15	12	41.0	54.0	10	6	14		24	20	62	9
IMPERIAL GEN.	29	25	9.7	1.9	20	28	33.4	7.6	12	28	55	91	34		11	
SIFTON*	28	20	6.7	5.5	24	21	23.9	27.5	16	12	36	44	64	56		
MONARCH*	26	22	11.5	10.2	17	14	44.2	46.4	9	7	28		53	86	19	14
COSTAIN*	24	22	20.2	13.6	9	11	84.2	61.8	1	3			88	61	10	39
CONSOLIDATED*	24	20	14.8	7.7	14	18	61.7	38.5	5	9	20	39	70	76	10	24
MAJOR*	23	21	3.4	2.3	27	25	14.8	10.9	22	23	5		77	84	18	16
PARAGON*	22	19	11.0	6.4	18	20	50.0	33.7	7	2	-23	6	80	94	43	
HEADWAY*	21	15	17.3	14.6	11	9	82.4	97.3	2	2	7	6	78	79	15	21
CORPORATE*	19	11	1.3	1.0	30	30	6.8	9.1	30	26	42	94	41		17	6
CAN.ALLIED	18	17	1.6	1.5	29	29	8.9	8.8	29	27	100	94				
TOTALS AND AVERAGES																
–Subtotal *26	$2,126.	$1,841.	$550.9	$448.1			25.9	24.3			9	8	12	14	4	4
–All –30	$2,304.	$1,991.	$578.8	$464.7			25.1	23.3			13	12	13	14	4	4
AVERAGES –30	$76.8	$66.4	$19.3	$15.5			25.1	23.3								

SOURCE: A.E. Ames & Co. LTD. in Canadian Real Estate Annual 1971 and 1972 editions, pages 70 and 97, respectively. Underlined percentages in "Source of Operating Profit" columns are the dominant sources of operating profit in that year.

NOTE: *Indicates inclusion in Development Corporations Survey.

Table 3 Development Corporations Survey Summary of Holdings, by City

CITY	NAME OF FIRM (ABBREVIATED)	ACRES	APARTMENTS BLDGS.	UNITS	COMMERCIAL BLDGS.	SQ. FT.	HOTELS	SHOPPING CENTRES
Halifax – Dartmouth	Trizec		4	826	2	147,100		2
	Halifax			306	5	154,000	1	
	Clayton	970		1,100				
	North American		2	234				
	Manufacturers Life		1	55				
	(5)	970	7	2,521	7	301,100	1	2
Quebec	Trizec				2	380,000	1	
	Cadillac						1	2
	Concordia							
	North American		1	45				
	Great Northern						1	
	Headway		1	786				
	Gtr. York Group							2
	(7)	0	2	831	2	380,000	3	4
Montreal	Trizec				14	5,480,650		2
	Campeau	146	2	267	3	351,513		2
	Cemp/Fairview				9			4
	Bramalea	365						
	Concordia			4,000	1		1	
	Monarch	935			2			1
	Marathon							
	North American		1	415				
	Metro Structures	300		4,000	5	200,000	1	
	St. Lawrence	1,435						
	Revenue					886,000		
	Great Northern	305						1
	Manufacturers Life		2	1,137				
	(13)	3,486	5	9,819	34	6,918,163	2	10
Ottawa – Hull	Trizec		2	510				1
	Campeau	6,945	11	2,773	4	1,676,500	2	2
	Cadillac	4	2	488				2
	Bramalea	11						
	Costain	826	3	353				
	Minto	758		8,000				
	North American		2	728				
	St. Lawrence							1
	Great Northern	261						
	Manufacturers Life		1	108				
	George Wimpey	397						
	Alliance			394				
	Cambridge							3
	City Parking					1		
	Gtr. York Group				3			1
	Olympia & York							
	Assaly	214						
	(17)	9,416	21	13,354	7	1,676,500	3	10
Kingston	Trizec				1	35,000		1
	Campeau				1	12,510		1
	Orlando							1
	Headway	34	1	676				1
	(4)	34	1	676	2	47,510		3
Peterborough	Marathon	6					1	1
	Headway							1
	(2)	6	0	0	0	0	0	1
Oshawa	Campeau				1	83,414		2
	Cadillac	20						
	North American		1	147				
	Orlando							1
	Cambridge							1
	(5)	20	1	147	1	83,414		4
Hamilton	Cadillac	41	1	175				2
	Canadian Equity	30						1
	Cemp/Fairview							1
	Bramalea	76						1
	Monarch			128	2	145,448	1	
	Great Northern	454						
	Manufacturers Life		1	280				
	Cambridge							1
	Gtr. York Group							1
	(9)	601	2	583	2	145,448	1	7
Guelph	Bramalea	242						
	Sifton	120		800				1
	(2)	362	0	800	0	0	0	1

CITY	NAME OF FIRM (ABBREVIATED)	ACRES	APARTMENTS BLDGS.	UNITS	COMMERCIAL BLDGS.	SQ. FT.	HOTELS	SHOPPING CENTRES
Kitchener – Waterloo	Campeau				1	5,742		1
	Cemp/Fairview	10						
	Costain	368						
	Major	2,600		544	4	270,900		3
	Buildevco	474						1
	Monarch	262						
	George Wimpey	65						
	Alliance	20		502				1
	Cambridge							1
	(10)	3,799	0	1,046	5	2,766,642	0	7
St. Catherines	Cemp/Fairview	116						1
	Costain							
	Cambridge							1
	(3)	116	0	0	0	0	0	2
London	Campeau							1
	Bramalea	1						1
	Sifton	1,000						1
	Monarch	400			1			
	Orlando							1
	Alliance							1
	(6)	1,401	0	0	1	0	0	4
Sarnia	North American							1
	Orlando							1
	Cambridge							1
	(3)	0	0	0	0	0	0	3
Windsor	Campeau							1
	George Wimpey	270						6
	Cambridge							7
	(3)	270	0	0	0	0	0	7
Thunder Bay	Campeau							1
	Cadillac							1
	Headway	1,190	6	307			1	3
	Gtr. York Group							1
	(4)	1,190	6	307	0	0	1	6
Winnipeg	Cemp/Fairview							1
	BACM Ltd.	2,032						
	North American							2
	Great Northern		1	203				
	Manufacturers Life		1	240				
	Headway	22	1	40				
	Ladco	1,426						
	(7)	3,480	3	483	0	0	0	3
Brandon	Trizec							1
Regina	Trizec							1
	Campeau				2	32,096		1
	Western	39	1	107	2	151,000		
	Corporate							2
	Markborough				2		1	
	North American				2			
	(6)	39	1	107	8	183,096	2	4
Saskatoon	Trizec							1
	Great Northern	234						
	(2)	234	0	0	0	0	0	1
Edmonton	Trizec				5	798,205		
	Cemp/Fairview	158						1
	Nu-West	44						
	Bramalea							
	Western	3,923	3	1,248	3	162,000	1	4
	Dawson	58						
	Paragon				1	37,000		1
	MacLab	911		2,623	4			6
	BACM Ltd.	1,500						
	Corporate				1	40,000		
	Marathon							1
	Great Northern	2,807	1	133				
	Allarco	8,803						
	Block	1,815		459		4,600		
	Melton					192,108		14
	(15)	20,019	4	4,483	14	1,233,913	1	14

CITY	NAME OF FIRM (ABBREVIATED)	ACRES	APARTMENTS BLDGS.	UNITS	COMMERCIAL BLDGS.	SQ. FT.	HOTELS	SHOPPING CENTRES
Calgary	Trizec		1	330	12	1,626,400	1	1
	Campeau	37			1	66,209		
	Cemp/Fairview							1
	Nu-West	1,759						
	Bramalea	211						
	Western	2,063	4	1,454	4	169,000	3	8
	Dawson	1,400						
	Paragon	30						
	Qualico			300				
	Corporate			309				
	Marathon			202	3			1
	Great Northern				1	75,000		
	Manufacturers Life		1	52	1			
	Headway		2	267				
	Carma	4,500						
	Melton	920						
	(16)	10,920	8	2,914	22	1,936,609	4	11
Victoria	Campeau							1
	Grosvenor-Liang							1
	Concord Group	96		30		16,000		
	North American		1	120			1	2
	(4)	96	1	150	0	16,000	1	2
Vancouver	Trizec				1	740,000	2	2
	Campeau				1	67,420		
	Cemp/Fairview				1			
	Nu-West	103						
	Bramalea	54						
	Western	757	3	559	1	92	1	
	Grosvenor-Liang	500			2			1
	Dawson	394						
	British	2,800						
	Marathon	125		605	1	25,000		2
	North American		1	266	1			
	Wall & Redekop	612		1,600				
	Manufacturers Life	90	1	150				
	Carma							
	Block			1,254		170,800		
	(15)	5,435	5	4,434	8	1,003,312	3	5
Toronto -General	Trizec	14			1	241,500	1	1
	Campeau		33	13,715				3
	Cadillac							1
	Canadian Equity	200		454	2	398,000		6
	Cemp/Fairview				4			
	Bramalea	229	1	91	1			
	Kaufman & Broad	1,080			1	25,000		
	Monarch	13		400	1	119,427		
	Corporate				2			2
	Marathon	92			2			
	Pinetree	812		329	7	405,850		
	Markborough			1,785	7	624,000		
	North American	550			1			
	Revenue	24						
	Hambros	62		1,268				
	Consolidated	100		1,557				
	Great Northern				1	164,000		1
	Orlando				15	1,578,000		1
	Greenwin			10,000				
	Manufacturers Life	230	3	707	5			
	George Wimpey			2,000				
	Headway							1
	Alliance	230		239	3			3
	Cambridge							1
	Gtr. York Group							2
	Morenish		3	590	45			
	Olympia & York				5			
	Y & R				4			
	(27)	2,326	40	24,216	99	3,555,777	2	21
Toronto -Ajax	Bramalea							1
	Consolidated			595				
	Great Northern	34						
	George Wimpey	950		1,750				
	Alliance							1
	(5)	984	0	34,215	0	0	0	1

CITY	NAME OF FIRM (ABBREVIATED)	ACRES	APARTMENTS BLDGS.	UNITS	COMMERCIAL BLDGS.	SQ. F.	HOTELS	SHOPPING CENTRES
Toronto -Pickering	Bramalea	745	1	97				
	Revenue	1,100						
	Runnymede	3,960						
	(3)	5,805	1	97	0	0	0	0
Toronto -Uxbridge	Revenue	6,600						
Toronto -Markham	Cadillac	125						
	Markborough	858						
	Great Northern	161	1	54				1
	(3)	1,144	1	54	0	0	0	1
Toronto -Richmond Hill	Cadillac	45						1
Toronto -Unionville	Bramalea	696						
	Monarch	505						
	(2)	1,201	0	0	0	0	0	0
Toronto -Brampton	Cadillac		1	246				2
	Bramalea	3,258	3	510	5	253,000		1
	Hambros	23						1
	Cambridge							1
	Gtr. York							5
	(5)	3,281	4	756	5	253,000	0	5
Toronto -Mississauga	Cadillac	90						3
	Canadian Equity	6,678						
	Bramalea	3						
	Trans-Nation	317						
	Markborough	3,900						
	McLaughlin	2,400		1,800	1			1
	Hambros	22						1
	Orlando	100					1	
	(8)	13,510	1	1,800	1	0	1	6
Toronto -Caledon Hills	Caledon Mt. Estates	2,100						
Toronto -Georgetown	McLaughlin	1,026						
Toronto -Oakville	Consolidated	120						
	Great Northern	1,038						
	(2)	1,158	0	0	0	0	0	1
Toronto -Scarborough	Cadillac		4	326				
	Western	260						
	Costain	396						
	Kaufman & Broad	82						
	Monarch	420						
	Markborough	140		425	1	310,000		1
	Runnymede	140						
	George Wimpey	396						
	(9)	1,834	4	751	1	310,000	0	2
Toronto -Etobicoke	Cadillac		1	464				
	Bramalea		1	76				
	Monarch							
	Corporate							1
	Trans-Nation	160						1
	McLaughlin	14						
	Gtr. Northern		1	233				
	Orlando		1	374			1	
	Alliance			50				
	(9)	174	4	1,197	0	0	0	2
Toronto -CBD	Cadillac				4	561,500		
	Bramalea	10		400				
	Consolidated							
	Cambridge							1
	Gtr. York Group				2		1	
	(5)	10	0	400	6	561,500	1	1

Table 4 Development Corporations Survey Concentration of Corporate Holdings at Head Office Location

URBAN REGION HEAD OFFICE	FIRM NAME	ACREAGE	AS %	APT. BLDG.	AS %	APT. UNITS	AS %	COMMERCIAL BLDGS.	AS %	COMMERCIAL SQUARE FT.	AS %	HOTELS	AS %	SHOPPING CENTRES	AS %
HALIFAX	Halifax					306	100%	5	100%	154,000	100%				
	Clayton	970	100%			1,100	100								
MONTREAL	Trizec							14	37	5,480,650	58			2	14%
	Cemp/Fairview							9	64					4	25
	Concordia					4,000	100	1	100			1	50%		
	Metro Structures	300	100			4,000	100	5	100	200,000	100	1	100		
	St. Lawrence	1,435	100												
OTTAWA	Campeau	6,804	97	11	85	2,773	89	4	28	1,676,500	25	2	100	2	17
	Minto	758	100			8,000	100							1	100
	Assaly	214	100											3	25
TORONTO	Cadillac	260	80	33	78	13,715	90							4	80
	Cdn. Equity	6,878	99			454	100	2	100	398,000	100				
	Bramalea	4,941	83	1	16	91	12								
	Kaufman & Broad					1,080	100	1	100	25,000	100			2	100
	Monarch	938	37			400	76	2	40	119,427	45			2	40
	Corporate							2	67						
	Pinetree	812	52			329	23	7	77	405,850	100				
	Markborough	4,898	100			2,210	100	1	25	624,000	67	1	100		
	N. American	550	100												
	Revenue	7,724	100			1,635	100							3	100
	Hambros	107	100			1,268	100								
	Consolidated	220	100			2,552	100							2	50
	Great Northern	1,233	23	2	50	287	46	1	50	164,000	69	1	100	1	20
	Orlando	100	100	1	100	374	100	15	100	1,578,000	54				
	Caledon Mt.	2,100	100												
	Greenwin					10,000	100								
	Manufacturers Life			3	27	707	22	5	83						
	Wimpey	396	21			3,750	100							1	33
	Alliance	1,180	52			289	25	3	100					2	10
	Cambridge							2	100			1	100	3	17
	Grt. York	1,000	100					45	100						
	Morenish			3	100	590	100	5	82						
	Olympia & York							4	100						
	Y & R														
	Costain	396	18												
	Trans-Nation	477	100			1,800	100	1	100					1	100
	McLaughlin	9,265	100												
	Runneymede	4,100	100			544	100	4	100	270,900	100			3	100
KITCHENER	Major	2,600	100											1	100
	Buildevco	474	68											1	50
LONDON	Sifton	1,000	89									1	100	3	60
THUNDER BAY	Headway	1,190	95	6	55	307	15								
WINNIPEG	Ladco	1,426	100												
	BACM	2,032	57												
EDMONTON	Western	3,923	64	3	27	1,248	37	9	90	162,044	33	1	20	4	33
	Allarco	8,803	100			2,092	69			286,000	100	10	100	3	100
	Melton	815	25			459	100			192,108	100				
CALGARY	Nu-West	1,759	65												
	Paragon	30	100												
	Qualico	2,500	62			202	20	3	37						
	Marathon													1	5
	Carma	4,500	98							1,160,000	100				
VICTORIA	Concord	96	100			30	100							1	50
VANCOUVER	Grosvenor-Laing	500	100					2	100						
	Dawson	394	17			700	100	2	100						
	British	2,800	100												
	Wall & Redekop	1,694	100			1,600	100								
	Block					1,254	62			170,800	97				

Table 5 Development Corporations Survey Development Projections — Various Firms

CITY	STATED DEVELOPMENT FIRM NAME (ABBREVIATED)	DEVELOPMENT PROJECTIONS PLOT SIZE (ACRES)	PLANNED HOUSES	TOTAL UNITS	TOTAL POPULATION
Halifax	Clayton	535	3,500	2,000	50,000
		400		1,000	50,000
	(1)	970	3,500	3,000	
Montreal	Campeau	146		8,000	59,500
	Metro Structures	300		15,000	49,500
	(2)	446		23,000	108,500
Ottawa	Campeau	120	1,000	600	10,000
		325		2,700	10,000
Toronto -General	Costain	2,600		3,300	
		769	1,000		
	(2)	3,814			
Toronto -Pickering	Campeau	14		25,000	12,000
	Revenue	24		1,650	22,500
	(2)	38		26,650	34,500
Toronto -Uxbridge	Bramalea	745			32,000
	Runneymede	3,960			
	(2)	4,705			
Toronto -Brampton	Revenue	6,600			125,000
	Bramalea	3,258			
Toronto -Mississauga	Canadian Equity	6,678		8,200	150,000
	Markborough	3,900			75,000
	McLaughlin	3,600			
	(3)	11,178		8,200	225,000
Edmonton	Western	2,188		532	33,000
	BACM Ltd.	1,500			20,000
	Allarco	803			73,000
	(3)	4,491			
Calgary	Paragon	30			
Vancouver	Marathon	90	400	3,000	
		35		180	
	Wall & Redekop	405		985	
		100	400		
	(2)	630		4,165	

SOURCE: Development Corporations Survey - 1973.

NOTE: These projections are based on varying time frames, but are all intended within twenty years.

Dawson, Paragon and Consolidated, are essentially builders who had gross annual revenues exceeding one-half of the total value of their assets, an indication of the rapid pace and growth of their operations. The growth force within this industry is also indicated, as the average gross revenue of these thirty firms was $15.5-million in 1970 and from their average tax payments it appears the firms circulate about 150 times as much money as they pay in taxes.[7]

Table 3 shows the distribution of the assets found in the Development Corporations Survey, by firm, among 24 cities including 17 metropolitan areas, with a further breakout of the holdings in the Toronto region. After the holdings of individual firms, the last row in each city section summarizes all holdings found in that city. The table demonstrates other aspects of the structure and diversification within this industry, as the largest firms operate both in various fields of real estate and across the country, while a few firms are major regional actors, and others operate primarily in one city. The extensive land and shopping centre holdings of the surveyed firms are evident, particularly in Montreal, Ottawa-Hull, Kitchener-Waterloo, Edmonton, Calgary and Toronto.

The considerable regional importance of some of these firms is exemplified by five of the surveyed companies whose holdings appear modest relative to the largest national developers. In 1972, if all businesses in British Columbia are ranked in terms of gross revenue, Dawson Developments Ltd. ranks 26th, Block Brothers Industries Ltd. ranks 30th, Western Realty Projects ranks 31st, and Wall & Redekop ranks 36th. In terms of profitability, the ratio of earnings to sales, Western Realty ranks 10th, Block Brothers is 24th, Dawson Developments is 40th and Wall & Redekop ranks 47th.[8] British Pacific Building Ltd. owns most of the prestigious mountain side of West Vancouver, a holding that involves over 10 per cent of the municipal area and whose development required that the firm build the famed Lion's Gate Bridge. It is interesting that most of the other large businesses in British Columbia were mining and forest products industries — economic sectors which attract government attention as they are recognized to affect the state of the entire economy and society.[9]

Table 4 highlights the single-city firms, as it shows the holdings of each firm in the region where its head office is located, and the percentage that this holding represents of the firm's total surveyed assets of this type. Forty percent of the firms, mainly smaller firms located outside Toronto, only operate in their head office region. Nearly one-half of all firms in the survey have head offices in Toronto, and of these twenty-eight developers, seventeen also operate in other cities. In most cases where a firm owns a square mile or more of land,

"... the surveyed firms hold sufficient acreage to provide all of the respective regions' new residential starts at current levels and densities for over 5 years, and to provide only low density starts at current levels for over 10 years."

the holding is in the same region as the owner-firm's head office.

Tables 5 and 6 demonstrate the use intended for the developers'land inventory and indicate the significance of the holdings in their respective regions. Table 5 contains some development projections of sixteen firms in seven cities, intended to provide housing for over 1,000,000 people within twenty years. This table is neither indicative of all developers' plans, nor all plans of the developers included in these cities. Nevertheless, the table indicates the immense volume of production intended by these firms, and is another manifestation of the increasing shift to large scale development projects. Table 6 compares the land holdings surveyed in each city, with an estimate of each city's current residential acreage consumption, to indicate the significance of the developers' acreage. In Ottawa-Hull, Toronto, Kitchener-Waterloo, Thunder Bay, Calgary and Edmonton, the surveyed firms hold sufficient acreage to provide all of the respective regions' new residential starts at current levels and densities for over 5 years, and to provide only low density starts at current levels for over 10 years. If densities were higher or the firms provided less than 100 per cent of new production, both of which are likely, these time periods would be extended. In general then, these tables demonstrate that the developers' land holdings are large, relative to local consumption, providing an assured supply of raw land to their owners for extended production, and this is translated into production projections that indicate the firms intend to maintain sizeable shares of the local housing market. As the firms hold this land inventory now, they can plan future operations with a base, in terms of location and cost, which are not subject to as many variable factors, or risk as their competitors. Finally, as current acreage prices continue rising,[10] any new purchases by these firms or their competitors will be more expensive. While the competitors must quickly turn over close-in, high-priced land to stay in business, the land bank companies can roll over their inventory, developing the close-in land and using the attendant capital appreciation to increase their inventory from

Table 6 Development Corporations Survey Comparison of Corporate Land Holdings, Using Various Development Assumptions with Estimates of Current Land Consumption, Metropolitan Areas

URBAN REGION	RESIDENTIAL STARTS - 1972 DETACHED AND SEMI-DETACHED (LOW DENSITY)	ROW AND APARTMENTS (HIGH DENSITY)	ESTIMATED LAND CONSUMPTION LOW DENSITY (@ 5 UNITS PER ACRE)	HIGH DENSITY (@ 25 UNITS PER ACRE)	TOTAL (CURRENT MIX)	CORPORATE LAND HOLDINGS NO. OF CORP. OWNERS	ACREAGE HELD	NUMBER OF YEARS OF LAND SUPPLY IN CORPORATE OWNERSHIP ASSUMING USE FOR LOW DENSITY DEVELOP. ONLY	ASSUMING DEVELOP AT CURRENT DENSITY MIX	ASSUMING IT PROVIDES ALL CURRENT STARTS, AT HIGH DENSITY ONLY
HALIFAX	1,187	1,353	237	54	292	3	970	4	3	9.5
MONTREAL	10,118	14,613	2,024	585	2,608	6	3,486	2	1	3.5
OTTAWA-HULL	3,188	11,699	638	468	1,106	8	9,416	15	8	15.8
KINGSTON	541	603	108	24	132	1	34	0	0	.7
PETERBOROUGH	299	536	60	21	81	1	6	0	0	.2
OSHAWA	1,137	695	227	28	255	5	20	0	0	.3
HAMILTON	3,254	5,067	651	203	853	2	601	1	1	1.8
GUELPH	415	184	83	7	90	7	362	4	4	15.1
KITCHENER-WATERLOO	2,134	3,215	427	129	555	1	3,799	9	7	17.8
ST. CATHARINES	2,099	2,120	420	85	505	3	116	0	0	.7
LONDON	2,097	3,347	419	134	553	1	1,401	3	3	6.4
WINDSOR	1,301	1,682	260	67	327	1	270	1	1	2.26
THUNDER BAY	552	587	110	23	134	3	1,190	11	9	26.1
WINNIPEG	3,713	5,421	743	217	959	1	3,480	5	4	9.5
REGINA	1,037	267	207	11	218	1	39	0	0	.7
SASKATOON	794	83	159	3	162	1	234	1	1	6.7
EDMONTON	4,290	5,208	858	208	1,066	9	20,019	23	19	52.7
CALGARY	4,743	2,311	949	92	1,041	8	10,920	12	10	38.7
VICTORIA	1,293	2,899	259	116	375	1	96	0	0	.6
VANCOUVER	7,679	8,531	1,536	341	1,877	9	5,435	4	3	8.4
TORONTO	14,585	24,110	2,917	964	3,881	24	41,198	14	11	26.6
TOTAL	66,456	94,531	13,291	3,781	17,072	47	103,092	8	6	16.0

1. Assuming all development occurs on this land, at current levels of construction.

cheaper acreage further out. This self-sustaining aspect of the land banks combined with their capacity for development in large scale integrated projects which are desired by local authorities, ensures that their owners will maintain a strong share of the housing market, and consequently, maintain the concentrated structure of the land development industry.

OWNERSHIP

Tables 7 and 8 summarize the principal ownership of 47 of the firms in the Development Corporations Survey as of early 1974. Most of the firms, and particularly the largest ones, are public corporations although a predominant proportion of their shares are closely held. At least thirteen of the 47 are involved in interlocking ownership. While most of the firms are Canadian-owned, nearly 40 per cent of them, and nearly 50 per cent of the public corporations are controlled by foreign interests, particularly British, nationality of owners does not appear to vary with firm size. The foreign owners vary from British families to public stock corporations in the United States to a German workers' investment fund, and are not readily categorized. Canadian private corporations are usually family businesses, or partnerships. In general, while the ownership of large development firms is varied in nature, across this spectrum of owners it is common that a controlling core of direct or share equity is closely held.

The survey demonstrates that foreign ownership is prevalent among the large real estate developers,[11] a situation which has drawn considerable criticism recently. While many people consider foreign ownership undesirable, a priori, it is useful to identify actual variances between foreign and non-foreign firms. Three variances are apparent, one of which may warrant further investigation from the viewpoint of Canadian land policy. Firstly, most foreign-owned firms have head offices in Montreal, Toronto and Vancouver. While there is a similar locational tendency among Canadian-owned firms, there are few exceptions among the foreign companies. This choice of locations probably reflects the international banking, finance and travel capabilities of the three cities, but regardless, the evident concentrations of developers' operations in their head office regions[12] implies that these firms help focus growth momentum on the largest metropolae. Secondly the foreign firms export some proportion of their profits, using up some Canadian foreign exchange credits and removing some money from circulation in Canada.[13] Finally, it is often claimed that foreign

"The average tenant in a 'profit basis' row house pays 72% more for 4% fewer rooms than a tenant in a 'non-profit' row house."

owners are satisfied with a lower rate of return on their investments than is typical here. As it is unlikely this would occur through altruism, it would require that the foreign firm has higher expenses than domestic producers. In land markets, this could imply that foreign buyers inflate prices by paying too much for unfamiliar Canadian property. If this inflationary situation does exist, it would constitute a significant disadvantage of foreign ownership. Otherwise the activities of foreign firms seem quite similar to those of domestic developers.

THE RENTAL BUSINESS

To complete this introduction to development corporations it is useful to review some information about two at their major residential activities — land development and the operation of income property. This brief review includes samples of operating data concerning income property generally, and several major developers' property.

Table 9 and 10 summarize some samples of financial and other data concerning various types of income property. Table 9 reports a small general sample of operating costs of properties in Canada's largest cities, published by the Institute of Real Estate Management. It indicates that, generally, 40-50 per cent of the gross rentals generated by all income properties goes to operating expenses, leaving 50-60 per cent for debt service, income taxes and profit. Expenses as a proportion of gross income are lower in row-type buildings, are becoming lower over time, and are lower in Ottawa, Toronto, Victoria and particularly Vancouver. The tenant appears to receive more rooms per rent dollar expended in large low-rise apartments generally, and in Montreal, Ottawa and Toronto generally. Expenses appear high in Montreal except in elevator apartments, and this high expense/low rent situation reflects the large competitive rental market in the city, while the converse low expense/high rents scenario in Vancouver may reflect the low proportion of apartments in this region's housing stock. Property taxes are usually the largest single operating expense, accounting

Table 7 Development Corporations Survey Summary of Principal Owners (Data from Published Sources, but Accuracy Unverified)

NAME OF OWNED FIRM, ABBREVIATED	OWNERSHIP DATA OWNERS NAME (ABBREVIATED)	OWNER'S NATIONALITY	% OWNED	OWNER'S NAME (ABBREVIATED)	OWNER'S NATIONALITY	% OWNED	NOTES
PUBLIC CORPORATIONS							
ALLARCO	Dr. C. A. Allard	Canadian	49				See also Markborough
ALLIANCE	Slater Walker	British	38				
ASSALY	Thomas & Ernest Assaly	Canadian	90				
BACM INDUSTRIES	Genstar	Canadian	58				
BRAMALEA	Bansco Ltd.	Canadian	15				
	Eagle Star Ltd.	British	10	Societe Generale Belgique	Belgium	19	Eagle Star Ltd. owns 18% of Star Holdings Ltd. (See Trizec)
	Br. Electric & Kayser	British	27	Portland Cement	British	11	
CALEDON MT. ESTATES	McLaughlin	Canadian	96				See also McLaughlin
CAMBRIDGE	Tabachnick Family	Canadian	33				
	Eastern Construction	Canadian	40				
CAMPEAU	Robert Campeau	Canadian	16				
CANADIAN EQUITY	Cadillac	Canadian	42				Cadillac and Cemp/Fairview have announced merger plans
	Cemp/Fairview	Canadian	30				
CARMA	Nu-West	Canadian	35				See also Nu-West
CONSOLIDATED	Bovis Ltd.	British	20				
	L. Shankman	Canadian	18				
CORPORATE	Vincent Paul	Canadian	40				
COSTAIN	R.Costain (Holdings)Ltd.	British	49				
DAWSON	North American Life	Canadian	30				
	J. Poole	Canadian	70				
FAIRVIEW	Cemp	Canadian	64	Bronfman Family Trust	Canadian	100	Bronfman Trust owns Cemp
GT. NORTHERN CAPITAL	Capital Countries & Prop.	British	54				See also Western
HALIFAX	J. Jodrey & F. Sobey	Canadian	42				
HAMBROS	Hambros Ltd.	British	61				
HEADWAY	R. Keenan & H. Ganja	Canadian	35				
LADCO	Borger Brothers	British	49				
MAJOR	Vavasseur & Co.	British	10				
MARKBOROUGH	Slater Walker	British	39				Campeau Corp., offering takeover
MCLAUGHLIN	B. McLaughlin	Canadian	51				See also Caledon Mt.
MORENISH	Lehndorff Group	German	48				See also Y & R
NU-WEST	Ralph T. Scurfield	Canadian	71				See also Carma
PARAGON	C. Smith & N. Steinberg	Canadian	50				
SIFTON	Taylor Woodrow	British	50				
	Mowbray Sifton	Canadian	65				See also Bramalea
TRIZEC	Star Holdings Ltd.	British	62				
WESTERN	Capital Counties & Property	British	62				See also Gt. Northern Capital
Y & R	Morenish	German	52				
PRIVATE OR WHOLLY-OWNED CORPORATIONS							
BLOCK BROS.	AJ & HJ Block	Canadian	100				
BRITISH PROPERTIES	Guinness Family	British	99				
BUILDEVCO	Dutchman Homes	Canadian	49				
	Harold Fruere	Canadian	49				
CITY PARKING	Bernard Herman	Canadian	100				
CLAYTON	L. E. Shaw	Canadian	100				
CONCORDIA	Concordia Inc.	U.S.A.	100				
GTR. YORK GP.	G.Shefsky & E. Cogan	Canadian	100				
GROSVENOR-LAING	Grosvenor-Laing Holdings	British	100				
KAUFMAN & BROAD	Kaufman & Broad	U.S.A.	100				
MACLAB	J.de la Bruyere-S.MacTaggart	Canadian	100				
MARATHON	Canadian Pacific	Canadian	100				
METRO STRUCTURES	Metro Structures	U.S.A.	100				
MINTO	Greenberg Family	Canadian	100				
OLYMPIA & YORK	Reichmann Family	Canadian	100				
PINETREE	Tanenbaum Family	Canadian	100				
WALL & REDEKOP	P.Wall,P.J. Redekop,B.Lee	Canadian	100				
WIMPEY	George Wimpey Ltd.	British	100				

for 30-60 per cent of all expenses with varying incidence among building types and through time. In general, these taxes appear lower in Vancouver[14] and higher in the eastern centres.

Table 10 reports similar data from a large sample of apartments in more cities during 1971-1972. The data is collected by CMHC from applicants for NHA loans, and includes both buildings operated on a profit and non-profit basis. There is a tremendous difference between the two financial strategies. The average tenant in a "profit basis" row house pays 72 per cent more rent for 4 per cent fewer rooms than a tenant in a "non-profit" row house. In a "profit" high rise, the average tenant pays 40 per cent for 19 per cent less room, while in a "profit" walk-up, the tenant receives 4 per cent more rooms for 26 per cent more rent. On a "per room" basis, the tenant in a "profit" row house or elevator apartment building pays a rent premium of about 75 per cent, while this premium falls to about 20 per cent in walk-up buildings. From the viewpoint of the owner, the actual dollar expense per room is 11 per cent and 12 per cent cheaper in row and walk-up buildings respectively, when operated for profit, but expenses per room in "profit" high rises are 20 per cent higher than those in "non-profit" buildings. Taxing authorities appear to have mixed feelings about the two types of buildings. Average property taxes per room on "profit" high rises are 19 per cent higher than on non-profit, while the walk-ups which are favoured by non-profit operators pay 20 per cent higher taxes than profit walk-ups and tax treatment of both types of row houses is about equal. The heaviest taxes apply to high rises and walk-ups pay the lowest tax. It should be noted that these figures and comparisons are based on national average data concerning new buildings, and do not necessarily apply to any city. However, these indications of the benefits of users of non-profit buildings invite further investigation; warrant a general commendation to the co-operatives, service and religious organizations, industries and builders who have chosen to build under the "non-profit" programmes; and suggest that muncipal governments might reconsider their taxing policies concerning non-profit walk-up buildings.

The city by city section of Table 10 aggregates profit and non-profit dwellings. In general, the data follows the pattern of Table 9, with expenses at about 40 per cent of gross income for high rises and row houses, and slightly lower for walk-up. Expenses appear particularly high in Kingston, and generally higher in smaller cities. Property taxes are the dominant expense, and are highest in the province of Quebec and smaller cities in southern Ontario. Nova Scotia, Alberta and British Columbia take the lowest proportion of gross income as property taxes. Net income reaches the highest proportions of gross income in: row buildings in

Halifax, Quebec, Hamilton, Kitchener, Calgary, Edmonton, Vancouver and Victoria; walk-ups in Halifax, Montreal, Hull, Toronto and Edmonton; and in high rises the proportion is quite constant around 59 per cent except in Kingston where it falls to 48 per cent.

Table 11 concerns the same buildings reported in Table 10 and contains averages of estimates made by both loan applicants and CMHC appraisers of the land cost per unit, and annual returns on equity, associated with these buildings. CMHC appraises buildings and sites to determine lending values. The variance between the CMHC estimates and the loan applicants estimates indicates the considerable and frequent extent that CMHC appraisers consider loan applicants overvalue their property. The objective of this overvaluing is seen in the "return on equity" columns, which are calculations of average annual yields using the loan amounts requested by the applicant, and those authorized by the Corporation. It is apparent that mortgage houses such as CMHC can exercise a considerable profit-limiting function in their lending activities.[15]

The two tables also demonstrate a general tendency for non-profit buildings to locate on much more expensive land than profit buildings. In general, non-profit buildings have higher land costs per unit, higher land to total cost per unit relationships, and more units per building. If further examination showed the non-profit sites to be superior locations, this would constitute another significant credit to this housing programme. On the other hand, if the sites are not superior, it would demonstrate a gross inefficiency (as the total land costs average 32 per cent higher for elevator buildings, 158 per cent higher for walk-ups, and 101 per cent higher for row houses).

It is interesting to note the levels of equity return anticipated by borrowers — these are quite similar to findings of two other recent studies of rates of return on income property. Woods, Gordon and Co. examined average annual rates of return, after tax, on apartment investment during the 1960s and determined: individual apartment owners averaged 57.2 per cent per annum; private corporations received 50.2 per cent per annum; and public corporations averaged only 19.2 per cent per annum.[16] It is notable that, in the late 1960s, about 50 per cent of all rental income was received by individuals. Walter Keyser, vice-president of Gardiner and Co. Ltd., reported in 1972 that ten to fifteen year old apartments containing 85 to 100 units and located in lower middle class districts of Toronto were yielding upwards of 35 per cent per annum, including capital appreciation and leveraging.[17] It appears, then, that while income property can yield very high returns, large corporations generally settle for lower annual yields. This sharply contradicts the widely-held notion that the large

Table 8 Development Corporations Survey Summary of Ownership, by Nationality

NAME OF OWNED FIRM	LOCATION OF FIRM'S HEAD OFFICE	PERCENTAGE OF DIRECT OWNERSHIP, BY NATIONALITY				
		CANADA	GREAT BRITAIN	U.S.A.	W. GERMANY	OTHER
PUBLIC CORPORATIONS --CANADIAN						
ALLARCO	Edmonton	49%				
ASSALY	Ottawa	90				
BACM	Winnipeg	58				
CALEDON MT.	Toronto	96				
CAMBRIDGE	Toronto	73				
CAMPEAU	Ottawa	16				
CAN. EQUITY	Toronto	72				
CARMA	Calgary	35				
CORPORATE	Toronto	40				
DAWSON	Vancouver	60				
FAIRVIEW	Montreal	70				
HALIFAX	Halifax	54				
HEADWAY	Thunder Bay	61				
LADCO	Winnipeg	35				
MCLAUGHLIN	Toronto	39				
NU-WEST	Calgary	48				
PARAGON	Calgary	71				
SUBTOTALS - 17	9	(17)56.8%				
PRIVATE OR WHOLLY-OWNED CORPORATIONS -CANADIAN						
BLOCK BROS.	Vancouver	100				
BUILDEVCO	Kitchener	98				
CITY PARKING	Toronto	100				
CLAYTON	Halifax	100				
GTR. YORK	Toronto	100				
MACLAB	Edmonton	100				
MARATHON	Calgary	100				
MINTO	Ottawa	100				
OLYMPIA & YORK	Toronto	100				
PINETREE	Toronto	100				
WALL & REDEKOP	Vancouver	100				
SUBTOTALS - 11	7	(11)99.8%				
PUBLIC CORPORATIONS - FOREIGN						
ALLIANCE	Toronto		38			
BRAMALEA	Toronto	15	37			
CONSOLIDATED	Toronto	18	20			
COSTAIN	Toronto		49			
GT. NORTHERN CAP.	Toronto		64			
HAMBROS	Toronto		42			
MAJOR	Kitchener		49			
MARKBOROUGH	Toronto		10			
MORENISH	Toronto					51
SIFTON	London	50	50			
TRIZEC	Montreal		65			
WESTERN	Edmonton		62			
Y & R	Toronto					52
SUBTOTALS - 13	5	(3)27.6%	(11)44.1%			(2)51.5%
PRIVATE OR WHOLLY-OWNED CORPORATIONS - FOREIGN						
BRITISH	Vancouver		99			
CONCORDIA	Montreal			100		
GROSVENOR-LAING	Vancouver		100			
KAUFMAN & BROAD	Toronto			100		
METRO STRUCTURES	Montreal			100		
WIMPEY	Toronto		100			
SUBTOTALS - 6	3		(3)99.6%	(3)100%		
TOTALS						
ALL PUBLIC - 30	11	(20)52.5%	(11)44.1%			(2)51.5%
ALL PRIVATE - 17	8	(11)99.8%	(3)99.6%	(3)100%		
ALL CANADIAN - 28	10	(28)73.7%				
ALL FOREIGN - 19	6	(3)27.6%	(14)56.0%	(3)100%	(2)51.5%	
ALL CORPS - 47	11	(31)69.3%	(14)56.0%	(3)100%	(2)51.5%	

23

Table 9 Sample of Apartment Income and Expense Data, Selected Canadian Cities — 1966, 1968, 1970

	1966					1968						1970					
	MONTREAL	OTTAWA	TORONTO	VICTORIA	CANADA	MONTREAL	OTTAWA	TORONTO	VANCOUVER	WINNIPEG	CANADA	MONTREAL	OTTAWA	TORONTO	VANCOUVER	WINNIPEG	CANADA
GARDEN TYPE APARTMENTS																	
Complexes sampled	2		3	3	7			2	2		5	3		2	4		10
1. Av. Apts. Per Complex	346		42.7	40	128.4			161.5	189.5		152	108.7		271.0	130.7		144.7
2. Av. Rooms per Apt.	4.1		4.3	3.0	4.1			4.2	4.5		4.5	4.1		4.7	4.0		4.3
3. Av. Rent per Apt.	106.55		138.55	97.55	112.48			131.87	196.83		164.55	117.89		158.33	214.47		170.04
4. Av. Ann. Net Income per Apt.	616.39		978.72	611.91	674.41			732.86	1630.35		1183.05	431.36		1130.82	1680.04		1185.38
% of Gross																	
– Net	46.0		56.7	51.0	48.7			44.3	63.9		55.9	29.1		55.3	62.1		54.9
– Expenses	52.6		42.9	45.5	50.1			55.3	34.9		43.2	58.3		43.4	35.8		41.6
– Property Tax	17.1		17.8	15.1	17.4			23.4	11.8		16.5	24.3		16.2	13.1		15.9
LOW-RISE APARTMENTS (12-24 UNITS)																	
Buildings Sampled	4	5			13		4		7		22	5	3		5		16
1. Av. No. per Bldg.	15.7	15.4			15.9		15.5		19.3		16.9	15.0	18.0		18.2		17.1
2. Av. Rooms per Apt.	3.6	4.1			3.7		4.2		2.9		3.4	3.6	3.1		3.0		3.3
3. Av. Rent per Apt.	117.53	102.38			107.02		107.33		111.80		118.57	117.45	118.02		116.72		120.72
4. Av. Ann. Net Inc. per Apt.	639.90	566.09			614.20		668.18		820.61		779.18	664.42	876.46		806.70		804.44
% of Gross																	
– Net	44.4	45.4					50.8		59.6		53.0	46.3	52.2		56.2		53.2
– All expenses	55.6	48.8					42.5		39.7		45.6	53.6	46.8		42.9		45.6
– Property Tax	14.9	20.4					19.5		13.3		15.9	17.6	18.1		13.6		15.6
LOW-RISE APARTMENTS OVER 25 UNITS																	
Buildings Sampled	3	5	4		16	6	3	7	3		16	2			11	3	16
1. Av. Apts. per Bldg.	28.7	40.4	58		42	25.8	41	60.1	36.3		46.4	25.5			56.1	66	49.3
2. Av. Rooms per Apt.	3.4	4.06	2.8		3.3	3.8	4.2	3.4	2.9		3.5	4.6			3.5	3.8	3.6
3. Av. Rent per Apt.	96.97	100.03	103.76		99.99	136.56	124.56	127.44	130.48		127.27	134.86			141.96	170.77	143.93
4. Av. Ann. Net Inc. per Apt.	589.32	614.03	607.85		612.61	738.83	810.77	796.42	1006.01		820.33	781.31			1081.39	994.31	1021.21
% of Gross																	
– Net	47.9	50.0	48.2		50.0	43.0	54.1	49.9	62.4		52.5	45.1			60.6	45.7	57.4
– Expenses	50.4	44.0	50.9		47.1	56.9	40.6	49.0	36.4		45.6	53.9			37.7	49.4	40.7
– Property Tax	14.1	19.3	23.4		19.2	18.0	17.5	21.3	12.7		18.8	18.1			13.8	17.3	15.2
ELEVATOR APARTMENT BUILDINGS																	
Buildings Sampled	6	3	10		24		4	7	3		25	6	5		6	2	20
1. Av. Apts. per Bldg.	61	113	77		79		113	87	180		99	136	101		134	70	117
2. Av. Rooms per Apt.	4.8	3.0	3.0		3.5		3.2	3.1	3.1		3.4	3.7	3.4		3.7	4.1	3.7
3. Av. Rent per Apt.	171.36	137.11	118.28		140.50		140.33	124.82	121.31		149.28	184.90	156.80		171.64	207.23	174.71
4. Av. Ann. Net Inc. per Apt.	823.06	703.95	819.78		818.19		910.43	814.06	1016.12		1008.81	1270.81	959.51		1351.09	1359.60	1247.75
% of Gross																	
– Net	37.9	41.1	54.4		45.2		50.1	51.1	59.0		52.1	49.6	47.2		60.7	52.1	53.1
– Expenses	61.9	41.6	43.4		47.2		45.6	46.7	36.3		45.3	43.9	46.6		36.7	45.6	42.1
– Property Tax	22.8	17.6	19.8		19.1		18.3	21.9	15.0		18.4	18.5	19.5		15.0	17.0	17.3

Source: Calculated from data in Institute of Real Estate Management, *Apartment Building Income/Expense Analysis*, 1967, 1969, 1971 editions.

Notes: Average Rents per apartments do not include parking and are monthly.
Average net income per apartment is net annual income before income tax and debt service, on a per apartment basis.

Table 10   Apartment Income and Expense Data, NHA Financed Dwellings Selected Canadian Cities — September 1971 to September 1972

	HALIFAX	QUEBEC	MONTREAL	HULL	OTTAWA	TORONTO	HAMILTON	LONDON	KITCHENER	KINGSTON	SUBURY	WINNIPEG	EDMONTON	CALGARY	VANCOUVER	VICTORIA	CANADA	CANADA Non-Profit	CANADA Profit
ROW – TYPE APARTMENTS																			
Buildings sampled	3	4	9	2	20	21	22	10	8	6	3	18	19	6	4	5	233	74	149
1. Av. Apts. Per Bldg.	24	20	63	42	38	82	39	36	26	49	52	31	59	25	44	28	43	48	40
2. Av. Rooms Per Apt.	5.7	5	5.2	5.6	5.7	5.6	5.4	5.2	5.3	5.5	5.6	5.4	5.3	5.7	5	5.1	5.3	5.5	5.3
3. Av. Rent per Apt.	$138	179	150	216	185	206	188	181	186	105	171	127	141	208	$177	185	165	111	192
4. Av. Net Ann. Income per Apt.	$997	1385	1053	1304	1313	1531	1493	1295	1550	424	1176	639	1015	1664	$1460	1471	1198	469	1560
% of Gross Income																			
– Net Income	60.1	64.6	58.4	50.1	59.0	61.9	66.3	59.8	69.5	33.8	57.1	42.0	59.7	66.6	68.1	66.4	60.5	35.1	67.7
– All Expenses	39.9	35.4	41.6	49.6	41.0	38.1	33.7	40.2	30.5	66.2	42.9	58.0	40.2	33.4	31.9	33.6	39.5	64.9	32.3
– Property Taxes	18.6	18.2	26.3	25.5	19.8	19.4	19.2	18.3	16.0	27.6	19.8	25.3	19.6	14.1	14.3	11.8	18.9	28.5	16.4
WALK-UP APARTMENTS																			
Buildings Sampled	2	16	107	8	9	2		10	3	3		34	38	13	6	3	638	64	574
1. Av. Apts. Per Bldg.	30	189	524	12	27	120		26	61	57		48	53	27	90	15.9	26	46	23
2. Av. Rooms per Apt.	4.4	4.7	4.3	4.3	4.6	5.1		4.5	4.3	4.6		4.0	4.3	4.1	4.1	4.4	4.1	4.2	4.4
3. Av. Rent per Apt.	$170	144	101	141	149	188	150	150	151	133		138	150	141	$172	158	125	105	133
4. Av. Net Ann. Income per Apt.	1362	1048	759	1083	1075	1596	1030	1030	1082	861		986	1128	1005	$1220	1114	935	618	1001
% of Gross Income																			
– Net Income	66.8	60.7	62.6	64.1	60.1	80.6	57.3	57.3	59.8	53.3		59.5	62.8	59.5	59.1	58.6	62.2	49.0	62.6
– All Expenses	33.2	39.3	37.4	35.9	39.9	29.4	42.7	42.7	40.2	46.2		40.5	37.2	40.5	40.9	41.4	37.8	51.0	37.4
– Property Taxes	14.1	18.7	19.9	19.0	20.4	12.0	19.4	19.4	17.2	18.2		15.6	15.0	15.4	12.2	12.9	17.7	19.5	12.9
ELEVATOR APARTMENTS																			
Building Sampled	3	8	18	15	30	70	23	10	5	4	4	9	6	8	23	16	301	13	288
1. Av. Apts. Per Bldg.	174	464	122	150	171	189	140	93	141	71	84	180	54	118	129	48	139	124	140
2. Av. Rooms per Apt.	3.6	3.7	3.5	3.8	4.0	4.2	4.3	4.0	4.3	4.3	3.9	3.6	3.9	4.1	3.8	3.8	4.1	4.9	4.0
3. Av. Rent Per Apt.	$176	169	164	164	188	178	159	155	178	135	151	154	184	160	$151	146	169	120	170
4. Av. Net Ann. Income Per Apt.	1326	1183	1096	1184	1338	1285	1094	1072	1252	782	1017	1104	1359	1186	$1048	1045	1203	593	1218
% of Gross Income																			
– Net Income	62.8	58.3	55.7	60.1	59.2	60.0	57.4	57.6	58.7	48.3	56.2	59.7	61.4	61.6	57.7	59.7	59.2	41.1	59.6
– All Expenses	37.2	41.7	44.3	39.9	40.8	40.0	42.6	42.4	41.3	51.7	43.8	40.3	38.6	38.4	42.3	40.3	40.8	58.9	40.4
– Property Taxes	14.1	20.0	24.0	17.0	20.7	20.6	20.2	18.7	18.9	20.2	18.2	17.6	15.7	14.9	14.0	14.4	18.7	25.6	18.6

Source: CMHC Appraisal Division

Table 11 Average Land and Total Costs per Unit, and Estimated Annual Return on Equity,

CITY	ROW TYPE BUILDINGS								LAND COST	
	NO. OF BLDGS.	LAND COST		LAND AS % OF TOTAL COST		ANNUAL EQUITY RETURN USING		NO. OF BLDGS.		
		OWNER ESTIMATE	CMHC ESTIMATE	OWNER ESTIMATE	CMHC ESTIMATE	OWNER FIGURES	CMHC FIGURES		OWNER ESTIMATE	CMHC ESTIMATE
HALIFAX	3	$2562	$2000	16%	13%	2%	4%	2		$ 919
QUEBEC	4	1114	1072	8	8	29	6	16	1189	893
MONTREAL	9	991	1011	8	7	8	9	107	1916	1929
HULL	2		2914	19	16	9	5	8	1264	996
KINGSTON	6	1364	1490	8	9		4	3	471	1265
OTTAWA	20	2139	1496	11	10	14	5	9	1462	
TORONTO	21	7354	6874	28	27	9	7	2		2498
HAMILTON	22	4264	3768	21	18	11	4			
LONDON	10	2840	2242	17	12	13	3	10	1506	1081
KITCHENER	8	7763	2643	16	15	12	4	3	1675	1458
SUDBURY	3	3939	2276	20	12	17	6			
WINNIPEG	18	2146	1972	11	10	17	5			
EDMONTON	19	3027	2677	18	16	15	7	38	2125	2005
CALGARY	6	2556	1733	12	8	12	6	13	1671	1813
VANCOUVER	4	2524	2454	15	15			6	2454	1876
VICTORIA	5	1748	1738	9	9	12	7	3	1357	894
NHA CANADA										
–NON PROFIT	74	4258	4044	20	19			64	1231	1565
–PROFIT	149	2807	2413	16	13	12	5	574	1355	1212
–ALL	223	3348	3028	17	16	12	5	636	1349	1225

SOURCE: CMHC APPRAISAL DIVISION

Table 12   An Approximation of Land Revenue and Land Costs, 1972-73, Nine Canadian Cities

ASSUMPTIONS:

1. One acre sells as 5 serviced lots.
2. Sale price includes 10% profit.
3. Servicing costs are carried for one year at 10%.
4. For each saleable acre (5 lots), 1.4 acres must be acquired and held.

SOURCES:

5. Five lots at average price of NHA-financed detached lots in 1972, given in CMHC, Canadian Housing Statistics, 1972, p. 70.
6. Lot prices in Ottawa Journal, 11 June, 1973, p. 3.
7. Lot prices in Toronto Star, 30 March, 1973, p. 1.
8. Lot prices in Regina Leader Post, 16 July, 1973, p. 3.
9. Lot prices in Calgary Herald, 10 July, 1973, p. 3.
10. CMHC estimates.
11. Lot price in Toronto Globe & Mail, 14 December, 1972, p. B-9.
12. Toronto Globe & Mail, 27 July, 1973, p. B-9.
13. Toronto Globe & Mail, 18 June, 1973, p. 29.
14. Regina Leader Post, 10 June, 1973, p. 25.
15. Letter H. E. Wellman, Director of Planning.
16. Mill Woods report.

	Halifax	St. John	Ottawa	
	NHA	NHA	NHA	Other
Revenue (Sale of 1 Acre)[1]	$28,385[5]	$23,725[5]	$42,000[5]	$75,000[6]
Less Costs				
–Profit Allowance[2]	2,583	2,159	3,822	6,825
–Servicing Costs	20,915[10]	16,500[12]	19,405[10]	19,405[10]
–Carrying Costs on Services[3]	2,090	1,650	1,941	1,941
Excess (For Land Acquisition Carrying Costs, Tax, etc)	2,794	3,415	16,832	46,829
Estimated Agricultural Value[4]	100	100	300	300
–Increase 40% for Gross Land	140	140	420	420
–Plus Holding Costs–10 Years at 8%, Taxes at 2%	371	371	1,114	1,114
–Implied Returns to Scarcity, or Speculative Gain	2,423	3,044	15,118	45,715
–As % of Total Revenue	8.5%	12.8%	37.2%	60.9%

NHA Financed Buildings, Canadian Cities, September 1971 to September 1972

| WALK-UP APARTMENTS | | | | | | | ELEVATOR APARTMENTS | | | |
| LAND AS % OF TOTAL COSTS | | ANNUAL EQUITY RETURN USING | | NO. OF BLDGS. | LAND COST | | LAND AS % OF TOTAL COSTS | | ANNUAL EQUITY RETURN USING | |
OWNER ESTIMATE	CMHC ESTIMATE	OWNER FIGURES	CMHC FIGURES		OWNER ESTIMATE	CMHC ESTIMATE	OWNER ESTIMATE	CMHC ESTIMATE	OWNER FIGURES	CMHC FIGURES
7%	6%	17%	7%	3	$1781	$1126	11%	7%	13%	8
11	8	18	5	8	1367	1363	10	10	11	6
16	18	18	8	18	1988	1698	13	12	13	7
11	9	11	8	15	1265	1029	9	8	11	8
4	10		4	4	1404	1163	10	8		4
10	10	13	7	30	1648	1128	10	7	12	6
17	17	10	21	70	3345	3196	19	19	12	7
				23	2201	1531	14	11	13	6
13	9	22	7	10	1615	1252	12	9	13	6
12	11	8	4	5	1444	1359	9	8	10	4
				4	1428	1382	10	9	12	7
				9	916	838	6	6	10	6
16	16	14	6	6	2630	2097	14	11	13	7
13	15	13	5	8	1266	1702	8	11	13	5
18	14			23	2111	1909	14	14	9	5
9	6	9	3	16	1825	1509	14	12	10	5
10	12			13	3039	2829	16	15		
11	10	14	7	288	2160	1894	14	12	12	6
11	10	14	7	301	2189	1929	14	13	12	6

	Toronto NHA	Toronto Other	Regina NHA	Regina Other	Saskatoon NHA	Calgary NHA	Calgary Other	Edmonton NHA	Edmonton Other	Vancouver NHA	Vancouver Other
	$57,535[5]	$110,000[7]	$16,545[5]	$25,000[8]	$16,285[5]	$31,600[5]	$35,000[9]	$34,565[5]	$45,000[10]	$48,335[5]	$70,000[11]
	5,236[13]	10,010[13]	1,506[14]	2,275[14]	1,482[15]	2,875[16]	3,185[16]	3,145[16]	4,095[16]	4,398[10]	6,370[10]
	20,000[13]	20,000[13]	15,500[14]	15,500[14]	10,437[15]	20,805[16]	20,805[16]	20,805[16]	20,805[16]	16,000[10]	16,000[10]
	2,000	2,000	1,550	1,550	1,044	2,081	2,081	2,081	2,081	1,600	1,600
	30,299	77,990	- 2,010	5,675	3,322	5,839	8,928	8,534	18,021	26,337	46,030
	400	400	80	80	80	150	150	250	250	300	300
	560	560	112	112	112	210	210	350	350	420	420
	1,486	1,486	297	297	297	557	557	929	929	1,114	1,114
	28,813	76,504	- 2,307	5,378	3,025	5,282	8,371	7,605	17,092	25,223	44,916
	50.1%	69.5%		21.5%	18.6%	16.7%	23.9%	22.0%	38.0%	52.2%	64.2%

developer/landlords commit the worst excesses in "ripping-off" their tenants. While there is not adequate data to determine rates of return by class of investor, the Woods, Gordon data certainly indicates that individuals and their private companies take the highest profits from real estate, and examination of income tax data for individuals and corporations certainly supports this finding.

DEVELOPER LAND BANKS

[In an earlier section of his report, Spurr explains the process by which farmland is transformed into urban land, and examines the costs and profits involved in assembling, holding, servicing and selling this land as building lots.]

The large appreciation in land value in the predevelopment process of urbanization is also illustrated by the figures in the accompanying table. The most common pre-urban use of land is agriculture, as slow contours, good drainage, and the absence of rock are prerequisites for economical farming and cheap urban development. The value of agricultural land is also a residual function, basically the capital value of the net income produced by a farm, prorated on a per-acre basis. While this varies across Canada it seldom exceeds $500 per acre, and is usually about $300 per acre. As these values are greatly exceeded by the residual values of acreage suitable for urban use, a parcel of urbanizing land appreciates through a wide range of values. People who buy and sell land during this period of rapid price appreciation are often known as speculators. In practice, there are relatively few pure speculators as many farmers do not sell their land until development is imminent, and many developers buy acreage in likely growth locations far in advance of need. In all of the higher price areas a builder can pay well above agricultural values for farmland, hold the land for ten years, and recoup all expenses when the developed acreage is sold. Alternatively, if the developer buys at agricultural prices, or the farmer holds the land, the accrued appreciation in the value of this land inventory gives the owner borrowing power to finance its development.

Table 12 is focussed on this appreciation in the value of urbanizing agricultural land. In this table, typical servicing costs and a profit of 10 per cent are subtracted from the average sale price of a developed acre, and the result is compared with agricultural values. In six of the nine areas in the table, separate estimates of revenue per acre in 1972-73 are shown, based on CMHC data and newspaper reports of average lot prices. Agricultural values are increased by 40 per cent to account

for that land in a development which does not produce revenue, and carrying costs and taxes are charged for 10 years to simulate the expense of holding this farmland. The difference between the cost of the held farmland, and the amount that sales revenue exceeds development costs, is identified as a return due to scarcity, and is shown as a percentage of total revenue. In other words, the table indicates the proportion of the selling price of a developed acre which is appreciation of land value above basic agricultural value. Using the lower, NHA revenue estimates, these proportions vary from 10-20 per cent in Halifax, Saint John, Saskatoon, Calgary and Edmonton to 37 per cent in Ottawa and over 50 per cent in Toronto and Vancouver. When the higher revenue estimates are employed, in the latter three cities, returns to scarcity exceed 60 per cent of the cost of a lot. The builder or developer who sells the lot does not necessarily obtain this entire return to scarcity as parts of it might have been realized by the original farm-owner, and any interim owners. However, in those increasingly common situations when developers buy land directly from farmers long before development, and hold it in banks for future use, it is likely that large proportions of the eventual selling price of their lots are returns to scarcity. This appreciation of land value or return to scarcity is often described as the social increment in land value, as the added value is created by the local society or economy, rather than the landowner. It is this social increment in the value of urbanizing land, and in the increase of the market value of developed property, that is usually the object of proposals to increase taxation on land.

Developers' land banks of farmland next to the urban fringe are increasing in size, value and importance. While the value of current or "on stream" land remains at about the same level each year, the value and size of land banks, and total land revenue are rising. Land, at cost, accounts for a progressively higher proportion of the firm's asset inventory even though land costs appear to be only 30-55 per cent of land value. Acquisition costs comprise 70-95 per cent of the total cost of banked land, interest or carrying costs run 3-12 per cent and taxes are 1-8 per cent. These raw land acquisitions are heavily leveraged, usually to 40-60 per cent of their cost, and generally at low rate mortgages between 6 per cent and 11-1/4 per cent. As the land moves "on stream" the scant data herein indicates the original acquisition cost constitutes one-quarter to one-third of total developed land costs, with development costs comprising 55-60 per cent and accumulated carrying costs amounting to 10-20 per cent. Land sales yield very high profits, and provide 5-40 per cent of the firms' total revenue, however, when grouped with all other sales the yield declines to 10-30 per cent and the firms' entire net income as a proportion of all costs, before taxes, is in the

> "The small builder, revered in the mythology of housing is an anachronism — the residential construction industry in metropolitan Canada can be recognized as paralleling the structure of the automobile industry during the 1920s, or the aircraft industry in the 1940s."

reasonable range below 15 per cent. While land operations are clearly big money-makers, it appears these large developers have sufficient costs in other sectors that their total returns are relatively modest.

This varied and complex data has many implications, a few of which shall be noted here. Developers' land banks are a valuable asset — nine large firms hold over thirty-three thousand acres costing over $200-million but leveraged by about one-half, and having a market value of at least two to three times its cost. It is sometimes suggested that governments should buy or expropriate developers' land banks — this data gives some notion of the magnitude of the price that such a change in ownership might entail, in the case of nine firms in about eight cities. It is sometimes proposed that large developers are withholding land from the market, and that a higher property tax would increase their carrying costs to the extent that they would be forced to sell. The data indicates the unlikelihood of this effect, as a major increase in taxes would be required to escalate carrying costs to a level comparable with land acquisition costs. The sum of acquisition costs, the sum of acquisition and cumulated carrying costs are not as large an expense as development costs for "on stream" land, and the total costs of land sales are so much lower than current market prices that incremental additions to cost do not appear capable of forcing the land bank firms to do anything. However, as the data also showed that these large land-banking, vertically integrated developers realize scanty profits if not losses in non-land aspects of their operations, and recalling the concentrated structure of the entire industry and the necessity that smaller, less-efficient firms have the added disadvantage of buying land at retail prices, it is apparent that any measures directed at increasing production costs will strongly affect the numerous marginal small producers.[18]

This brief examination of private developers has yielded considerable insight into the nature and operations of this industry. Metropolitan land de-velopment is dominated by relatively few, big vertically integrated diversified producers who hold five-to-twenty year banks of land for future use, considerable residential and commercial rental property, and a large number of smaller, subsidiary firms. The largest of the firms are active across Canada, and most of these have headquarters in Toronto. Others, particularly western firms, have major regional operations. Inter-corporate ownership is frequent. While the corporations include public, private, foreign and domestic owners, ultimately the controlling shares of each firm are held by a small group, usually the firm's directors. While these firms are vertically integrated, efficient organizations, which have lower costs than their smaller competitors, they do not receive particularly high profits. They appear to obtain lower rates of return on income property than smaller investors, and while they receive very high returns on land development, there are sufficient offsetting expenses and reinvestments in their operations that their net pre-tax income constitutes a modest return on current expenditures. The combination of these factors — modest current returns, large and expanding asset portfolios (land banks and income property holdings), frequent acquisitions of smaller firms, extensive vertical integration in production, financing and marketing, mergers and the top-heavy industry structure, with broad-based financing and close control manifest the predominant growth strategy in the industry. Metropolitan land development has been taken over by the giants, who are now consolidating their position by buying up their competition, and the suppliers and materials in their production processes. The small builder, revered in the mythology of housing, is an anachronism[19] — the residential construction industry in metropolitan Canada can be recognized as paralleling the structure of the automobile industry during the 1920s, or the aircraft industry in the 1940s. The understanding of this reality could lead to several different objectives for public policy, ranging from the break-up of the evolving cartel, to the nationalization of the firms, to increased public supervision of their products and prices. Of the three, the latter seems most directly related to the quality of life and substantive needs of this society.

[1] Calculated from the membership list in *The Canadian Real Estate Annual*, 1973 edition, Toronto: Maclean-Hunter, 1973, pp. M-34 to M-47.

[2] Table 4.2.

[3] *Canadian Real Estate Annual*, 1973, *op. cit*, pp. M-65 to M-68.

[4] The Cemp Investments portfolio illustrates the understatement contained in the commercial assets as reported in the survey. While the survey found about 26,000,000 square feet of commercial space, and 223 buildings, with only 14 buildings held by Cemp Fairview, this company holds over 10,000,000 square feet of

space, including about 6,000,000 in 10 of its office structures. See Ludwick, A. M. and K. W. Simpson "The
Case of the Missing Property, OR, When Does 50% =
1/2?" pp. 17-29 in *Canadian Chartered Accountant*, April
1973.

[5] Reported in Canadian Council on Social Development,
Housing and People, Volume 2, Number 1, Ottawa 1971,
p.7.

[6] Statistics Canada. *1971 Census of Canada-Housing*,
Catalogue No. 93-729, Volume 2, Part 3, p. 6-17.

[7] The accompanying table showed that in 1970, the average taxable income of firms having over $5-million in
assets was $279,000. If an average of 35% of this income
went to taxes, each of these firms would have paid
about $100,000 in taxes in 1970.

[8] *Financial Post*, 28 October 1972, p. 33.

[9] It is also interesting that government regulates these
other regional industries by control of land (mining and
timber leases, royalties charged on an areal or volume
extracted basis, etc.). In the development sector the
firms own the land and may construct their operations
around this control.

[10] Section 2.2 discussed the mechanism which produces
rising raw land prices.

[11] Similar indications are seen in the following:
   a) Canada's largest realtor, A. E. LePage Ltd., esti-
      mates that 35% of its corporate time is spent with
      European and Asiatic investors (*Financial Times*, 9
      April 1973, p. 18.)
   b) Thirteen British-owned developers own 20,000
      acres between Oshawa and Burlington (*Ottawa
      Citizen*, 12 August 1973, p. 6.)
   c) It is estimated that $1,000 million has been in-
      vested in Canadian real estate by German citizens.
      (*Financial Post*, 16 June 1973, p. 3)

[12] This concentration was described in connection with
Table 4.

[13] Reduced circulation in the sense of lessened multip-
lier effect and perhaps reduced re-investment.

[14] Another study of 65 apartment buildings in metropolitan Vancouver in 1970 found 66% of apartments
paid between 13%-16% of their gross income in
property taxes, and only 12% of buildings (mainly
frame structures) paid a higher proportion. White and
Hamilton, *The Real Property Tax in British Columbia*,
op. cit. p. 43.

[15] The extent of this activity is suggested by the coverage
of Tables 10 and 11, which involves 10,019 rentable
units in 223 buildings.

[16] Woods, Gordon and Co. *Comparative Survey of the
Rates of Return on Apartment and Stock Investment,
1960-1969*, 1970 as reported in a paper presented by
Frank A. Clayton, Canadian Real Estate Research
Corporation to the 23rd Tax Conference, Canada Tax
Foundation, Vancouver, 17 November 1971.

[17] Quoted in Belford, Terrence "Investment Properties. .
. .", *Globe and Mail*, 12 May 1972, p. B-3.

[18] There are two significant points here — that the primary consequence of a policy supposedly directed to
increasing holding costs for large firms would be the
elimination of more small firms, and that the elimination of small firms bars entry to land development
thereby increasing concentration and decreasing
competition in this industry.

[19] Small builders are still active in smaller centres, rural
areas and in the renovation field, but it is simply
inaccurate to continue to describe them as the basic
producers of new urban housing.

Ottawa: Endorsing monopoly land ownership

Brian Bourns

As is the case in most urban municipalities, residential development in the Ottawa-Carleton region is very tightly controlled by a small number of major landowners, who also function as their own developers. In this way, the small group can control the rate of housing production, and therefore to some extent the price they receive for their product, very easily.

Ottawa-Carleton is also a textbook case of how "co-operation" between the private sector and various levels of government has legitimized the oligopoly control of land by a small number of individuals and companies.

The urban policy map on this page illustrates the areas designated for major residential development in the next twenty-five years. There are only four major areas left within Ottawa's "Greenbelt" available for residential development. These are shown on the map as Lebreton Flats, Woodroffe-Baseline and the eastern and western communities of South Ottawa. The first two of these are federally owned and now in the planning stages.

The eastern and western communities are both shared by the same two developers (see enlargements).

Outside the Greenbelt there are four major areas (identified on the map) that were considered for major development. By sheer coincidence, no doubt, they roughly correspond with the major land assemblies outside the Greenbelt.

Three of these areas were chosen for development — the three privately owned areas. The Carlsbad Springs, federal/provincial land assembly was relegated to development at some undetermined time in the future.

The southern growth area (chosen in preference to the federal/provincial land assembly) was selected despite objections concerning its proximity to the airport, the need for its storm sewage to dump into the Rideau River as it heads into Ottawa, the lack of available transportation corridors to the central area and the good agricultural value of much of the land contained within it after the four major owners of land within the area appealed to the Regional Planning Committee and Council with the usual slick consultants' presentation.

The chart below, and the accompanying detailed maps of the five areas designated for major development illustrate how this gives a very small number of private companies control over that development.

12,751 of the 16,898 acres in the five major developing areas are controlled by eleven private corporations. In fact, just seven corporations own 11,847 acres, or over 70 per cent of the land within these areas. (These figures understate the situation in the three areas outside the Greenbelt as already developed land, or land already purchased by municipalities for park, recreation or conservation purposes are not deducted from the totals listed as available for development.)

Even more impressive are the holdings of the Campeau Corporation, Ottawa's homegrown wonderboy. Campeau alone owns one-third of all land available for development and controls major holdings in the two areas inside the Greenbelt and in the Kanata-Glencairn growth area. Campeau's strategic holdings make him a crucial actor in every major planning exercise in the region and leave him with tremendous power to determine the kind of housing we get, the rate at which it is produced and price at which it sells.

Campeau's power today is the result of some very skilful long-term planning on behalf of the Corporation. With the exception of Kanata-Glencairn holdings (acquired from Bill Teron in bulk a couple of years ago), most of Campeau's parcels were acquired a decade ago. This foresight, coupled with the political power to ensure designation of the holdings for development has now given Campeau the financing and resources to extend his operations to other areas of the country. I

	Kanata-Glencairn Growth Area	South Urban Area	Orleans Growth Area	South Ottawa		Total for Corporation
				Eastern Community	Western Community	
1. Costain Estates	715		774			1,489
2. Minto Construction		310	427			737
3. Campeau Corporation	2,340	2,370	165	400	206	5,481
4. Cadillac	227					227
5. Johannsen		175				175
6. Queenswood Home Association			185			185
7. Admiral Leaseholds	*317					317
8. Wes Nicol (various corporations)		328		350	87	765
9. Shenkman Corporation		1,600				1,600
10. Urbandale		975				975
11. Jockvale		800				800
12. Public Ownership (Schools, Federal/Provincial)	?	?	?	177	55	232
Total Majors	3,599	6,558	1,551	927	348	12,983
Total Designated	4,400	9,700	1,500	946	352	16,898

*Industrially Designated Land

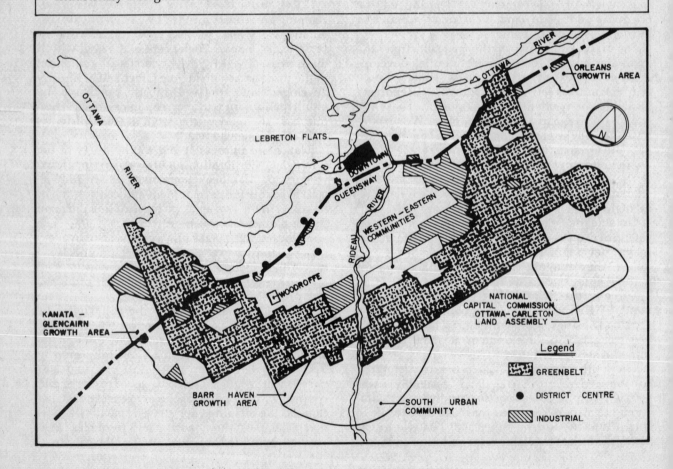

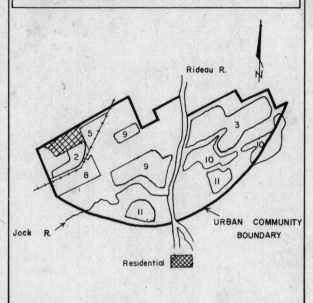

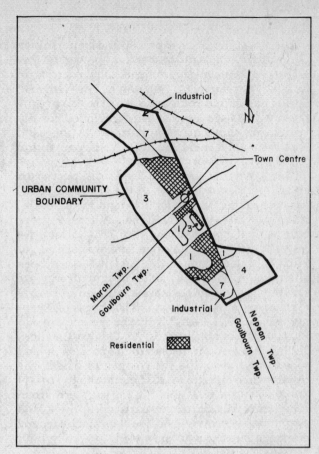

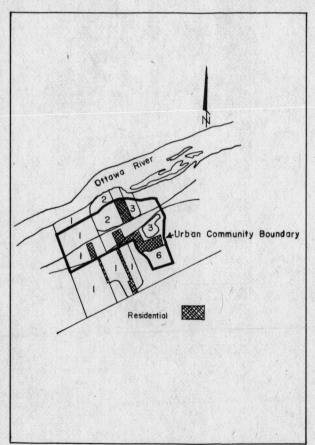

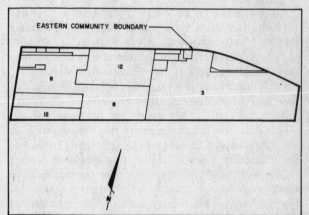

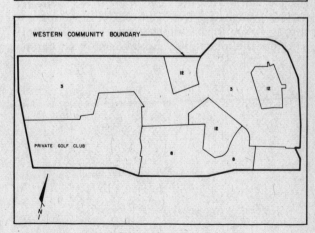

hope you enjoy him.

The most interesting aspect of land ownership in Ottawa-Carleton is the tremendous power the federal and provincial governments could exercise on housing development but don't. The Carlsbad Springs assembly contains 5,300 acres owned by the provincial government and intended for development. Obviously the entrance of this land onto the market could provide severe competition to the private sector.

This government-owned land was purchased and expropriated at prices in the $1,500 to $2,500 per acre range. As late as 1970 land in the designated growth areas was being sold by farmers for as little as $2,400 per acre. By April 1973 (latest price research available) this same land was selling for $40,000 per acre. Since the land has since been officially designated as part of the growth area, we can only assume prices have continued to rise.

Even assuming prices at $40,000 per acre, keeping the Carlsbad assembly off the market will add $200,000,000 to housing costs in Ottawa-Carleton, adding that amount instead to the pockets of land speculators, including the companies listed. The result will be an extra $8,000 per unit, to the cost of the 25,000 units now going in the southern urban community instead of the Carlsbad Springs land assembly. This cost will no doubt be met by federal mortgage subsidies to ensure the privately built housing can be sold.

Although the three levels of government clearly have the power to be a major force in stabilizing land and housing prices, none of them has chosen to do so. The federal government has left its two major holdings inside the Greenbelt (Woodruffe-Baseline and Lebreton) vacant for more than a decade, a period that includes the recent "housing crisis" and rapid price escalation that involved.

The provincial government has done little to push its Carlsbad Spring assembly and, in fact is likely to ratify a Regional Plan that does not permit its development for decades. And the municipal level has developed plans, including the major Regional Plan which clearly favour development of private lands over the development of publically owned lands. And the "control" of development through planning has rapidly come to mean endorsation of the monopoly land ownership situation.

Calgary:
Housing market control revealed

Mike Cooper

In late 1972 the then Chief Commissioner of the City of Calgary engaged a law firm and a management consulting group to prepare a report on the impact of the Genstar group of industries on development activity in the Calgary area. Despite the fact that the report was completed before the end of 1973 it has only just been released to the public. The contents of the report and the manner in which the city has dealt with it provide an interesting insight into the functioning of Canada's fastest growing city.

Genstar is a foreign owned and controlled company. Controlling interests are held by Societe Generale de Belgique and Portland Cement Manufacturers, a multi-national enterprise based in the United Kingdom. Genstar's initial investments in Canada were in the mining field, but since the mid 1960s it has established itself as one of the top forty companies in the manufacturing resource and utility category in Canada. Genstar's activities in western Canada include: the manufacturing of Portland cement; the production and distribution of building materials; land and housing developments; heavy construction; and the import, export and distribution of steel products.

The report on Genstar, prepared by the law firm, Burnett Duckworth Palmer Tomblin and O'Donoghue and the management consulting group, Laventhol Krekstein Horwath and Horwath, concluded that in the Calgary area Genstar has succeeded in achieving market dominance in the land development, construction and housing industries. Based on the evidence the consultants could obtain from public documents, they concluded that a prima facie case could be established against Genstar that would warrant the City of Calgary pursuing the matter under the federal Combines Investigation Act.

In outlining the extent of Genstar involvement in Calgary, the report focuses on the role of British American Construction and Materials Limited (BACM). Through BACM and several other sub-

sidiaries, Genstar is in virtual control of the concrete and concrete products industry in the Calgary area. In addition, BACM is considered to be the largest home builder in the prairie provinces and one of the largest heavy construction enterprises based in the prairie provinces.

The report notes that during 1973 three house builders accounted for 45 per cent of all housing starts. Nu-West Developments led the way with 18.9 per cent followed by BACM with 17 per cent and Qualico Developments with 9 per cent. The report also identified the current pattern of land ownership in the Calgary area and BACM is the largest land developer in Calgary with extensive holdings in the south-east quadrant of the city. CARMA, the second largest land development company, is in virtual control of the north-west quadrant of the city. An interesting interlocking relationship between BACM, CARMA and Nu-West is also identified in the report. Nu-West owns 35 per cent interest in CARMA and BACM is the second largest registered shareholder in CARMA with 7 per cent interest in that company. A rumoured CARMA-Nu-West merger (which subsequently fell through) was cited as a further indication of the tight control of the land development industry in Calgary.

The City of Calgary's involvement in the preparation of the report can best be described as a comedy of errors. The former Chief Commissioner, G. Hamilton, commissioned the report in the fall 1972 but the Board of Commissioners was not notified of the existence of the report until July 1973 when the new Chief Commissioner, G. Cole, was presented with bills from the consultant. The total cost of the study ($78,000) was not exorbitant, but it is difficult to understand why the study was originally requested. Apparently, prior to the time the study was commissioned, top officials of BACM met with the Board of Commissioners (which includes the Mayor) to describe the company's activities in Cal-

BACM and CARMA are the two largest land holding development companies in Calgary and region. The two companies appear to have concentrated their efforts into separate quadrants of the city.

During 1972, BACM purchased an approximate 7 per cent interest in the issued shares of CARMA apparently placing it as the second largest registered shareholder in that Company (Nu-West holding 35 per cent). The resultant inter-relationship of the three largest land development companies, two of which are the dominant house building companies, could lead to an oligopolistic position in the land development industry and a strengthening of the oligopolistic situation in the house building industry.

BACM's concentrated land position in the south-east quadrant of the city and the area immediately outside the city limits follows the same concentration of CARMA's land position in the north-west quadrant of the city and the north-west periphery outside of the city. The land position of Nu-West outside the north-west periphery of the city limits appears complementary to the activities of CARMA in the north-west quadrant. From this analysis the writers have concluded that these developers are anticipating the extension of the city boundaries in the growth corridors chosen by them. Should their anticipation prove correct the companies face the prospect of windfall profits and control of the developable lands and serviced lots supply.
—pp. 36-37, Genstar report.

The land investment of Genstar, together with the apparent emerging patterns of the chief land development competitors is possibly placing the city in a vulnerable position with respect to future controllability of residential lot prices. The proposed CARMA-Nu-West merger could have severe effects on the City of Calgary with respect to the land development and housing industries. Should the proposed merger take place, the city would be well advised to study the effects which would inevitably flow from the integrated positions of Genstar, Nu-West and CARMA.
—p. 43, Genstar report

---

gary and at that meeting they invited the City to ask the company for further information at any time.

On February 28, 1974, Mayor Sykes received a copy of the report and a copy of the letter of transmittal to Mr. Cole which was dated December 11, 1973. The commissioners and the Mayor decided to keep the report secret. Several weeks prior to the municipal election in Calgary (October 16) rumours circulated through city hall and in the press about a devastating secret report. Pressured by city council, the Mayor and commissioners reluctantly agreed to make two copies of the report available to the aldermen (in the Commissioner's office), and subsequently to hold an in camera meeting to discuss the contents of the report. At the October 4 closed meeting the council heard the recommendations of the city solicitors, two outside legal firms and the Board of Commissioners that the report should not be released. Finally, council voted nine to four in favour of releasing the report and the veil of secrecy was lifted.

This action resulted in an initial flurry of activity. The Mayor (and subsequently BACM) warned of lawsuits against the city because of the council's irresponsible actions. The Mayor disclosed that he had sent the report to Ottawa (after it received press coverage), and that the seven-month delay in forwarding it was due to delays in getting legal opinions on the document. Federal and provincial opposition members raised a hue and cry about the monopolistic situation in the development industry and the government ministers responsible cheerfully agreed to study the matter. Newspaper editorials criticized the commissioner system and stressed the need for more control by elected representatives.

Release of the report finally cast some light on the real meaning of a battle over annexation which had set local politicians at each others' throats for months previously.

The annexation proposal, adopted by a majority of Calgary's city council, called for an extension of the city's boundaries to include another 125 square miles of mostly vacant land to the north and south of the present city limits. This move would double Calgary's present size, and many citizen groups expressed their opposition to the proposal. The Housing and Urban Development Association, a developers' lobby, countered with a massive advertising campaign to promote annexation.

Residents of Calgary were worried about the additional tax burden which might come as a result of servicing the annexed land, and about the urban growth it would inevitably encourage. Citizen opposition led to a referendum on the matter.

The Genstar report established quite clearly who stood to benefit if annexation was approved. At the north-west end of the city just outside present boundaries the report identified a major land assembly by CARMA and Nu-West. At the south end is a similar major assembly by BACM. Annexation of these lands would put millions of dollars of profits into the pockets of these developers, since it would be a major step towards opening up these assemblies for development.

Annexation was rejected by an overwhelming 75 per cent of the Calgary electorate. So BACM and Genstar have met with a temporary roadblock to one aspect of their expansion plans in the Calgary area. But, as the report prepared for Calgary City Hall demonstrates, they are left with a position of enormous power in determining the future of housing, house prices, and urban development in that city.

Since this article was written, there have been several interesting developments. Following public consideration of the report by city council, Mayor Rod Sykes convened a secret meeting of the aldermen in the aldermen's lounge at city hall. At this meeting the aldermen were informed of several potential lawsuits arising from the preparation of the report. Faced with this challenge the aldermen decided to reverse their earlier decision and authorized the Mayor to write a letter of apology to Genstar. At the following council meeting, the aldermen formally authorized the Mayor to apologize to Genstar for having prepared the report, but the contents of the letter have not been made public.

The status of the report has also changed. According to the city clerk the report, which was originally available to the public for twenty-five dollars a copy, is no longer being published. In addition, there are no copies of the report available for public perusal at city hall. For those of you lucky enough to have purchased the report—save them. The City of Calgary has officially declared them "collectors' items".

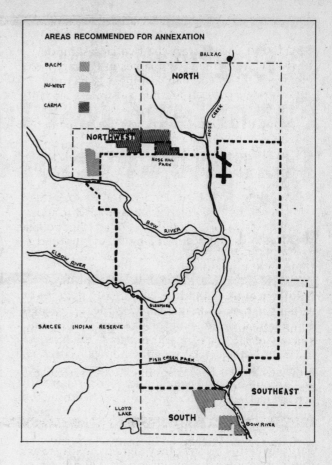

AREAS RECOMMENDED FOR ANNEXATION

BACM

NU-WEST

CARMA

NORTH

BALZAC

NORTHWEST

NOSE CREEK

NOSE HILL PARK

BOW RIVER

ELBOW RIVER

GLENMORE

SARCEE INDIAN RESERVE

FISH CREEK PARK

SOUTHEAST

LLOYD LAKE

SOUTH

BOW RIVER

St Catharines: Farm land lost to Toronto developers

Peter Coda

The name of St. Catharines conjures up pictures of verdant orchards, vineyards and gardens. Situated on a plain at the base of the Niagara escarpment, this city of 115,000 is near the heart of the Niagara fruitbelt, famed for its strawberries, cherries, plums, peaches, pears and grapes. Small wonder that recent concern over the loss of farmland in general has been particularly strong concerning the fruitbelt around St. Catharines. It has already been severely depleted by the road projects associated with the Queen Elizabeth Highway which runs the length of the plain, the eastward industrial expansion of Hamilton and residential sprawl.

When in the late 1960s "citizen participation" was introduced into planning at various levels in Ontario, the newly-established Niagara Regional Government involved "opinion leaders" as well as the public at large in the formulation of area planning policies. The resultant policy plan proposals for the Niagara region drew much praise for its progressive stance regarding farmland preservation. The proposed plan advocated the shifting of future development onto less desirable soils south of the escarpment and scrupulously preserving all land suitable for farming wherever possible.

In December 1973 Niagara Regional Council adopted the text of the draft policy plan.

In September 1974 the actual plan constructed from these goals was shot down in flames. Only a few of the original words and phrases remained. The substance of the final version of the plan contradicted the input by the area's citizens on opinion panels as well as at several well-attended public meetings. Several thousand acres more than the proposed plan allowed were designated for urban development on the Lake Ontario plain from Lincoln East to Niagara on the Lake, with the support of a large majority of regional councillors. Councillor Don Alexander summed up the result on behalf of himself and two other politicians, Councillors Mel Swart and John Buscarino, who had unceasingly championed the original goals. Said Alexan-

der: "The score is speculators 23, Niagara 3."

The reference to speculators made by Alexander, a councillor from St. Catharines, is well-founded. One large developer controls almost 1500 acres of the 2,400 acres comprising two blocks south of St. Catharines in the Thorold area, while a considerable parcel of prime agricultural land west of the St. Catharines urban area is already largely in the control of two groups of local developers. That the rural "land-grab" far exceeded the requirements for St. Catharines population growth to 1991, the end of the planning period, is suggested by the figures in the accompanying table.

Planning for growth in St. Catharines		
	Regional plan figures	Alexander figures
Population, 1974	112,000	112,000
Projection, 1991	155,000	140,000
Population capacity of plan development area	185,250	185,250
Overcapacity as of 1991	30,250	45,250

Note: Calculations of the capacity of urban-designated land in St. Catharines do not include any estimate of potential higher densities which could be achieved by redevelopment of older residential areas.

The town of Thorold and its new urban areas are located south of St. Catharines and the Niagara escarpment. At first it might be thought that locating new urban development in that location might save some of the very best of lands below the escarpment. However, besides the fact that considerable acreages of vineyards situated there would be lost, there are other factors to be considered.

While St. Catharines was given an area for urban

expansion far beyond its estimated needs, the area granted to Thorold is even more incongruous. In the last few years, of all the centres in the Niagara region — including Niagara Falls, Welland, Port Colborne, Fort Erie and Thorold — only St. Catharines had experienced a population increase. Regionally there has been a net population *decrease*. Why was one developer so keen on acquiring so much land if no population growth would occur under present trends? Questioned by Councillor Mel Swart, the president of this development company suggested that people in Toronto would eagerly buy in the Thorold area even if it was 80 miles away. Incredible to commute that distance? Not so incredible perhaps if the 406 Expressway now forming a corridor between Welland and St. Catharines were extended through the St. Catharines downtown and across the farmland west of the city, as is planned, and if the Queen Elizabeth Highway were widened. It seemed to urban growth critics that planning for the region was being done from the outside by Toronto-based developers and the Ontario government in collusion with a narrow group of local interests who had no intention of conserving farmland.

It wasn't entirely smooth sailing for the politicians who advocated the policies adopted in the official plan of regional Niagara. They encountered an alert and informed opposition at sessions of Niagara Council through councillors Alexander, Swart and Buscarino and from a citizen-based group called Grapevine which researched and documented the conservationist point of view and assisted other individuals and groups to lobby more effectively.

The opposition created considerable public awareness about the monopolistic land ownership pattern in the new urban areas and thereby disputed the common promises made to the public by the growth-oriented politicians. For example, Councillor William Marshall, a United Auto Workers staff representative, warned the industrial workers of the St. Catharines area that to limit the supply of land for development would create "instant millionaires" of a few developers. But Grapevine critics proved that new development lands in the Thorold-St. Catharines area was even more monopolistically held than previously and by interests which also held properties in the older urban areas. His fellow regional councillor, John Buscarino, himself a real estate agent prior to becoming mayor of Port Colborne, warned of giving in to the "land syndicates" who, he alleged, would keep the supply of building lots to a trickle so that they could guarantee themselves $15,000 or so per lot. Charged Buscarino: "Under the current system there is effectively no competition, with a few developers monopolizing land and construction."

Other councillors spoke of expanding the tax base by granting more land for development without ever substantiating how this would occur.

Harvesting grapes in the St. Catharines fruitbelt. Photo: Ministry of Industry and Tourism.

Conservationists argued that, instead, taxes would probably rise since the population foreseen would be commuting to commerical and industrial places of employment outside the Niagara region and suggested that growth policies must at least be based upon keeping a balance between population and employment opportunities within the area.

The opposition case presented was a major factor in 1974 local elections. On St. Catharines' council two allies of developers — both associated with development companies — David Lewis and John Taliano were defeated. Regionally, the 1974 election was inconclusive. The city voter turn-out was only 23 per cent. Development critic Don Alexander was re-elected by the voters of St. Catharines despite some virulent attacks on his position by most of the other politicians.

Subsequently there were apparently some second thoughts about land-use planning for the Niagara region at Queen's Park. The rumoured cancellation of the 406 highway extension on which much of the land development in St. Catharines hinges, is likely a consequence of severe budget restrictions combined with a concern for votes in this traditionally Tory area.

Among the important land-holders and developers operating in the St. Catharines area is a large Toronto-based firm with some unsavoury

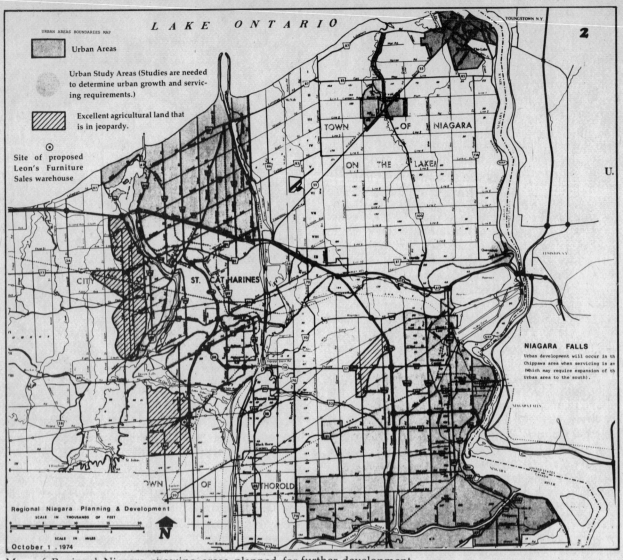

Urban Areas

Urban Study Areas (Studies are needed to determine urban growth and servicing requirements.)

Excellent agricultural land that is in jeopardy.

Site of proposed Leon's Furniture Sales warehouse

TOWN OF NIAGARA ON THE LAKE

ST. CATHARINES

NIAGARA FALLS
Urban development will occur in the Chippawa area when servicing is av (Which may require expansion of the Urban area to the south).

Regional Niagara Planning & Development
SCALE IN THOUSANDS OF FEET
SCALE IN MILES
October 1 , 1974

Map of Regional Niagara showing areas planned for further development.

connections. This is the DelZotto group of companies, which has operated under as many as 168 names at one time. For all practical purposes DelZotto monopolizes all of the new urban land in the Thorold area south of St. Catharines. It furthermore holds properties in new urban areas west of St. Catharines as well as inside the city proper. DelZotto operates under the names Deltan Realty, York Speculative Realty, Effingham Investments, as well as trust holdings under James H. Climenhage. The use of at least six different names locally had made it less obvious just how commanding this group is. Furthermore, by being represented locally by a fairly prominent local businessman, James Climenhage, it has generally been regarded as a locally-based enterprise. The unsavoury associations of Angelo DelZotto of Toronto documented by the Ontario royal commission on construction violence has not been covered by the local media, particularly the *St. Catharines Standard*, which has had harsh words for citizen reform advocates on many occasions.

Through partnership with a company with connections to enterprises partially held by the Toronto-based Tanenbaum brothers (Runneymede-Taro Homes), the second most significant holder of property in and around St. Catharines is a "distant cousin" of the DelZotto companies. It is Taro, heading Fox Hill Taro Investments, Vonler Construction Ltd., Runneymade-Taro Homes and Mclaughlin-Taro Developments Inc. Through its connection with the city law firm of Cairns, Chown, Edgar, Huska and Taliano it has had very effective relations with local government through Chown as mayor between 1968 and 1972 and through Aldermen Taliano and Lewis for a number of years until 1974 when they were defeated.

The third major developer and holder of properties in the newly-designated development area west of St. Catharines is a group of companies grouped around Birchwood Builders. They include the names Langendoen, Vector, Paramount, and are probably linked to several others. Again, in terms of directors there appears to be an overlap with a city-based legal firm of Willson, Miller, Fullerton, Partington and Robins.

There are a number of other firms involved both locally based as well as being directed from other centres. But the evidence indicates that a very few developers have managed to gain control of most of the land designated for urban development in the St. Catharines area, and to obtain exactly the regional planning policies which favour their interests and promote urban growth and sprawl generally. The official plan offers a very weak justification for all of this:

In the interest of encouraging competition and choices of location for new development and thus assisting in minimizing housing costs, a surplus of designated lands over minimum needs is desirable.

There is no evidence that the increased supply of land designated for development has made the cost of building lots any lower in St. Catharines. But elsewhere this policy has facilitated unwanted growth which citizen groups have had little success in opposing.

Lucerne: Politicians share in land profits

Guy LeCavalier

In mid-December, during a debate in the Quebec National Assembly on the bill on reorganization of municipal government in the Outaouais area, Marcel Leger, *Parti québécois* member for Montreal-Lafontaine, revealed details of extensive land speculation in Lucerne which involved some potential conflicts of interest for politicians at several levels. Lucerne is located next door to Hull in the Outaouais regional district.

Leger accused several Liberals of being involved in this land speculation. He named federal Minister of Supply and Services Jean-Pierre Goyer and some local Liberal organizers and highly placed public administrators: Messrs. Marcel Beaudry, Maurice Marois, Fernand Philips, and Edouard and Pierre Bourque. The latter were, by the way, directly involved in another scandal, the Dasken affair.

Leger claimed that Jean-Pierre Goyer had sold for the amazing amount of $8-million land in Lucerne for which he had previously paid $400,000.

Leger asked the Quebec minister of municipal affairs, Dr. Victor C. Goldbloom, if he was aware that such transactions were undertaken mainly by Liberal organizers who were, at the same time, promoting the reorganization of the Outaouais territory in a way that could make these transactions even more profitable. Dr. Goldbloom said he was unaware of the transactions and did not know to whom these lands belonged. He promised an inquiry if Leger could provide the facts in writing. Leger promised to do so.

Meanwhile, federal minister Goyer categorically denied the accusations. "I don't only deny these charges," he said during a phone conversation with a representative of the Canadian Press, "but I defy him to prove them." "Personally," he added, "I find Mr. Leger's charges dishonest and libellous, and I believe that he should prove them right away or deny them and make public excuses."

Leger proceeded to provide the facts in writing to the minister of municipal affairs, as promised. And the latter kept his word in calling for an inquiry.

Before the emissaries responsible for Goldbloom's inquiry could reach Hull, *Le Droit*, Ottawa-Hull's French-language daily, carried out its own inquiry from public records on land transactions in Lucerne. This investigation also found the names of Liberal organizers mentioned by Leger as being involved in these transactions. Other names were added to Leger's list, and many transactions documented. Major land value increases had occurred in a few years, sometimes in a few months. Most of the time, these increases were not related to any construction on the land. And Liberal party members had made enormous profits in the transactions.

The two brothers, Edouard and Pierre Bourque, for example, sold for $1,875,520 in 1974 land which they had purchased at $375,000 the previous year. The brothers had also bought a 40-acre parcel in 1972 for $80,000 and sold it two years later for $475,000.

Two other men named by Leger, Maurice Marois and Fernand Philips, both highly placed members of the Outaouais Development Corp., were also found to be involved in land speculation. Marois's property increased in price from $142,000 to $1,282,608 in three years. Philips did not do so well, receiving an increase only from $210,000 to $375,000. Antoine Gregoire, president of the corporation, said that the transactions were made before the two men became members. However, Philips is presently a shareholder of many enterprises, including the Gatineau Westgate, a society still heavily involved in Lucerne land speculation; Mr. Marois is the president of Investments Mirage, Inc., also involved in such transactions during 1974.

Other names were added to the list. Two highly placed public administrators, this time members of the Outaouais Regional Community, Mr. Roland Stevens and Mr. Taoufik Zeribi, were found by *Le Droit* to be involved in these transactions. Records indicate they made a $290,000 profit in one year on an investment of only $87,500. The president of the Outaouais Regional Community, Jean-Marie Seguin, revealed to *Le Droit* that he had been aware of the transactions made by his two colleagues for some time. He assured the newspaper that he personally did not find this involvement "normal." He even said that he himself had informed the Quebec Municipal Commission as well as the minister of municipal affairs of these transactions. Seguin's declaration appeared to conflict with the municipal affairs minister's declaration to Leger, a few weeks before in the National Assembly, that he did not know who was involved. Seguin added that he was told that these transactions were legal and that until it was proven without any doubt that his two colleagues had taken advantage of information provided by their position for their own personal interest, nothing could be done.

On top of the problem of proving the presence of potential conflict of interest, *Le Droit* also found that many of the names of persons involved in these transactions were not available in public records. Many transactions were made as "in trust" and "in fiducie" arrangements. In some cases, neither the names of the sellers nor the buyers were known.

According to *Le Droit*, the land speculation in Lucerne permitted 20 speculators to realize a profit of nine million dollars on 2,000 acres between 1970 and 1974. Excluded from this "preliminary" investigation carried out by *Le Droit* were all the farms that were divided and sold into acre lots for prices ranging from $1,500 to $10,000. According to newspaper estimates, the profits varied between 200 per cent and 1,000 per cent in most transactions. The actual average profit on the 2,000 acres examined was no less than 400 per cent.

Holding costs for land held by speculators are minimal, due to outdated assessments and tax concessions aimed at retaining farming in the region. According to the director of land assessment for the Outaouais Regional Community, Roland St-Cyr, the real estate taxation has not kept up with the land market trend, as the last assessment (on which taxes are based) was carried out in 1971.

In terms of dollars, for instance, one lot in Lucerne was sold three times in four years: first for $26,000; then $185,000; and $420,000 in September 1974. Its assessment for municipal taxation remained at $30,625 through this period.

On top of this gap between the actual (though speculative) value of the land and its official assessment value, a speculator in Quebec can save on taxes by renting his land to a farmer. In Quebec, this means a reduction of 40 per cent on municipal taxes and 35 per cent on school taxes, with a maximum payment of 1 per cent of the roll value or $150 per acre.

The official inquiry called by Goldbloom started in late January. This investigation was, in fact, a preliminary—and maybe also final—examination. The two emissaries sent to Hull had been directed to discover whether a thorough study was necessary. Their task was to get a general idea about the situation and to determine whether or not some cases of conflict of interest existed. This process was expected to last several weeks and consisted of compiling documentation on land transactions in the Outaouais region, especially in Lucerne. It included checking various land deeds at county registration offices and questioning various local officials. By the end of March, a report of their finding was to be presented to another group of experts and to Dr. Goldbloom who would decide whether or not to pursue the matter. In fact, their mission lasted three weeks and was completed in mid-February. Their report, presented to Dr. Goldbloom, has not yet been released.

The two ministry representatives were not given the power to force area notaries to reveal information. Consequently, they could not find out who was involved under the cover of "in trust" and "in fiducie", which means that a large proportion of the transactions were not accessible to them. Their investigation was practically limited to what *Le Droit* had already found out.

Whatever the outcome of the investigation, however, the results of the speculation itself are quite clear. Development in the Outaouais area will be speeded up by the adoption last December of the bill reorganizing local government by replacing 32 original municipalities with eight new ones. Also expected in the near future is annexation of a portion of Lucerne to Hull. Lucerne is the area where most of the speculative transactions occurred. There seems little doubt that this land will turn out to be directly in the path of Hull's development.

Gilles Paquin, the reporter who carried out most of the *Le Droit* investigation, believes that this speculation will inevitably force up the cost of housing in the area. It is making land so expensive that many residents will only be able to afford to live in high-rise apartments. And area residents will find that their local governments are paying very high prices for the land required for schools, housing for the aged, and low rental housing projects.

The facts brought to light, however, demonstrate how people involved in the ruling Liberal party, from a federal cabinet minister on down, are themselves implicated in forcing up the cost of land by their land speculation activities.

The last news made public about the Lucerne inquiry appeared in November 1975, about eleven months after the opening of the investigation which was to have taken a few weeks. In answer to a question posed by an opposition member of the Quebec National Assembly, Minister Goldbloom promised that a public report based on the inquiry would appear sometime in the future.

II The experts

Planners as professionals

Ron Clark

There is a crisis in Canadian city planning. It is not simply a dilemma of which coloured pencils planners should use, the appropriate design for residential subdivisions, or the proper contents of an urban development plan. Instead, the crisis is one of the performance, role and function of planners and planning in contemporary Canadian society. Canada's planners and their professional club, the Canadian Institute of Planners (CIP), have adopted a position which reinforces the status quo, often facilitates the narrow interests of the property development industry, and enhances their own professional status — to the detriment of Canadian urban places and the majority of their inhabitants.

The process of urbanization in Canada, since the end of World War II, has focussed attention on the need for city planning, to the point where today planners and their agencies affect the lives of millions of urban Canadians. Although criticism of planning in Canada has occurred in the past, the profession has always ignored the call for change. As the importance of city planning continues to increase, therefore, the need to re-examine the activities of planners becomes critical.

The current behaviour of planners and of the Canadian Institute of Planners has not come about as a result of social uncertainty, professional unawareness or even institutional drift. On the contrary, Canada's planners and their sacred profession have constantly been warned of their continuing withdrawal from urban reality. Yet, in the face of considerable criticism and countless danger signs, planners have consciously responded not with re-form, but rather by becoming increasingly smug and aloof at the level of their individual practice and by accelerating their self-serving elitist pursuits at the level of their professional institute.

NORMAN PEARSON'S ONE MAN CRUSADE

An important voice in the call for change within Canada's planning profession was that of Norman Pearson of British Columbia. As editor of *TPIC News*, the newsletter of the Town Planning Institute of Canada (since renamed Canadian Institute of Planners), in the late 1960s and early 1970s, Pearson was a harsh and persistent critic of planners and their professional institute.

It was Pearson who, as he himself characterized it, continually "rattled the bell on the sacred cow." Critical of the profession's elitist tendencies, he once observed that, "when the chips were down, the old guard votes clung successfully to the conservative protectionist threads of 'professionalism' and carefully skirted outward oriented innovations."

One memorable Pearson editorial included a characterization of the planning profession which is still appropriate today.

If the Institute is to survive, it will have to change its ways. It can no longer obstruct the development of society and the solution of its problems; it must aid in their solution as its first and most important objective – through developing constructive views on national public issues, and through aiding and encouraging citizens to participate in solving community problems. If the Institute is interested in retaining its younger members and attracting the involvement of the students – and it had better be – it will offer them not paternalistic lip service, but sincere and responsible involvement in tackling the public issues that are relevant to them ....

If the Institute is serious in its desire to maintain the competence of its members – and it has to be – it will start financing upgrading programmes across the country and expel those members who fail to take part. Indeed if the Institute is serious at all it will drop its pomp ... and strive to involve all the members in these broad concerns. If it does not, it will become or remain, the "Old Boys' Club."

Probably no one before or indeed after Pearson has strived as hard to influence the future direction of planning in Canada. He recognized the misguided priorities of the planning profession and realized where they were leading. However, even his constant haranguing of the profession produced nothing more than paternalistic "well dones" at each annual general meeting. Finally, in 1972 Pearson resigned as editor of *TPIC News*, quit the profession, and directed his energies toward improving social and urban conditions in British Columbia.

WARNINGS IN SASKATOON

The planning profession's next significant encounter with an advocate of change was at Saskatoon in the summer of 1972. The setting was the profession's annual get-together. Kent Gerecke, a doctoral student in planning at the University of British Columbia, was invited to TPIC's Conference to present a report on the future of planning in Canada. In doing so, Gerecke essentially called for change in the profession. The substance of his paper had been gleaned from extensive research on Canada's planners — the way they operate, the things they do, the methods they use. In fact, Gerecke's analysis revealed what he called "the paradox of Canadian city planning" — the emerging incongruence between the type of planning that has been created and changing Canadian society, which he illustrated with a simple diagram. Gerecke's research showed that today's planning is based on a bureaucratic model that emphasizes day-to-day administration, shuns citizen participation, uses an inward methodology and places more faith in planning per se than in the content of the plan.

Gerecke offered a clear challenge to the planning profession: "We must seriously ask whether there is a crisis in Canadian city planning. Obviously, such depends on one's interpretation. If you want planning to maintain and expand its role as a major contributor to public policy, then there is a crisis. On the other hand, if you wish the profession to stabilize and merely act to facilitate urban growth, then there is no crisis." Having raised the question, Gerecke made clear his own position: "I accept that there is a crisis in Canadian city planning, which relates to our infatuation with power and our inability to adapt to changing times." The planners gathered in Saskatoon were not, however, at all receptive to Gerecke's findings and were quite unprepared to accept his challenge. This was made quite clear to Gerecke during an evening social function when he was attacked and insulted by two past presidents of the institute.

Despite the profession's rejection of their colleague's message and his research findings, Gerecke's work represents an important contribution to the understanding of Canada's planning practice and a major benchmark in the struggle for change in planning.

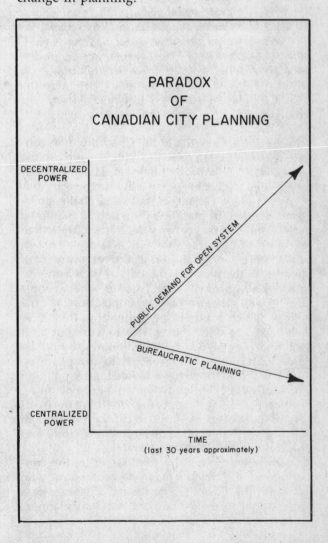

PARADOX
OF
CANADIAN CITY PLANNING

DECENTRALIZED POWER

PUBLIC DEMAND FOR OPEN SYSTEM

BUREAUCRATIC PLANNING

CENTRALIZED POWER

TIME
(last 30 years approximately)

THE CHARLOTTETOWN CHALLENGE

The most recent challenge to the planning profession occured during the 1973 gathering of members of the Canadian Institute of Planners for their annual conference. The planners were confronted by a few of their number with the following critique of their activities:

Planners have done little to challenge or question the activities and motives of those development interests operating within the urban environment, and in fact mounting evidence would seem to indicate that a conscious or unconscious alliance has existed between planners and the property development industry.

Planners even when given a free hand to author new provincial planning legislation, to develop municipal planning and subdivision standards, and to prepare zoning by-laws, have failed miserably in their task of improving the quality of urban development and as a consequence have contributed very little to the habitability of urban places.

Planners as a professional body in this country have not only failed to speak as a unified and socially responsible voice on urban issues of national significance, but have instead endeavoured to acquire professional, intellectual and societal credibility through the establishment of a professional organization (TPIC/CIP) imbued with a philosophy of elitism, conservatism and self-preservation.

In the special session at the Charlottetown conference, designed to raise the issues relating to the failures of the planning profession, James Lorimer was invited to give his perspective on the activities of city planners. Lorimer initiated the challenge by observing that the planning profession has aligned itself solidly with property interests rather than reflecting the diverse interests that now exist in urban affairs, and that, in fact, the commitment of planners to the property industry is increasing. In cities like Vancouver and Toronto when people have found themselves in opposition to the policies which planners are promoting, they have been forced to start from scratch to work out their own analyses of what city planning should be doing and their own approaches to city planning problems. And they have arrived at a position which is more or less independent of the planning position and often in opposition to it. Yet the planners in most cases continue to carry on as though nothing has happened to question the validity and propriety of their work.

Lorimer was joined by Kent Gerecke, the constant critic of Canada's planning profession, who in examining the rationale for the existence of a professional institute, pointed out that planners are far more interested in careers, salaries and licensing than helping ordinary citizens. The institute, in his opinion, was more or less an economic union. In an amazing confirmation of this statement, Michael Kusner, chairman of the planning program at Ryerson Polytechnical Institute (one of the schools of planning in Canada "recognized" by CIP) told the audience that they were naive if they thought that CIP was anything but an economic union.

In the end, the Charlottetown deliberations produced nothing in the way of change within the Canadian Institute of Planners. This was, perhaps to be expected, since less than a month prior to the Charlottetown showdown, CIP's president Bill Thompson (Commissioner of Planning for the Region of Waterloo in Ontario) had set the intellectual climate by branding professional self-evolution as "navel gazing" (planners' favourite cop-out when faced with any activity which resembles a scrutiny of their behaviour or performance.) In any case, the much hoped for dialogue and subsequent action on the issue of planning and society turned out to be a monologue by those advocating change. Change was the last thing the profession wanted to entertain. It was Lorimer who provided a fitting end to the Charlottetown charade.

For those of you who feel fairly comfortable with what city planning had done and what it is doing now – well, I'm pleased to discover that there are situations where you are able to get together and say these things to each other and to reinforce your strength to deal with us when you come across us in political debate. This is a fight for power. I think there is no doubt that there are some of us on one side and there are a lot of you on the other side. All I can say at the moment is that we are not winning but we soon may be.

CIP — GROWTH WITHOUT MATURITY

Taking these rather futile efforts at effecting change within the planning profession as a point of reference, let us look at some of the profession's most recent activities.

Recently, the planning institute has been determined to strengthen and expand its geographic dominance in Canada. The planning profession in Quebec — le Corporation des Urbanistes du Quebec — had long been a holdout from CIP. However, by 1974 CUQ had been persuaded to align itself with CIP and Quebec City became the host for the 1974 conference and annual general meeting. This affair was calm and collected with most sessions amounting to little more than an English Canadian exercise in flag-waving, the main effort being to convince the Quebec planners of their good fortune in finally being part of CIP.

About this same time, however, CIP did launch an interesting in-house project. A questionnaire, designed to "gather some basic information on the nature of our membership and their expectations of the Institute", was circulated to all members. The results offer some interesting perspectives on the planning profession. When asked, "Why did you join CIP?" or "What do you feel are the main benefits in CIP?", the most predominant response was "communication". This is a rather strange response, however, in view of the kind of communication which actually occurs within CIP. The major means of communication are the newsletter, *Plan Canada* and the annual conference. The newsletter is published regularly (about 10 issues a year) but its contents are decidedly mundane, discussing few things of any consequence. *Plan Canada*, a rather scholarly review, appears on a very irregular basis and is read by less than one quarter of CIP's membership (according to a survey conducted a few years ago). In terms of face-to-face contact, the annual conference is merely a meeting ground for the profession's mandarins, since few younger and junior members can afford to come on their own and fewer still are sent by their agencies. Thus, communications would seem to be a motherhood issue masking other motives.

In the survey results, "professionalism" and "credibility" were also singled out as major reasons for membership in CIP. Fearful of their tenuous public and professional status, planners respond not with efforts to display their social utility but rather seek to assure their identity with the initials "M.C.I.P." and other institutional paraphernalia which they can display on their walls or place in their wallets.

There have been moves afoot to legislate and hence legalize the planners' perceived "right" to professional status. The survey indicated that many planners favour licensing and registration of their profession. Supporters of such action claim that tightening up the profession would improve "public responsibility." This is a strange perspective, since the public will hardly be better served by a group determined to become as elitist and aloof as some of today's "senior" professions. In reality, the licensing and registration of planners is a ploy, designed primarily to strengthen their ability to bargain more successfully in the market place; it has little to do with "public responsibility."

Meanwhile, things continue to get worse. The 1975 meeting of Canada's planners in Vancouver produced more of the same type of petty, institutional thinking. But more of the same thing is more of the wrong thing, despite the belief of Mark Dorfman, the current president of CIP, that planning is now on the threshold of renaissance.

On the contrary, planning in Canada today is in a more critical state than ever. Planners have consciously aligned themselves with the forces of the status quo, and have, through their daily activities and professional posture, clearly decided to ignore the planning paradox cited by Gerecke.

What are the reasons for planners having adopted such a position? While one could engage in endless intellectual or professional nit-picking, it seems that the fundamental problem is that planning was never founded with any supporting ideological principles of its own.

Instead, planning took its lead and developed its role in response to the whims of the market place and those key actors in whose interests it was crucial to retain the socio-economic equilibrium of power. Hence planning, determined to curry the favour of society's power brokers, was not interested in developing independent theories or courses of action which might jeopardize their socially-secure niche. In this respect, Dennis Hardy's comments are significant.

No amount of reform of the planning machinery can alter the fact that it operates within a system devoted to private gain and the perpetuation of a class system. Planning has been able to survive and extend its activities because, far from standing for socialism, it has become an important part of bourgeois ideology. In the post-war period its policies have been consistent with the emergent ideal of a stratified property-owning democracy, and a consumer-based system of priorities. Intervention in the inner city, where planning has been most comprehensive, has been manifestly unsuccessful in social terms but has cleared the way for massive private investment and construction. It is no longer necessary for the ruling interests to oppose planning and, even in those cases where it exceeds its permitted limits, policies and legislation can be easily revoked. Goodman's comment on the American situation is not

Licensing planners in Quebec

While only the provinces of Saskatchewan and Quebec have legislative acts which permit the licensing of planners, other provinces are feeling the pressure from provincial affiliates of CIP to institute similar legislation.

But does the licensing of planners generate increased public responsibility, as advocates of such legislation would suggest? Two brief instances from Quebec would seem to indicate that it produces little more than professional watchdogging of the pettiest nature.

One professor of planning teaching, in a "CIP recognized program", in a Quebec university, is constantly troubled by the Quebec affiliate of CIP because he has chosen not to become a member of CIP. The professor in question has an acknowledged national reputation in planning and possesses an outstanding educational background in urban planning, architecture and urban design. What seems to be particularly unsettling to the Quebec planners, is that his classes are always overloaded with students wishing to share in his knowlege of urban issues. A sad state of affairs when the excellent are harassed and the uninspiring are protected all because of the existence of supposedly public serving legislation.

The second account of planners protecting the public through licensing again occurs in Quebec. This story would be humorous if it weren't such a sad revelation of what self-serving professionalism produces.

In this case, a person with an excellent academic career in both planning and architecture set up a consulting practice in Montreal. By choice the individual chooses not to belong to either the professional planning or architectural "clubs". Consequently, when the firm was to be registered in the yellow pages of the Montreal telephone book, the person asked that it be located under "Urban Design". When the yellow pages came out, the firm was listed under "Planners". A subsequent explanation from the telephone company indicated that they had no such category as "Urban Design" and they were not about to create one. Hence, the firm, one of Canada's most innovative and competent, came under immediate pressure from (you guessed it) the Quebec affiliate of CIP. It seems that Bell's intransigence about creating a new category, coupled with their decision to lump them under the heading Planners, has brought the wrath of CIP on its head. Strange behaviour. In a country beset with urban problems, we have an organization apparently more concerned with scrutinizing the yellow pages of telephone books than shaping creative responses to the problems at hand.

---

inappropriate: *Contrary to popular mythology, planning did not bring socialism – in fact, it became a sophisticated weapon to maintain the existing control under a mask of rationality, efficiency and science.*

In short, planning is not a value-free, apolitical activity. Again Hardy's comments are pertinent:

This is a critical point in contemporary debate because it separates those who take a neutral view of science, and have attempted to develop planning as a value-free technical activity which provides a basis for political decisions, and those who see reality and ideology as inseparable and all inputs to the planning process as being value-laden.

As long as Canadian planners refuse to understand this, they will continue to do nothing more than aid and abet the aspirations of the property development industry, and support the advocates of growth. Planning offices, and city halls, still appear to operate on the premise that "whatever is good for (Trizec, Genstar, Cadillac-Fairview, Daon, etc.) — is good for our city." Under the euphemisms of "implementation" and "practicality", planners are moving further away from a concern with the equity of planning (as Harvey Lithwick has so cogently observed, "Planning offers security for the rich and guarantees insecurity for the poor.") and closer to becoming willing participants in potentially undesirable growth and development. The match-cover message of the Hamilton-Wentworth Planning Agency — a public agency — while more blatant than most planning departments, underscores this point.

Unquestionably, the planning profession in Canada has grown. Its membership ranks become larger each year (now over 1600 members). However, this process is more akin to bloating, since it assumes no intellectual or societal maturation. As Richard Bolan so succinctly notes, "The maintenance of the specialist group becomes of paramount concern to its members and the group is seen to become an interest bent on promoting its own status, power and resources within society." Canada's emerging planning profession certainly fits the Bolan organizational model.

ROOTS OF THE CRISIS

There are many reasons — both historic and contemporary — which account for the current crisis in Canadian city planning.

Historically, Canada's planning tradition is not rooted in this country, but rather is a "heritage" of British and later American influence.

Under the leadership of Thomas Adams, a British planner working in Canada between 1914 and 1921, the Town Planning Institute of Canada was formed in 1919. Consisting principally of surveyors, engineers, architects and lawyers who were interested in the new field of town planning, the Canadian planning profession began to thrive. But between 1932 and 1946 the profession vanished, giving way to the two national priorities of that era — namely depression and war. Then in the late 1940s, planning experienced a significant rejuvenation. What occurred at that point established a trend in Canadian city planning which still pervades much of the planning field today. Anthony Adamson excellently depicts these events.

"It was then found (after World War II) that there were no planners in Canada. They taught the British the rudiments of colonial life and then let them loose in the blood stream of the country .... We put up the greatest song and dance today if an American is made chief of police or an art gallery curator, but the British takeover of planning in the 1940s was massive and we did not object."

The significance of this early infusion of British-trained planners into Canada cannot be overstated. For, the British imports, facing no Canadian opposition, advanced quickly and soon occupied many senior positions in all the major public planning and housing agencies in Canada. Also, in the years which followed, as Canada endeavoured to develop its own education programs in planning, many British-trained planners gravitated toward these new academic posts.

Unfortunately, the British training and experience were not (and indeed are certainly not today) appropriate for Canada's emerging urban problems. Sadly, the British preoccupation with the physical details of land use and their extremely narrow view of the complex interrelationship among the multitude of variables which influence the quality and form of cities, became deeply ingrained in Canadian planning thought and practice.

Perhaps, most serious of the deficiencies in the British approach to planning was the relentless desire to accumulate, centralize and legislate more and more planning power and control. Accompanying this emphasis on the expansion of planning authority, the British ignored the role of the public in planning. Consequently, what emerged in Canada throughout the 1950s and early 1960s was a planning model in which planners were totally detached from the dynamics which characterize urban issues. The British belief that planning is a value-free, apolitical science to be practiced with rigorous precision, employing a grab bag of pseudo tools and having a "New Town" fixation was the unfortunate legacy the British planners bequeathed to Canada. This approach continues to haunt — both intellectually and practically — planning in this country today.

While the British planning model established the basis for Canadian city planning, the American influence must also be considered. The influx of U.S. planning into Canada tended not to significantly affect the narrow practice of planning as introduced by the British. Certainly, there is no event in the history of U. S. involvement in Canadian planning which parallels the British invasion of the late 1940s.

Nevertheless, the U.S. influence had its impact. First, the substantial U.S. takeover of Canadian universities which peaked during the 1960s, included schools of urban and regional planning. This U.S. input into planning education and practice brought about a slight shift away from the British concern for efficient patterns of land use, and introduced pluralism, public interest and advocacy to the vocabulary of Canadian planning. However, the American notion of planning and public interest was merely a microcosm of the broader social and economic injustices which characterize the United States. As Herbert Gans succinctly noted when discussing planners and public interest there, "The public interest turns out to be primarily their own (planners) interest and that of their business and upper-middle class constituencies". Or as Henry Fagan later acknowledged, "The truth is that for half a century our profession has specialized predominantly in advocacy planning for the business community." Of course, Robert Goodman's later characterization of planners as "the soft cops" was the ultimate condemnation of planning in the United States.

As a result of these influences, we see, in 1975, a planning profession in Canada which, at the practitioner level, continues for the most part to be dominated by British trained planners in senior positions, and which, at the academic level, is directed by Americans. There are, unfortunately, still only a handful of Canadian-education specialists

in urban planning currently teaching in our planning schools.

While these historic events account for much of what has already occurred in Canadian urban planning and characterize this country's response to urban issues, numerous contemporary circumstances continue to perpetuate and in fact reinforce these earlier directions in planning.

JOBS, MONEY AND CREDIBILITY

As Canada urbanized and accordingly as governments mobilized themselves to cope with the perceived need to plan and manage growth in a "rational" and "holistic" fashion, people educated in planning became a sought-after commodity. At the same time, the private sector began to engage planners so as to feign a commitment to public interest and community goals. And to accommodate these varying needs for planning expertise, a very active urban consulting fraternity developed. Consequently, in the past few years there has been a notable acceleration in the number of positions available to individuals with backgrounds in planning. As a result of this increased demand there has been a rather rapid and significant elevation in the salaries paid to planners.

Of course, one might say that the increase in job opportunities and money offered is not necessarily bad, for clearly this country requires planners. However, this recent demand for planners has had two perverse effects on Canadian planning. First, the general acceptance of planning has enhanced and indeed entrenched traditional approaches to planning, which are now being called into question. This makes it increasingly difficult to dislodge the planning mandarins who, while they consciously ignore the need for social change, will now work even harder to protect their well-paying, influential positions. Secondly, the growing acknowledgement of the planning function has tended, unhappily, to pervert contemporary attempts at restructuring and reorienting Canadian planning education. As one professor of planning recently pointed out, the major preoccupation among planning students is the need for "tools" that will be marketable. Interest in a philosophy of planning or a planning ideology has apparently been dropped by the wayside in recent years.

Hence the prospects for change in the planning profession are dismal. As planning becomes more and more widely acclaimed as a useful social function, and as schools of planning turn out more aspiring MCIP'ers, the gap between planners and the people with real urban and social problems grows.

Efforts to influence and persuade practicing planners of the need for change, as we have seen, have failed. The question now is whether it is possible to influence and indeed change the approaches to planning in the future by achieving a substantial shift in the education offered in planning schools. Unfortunately, there is little reason for optimism in this respect. Writing recently in *City Magazine*, Gerald Hodge, Director of the School of Urban and Regional Planning at Queen's University, observed that, "it would be both arrogant and irrelevant to teach planning courses for the ideology of the day, no matter whose."

To suggest as Hodge does, however, that the Canadian planner of the future can be "all things to all men" is surely ridiculous in an era when the social, political and economic inequities of our present society are becoming more and more sharply defined. As Aaron Wildavsky so neatly summarizes, "If planning is everything, maybe it is nothing."

THE URBAN FUTURE: A PLACE FOR PROFESSIONAL PLANNERS?

The underlying issue in this discussion is: what is to be done to redirect urban policies at all levels so as to begin to redress the inequities that continue to characterize urban Canada? The fundamental question for planners is: what role will planners play in solving this issue and in formulating the necessary new directions for urban policy? For an answer to these questions, there seems little point in looking to the schools of planning which have opted for an educational curriculum designed to affirm the status quo. Nor is there much point in looking to the planners' professional club, CIP, which seems quite content to ignore everything but self-serving professional interests. The establishment planners have worked long and hard to discount the critics who tried to promote the debate on the need for alternative approaches to planning. In the past, they have been able to shrug off with no apparent difficulty the challenges from insiders to open their work up to more critical scrutiny. As these planners work to improve their bargaining power as professionals through the introduction of licensing and registration measures, it becomes more important than ever to break through their monopoly for status quo planning and its derivative intellectual tradition in Canada.

Planning and professionalism: A view from the south

The results of an informal poll of U.S. planning students by the American Institute of Planners' (AIP) Student Coordinator, (reported in the February-March 1975 issue of *AIP Newsletter*) indicates that, like those in Canada, American planning students of today are demanding to be trained simply as qualified technicians. They want the "tools" that will get them jobs and let them "do" planning. They have little interest in receiving an education which would include discussion of the values and purposes that ought to guide the use of those tools. The idea of planners as "social activists" or as "agents of change", which began to emerge in the sixties, seems now to have given way under the pressures of job and economic insecurity. It seems that once more the technocrats have won out. The new generation of planners in the United States, if the poll was indeed representative, will be technicians and clock-punchers, possessing no underlying philosophy for planning and placing personal security above all other concerns.

The fact that AIP has undertaken this year certain actions to institute certification as a means of ensuring professional planning "competency" would certainly seem to reinforce the impression that so-called professional planners in the United States will increasingly define their role as technocrats.

The January 1975 issue of *AIP Newsletter* reports that AIP's Board of Governors has taken formal steps toward setting up the institute as a "professionally tight circle" which would act as the nation's single "source of competency in planning." In making this decision, the Board of Governors (in a masterful piece of self-serving logic) concluded that because of the increased pressure being felt by all professions during the past decade, for more direct accountability to the public they serve, "pressure has increased for some form of certification."

Another article in the newletter, "A Sense of Direction" by Robert C. Einsweiler, the immediate past president of AIP, indicates that the institute's major concerns, at a time when "the number of new professionals coming into the field" is growing, are to "restrain the move to state licensing and registration" and to create some sort of "limitation on entrance to the profession" at the national level. "Certification" was seen as the alternative to be sought in the immediate future. AIP becoming the national accrediting organization was deemed not only inevitable but desirable.

In looking at the implications of these moves on the part of AIP, what is distressing about the Board's actions (among other things) is what they say to the aspiring technicians being produced by the planning schools — that is, that the general welfare we should be most concerned with, fellow planners, is our own.

The question planners, and the public, should ask themselves is, just what will licensing, or "certification", as AIP would have it, do for planners and the planning profession? AIP asserts that it will increase the competence of planners as well as their "accountability" to the public they serve. Will it though? Doctors and lawyers have been licensed or certified for years and engineers and architects more recently. Yet we still have too many doctors who kill or maim their patients, or, at best, do nothing for them; too many lawyers who use Perry Mason theatrics in the courtroom to try and cover their sloppy research; too many engineers whose highways destroy rather than make use of their surroundings, and sometimes promote accidents; and too many architects who design inhuman buildings for which their colleagues award them prizes when they ought to censure them.

Moreover, is planning a profession in which competence can be determined by an examination? In a profession based on innovation, change and ambiguity, who is to prepare the examination, to determine which are the "right" questions and, worse still, the "right" answers?

The licensing or certification of planners will not guarantee or even promote competence and accountability. What it will promote, or possibly guarantee, is that a small and exclusive "club" will be created, that innovation and creativity in planning education will be smothered and that incompetence on the part of members of the "club" will be covered up more frequently than it will be exposed.

The AIP Board of Governors asserts that "planners cannot win in state level credentialing" and proposes instead AIP certification. If I am to be hung, the question of who is to spring the trap makes little difference to me. The end result is the same.

The certification or licensing of planners, in my opinion, is aimed at improving not their performance but their economic and social status. And the question which must then be answered is how can individuals who are primarily concerned with their own economic and social status ever hope to serve as agents of change?

Richard M. Grout

Arthur Erickson:
The Corporate Artist-Architect

Donald Gutstein

Arthur Erickson is often considered to be Canada's greatest architect. For projects such as Simon Fraser University atop Burnaby Mountain, and the Canadian Pavilion at Expo '70 in Osaka, Erickson has been showered with every major professional award in Canada. He was on the cover of Time Magazine in 1972. And he has won the prestigious $50,000 Royal Bank Prize and the $15,000 Molson's Prize.

Yet Erickson has also been responsible for a long string of controversial projects which have generated enormous public opposition. Often, in fact, the opposition has been so strong that the projects haven't been built. But even though this experience has made many ordinary citizens wary of Erickson, particularly residents of Vancouver who are most familiar with his work, somehow it doesn't seem to have harmed his professional reputation. In fact in some cases the very projects which have caused public uproar—like a controversial scheme for a ' see-through ' high-rise apartment in Vancouver's False Creek area which won an award from Canadian Architect magazine—are those which are lauded by the architectural profession.

Erickson's career is a lesson in the function of architects in Canada today. His mastery of the art of finding clients, of pleasing them, and of producing buildings which look good even though they often ignore or positively work against the needs of the people using them and of others they affect seems to be the combination of qualities that is admired in Canadian architects.

The design for Vancouver's Simon Fraser University was the beginning of a formal 10-year partnership between Erickson and Geoffrey Massey which began in 1963 and ended in 1972 when they went their separate ways.

Massey brought to the partnership the right connections. Son of Raymond, the actor, and nephew of Vincent, the Governor-General, Geoff was related to the Massey-Ferguson farm machinery millions. Geoff consolidated his position in 1956 by marrying into further wealth—Ruth Killam, niece of Izaak Walton Killam, Royal Securities chief, who made his millions by extracting huge profits from his power utility companies in South America. Arthur Erickson designed the residence for the Massey-Killam alliance.

SIMON FRASER

As you ascend from the chaos and confusion of the city below, your first impression of Simon Fraser University is a strong one. The University has been called a 'masterpiece of siting and composition' and you can see why. You park your car, you take the well-worn tour through the series of spaces carefully designed for such tours, you get back in your car, and you return home favourably impressed.

Such is the trek made by thousands of tourists and visiting art critics. One of the latter was the late Ada Louise Huxtable who was inspired to comment that SFU was 'consummate urbanity on a mountain top' (whatever that means). Simon Fraser was de-

Simon Fraser University on its mountain-top setting in Burnaby, with "portable" additions which weren't part of the master plan in the foreground.

A conversion of what was a "communications area" in the Simon Fraser master plan into a student study area.

An exterior detail of the "noble" concrete used so extensively at Simon Fraser.

signed for the visitor, to evoke comments such as that made by Huxtable, who had come to see it as a *thing*, an object set in a landscape.

However, for the people who actually *use* the place, things begin to look a little different after a while. Instead of being *impressed*, you begin to feel *oppressed* —by the vast unrelieved stretches of concrete, by the total lack of privacy, by the all-pervading presence of the place.

Erickson selected concrete as the only material for both structure and finish because he considered it to be so *noble*:

[Concrete] becomes as noble a material as limestone. There is no paint to mar its surface or contrasting materials to distract from its inherent beauty. As in all serious architecture, the structural material is consistent, pervasive and unadorned and the floors which should be more like a carpet, are of clay tile of various colours. Colour is used intensively only in the interiors, where it is appropriate and does not disturb the harmony of the composition of masses. [emphasis added]

In practice, however, for the students, faculty and staff who work surrounded by this nobility, the reality is coldness and a sense of sterility. When the concrete is wet—and that is much of the time—it has an omnipresent odour, resembling burnt toast. And of course the lack of finishes means that it is getting progressively dirtier with stains from coffee and other spilt liquids. Those are the realities that are rationalized away in Erickson's rhetoric.

In the photographs which are usually published

in architectural magazines, the realities of life and work at Simon Fraser are not very obvious. But to get those photographs, the photographers certainly come up hard against those realities. First there is the constant difficulty posed by portables. They have to be excluded from the photographs because they look so messy beside Erickson's grand design. Then there is the problem of ongoing construction. One of the few really perfect photographic compositions turns out to be a worm's eye view from the bottom of the stairs at the end of the mall looking up at the rotunda—a view that you would see in reality only if you had fallen down the stairs, broken your head, and couldn't move. But it sure makes a nice picture.

Portables are, of course symptomatic of the inflexibility of the master plan, which was conceived as a finished thing. Simon Fraser is constantly under construction—new residences, alterations, new academic facilities. Although each construction job is temporary, in total they present a constant disruption of the famous circulation patterns as well as continual noise and discomfort.

Within the main structure, many other 'temporary uses' not in the master plan, have appeared: an area which was once a cafeteria has become a lounge; the concourse, the so-called 'communication area,' has been turned into the exact opposite, a study area. The structure is so inflexible and fixed (partially because of the famous concrete finishes) that when the use of a space is changed, the original environmental controls—the lighting, acoustics, mechanical services, and surface finishes—are often next to useless. Generations of Simon Fraser students have responded to the inhuman and inflexible environment in a number of ways, not the least of which has been by 'trashing' the place.

THE CHINATOWN FREEWAY PROJECT

After Simon Fraser, the Erickson-Massey partnership remained visible in Vancouver through its design for the headquarters of MacMillan-Bloedel, B.C.'s largest corporation, in downtown Vancouver. And in 1967, they put themselves right at the centre of a major civic controversy by acting as architectural consultants for part of Vancouver's freeway system.

What happened was that Vancouver city hall decided to start construction on a section of its overall freeway plan which would connect a new freeway-scale Georgia Viaduct to a proposed waterfront freeway by cutting through the western part of Vancouver's Chinatown.

The City had been trying to build a network of freeways for 15 years, but it had been frustrated in almost every attempt by senior governments unwilling to put up large amounts of cash and a hostile

What the photographer sees: a dramatic view of Simon Fraser, taken from a difficult location.

citizenry. This time too there was massive public opposition, led by the Chinese community and University of British Columbia academics. The freeway plan was widely attacked, not only for the design itself—called 'a concrete knife through the heart of Chinatown'—but also for the complete lack of a planning framework.

Erickson-Massey were hired as the architectural consultants for the Chinatown freeway. Their job: to integrate the 120-foot wide, 30-foot high elevated freeway, into the 'urban fabric'. Their proposal: to put an arcade for shops and elevated restaurants under the freeway. Of course the assignment was ridiculous; there is just no way that a freeway can be 'integrated' into the urban fabric. So it was inevitable that Erickson-Massey's plan would also be ridiculous.

To a certain extent, Erickson recognized this. Soon after he produced his scheme, he warned that a freeway could destroy Vancouver's greatest asset—its beauty. But that did not lead him to oppose it. Instead he went on to say that 'maybe there has to be a freeway,' and to produce his design for it. Rather than fight the issue head on, or refuse the commission, he retreated into nonsense—by saying, for instance, that the way to overcome the need for freeways was to change public attitudes toward city living. That was little consolation for the Chinese community which was fighting for its life. But the citizens of Vancouver combined to stop the

58

The Shannon Estate mansion, surrounded by luxury town houses in a scheme designed by the Erickson-Massey partnership.

Chinatown freeway, and so Erickson's 'beautification' project was not implemented.

THE SHANNON ESTATE

The Erickson-Massey approach to smaller residential development was well-illustrated in their plan for the Shannon Estate. The estate was a mansion located on South Granville Street in Vancouver, the home of mining magnate Austin Taylor. After Taylor's death in 1966 the property was acquired by a Vancouver real estate and land development firm, Wall and Redekop. Founded by two cousins, Peter Wall and Peter Redekop, the firm had originally dealt solely with real estate sales, but gradually moved into the area of land development and apartment rentals. Over the years Wall and Redekop have become particularly unpopular in Vancouver. They created a furor by their practice of evicting welfare recipients from their apartment units. They were exposed as one of the major conduits for the flow of South-East Asian money into Vancouver real estate. But their most unpopular action was their handling of the Shannon Estate project.

The original plan for the property was to demolish the beautiful old mansion and to redevelop the whole site with luxury townhouses.

Because the mansion was undoubtedly an historic monument, there was considerable opposition to its destruction. Wall and Redekop's response was to encourage the vandalism of the property and to allow it to fall into a state of disrepair. That would allow them to tell a sympathetic city council that the building was beyond saving and had to be torn down. However, public pressure was so intense that they were forced to include the mansion in the project.

Bruno Freschi, an Erickson associate, was the project architect. He produced a design for luxury town house units which included the mansion but the residents of the surrounding area—mainly upper-middle class—still fought the project. They claimed that the project was not in keeping with the single-family character of the neighbourhood; and that *any* development on the property would destroy the historical value of the buildings.

The pro-development Non-Partisan Association Vancouver city council helped Wall and Redekop along at every stage of the process, frustrating the efforts of the opponents. When TEAM came into power in 1973, one of their campaign promises had been to stop the Shannon project, but despite some half-hearted attempts the project was not stopped and has now been built.

THE WOODCROFT ESTATE

Another unpopular project in which the Erickson-Massey partnership has been involved in Vancouver is known as the Woodcroft Estate project. In this case, Erickson's public reputation for quality was helpful in promoting a design for a controversial project which, while dressing it up and making it look much fancier and elegant, greatly increases its density and potential profitability.

The site is a chunk of North Vancouver which projects across the Capilano River into West Vancouver, across the Burrard Inlet from the City of Vancouver itself. It is surrounded by upper-middle-class single-family homes and parkland. In 1966 it was rezoned for seven high-rise apartment buildings by a development-hungry North Vancouver Council—over the strenuous objections of area residents and the West Vancouver Council. In an unsuccessful attempt to quell the opposition, North Vancouver made a condition of their approval the construction by the developer of a bridge across the Capilano River so that traffic from the project would use North Vancouver's road system rather than the suburban streets of West Vancouver.

For several years the project lay dormant. Then one of the original partners, Daon Developments Ltd. (called Dawson Developments until 1973) bought out the other two partners and hired Erickson-Massey to prepare a new plan for the site.

Daon is one of the most aggressive developers on the west coast. Formed just 10 years ago by Graham Dawson of Vancouver and Jack Poole of Edmonton, the sons of multi-million dollar construction families, Daon has become the largest public real estate company in Western Canada with assets of $100-million at the end of 1973, and profits on invested capital of up to 200 per cent.

Two factors are important to the Daon success

Sketch of Village Lake Louise: room for doubt remains

A sketch of the Village Lake Louise proposal.

story: its sometimes dubious development tactics; and its connections with the Vancouver business establishment—the Vancouver Board of Trade, the Non-Partisan Association (NPA) and The Electors Action Movement (TEAM), the Liberal Party, and powerful old families.

Daon achieved notoriety in Vancouver in 1973 through its practice of buying apartment buildings and converting them into condominiums, to bring in immediate cash rather than tie it up in long-term rental housing. The strategy was good for Daon's liquidity, but bad for some of the people living in those buildings. One of the buildings was the Crescent View Apartment in West Vancouver. The tenants were offered the choice of buying their apartments or getting out. They were all elderly. One woman had a stroke after hearing about Daon's plans. Many of the tenants were widows who had lived in the building for years and could be bullied into buying rather than change old habits and move. After several such outrageous cases came to public attention, the municipal government put a freeze on further conversions.

Erickson's 1973 proposal for Daon's Woodcroft property was composed of two crescent-shaped structures, one of them rising in a stepladder design to a height of 30 storeys. The previous scheme had 943 suites; Erickson's had 1322. The previous scheme had included some family-oriented accommodation, appropriate to its semi-rural setting.

In Erickson's proposal this was all eliminated for more profitable bachelor and one bedroom units, also adding more cars to the project; the height of the original scheme was 170 feet, Erickson's design increased the height to 300 feet which would have made it the tallest residential structure in B.C.

A public hearing had to be held because of these major changes in the design. Perhaps Daon and Erickson were not prepared for the public reaction, a reaction so strong that none of Daon's connections to the Vancouver establishment could keep the project on the rails. All of the charges which had been levelled at the original proposal were reiterated, but there were some new ones for the Erickson scheme. Due to the intense public pressure, North Vancouver Council had to reject Erickson's design, and Daon, perhaps figuring that it wasn't worth the effort to push further, went back to the original seven high-rise design, which is currently under construction.

VILLAGE LAKE LOUISE

Arthur Erickson's controversial projects have not been limited to Vancouver. The Village Lake Louise proposal, which brought one of the largest U.S. corporations into Banff National Park as a developer of a jet-set style development, roused protests from across the country.

In early 1971, Imperial Oil Ltd., in partnership with Lake Louise Lifts Ltd., revealed a proposal for a $37-million year-round resort village in the heart of Banff National Park. For both partners the project had many attractive features. Several years earlier, Imperial Oil had decided to diversify into the promising areas of property development (using up some of its extensive land holdings) and the recreation-leisure market (promoting travel and gasoline sales). Imperial had set up Devon Estates Ltd. to do its developing, and Devon was looking after Imperial's half of the project.

The other partner, Lake Louise Lifts, was the operator of ski lifts in the Banff area, and hence stood to gain enormously from any development. Control of Lake Louise Lifts had been acquired in 1968 by an alliance of eastern businessmen, led by the Toronto law firm of Borden and Elliot, and western businessmen, such as the Seaman family of Calgary (Bow Valley Industries Ltd.).

Also on the board of Village Lake Louise was Victor S. Emery of Montreal, market development officer for Air Canada. Emery's presence on the board was convincing proof, if any were needed, that the development was not intended for local residents, but rather for eastern and international jet-set holidayers. In fact, the proposal was referred to as 'Canada's recreational challenge to the Alpine villages of Europe and the great ski resorts of the United States.'

Erickson-Massey and Ray Affleck of Montreal were the architectural and planning consultants for the scheme.

Public reaction was hostile—and no wonder. Here was a foreign-owned corporation—the Rockefeller's Standard Oil of New Jersey —planning a massive development—a population of 6,000 was projected—for one of Canada's most important national parks. No major environmental studies had been done prior to planning for the development; the scheme was definitely for jet-setters, not for the large majority of low-and middle-income Canadians who need improved recreational facilities; the proposal was on far too large a scale and would concentrate too many people in a very delicate environment.

Apologists for the Village Lake Louise project tried to use Erickson's involvement to advantage; they argued that the opponents of the scheme must be wrong in their assessment of the environmental impact of Village Lake Louise because after all it was designed by Canada's most prestigious architect. Erickson, however, addressed himself mainly to a formal problem: how to visually integrate an Alpine village-looking development into a mountainous landscape.

Outraged Albertans would have none of it, and started a mail-your-credit-card-back-to-Imperial-Oil campaign. When the federal government held public hearings in Calgary in March 1972, 195 briefs were presented, almost unanimously against the project. Altogether, 2,500 briefs and statements were mailed to the government. The Alberta government itself was strongly against the project. In July 1972, Minister of Indian Affairs and Northern Development Jean Chretien bowed to the public pressure and rejected the plan. It now sits on the shelf gathering dust with other rejected Erickson designs.

CHRISTCHURCH CATHEDRAL

Erickson had another opportunity to demonstrate a concern for the urban fabric and for important old buildings when in 1971 he was called on by Anglican church officials who had encountered problems with a scheme they had to demolish Christchurch Cathedral in the centre of downtown Vancouver and to erect a money-making high-rise office development in its place.

Located on the north-east corner of Georgia and Burrard, the site of the church building was one of the few open spaces remaining in downtown Vancouver. But attendance at the cathedral was declining and its operations were costing the Anglican Church money, so the hierarchy decided on the demolition scheme.

There was immediate opposition to this plan to destroy another part of Vancouver's small supply of important old buildings. Church officials were able to win a vote on the project amongst the congregation, but charges were levelled that they had manipulated the results of the referendum.

At this point, with opposition to their scheme increasing daily, the church turned to Arthur Erickson to prepare a design for a new building on the site which would disarm their opponents and win support for the project. This happened in 1971 when Erickson was very much in the public eye as a result of his design for the Canadian pavilion at the 1970 Osaka world's fair.

Erickson came up with a plan for what he called a 'tower of light'—which in fact was an 18-storey high-rise office building, covered with mirrors and glass, and including a multi-storey public area and a partly-underground cathedral building. The design caught many people's fancy, but it did not distract from the basic issue: redevelopment versus conservation, Manhattan or a more human city. The opposition to the church's proposal was not deterred by Erickson's plan, and within a year the whole thing was scrapped.

THE MUSEUM OF MAN

Though some of Erickson's controversial schemes have been stopped, many others have been built.

A publicity photograph of a model for the Museum of Man, complete with the reflecting pool (in the foreground). The pool had later to be abandoned because of site problems. The photo does not give a very strong impression of the drop-off of the cliffs to Wreck Beach.

One of the latter is his design for the Museum of Man, now under construction on the Point Grey Cliffs on the University of British Columbia's property.

The site is considered the most magnificent in B.C. It has a spectacular view of the North Shore mountains and of Howe Sound. What was more appropriate for the most magnificent site to be given to B.C.'s most famous architect?

But what's a Museum of Man—housing an extensive North-West Coast Indian collection —doing out at the university, miles from the city? Shouldn't it be downtown, where it would be accessible to more people, especially to Vancouver's Indian population, many of whom do not have automobiles to get out to the University? In fact, part of the financing for the museum had come from a federal government Centennial grant which had stipulated that the museum be in the downtown area.

The full story of how the museum ended up at UBC, on a site that had been designated as provincial parkland, has never been revealed publicly. Somehow, somebody got the site for Erickson.

As it happened, this ideal site gave Erickson some problems. The Point Grey Cliffs are eroding and have been for a long time—another good reason, one might think, not to build the Museum there. Because of the erosion danger, Erickson was forced to eliminate the central feature from his design—an extensive reflecting pool which, when viewed from the museum, was meant to merge with the seascape.

Another implication of this site stems from the fact that at the base of the cliffs is Vancouver's famous nudist beach—Wreck Beach. Although there are at least five different causes of the cliff erosion, the Parks Board and the UBC administration chose to deal with the least important one—high winter tides washing away cliff material. Their solution was to cover the beach with a sand-and-gravel 'erosion-control' blanket. UBC brass and the other sponsors of the museum couldn't stand the idea of having naked human

The award-winning scheme for the False Creek see-through high-rise.

bodies just down the cliff from Erickson's prestigious museum. They went ahead with their scheme in the spring of 1974, although beach users, UBC students and concerned environmentalists fought them all the way to the B.C. Court of Appeals. The beach has now been covered with sand and gravel, but this action neither stopped the erosion nor forced out the nude bathers.

THE SEE-THROUGH HIGH-RISE

Virtually all of Arthur Erickson's work, built or unbuilt, has been for major corporate clients like Imperial Oil or for organizations and institutions like UBC which are closely tied by interlocking boards of directors to the corporate hierarchy. But there is one project where the Erickson-Massey partnership had the ideal architect's client—themselves. Together with some close associates, they acquired six acres of prime land on the False Creek waterfront in Vancouver, and produced a plan for a $40-million high-rise apartment which they would design, build and own. The False Creek site has an interesting background. False Creek is really a bay which separates the downtown Vancouver peninsula from the inner residential neighbourhoods. For 80 years, it was a heavy industrial area, owned mainly by the CPR who leased its land to those industries that generated the most traffic for the railway. During the mid-sixties, however, the CPR decided it would be far more profitable to devleop some of its extensive inner urban land holdings in Vancouver for high density residential and commercial accommodation. The City, following its long-standing policy of giving the CPR everything it wanted, designated the whole False Creek area for residential-recreational-commercial uses. The Erickson-Massey consortium were able to get their hands on six prime acres of the False Creek land. The most profitable type of development, of course, would be high-rise apartment buildings, but there happened to be thousands of people living behind the proposed development who would have their view of downtown and mountains totally cut off by such a project.

Erickson-Massey had the ultimate solution for a view's problem: the *see-through high-rise*—800 feet long, varying from a height of 40 storeys at one end (there are still no buildings in Vancouver that tall), to a height of 20 storeys at the other end, with see-through holes and sections interspersed throughout the length, so that you would be able to catch a glimpse of something, although it's not clear what.

Canadian Architect magazine awarded Erickson-Massey a prize for the design, but even the pro-development city council couldn't accept this one. A high-rise is still a high rise whether you cover it with mirrors or punch holes in it. So the scheme was buried, and the land sold to another developer.

THE ARCHITECT AS ARTIST

There is a consistency in Arthur Erickson's work which applies to the projects that have been built—like Simon Fraser and the Museum of Man—as well as to those which have aroused so much opposition that they have been shelved. His buildings are artistic creations, solutions to problems of form, space, light, scale and massing. They are three-dimensional formal compositions set out in the natural landscape. That is what leads critics like *Time* magazine's architectural writer to say that his design for the University of Lethbridge campus is 'a tour-de-force of form, scale and siting.' Erickson's most famous creation, the Canadian Pavilion at Osaka, was not really a building at all, but an objet d'art to be looked at, admired, photographed and written about. It was not conceived of as a place in which to live or work.

Yet, no matter where Erickson's interests or talents may lie, the fact remains that his buildings are places where people have to live or work. Architects may choose to see themselves as artists, but unlike writers or painters their creations often can't be avoided, or ignored, or put down when they are uninteresting or unhelpful. Like it or not, their buildings will serve, or ignore, or work against the interests and needs of the people who have to use them. For an architect concerned about those people, this creates an obligation to consult with users of his building, and of course this consultation takes him far beyond the elitist world of the artist and into the realm of social process and human need.

Another problem faced by artist-architects is that, whereas painters and writers can provide themselves with their own materials for their work—their paper, or their paint, architects have to rely on clients to provide their materials, and pay for the execution of their work. The interests of the client may of course differ—and may conflict—with the interests of both the designer and the users. If the designer preoccupies himself with questions of form and composition, leaving all other aspects of his building to his client, he becomes a willing or unwilling dupe of those interests, particularly if his client represents corporate concerns in their quest for maximum return on invested capital as the sole object of any building project. Corporate clients may well consciously make use of famous architect-artists in order to make their profit-maximizing projects more palatable to the public. Concerns of this kind should lead architects worried about the public interest to refuse commissions or to resign from projects when they find their work being used for purposes of which they do not approve.

In Arthur Erickson's case, both elements of the architect-artist's situation are present. There is a lack of concern for the needs, interests and values of the users of his buildings best illustrated by his design for Simon Fraser University. And there is a history of involvement in controversial projects where corporate clients ranging from the Anglican Church to Imperial Oil have relied on his reputation to over-ride strong public opposition to their profit-maximizing development plans.

As Arthur Erickson's career well illustrates, this kind of architecture when stylishly executed brings substantial rewards. It has made Erickson a star amongst Canadian architects and created a public reputation for him which extends far beyond his profession. But it is no accident that his work has also generated so much opposition from people who saw his projects as harming their interests, or depriving them of amenities they cared about, or impoverishing a city's heritage.

In 1972, Douglas Shadbolt, director of the School

—Bill Cunningham photo
Arthur Erickson with award.

Man of the year

Arthur Erickson, prominent Vancouver architect, was presented with the Greater Vancouver Visitors and Convention Bureau's "Man of the Year" award Thursday.

The award, in the form of a Captain George Vancouver bronze bust, is presented annually in recognition of an outstanding contribution to Greater Vancouver.

The new president of the Bureau, elected at the directors meeting Thursday, is Victor Burt, general manager of

of Architecture at Carleton University, said that he wished that Erickson 'would do some things that have more to do with people.' It is two years later, and the prospects of Shadbolt's wish coming true are more remote than ever.

Waterloo's Bill Thomson: Planning for power

Kent Gerecke

not houses finely roofed,
nor the stones of walls well-builded,
nor canals or dockyards make the city,
but men who use their opportunity.
(Alcaeus, 585 B.C., quoted by Bill Thomson as his view of planning.)

What makes Bill Thomson's career as a city planner so intriguing and worth examining in detail is his embodiment of active, dynamic service for city government and the interests which control city government. Many other Canadian planners suffer from self doubts about what characterizes the public interest, what are the best policies for the city, and what power planners should have. Not Bill Thomson. He exaggerates the ideal qualities of the city planner in a dynamic style. So the man himself, and the things he has done, say a lot about what underlies city planning in Canada.

Thomson's self-assurance is stunning:

Sitting around discussing 'Who am I?', 'What do I do?' 'What is planning and planners?' thrills me about as much as sniffing the aroma of Andy Campbell's special 'seegars' (a reference to a former president of the Canadian planners' association). I happen to know who I am, what I do, what my profession expects from me, what planning is, and I'm not interested in your belly button....

This was Thomson's comment after a year in office as president of the planners' organization, the Canadian Institute of Planners, and at a time when a small group of members were raising questions about the profession's role in Canada. Its style is typical of the man.

Thomson graduated from the University of Toronto's planning school in the 1950s. He spent some time working in Hamilton's planning department and arrived in Kitchener in 1962 as the city's first Director of Planning. Comments one of the members of the planning board that hired Thomson, 'He brought planning to Kitchener.' In 1973, Thomson became the Commissioner of Planning and Development for the new Waterloo regional government which includes the cities of Kitchener, Waterloo and Cambridge.

The Kitchener-Waterloo area is 65 miles west of Toronto. It has a rapidly growing diversified industrial base which combines substantial locally-owned industries (Electrohome, Greb Shoes) with branch-plant factories of major U.S. corporations (Uniroyal, B.F. Goodrich). There are also two universities (Waterloo and Wilfrid Laurier) and a community college (Conestoga) which were all set up in the sixties. The population of Kitchener went from 43,000 in 1950 to 107,500 in 1970.

Bill Thomson arrived on the scene in the midst of rapid growth. His term as Planning Director for Kitchener, between 1962 and 1972, was dominated by three major planning projects: a freeway, a civic centre and an urban renewal program. Thomson stimulated action on all three; the duration of each filled most of his eleven years in Kitchener. Thomson's planning style, as it emerges through these projects, sets the stage for the second period of his career. His recent work as chief planner for the Waterloo Region (1973 to the present) has been dominated by the creation of a regional plan, hopefully the second regional plan in Ontario. Since this plan represents Thomson's most important work, and since it has been his first priority over the past two years, it serves as an important example of professional planning expertise. Altogether the record of Bill Thomson's work describes the style and expertise of a successful and dynamic Canadian planner.

Waterloo's Bill Thomson

FREEWAY TO NOWHERE

In 1949, the Kitchener, Waterloo and Suburban Planning Board adopted a ring road plan as submitted by a consultant. The ring road would encircle the cities, providing a bypass route for all approaches and would drain traffic away from busy downtown streets. Throughout the 1950s the Board kept the ring road idea alive, and in 1961 a joint Kitchener and Waterloo committee of aldermen sought provincial aid for the scheme. Provincial commitment was not forthcoming.

Shortly after his arrival, Thomson criticized the community for inaction on the ring road which led to his appointment to a three-man committee of experts composed of the city engineer, traffic director and himself. This committee of experts began negotiations with provincial bureaucrats and in June of 1963 the province agreed to pay 75 per cent of the costs subject to the road being built to provincial standards. A larger committee of experts to work out the details of the ring road was then established. It included representatives from the Department of Highways, Kitchener's and Waterloo's city engineers and solicitors, and Thomson. About one year later a plan emerged which abandoned the ring road idea in favour of a road half way around the cities and estimated the cost at $22-million in contrast to the original estimate of $6-million.

Opposition immediately arose from the Kitch-

ener, Waterloo and Suburban Planning Board which had long supported a full ring road. They claimed the original ring road 'has been perverted into a $22-million expressway connecting provincial highways passing through the area.' Thomson countered strongly in defence of the half ring road by discrediting the board. He said the board had done nothing for fourteen years. 'We have moved from the horse and buggy to the motor age in that 14 years. If we build it the way it was planned, we'd have a hell of a mess.' Kitchener and Waterloo Councils approved the new road as Thomson negotiated it.

The matter of meeting provincial standards turned a proposed 120-foot wide ring road into a major four-lane divided freeway several hundred feet wide with gigantic interchanges. By 1966 it was thought that final costs would be $38-million. Concerned citizens began questioning the rising costs. Thomson rebuked them harshly. For example, Dr. Diem, a geography professor and former Planning Board member criticized the rising costs and the failure to integrate the freeway into a total transportation system. Thomson publicly replied, 'You shame me, Mr. Diem, by your intellectual ignorance. Instead of emulating a few of your fellow lecturers, I suggest you delve into your subject more deeply, especially one which is so foreign to

Kitchener's Civic Centre site: where things stand now, after a decade of planning progress.

Kitchener's Civic Centre site. Note the paint peeling on the sign.

... 'You shame me, Mr. Diem, by your intellectual ignorance. Instead of emulating a few of your fellow lecturers, I suggest you delve into your subject more deeply, especially one which is so foreign to your intellect, before running off at the quill.'

your intellect, before running off at the quill.'

Criticism continued as did the rising costs. The final bill was $54-million for half a ring road which now ends in a two-lane road to the villages of St. Jacobs and Elmira. Thomson, however, had the final say. In his annual report to city council in 1967 he said:

The Expressway is also part of our overall planning in this city — not foreign to it as many people throughout the area seem to believe. It always seems strange to me how there are always so many experts in the field once a project is approved and underway. Where are these nimble witted experts when the public meetings are held and where are they when we are seeking even further help? Hiding behind fake names on the letters to the editorial page certainly offers little help to the city.

Thomson may also add further to this subject. In 1971 he announced he would write a book merely called 'Expressway'. He said it would reveal the full story about the behind the scenes work: 'the public relations, fairness to the property owners, the battling of wits to keep the Twin Cities and their residents first on the list, the astute negotiations for land, the discussion over design, planning and politics and so much more.'

SELLING A CIVIC CENTRE

Sporadic proposals for a Kitchener civic centre date back to 1912. A draft plan was proposed by the Mayor in 1956 and was rejected by an eight to two vote by council. From 1958 the Chamber of Commerce again pushed for a civic centre which resulted in a 1961 Civic Centre Committee to study the matter. Membership of the CCC was from the Chamber, city staff and aldermen.

In August of 1962, Thomson criticized the CCC for lack of activity and an absence of co-ordination. He followed this with the public release of a report directed at the CCC suggesting a number of civic centre alternatives. His public charges caused the CCC to become active and catapulted him to the position of Secretary of the CCC and onto a new steering committee. From this moment on Thomson designed the civic centre strategy.

In 1963 he engineered the creation of two additional committees to assist the Civic Centre Committee. The first was an advisory committee composed of potential future users or general beneficiaries. It included local branches of the Canadian Opera Guild, Little Theatre, Art Gallery, Red Cross, Jaycette Club, Public Library Board, Children's Aid Society and others. The second was a committee of architects which was formed through quiet, informal talks over several months between Thomson and local architects. Eight architects finally formed the committee and later they received a contract to prepare the civic centre plan.

Through a coalition of four groups, the Civic Centre Committee, the advisory committee of beneficiaries, the committee of architects, and the Planning Board, all guided by Thomson, a civic centre site was selected and a conceptual plan was prepared. In February of 1964, without contacting the citizens living on the site and without holding a plebiscite for the necessary financing, city council approved the civic centre, which would include such public facilities as the courthouse, police station, public library and an auditorium. One week later Thomson secured approval from the Planning Board for an amendment to the zoning by-law freezing existing land use on the site to keep the city purchase prices down. The following day he made his first official contact with area residents sending a letter which gave them ten days to comment on the zoning freeze. Only five responses were received from the 61 owners.

Both the land purchases without a plebiscite and the zoning freeze required approval by the Ontario Municipal Board. The Board considered these matters at hearings in the fall of 1964. At the hearings, the City claimed it had done exhaustive studies and had involved citizens. Therefore, no plebiscite was necessary and approval should be given. Principal opposition came from the Kitchener Taxpayers Association. Their legal counsel argued for a plebiscite because the Planning Department's report was incomplete and mere 'window dressing', because council had never approved the scheme, and because the zoning freeze was causing an economic hardship for owners. In December 1964, the OMB decided in favour of the city stating that the proposed civic centre was:

a scheme which has had a lot of study by the planning board and council as well as by groups of interested citizens; it has been well publicized, discussed at public meetings and there would appear to be no doubt that it has general support.

The OMB also placed a one-year limit on the zoning freeze.

Slowly the city began purchasing properties and razing them. Extensions of the zoning freeze were requested by the city for the next six years all of which were granted by the Ontario Municipal Board. In 1971 the Board decreed that the city must complete their land purchases during the next three years. Altogether residents of the future civic centre site had to endure a decade of the zoning freeze while being subjected to pressures to compulsory sale of their homes. Today most of the site stands vacant.

In short, Thomson's civic centre strategy created false public support by co-opting beneficiaries, overriding neighbourhood interests and using blockbusting tactics to achieve ownership at low cost without expropriation. Public blockbusting, as used by Thomson, stands as a new form of urban renewal.

CLASSICAL URBAN RENEWAL

The third, and major, project of Thomson's Kitchener tenure was an urban renewal scheme that he initiated in 1962 and pursued for the next ten years. In a now familiar style, he provoked the community to action by 'shooting from the lip' as the *Kitchener-Waterloo Record*, the local newspaper, termed it. Addressing the Kitchener-Waterloo Kiwanis in July of 1962, Thomson delivered a scathing attack on downtown merchants. He characterized downtown Kitchener as 'a long, linear facade of buildings that remind me of a skid row in Chicago' and the stores as 'one storey high with the rest filled with junk used as warehouses, dirty cramped offices or filled with families living almost in squalor.' Again the community was off and running to Thomson's tune.

Urban renewal, for Thomson, was a tool to provide cheap land for the developers. He rationalized urban renewal as follows:

If [a developer] went out to buy land on the market, he'd have to buy the land, the building that sits on the land; he'd have to buy the business the man has . . . he has to buy what the business is worth, and, if there is a tenant in the building that has, say, a ten year lease, the developer has to buy him out — which amounts to a tremendous amount of money. Now this is one of the reasons why there is urban renewal: so the federal, provincial and municipal governments can go out and buy buildings and leases and businesses and rip 'em all down and then put a value only

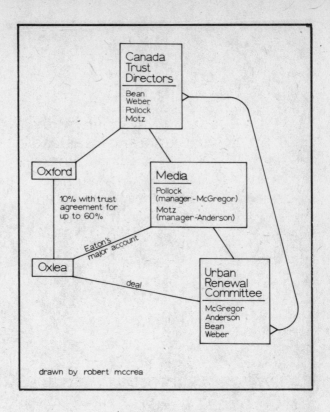

drawn by robert mccrea

on the land — which is a lot less than all the other stuff — put that on the market, and sell it to a developer. The developer will come in under those conditions.

The unfolding of the urban renewal story in Kitchener over the past few years demonstrates well how Thomson used urban renewal to aid the development industry. Since this story is told in a recent book by Jack Pasternak, *Rot and Renewal: the Undoing of a City,* only a brief chronology of events will be presented here. Following Thomson's initiative in 1962, a 48-member Urban Renewal Committee was formed in 1963. Although referred to as a 'citizen's committee' by Thomson, all but three academics and one cleric were downtown merchants and investors. From 1963 to 1965 Thomson's staff and consultants conducted studies. The first study was an economic study of downtown paid for half by the city and half by Waterloo Trust (owned by Canada Trust) and the *Kitchener-Waterloo Record.* In 1965 Thomson proposed an urban renewal plan for downtown redevelopment to attain 'a core of concentrated retail uses, including amusements, surrounded by tall office blocks and apartment buildings.'

After the plan was approved by Kitchener Council, federal and provincial assistance was sought for preparation of a detailed renewal scheme covering 450 acres. In 1968, while these further studies were underway, a freeze on urban renewal funds was set by the federal government.

Prior to the freeze, however, Walter Bean, chairman of the Urban Renewal Committee, proposed Oxlea Investments to Thomson as a prospective

Kitchener's old farmers' market, before urban renewal.

An apple cider counter in the old farmers' market.
Photos this page: Myfanwy Phillips

70

Kitchener's new farmers' market, built as part of the Oxlea development supported by Bill Thomson and Kitchener's city council. Rising above the market is a parking garage which serves the stores in the new project.

developer, and a URC subcommittee composed of Jack Young, a former alderman and PC federal candidate, James Darrah, Kitchener City Coordinator, and Thomson started working out the details of the deal with Oxlea. During this period, 1970-1971, the real estate division of Canada Trust obtained options to buy property for Oxlea. At the time Bean was deputy chairman and vice-president of Canada Trust. The media, well aware of the renewal deal co-operatively withheld the news from the public while the options were being taken (the *Kitchener-Waterloo Record* instructed its writers to ignore this matter.)

The 'Oxlea deal', in which Thomson was a principal negotiator, shows how planners and planning mechanisms serve development interests. In the corporate web diagram, it can be seen how the Urban Renewal Committee had substantial representation from Canada Trust which in turn controlled Oxlea Investments which got the urban renewal deal.

Kitchener City Council was presented with the renewal deal in two caucus meetings, May 31 and June 21, 1971; the media attended but still maintained their conspiracy of silence. The Oxlea deal was to trade away Kitchener's city hall and the traditional Farmers' Market in return for a new department store (Eaton's), an office tower which would house the city staff, lease back of a parking garage and $1,000,000. (An estimate of the redevelopment value of the city hall site alone was $3.9-million.) A special council meeting to approve the deal in public was set for June 28th.

On the Friday before this meeting, the University of Waterloo student newspaper, the *Chevron*, broke the story which the other media had held back for at least five months. Boisterous opposition faced city council on the 28th, but they approved the deal anyway. Opposition to the renewal continued and citizens obtained a ruling from the Ontario Municipal Board to hold a plebiscite on the scheme. Assisted by media falsification, (for example, the *Record* wrote its own letters to the editor and forced its writers to rewrite material to favour the scheme,) a plebiscite vote of about 35 per cent turnout favoured the renewal by 15,689 to 11,513 votes.

> ... 'During 1971 a group of misguided souls from the university area banded together into what they called A Citizens Committee for a Better County Core. We all know what happened to this group who now have so few members that meetings are held in telephone booths.'

OMB chairman Kennedy indicated that according to the rules of the OMB he would not have approved the scheme, but he must do so because of the plebiscite outcome.

Today, the Oxlea urban renewal scheme is a reality in Kitchener. Thomson predicted that 'the critics will be lost in the ring of cash registers and new buildings.' While the scheme has been an unbelievable financial success, the new market has turned into a tourist trap causing most locals to search for other markets outside of town. Many residents of Kitchener are now extremely upset by the artificial and commercial atmosphere of downtown Kitchener. As a planning case, each further documentation identifies this action for the disaster it is. Regardless, Thomson has given us his verdict in his 1971 annual report to city council; a verdict which reveals his tactic of discrediting citizen participation as an anti-democratic activity conducted by misfits and radicals. He says:

During 1971 a group of misguided souls from the university area banded together into what they called A Citizens Committee for a Better County Core. We all know what happened to this group who now have so few members that meetings are held in telephone booths. The beginning of the end for this committee was seen when democracy reigned supreme and the people of the City of Kitchener again voted for the whole urban renewal plan. As the committee dwindled, they still took a few kicks at the cat, but were spanked politely by the powers to be .... It does seem a shame and it is a disappointment to the planning director that the leader of this ill-fated group (reference to Alderman Morley Rosenberg) then thwarted by the people and the plans prepared by the people for the people can only holler 'How much are they paying you?'

STYLE OF PUBLIC SERVICE

Thomson's style of public service is characterized by a thirst for power and a catering to an elite power group. In all three projects, the freeway, civic centre and urban renewal, he attacked existing authorities for inaction in order to place himself in a key position. Then he took control of the project, attacking opponents by ridiculing them in order to avoid the issue at hand.

Thomson knows what is best for us and he carries it through. He is very clear about his elite concept of leadership:

This is the age of citizen participation, or so we have heard. But really, what have the citizens of this city got to crab about? Most of them are spoiled. They don't know what pollution is all about. They don't know what the word slum really means. They don't know what crime is all about. And if our council keeps moving ahead as they have in the past, the citizens will remain spoiled, and why shouldn't we be spoiled.

Not only does his style reject real citizen participation but it also rejects all but the interests of the elite elements in Kitchener-Waterloo.

Kitchener-Waterloo has a particularly strong business and industrial elite which feels a concern and responsibility for local political affairs. This has led to the formation of an informal group which calls itself the Saturday Morning Club. The group apparently does not function continuously but gets together whenever its members feel they have a problem or there is a need for action. The club, according to one researcher, was founded in the mid-fifties and was primarily concerned with city politics:

In the course of praising the quality and integrity of a number of the members of the Planning Board and city council, one respondent boasted that this was not simply due to chance. When asked to elaborate he explained that in the mid-fifties he and twenty-one other 'industrialists, executives, and professionals' had organized what was to be known as the 'Saturday Morning Club'.

The club looked for likely candidates willing to run for municipal office, and then provided campaign funds. On one occasion, when a downtown parking ban for both Kitchener and Waterloo was gaining favour amongst incumbent aldermen, the Saturday Morning Club responded to the occasion by getting eight new local aldermen who were opposed to the ban elected. For the 1974 Kitchener civic election, the Saturday Morning Club is rumoured to have run two candidates for seats which had become vacant.

There has never been any public discussion of the Saturday Morning Club's existence in Kitchener-Waterloo media. Most city residents, and some of the candidates it has run for office, are unaware of its existence. But it has played an effective role in ensuring that the towns are run as the local business and industrial establishments want them.

Bill Thomson is of course a key figure in Kitchener-Waterloo local government. And he has a history of close association with the Saturday Morning Club. During the controversy over the demolition of the Kitchener market, for instance, a second researcher reports that regular Saturday Morning Club meetings were held and Thomson attended at least some. No doubt contacts of this kind have helped Thomson to protect the interests of the local elite in the many controversial planning policies he has been involved in.

ON TO THE REGION

Bill 167 created the new Regional Municipality of Waterloo including Kitchener, Waterloo and Cambridge. Jack Young, a former Kitchener alderman and PC candidate and co-negotiator of the Oxlea deal with Thomson, was appointed as the first regional chairman as had been rumoured for some time. Young wanted Thomson as his regional planner, Thomson wanted more power, and they both got their way. Thomson did not get the regional job without adopting tactics to overcome fears created by his style in Kitchener. For the 18-month period prior to the establishment of the new region, Thomson hid his 'pop-off' attitude. To improve his image he suddenly changed from W.E. Thomson to 'Bill' Thomson which was quickly picked up by the media. Also he actively sought the presidency of the Professional Planners Association. In April and May he attacked critics of planning in the Professional newsletter:

Several times I have started to reply to the comments of a number of our members across Canada, especially those that have academic leanings rather than the practical, and who apparently feel that participatory democracy and public participation is the end to end all. It is these people who do not know what citizen participation is all about for they speak from the protection of the typical ivory tower instead of actual experience.

Then at the national conference he made the unprecedented move of challenging the appointment of the president-elect as the next president. With the help of friends, he forced an election and won.

Once appointed to Regional Commissioner of Planning and Development in January of 1973 Thomson began to establish himself as 'planner-king' over his former peers. He initated monthly meetings for the chief planners of Kitchener, Waterloo and Cambridge. Cambridge planning director, Sally Thorsen, and Kitchener planning commissioner, Sam Klapman, have called these 'show and tell exercises' and 'teacher-pupil relationships.' In addition, Thomson started to act as if he were planning under a one-tier government, an idea both he and Jack Young have long supported. Kitchener co-ordinator Jim Darrah has said that Thomson should be fired if he continues to act in this way and Mrs. Thorsen has also been critical of Thomson's one-tier attitude. Thomson has responded to these criticisms in a 16-page report which says 'the regional planning staff are not interested in becoming

... There has never been any public discussion of the Saturday Morning Club's existence in the Kitchener-Waterloo media. Most city residents, and some of the candidates it has run for office, are unaware of its existence.

involved in the continuing puerile, chimerical drivel from Mr. Darrah and now Mrs. Thorsen.' As reported in the *Record*, these words mean 'juvenile, immature, weak, silly and absurd.' Thomson's insults, however, are not limited to written reports. At a staff meeting, subsequent to the above exchange, he ironically greeted Mrs. Thorsen with 'well if it isn't the mouth from the south.'

THE FIRST REGIONAL PLAN: CHOOSE ONE OF ONE

Provincial legislation establishing the Waterloo Region requires a draft regional plan before December 31, 1975. Thomson wants to get his plan done as quickly as possible to demonstrate his superior planning ability.

In the first attempt at a regional plan, a number of vague and loosely-phrased 'goals' were identified, and from these were derived a long list of 'objectives' and possible policies. Then four alternative patterns were presented labelled satellite growth, linear growth, decentralized growth, and centralized growth. These were presented to the community in a 12-page tabloid newspaper-style plan, and citizens were asked to rate the four patterns on the basis of given criteria.

At the public meetings, many local residents realized that the four alternatives offered were simply different versions of plans for rapid growth by the same private development process that Kitchener-Waterloo has experienced over the last two decades and more.

Twenty-six public meetings were called in October and November of 1973 to discuss the proposals. The dominant response at all meetings was a desire for a zero or slow growth option. For example, John Taylor, general manager of Edgar Motors, challenged the planners at several meetings, to indicate whether the region had reached an optimum

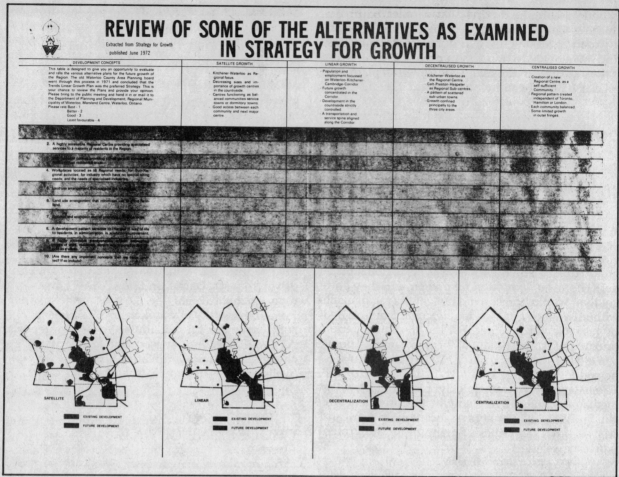

REVIEW OF SOME OF THE ALTERNATIVES AS EXAMINED IN STRATEGY FOR GROWTH

Extracted from Strategy for Growth
- published June 1972

DEVELOPMENT CONCEPTS	SATELLITE GROWTH	LINEAR GROWTH	DECENTRALISED GROWTH	CENTRALISED GROWTH
This table is designed to give you an opportunity to evaluate and rate the various alternative plans for the future growth of the Region. The old Waterloo County Area Planning board went through this process in 1971 and concluded that the Trends Linear Growth Plan was the preferred Strategy. This is your chance to review the Plans and provide your opinion. Please bring to the public meeting and hand it in or mail it to the Department of Planning and Development, Regional Municipality of Waterloo, Marsland Centre, Waterloo, Ontario. Please rate Best - 1 / Better - 2 / Good - 3 / Least favourable - 4	- Kitchener-Waterloo as Regional focus. - Decreasing sizes and importance of growth centres in the countryside. - Centres functioning as balanced communities service towns or dormitory towns. - Good access between each community and next major centre.	- Population and employment focussed on Waterloo-Kitchener-Cambridge-Corridor. - Future growth concentrated in the Corridor. - Development in the countryside strictly controlled. - A transportation and service spine aligned along the Corridor.	- Kitchener-Waterloo as the Regional Centre. - Galt-Preston-Hespeler as Regional Sub-centres. - A pattern of scattered sub-urban towns. - Growth confined principally to the three city areas.	- Creation of a new Regional Centre, as a self-sufficient Community. - Regional pattern created independent of Toronto, Hamilton or London. - Each community balanced. - Some limited growth in outer fringes.

A double-page spread included in the promotional tabloid newspaper describing the four alternative plans for the Waterloo region. City residents were asked to fill in the blanks and make their own decision about which of the four was best.

size. Thomson's response was to ridicule Taylor advising him flippantly to 'hang in there' for the rest of the meetings, and he later said these slow growth people 'are really just talking through their hats.'

Kitchener alderman Morley Rosenberg attacked this attitude: 'Thomson has already made up his mind about major growth policies for the region, and has no real intention of listening to what people want.' Although Thomson goes through the motions of citizen participation, as he himself says, citizens can have their say but the planners make all the final decisions.

In the end, the planner must place the alternatives of the future, the locations, the involvement of the public and private sector and the types of industries before the region. Right at the end he is charged with the responsibility of recommending one of the various choices for action. If all the work has been done correctly, then the proper choice between job opportunities versus good farmland will be made; the right alternatives for use and standards will be articulated, the best role for the region to play in industrial development made.

Rosenburg followed up his criticism by moving in the regional planning committee that Thomson's $30,234 salary be cut to $1. The motion failed for want of a seconder.

Having failed to bamboozle or stifle all citizen opposition in the first stage of developing the regional plan, Thomson was forced to alter his strategy somewhat. Instead of proceeding immediately to produce a detailed plan for adoption, he had policy papers prepared for further public discussion on regional planning issues.

THE SECOND ROUND: WEAR THE PEOPLE DOWN

Public rejection of the growth plans set Thomson and his staff on a different approach in 1974. Between January and September seven long policy papers were issued dealing with growth, settlement patterns, economic development, housing, sand and gravel pits, open space, and transportation. These policy papers provided more background and justification for the same approach to regional planning that had been reflected in the four-alternatives plan.

In the paper on growth, for instance, the recommended policy was that growth in the region should continue at exactly the same rate as it has occurred in the past. A cursory examination of a slower-growth policy led to dismissing that possibility by claiming that it would require tight controls on all movements of people from city to city, and state-imposed birth controls. Interestingly enough, these cheap-shot arguments are also used by development industry spokesmen in responding to critics calling for controls on growth. And it is astonishing that the growth policy paper makes no reference to the issue of water supply which is, in the Kitchener-Waterloo situation, a crucial determinant of how much urban growth can take place in the region. A $98-million water pipeline to the area from Lake Erie is already under study by the provincial government, and if built would allow a doubling in population. The justification for the pipeline is that the growth is going to occur, but of course, any rational consideration of growth policy for Kitchener-Waterloo would involve taking account of the costs and benefits of this expensive project.

The policy paper on housing said that the region's housing problems stem from the 'imbalance between shelter cost and disposable income', i.e., from the fact that people don't have enough money. The report goes on to propose no less than 75 different policies to deal with housing problems, and the sheer quantity is perhaps expected to give the impression that so many solutions are bound to solve one big problem. But the solutions add up to exactly the approach Thomson would be expected to take: more of the same, continued control of the supply of housing by developers, and in Kitchener-Waterloo this means a small number of very big developers who together control the supply of new land. Nowhere are policies identified which could have a dramatic impact on housing problems. An ordinary reader would be left with the conclusion that there are no alternatives to present housing policies.

Predictably, public attendance at meetings called to discuss these papers waned. For one paper sixteen meetings were held with an attendance ranging from zero to six. Altogether only a few hundred citizens participated. Simultaneously the development industry spent less energy in presenting its case. For the first policy paper, the developers submitted 628 written comments, almost ten times the quantity submitted by individuals and other groups. The number quickly dwindled.

While the public meetings were being held, Thomson's staff was busily drafting the final version of the proposed plan. On October 21, one month and three days after the last public meeting, a 50,000-word draft regional plan was published,

and Thomson set November 28th for final approval by regional council. Again the plan was printed in tabloid form. In an almost incomprehensible planners' language, 347 policies were presented for adoption.

Examined carefully, the plan proved faithful to Thomson's original commitment to continued rapid growth but this time hidden behind a mask of slow growth. The plan explicitly proposes that growth continue at the present rate for the next seven years after which growth should be slowed down: 'encourage through the use of policies in this plan a decline of the population rate from 3.4 per cent per annum to 2.5 per cent after 1981 and 2.2 per cent per annum by 1991.' Other policies in the plan, however, indicate that no growth control is intended. Housing targets are to be set and the region will have many powers to ensure they are met. And the Lake Erie water pipeline is proposed for construction in fifteen years which would bring an explosion in growth.

Part of Thomson's strategy in writing this regional plan is to disguise the real intent of the plan through a smoke-screen of motherhood policies. Of the 347 policies 125 have 'recognize', 'encourage', or 'consider' as the key word. Some examples of these vague policies which have questionable power within this legal document are:
— recognize the urban core of the cities, towns and villages as regionally significant
— recognize that adequate facilities and services are required to accommodate offenders of all age groups and of varying range of offences and to provide for the rehabilitation of offenders
— recognize the importance of horse-drawn vehicle traffic along regional roads (There is considerable Mennonite settlement in the region.)

Another strategy of the regional plan is to defer basic studies which should be in the plan of the future. Eighty-seven such policies identify studies the region will complete including such basic matters as housing, transportation, water resources and health services. Also many of these policies imply a commitment to a vague future without any indication of what this might be. For example, 'support the immediate commencement of a total transportation planning policy for regional transportation systems that can be complementary to the private vehicle and compatible with the social and economic needs of the people.' What can this mean?

The dominant strategy of the regional plan however, is the use of the plan as a vehicle for centralized power in the regional government and in Thomson's department. Key to achieving this is the provision that the regional plan pre-empt all local plans, and that all local land-use decisions on everything except the smallest matters must conform to the regional plan. What the plan calls 'the establishment of a new settlement', for example, must conform to regional planning and be approved by

Hi there!

Now is the time to express your views.

Hope to see you at the public meetings listed on the back page.

After 23 pages of solid type and maps, this diagram was used by Waterloo regional planners to promote citizen interest and involvement in regional planning decision-making. The cartoon figure, incorporating the region's logo based on a W and a maple leaf, is the closest thing to a human figure which appears in the tabloid newspaper containing the second and final draft of the plan which was circulated to every household by the regional government.

the regional council, and this turns out to mean any development of three houses within 1000 feet of each other. The same control applies to what the plan calls 'the expansion of an existing settlement', which might well mean the addition of a single house to any existing group of three or more houses in the region, wherever located. In addition to this dominance, the region will have power to require local municipalities to implement the growth policies included in the plan, establish maintenance and occupancy by-laws, prepare secondary plans, and handle citizen participation for the region. As well new control mechanisms are proposed in a regional housing authority, a transit co-ordination structure, and a health and social planning council.

In many instances, the power which the plan confers on the regional government is open-ended, and hence more difficult to criticize or attack since no specific proposal is made. For instance the plan gives the region the power to implement an interim regional housing policy which establishes regional housing targets, and to enter into agreements with developers to fulfill these targets. Yet what these targets will be and how they will be allocated is not known, so it is impossible to criticize this proposal on the grounds that it is being used unwisely.

Included in the many powers conferred on the

regional government is the power to approve all public works by every local government in the region, the power to approve all site plans, the power to establish standards for zoning and subdivision plans of local municipalities, control over the federal government's Neighbourhood Improvement Program, the power to co-ordinate transportation and to designate regional roads. The regional government is given land-use control within 140 feet of all regional roads, which means regional control of downtown Kitchener, Waterloo and Cambridge.

WHAT IS CITY PLANNING?

Thomson's overt style allows us to obtain a clear picture of city planning. It is an activity obsessed with power to the extent of creating long-range plans, not intended to be amended for the next 25 years according to Thomson's desire. It is an activity which promotes the centralization of power as in the constitution for one-tier government hidden in the draft regional plan and in the concentration of power with planners. It is bent on serving business and the development industry in the promotion of growth. And, finally, it promotes optimum public confusion to avoid citizen participation. Bill Thomson has no doubts about these matters. That is what makes him an ideal planner for the local business elite. Whether he is ideal for the ordinary citizen of the Waterloo Region, however, is entirely another matter.

In total, Thomson's regional plan allows him to do just as he pleases. One senior planner close to the scene says, 'Thomson's strategy is to require everyone to have to ask him before they can move a muscle.' If the plan is adopted, many people will be asking for Thomson's permission, for matters they know not why, for a long time. He has deliberately designed the plan so that once approved it will not require amendment for 25 years. Thomson, or his successor, will thus have in the regional plan a long term constitution for planner power. How will this power be used?

It is one year since my Thomson article. After the smoke cleared, many professional planners strongly defended Thomson's style — supporting the bureaucratic stance, loyal servant role, belief in representative democracy, and planning for power. One planning director said he used the article as a guide to his own planning (and by some strange accident he has since been fired). As well some of my students openly supported the role of the planner as "benevolent dictator" which was an unexpected result. However, the largest impact, as I have received it, has been to clarify the distinction between planning in practice, primarily a mindless bureaucratic activity, and the challenges of planning which require humanism, a spirit of reform, and the rescue of city hall from the corporate interests. This distinction is becoming better understood by both students and practitioners, and the struggle between these two alternatives is increasing.

Diamond and Myers:
The form of reform

Bruce Kuwabara and Barry Sampson

For a relatively small and young firm, Toronto-based architects and planners Jack Diamond and Barton Myers have attained remarkable public prominence not only in Toronto but also across Canada and abroad. More than that of any other Canadian firm of practising architects, their work combines a commitment to serious design with a commitment to social action. They have had impact in Toronto and elsewhere both through their design work and through their role as activists taking public positions on urban issues.

Diamond & Myers' early buildings, including Toronto's York Square (1969), the Ontario Medical Association building (1971) and the Myers' house (1971), were considered "radical" at the time of their realization, challenging the conventionally smooth "modern" styles of the prevailing Canadian architectural establishment. Now, eight short years later, the style of these earlier Diamond & Myers' buildings has been popularly assimilated and widely imitated. The exposed round ducts and industrial fittings that typify Diamond & Myers' work are now fashionable decor in countless commercial and domestic interiors and "warehouse" renovations. The round windows which they made

prominent years ago in the then celebrated York Square are now a feature of facades from deluxe suburban houses to downtown boutiques.

This flattery through imitation amounts to a consumption of architectural style that is devoid of the political sensibility that Diamond & Myers have developed in their recent projects and professional activity, both of which explicitly support reform politics and policies. Particularly after the Crombie-reform victory in the 1972 Toronto election, Diamond & Myers came to be publicly identified in the media and professional circles with the general reform movement in city politics. In Jon Caulfield's book on recent Toronto city politics, Diamond & Myers are the only practising architects noted for their active, visible roles. Their case studies and design proposals for low-rise, high- and medium-density "prototypes" as alternatives to high-rise development, their public criticism of high-rise and urban sprawl development patterns, and their testimony as expert witnesses at numerous governmental hearings have been relevant and timely to both moderate and hard-line reformers. Diamond & Myers' reform role stands in strong contrast to mainstream architects in Canada who mostly remain actively aloof and politically non-committed, operating comfortably and lucratively within the status quo of the development industry.

Looking at the work of Diamond & Myers chronologically, it becomes obvious that the scale of the projects has increased, and their content has shifted. Prior to 1972, single, complete buildings were executed for private clients, and have implicit "reform" value in terms of changing public and professional attitudes about architectural design. Since that time, however, the work of Diamond & Myers has become much more broadly-based, and has been undertaken in a more explicit "reform" political context, dealing with issues of city-building and fabric. This later work includes infill housing strategies and major urban design and planning studies.

THREE COMPLETED BUILDINGS

Toronto's York Square, the Ontario Medical Association Building and the Myers house are all lived-in buildings which play particular roles in specific urban settings. However, all three were conceived by Diamond & Myers as prototypes of urban infill projects. They all use an "atrium" or interior courtyard organization, though in each case this is adjusted to existing local contexts and to particular programmatic demands.

Diamond & Myers have consistently argued publicly for low-rise, high- and medium-density prototypes that start from typical conditions within this historical urban pattern of Toronto, and which function conceptually and physically, as infill forms at various scales appropriate to particular renewal contexts. The underlying premise for designing buildings as prototypes is that a particular design situation represents more general, pervasive physical and social conditions. The role of the architect becomes one of furnishing society with innovative ideas and forms potentially capable of reproduction and execution by others.

Early in the Modern Movement in architecture, theorists became preoccupied with prototypes. Originally this grew out of confidence in the power of industrialized mass-production to transform the social, moral and physical fibre of society, and a vision of the machine as a metaphor for rationalism, modernism, liberation and universality. In the case of Diamond & Myers, the uniqueness of any single building is structured by the ongoing formal and material preoccupations of the designers, but is strongly influenced by a consistent working vocabulary of forms which they all use.

Diamond & Myers configure their buildings in ways that follow, to a high degree of consistency, three salient formal tendencies which originate in the work of major figures in modern architecture.

First, there are the Purist forms, particularly the square, circle, cube and cylinder, and Heroic volumes, particularly the two-storey open interior space. Use of these forms was advocated in Paris in the 1920's by "Modernists," most notably le Corbusier. Primary forms were considered to represent an ideal Platonic order and to have a metaphysical meaning in themselves that had been tested by successive civilizations. The double height space represented the athletic vigour of a new social order, and evoked an image of an heroic everyman, living and working in a bright open room.

The formative role of the circle and square in Diamond & Myers' facade designs is most obvious at York Square, a commercial redevelopment and renovation project located at the corner of Yorkville Avenue and Avenue Road in Toronto. The representation of formal meeting spaces by circular and cylindrical forms, often set up to contrast with the dominant rectangular volumes of the overall building configuration, is most evident in the boardroom of the Ontario Medical Association building, located in Toronto's Annex area. A fascination with cubes of space is evident in a number of buildings but particularly in the Myers' house on Berryman Street (just north of Toronto's Yorkville) which is designed within three perfect cubes in tandem between two concrete block sidewalls. Double height clear volumes are repeatedly used to promote distribution of sunlight and the opportunity of overviews from one area of activity to another. This striking openness and subsequent viewability between parts of the building are most strongly perceived in the complex interplay of interior volumes at the OMA Building, and in the formally simple organization of the Myers' house.

A second major formal tendency in Diamond & Myers' buildings involves particular building "servant" elements like stairs, chimneys, driveways, etc. being splayed at an angle of 45 degrees to the main building plans. The square stairtower that is pulled out from the mainbody of the OMA Building at the 45-degree angle, and the two square stairwells buried in the corners of the new addition at York Square are the most pronounced expressions of the use of formal devices that follow from the "served versus servant" space distinction first advocated by American Lou Kahn.

Elements of structure such as columns, beams, piers and walls, which are traditionally the permanent static primary elements in architecture, tend to be de-emphasized in Diamond & Myers' buildings. At the OMA Building for example, the structural skeleton of the building is conventionally ordered and then mostly covered over while clear volumetric relationships and distinct servant elements that include exposed industrial mechanical

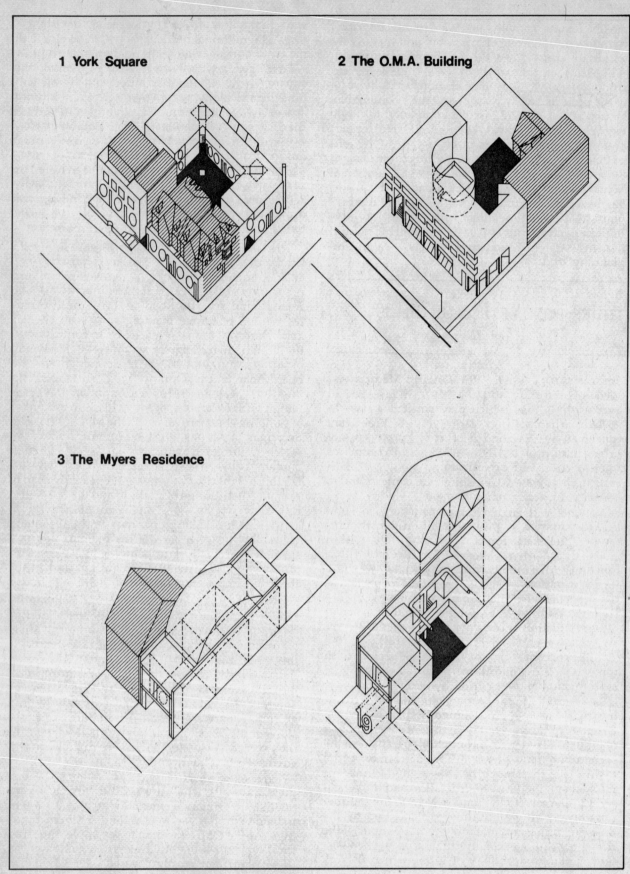

1 York Square

2 The O.M.A. Building

3 The Myers Residence

Three Diamond & Myers urban infill prototype projects.

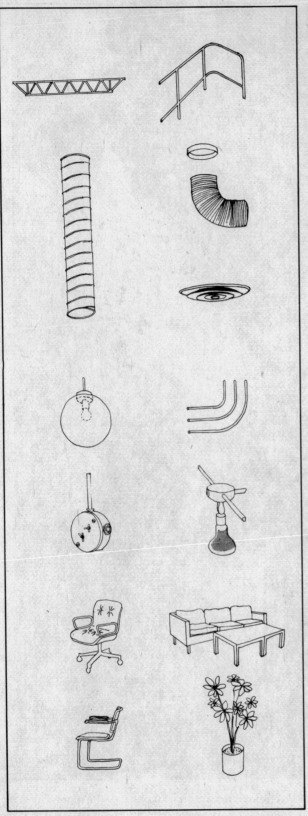

Typical elements of mechanical and electrical equipment, fittings, and furniture from Diamond & Myers buildings.

and electrical equipment and fittings are elaborated.

The third significant formal preoccupation of Diamond & Myers can be traced to the work and writings of Robert Venturi, an American architectural theorist. However, the full scope of Venturi's intentions to create complexity and contradiction in architecture is limited in Diamond & Myers' work, and applied mainly in the design of the public faces of their buildings. Once past the facades, the predominant ordering systems including the use of the "atrium" model, the use of Purist geometries, axiality created or reinforced by large round exposed ducts overhead, and evenly-spaced repetition of lighting or glazing systems are clearly perceptible. Adjustments to the particular or individual circumstances are often over-ruled in the pursuit of the dominant formal objectives. As a result, Diamond and Myers' buildings are singular, simple and orderly, as opposed to complex, and have little room for ambiguity or subtlety.

Throughout their work, it is evident that Diamond & Myers see themselves creating a rich mix of architectural tendencies and references, sometimes in a deliberately contradictory way, rather than following strictly particular architectural canons. Within the application of courtyard infill prototypes, each of the three buildings represent different hybrids of the same formal influences. At York Square, it is a combination of Venturi, especially on the public face, and Kahn. At the OMA Building, it is the most developed integration of Venturi, Kahn and Purist geometries. At the Myers' house, the references to Venturi are weaker while the predominant order is one of Purist cubes, with the influence of Mies van der Rohe and Charles Eames at the level of building detail and assemblage.

The outfitting of Diamond & Myers' buildings, particularly the interiors, conveys a sleek industrial look. This stems from the abundant and consistent exposure of mechanical and electrical equipment and fittings — pipes, switches, ducts, electrical fixtures and conduits — that the norms of mainstream practice would have smoothly concealed above suspended ceilings or within anonymous service walls. In addition to opposing the banality of the prevailing suspended ceiling style, Diamond & Myers have raised the notion of exposed industrial mechanical and electrical elements to a level that demands much more precise installation and workmanship as well as a higher degree of finish than is involved where they are simply covered over and hidden.

Clearly this aspect of Diamond & Myers' work pursues what has been called the Eames Aesthetic — the *select and arrange* technique for equipping and furnishing buildings whereby the integrity of individual objects chosen is intended to be enhanced through *assemblage*. The Eames house, de-

On the main floor of the OMA Building, looking from the main entrance towards the lounge past the round boardroom (left) and the committee room (right).   Photo by Karl Sliva.

The Boardroom of Diamond & Myers' OMA Building.

Photo by Ian Samson.

signed in 1949 by the American designer Charles Eames, employed in an original way pre-existing standard, industrial building components selected from building catalogues. The Eamesian grafting of industrial images and objects onto a domestic, urban situation produced an equally-weighted juxtaposition of evenly exposed industrial components and domestic and folk objects.

Compared with the calm repose of the Eames houses in which industrial elements are controlled as background, Diamond & Myers expose them obtrusively — and with sparkle — in chrome and enamel finishes. Against the retiring background of the de-emphasized physical structure, their fascination with the forms of industrial fittings replaces structural exhibitionism with a mechanical/electrical exhibitionism. This stance against displaying structural elements for their own sake is a somewhat rhetorical shift in emphasis, and avoids the complex issue of finding appropriate cultural roles for technological elements whether they are structural, mechanical or electrical.

The use of deluxe custom-finished fittings and the omnipresence of the industrial look used by Diamond & Myers erode the educational potential of revealing a building's workings to its daily users. Instead, the glamorous aura created by their overexposure turns them into excessive decor. Their obtrusiveness does not grant us the pleasure of choosing to ignore them, and their primary functions are not followed by secondary uses and meaning. For comparison, consider the cast-iron hot-water radiator commonplace in old houses as a free-standing, exposed but less obtrusive and more matter-of-fact service element. The complete package of exposed items in Diamond & Myers vocabulary of building is uniformly weighted so that making single evocative gestures is unavailable to

their schema.

The formalization of mechanical and electrical systems as integral elements of building design has been seriously pursued by others in modern architecture. In the work of Diamond & Myers, the use of the large circular overhead duct in a pseudo-monumental role of defining axes inside a building is a conscious inversion of the conventional defining role of permanent structure. In part, this can be explained as expressing recognition of the fact that mechanical services take up proportionately more of construction budgets in contemporary building. As well, it acknowledges the increasingly rapid technological and market obsolesence of contemporary buildings as a whole by presenting mechanical and electrical elements as detachable and replaceable.

Each completed Diamond & Myers building projects a distinct image of completeness with an aura of style and glamour that affects the ability of occasional and daily users to derive meaning from them. The process of taking possession through daily habits and perceptions is the way inhabitants "infill" a building with personal belongings, objects and associations alike, and in turn become attached to it. This personalization of buildings is a daily extension of the issue of user involvement in the design of the building.

The "completeness" of a building's image limits its ability to invite this day-to-day process of infilling. This is not to say that a building must always appear incomplete to its users when they move in. Rather, it is a recognition of the varying expectations and personal commitments held by them. The image of a building must support people in making the places where they live or work their own, if architecture is not to be a tool for manipulation.

At York Square, individual shop enterprises are responsible for making their own interior designs within the raw space rented from the complex owner. At the other end of the spectrum, the Myers house is lived in by Barton Myers himself, and consequently its furnishings, decor and atmosphere are highly tuned to the user in the first instance.

The OMA building interior is a good example in which to look at this question of completeness and the implications of a glamorous interior image. In spite of Diamond & Myers' claim that architectural "judgments made were in reference to the importance of activities and user work requirements," the image and use of the OMA building appears better tuned to the corporate self-image of the administration than to supporting the interests and tastes of people working in the building.

The building does have paintings and wall graphics chosen by an art committee and added to the assemblage of furnishings and large potted plants that Diamond & Myers have chosen. But

The secretary pool on the second floor of the OMA building.

although the building has been occupied for over four years, there is very little evidence of personal occupancy — postcards, calendars, clocks, pictures, plants, posters, artwork, books — in the open work areas. (This is less true of the executive offices.) The subtle suppression of any ongoing personalization of places is not just a manifestation of administrative control, but also reflects the consequences of architectural decisions about form and material. Rather than subverting such control and the conventional hierarchy of office administrators and workers that such control symbolizes, Diamond & Myers' work has, in this case, tended to affirm it, in spite of their intentions.

The very chi-chi style of the architects' assemblage of furniture, plants and other items of interior decor tends to make additional objects and their users appear out of place or lower in status. The premise for having architects choose furnishing for a building they have designed is the client's confidence in the designer's tastes. In the OMA building, Diamond & Myers chose classic chairs designed by previous outstanding modern architects. The effect of the selection of such high-calibre classic furniture is that it imposes this very high level of quality and cultural acceptability on any subsequent additions of furnishings by the occupants of the building, even when people want these to be

modest, or low-keyed, and especially when they are to be of a different style. Workers at the OMA building are either too unprovoked by the nature of their workplaces, or simply too intimidated by them, to bring personal objects to the overpowering assemblage completed for them by the architects and the art committee.

In their failure to deal successfully with the issue of appropriation of form by users of their buildings, Diamond & Myers have not transcended the attitudes of mainstream architecture.

A similar question of infilling, this time involving the public with the building face and image, arises at York Square. As a prototype it renews and unifies the street face of pre-existing buildings along Avenue Road by the addition of a new and apparently free-standing facade. The backyards of the one-time Victorian houses are used as the building site for a new court building that encloses and creates the square, with an attempt to make an optional pedestrian route between Avenue Road and Yorkville. In behind, the court makes a second front for more shops while out front, the Avenue Road and Yorkville facades project to passers-by a singular image of a new commercial complex.

The facade bears the influence of Robert Venturi in that it attempts to make the "point of change"

The courtyard of Diamond & Myers' York Square.

between inside and outside of a building by synthesizing the demand of the interior shops to be seen, and the exterior demand of the developer for the complex to promote a recognizable image, into an "architectural event" of Purist geometries — alternating circular and rectangular openings punched out of a continuous brick "cardboard" plane. Unlike the Myers house prototype, which if repeated in rows would mark individual houses by the appearance of party walls with potentially differing infill facades visible on the public face, the face of York Square gives uniformly mute or "dumb" expression to the individual shops behind. Without the normally extensive array of shopfront signs — lighting, awning, the degree of transparency, sidewalk stands, articulated entrances, and so on — the shopkeepers have to depend on the corporate iconography of the front wall to tell passers-by about the exclusiveness, cost, service and style of their stores.

Similarly the two entrances to the "square," one off each street, were intended to be modestly marked by breaches in the otherwise flat, continuous facade. Since completion, the developer has, against the architects' wishes, installed a projecting canopy over one entrance and an illuminated sign over the other to alert unnoticing shoppers. On the one hand, this dramatic move represents commercial expedience, but on the other, it is a manifestation of the inherent limitation of the second front established in the court. While the outdoor court of the OMA building, or the more private interior court of the Myers house work well as retreats insulated from the hurly-burly of streetlife, the commercial court of York Square depends on access for casual public activity to maintain shop trade. Its throughroute is not really a short-cut but is intended to offer momentary relief from traffic and noise to attract would-be customers off the streets. The route through York Square lacks the primary conditions held by genuine public spaces in Toronto such as streets, that would generate habitual patterns of use and casual public activity. (Compare York Square with the way the through-

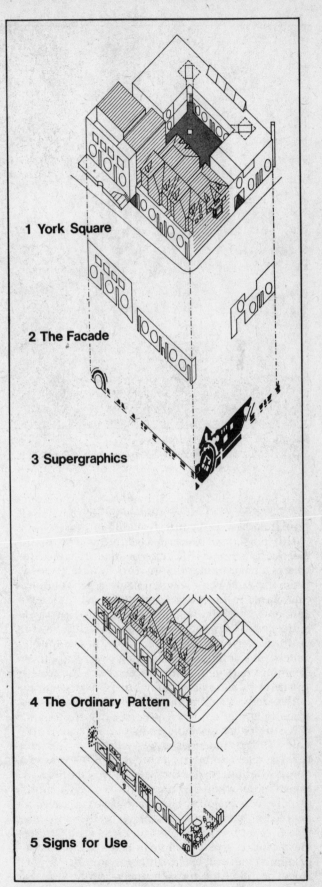

1 York Square

2 The Facade

3 Supergraphics

4 The Ordinary Pattern

5 Signs for Use

York Square.

The public face of York Square.

route works as a short-cut at Lothian Mews, a similar commercial court development.)

This tension between marketing necessity and the clearly second-level role of its optional route creates a crisis of identity for York Square. Indeed, Diamond & Myers designed some of its commercial spaces to front onto both the existing streets and onto the square. Since then, most of those entrances in the square have been closed in favour of those opening onto the more active public streets. The ambiguity of making two public faces is symptomatic of the equivocal role of the square as a semi-public space and its inability to generate public activity without programmed events and attractions.

As the flagship of the transformation of Yorkville, York Square has now settled into a more retiring role. It remains of interest, however, as a demonstration of the limitations of Diamond & Myers' somewhat rhetorical use of the "atrium" prototype as major public space at larger scales in later Toronto projects. Where such attempts were made, in a proposal for Union Plaza for example, the model usurps rather than reinforces or complements the use and primary symbolic importance of the existing genuinely public streets, spaces and structures.

STREET/BLOCK AND NEIGHBOURHOOD

High-rise apartment developers with their techniques for blockbusting neighbourhoods and their off-the-shelf plans for tall buildings of small, expensive apartments mounted an assault on older working-class neighbourhoods in many Canadian cities in the 1960s. When residents organized to oppose the developers, they were met with arguments about high-rise being the only way to achieve high densities. Most conventional architects worked happily with the development industry designing high-rise projects, and more prominent ones offered only safe pronouncements about "good urban design," "quality of life" or the mystical need for design inspiration. In contrast, Diamond & Myers mounted an effective counterattack by designing low-rise "infill" alternatives which conserve existing buildings instead of demolishing them, respect existing street patterns, and succeed in providing housing for more people on less land.

Diamond & Myers developed two basic infill prototypes. The first involves building new dwellings along the back lanes which run through many residential blocks. The lane becomes a minor street for the front doors of the new, compact low-rise rowhouses. Existing houses on the block remain, though they lose a large portion of their backyards and access to the lane.

The second infill prototype involves a five- to seven-storey wall-type apartment building that, in its idealized form, would be built along the street frontage of an entire city block. Family apartments, located at ground level, front onto the existing streets and have small private backyards. Smaller apartments higher up are reached by outdoor walkways served by stairs and elevators located in the corners. In the centre of the block is a large open space accessible to all block residents.

There are of course precedents for these relatively low-rise, medium-density, courtyard apartment buildings in the urban formations of 18th and 19th century European cities, particularly Paris. And in the 1920s, le Corbusier proposed several variations for "immeubles-villas" based on his 1922 prototype "Freehold Maisonette Scheme" for comprehensive block development of new housing which included upper-level pedestrian decks as an alternative to the interior corridor.

Diamond & Myers popularized the idea of infill housing with alternatives they developed for areas of Toronto faced with high-rise redevelopment. They applied the wall-type apartment prototype to a scheme for the Hydro block, a site just west of the downtown core which was purchased by Ontario Hydro for a transformer station, but which was turned over to the Ontario Housing Corporation in 1971 when the local MPP, Conservative revenue minister Allan Grossman, sensed that the project was going to cause him serious political trouble in his constituency. The Hydro block plans have been stalled by reluctant government housing agencies.

Toronto's Dundas-Sherbourne Project is the first of Diamond & Myers' infill schemes to be constructed. The project arose out of a major local victory by local citizens (supported by preservationist groups) over a small-time developer who had assembled a half-block of large old houses occupied by tenants and roomers which he proposed to demolish for a high-rise building. Residents and their local ward aldermen, John Sewell and Karl Jaffary, fought the project at city hall and the Ontario Municipal Board, but the developer received his final go-ahead only after the December 1972 election which made David Crombie mayor and changed the political make-up of Toronto city council. Demonstrations and picketing stopped the demolition of the houses when the developer attempted to get his project underway. Crombie attempted a half-hearted compromise which still

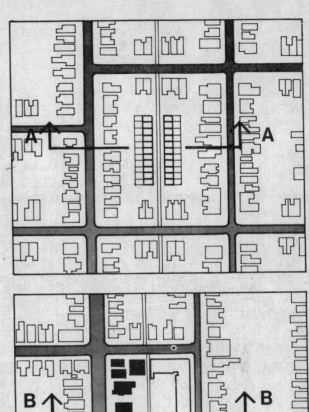

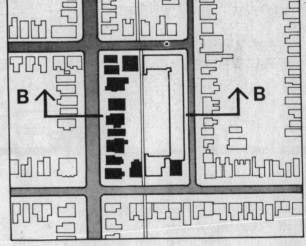

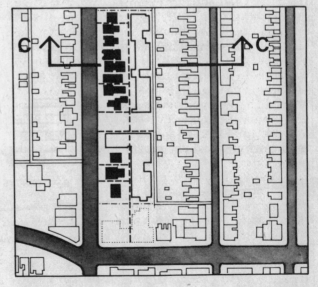

Plans for three Diamond & Myers infill housing projects, indicating where the sections (on the next page) have been taken.

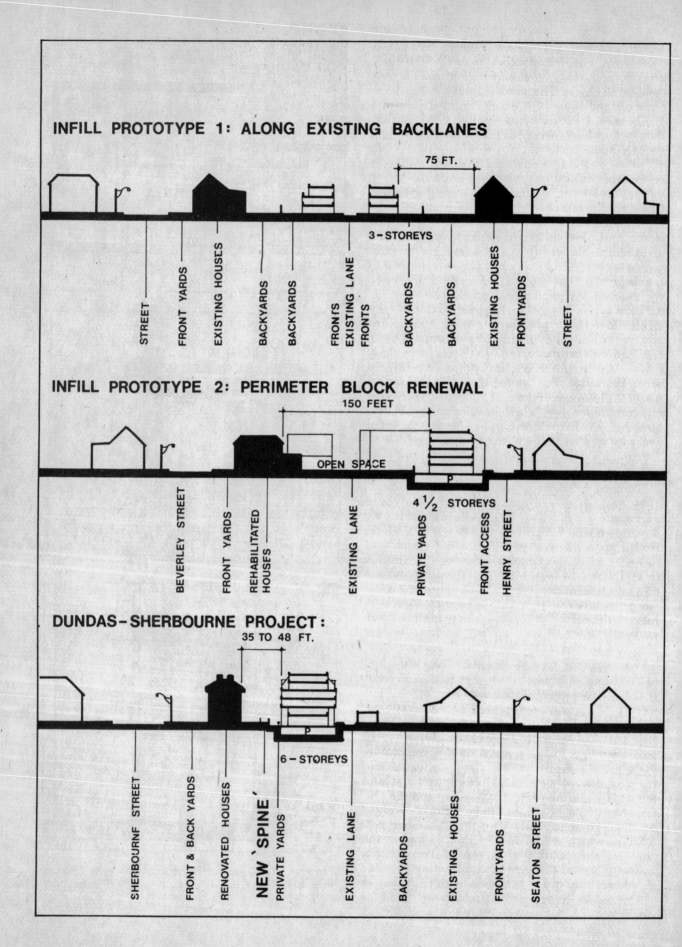

INFILL PROTOTYPE 1: ALONG EXISTING BACKLANES

75 FT.

3 - STOREYS

STREET · FRONT YARDS · EXISTING HOUSES · BACKYARDS · BACKYARDS · FRONTS · EXISTING LANE · FRONTS · BACKYARDS · BACKYARDS · EXISTING HOUSES · FRONTYARDS · STREET

INFILL PROTOTYPE 2: PERIMETER BLOCK RENEWAL

150 FEET

OPEN SPACE

P

4 ½ STOREYS

BEVERLEY STREET · FRONT YARDS · REHABILITATED HOUSES · EXISTING LANE · PRIVATE YARDS · FRONT ACCESS · HENRY STREET

DUNDAS – SHERBOURNE PROJECT:

35 TO 48 FT.

P

6 - STOREYS

SHERBOURNE STREET · FRONT & BACK YARDS · RENOVATED HOUSES · **NEW 'SPINE'** PRIVATE YARDS · EXISTING LANE · BACKYARDS · EXISTING HOUSES · FRONTYARDS · SEATON STREET allowed high-rise apartments, but the hard-line reform politicians and local groups forced city council to support a demand for a low-rise high-density project which would accommodate families and roomers at moderate rents.

This pressure led the city and OHC to form a partnership which purchased the residentially-zoned part of the site at a price which reflected its market value at its high-rise zoning, and gave the developer a very comfortable profit. The development on the site, it was decided after long discussions, would be done by a non-profit corporation set up by the city, using financing under section 15A of the National Housing Act and federal-provincial rent supplement arrangements to keep rents in the project within reach of local area residents.

Diamond & Myers, who were selected as project architects in spite of opposition from OHC, were faced with several severe constraints in their planning for this project. First there was an overriding commitment to retain and use the fine old houses on the site. Second, the price paid for the land by the partnership — the market value of the site at its new, rezoned, high-rise value — meant that a relatively high density had to be achieved if the land cost component of the housing was to be kept low enough not to push eventual rent levels sky-high. Third, the site encompassed only one side of a block, from street front to backlane, and the working committee of residents and city officials to whom the architects were responsible felt that the lane should not be used for access and address for the new housing, but remain as a back lane.

Looking south towards Dundas Street on a model of the Diamond & Myers Sherbourne-Dundas project. Existing houses are white; new construction is grey.

The requirement of retaining and using existing houses fell completely within Diamond & Myers' prototype infill projects. But the density required as a result of land costs and rent maximums, two times coverage, was very high for a site with such restricted scope, and the fact that the architects were working with only half a block also limited the extent to which their prototypes could be applied.

The resulting design involves five, six, and seven-storey apartment buildings built along the lane with the seven-storey building being "L" shaped with a wing perpendicular to Sherbourne Street. Of the 17 old houses on Sherbourne Street, 16 are retained and converted into flats for families.

The fundamentals of the Dundas-Sherbourne design are consistent with the political objectives of the citizen group and reform politicians whose cause Diamond & Myers supported. It does not involve high-rise buildings; it accommodates families; it retains and uses existing buildings; it uses the opportunities created by the traditional grid of streets and lanes. Moreover, the design process involved representatives of the surrounding community and potential residents. Financing and ownership was a departure from the develop-

ment industry with its profit-maximizing; the houses would be lived in by moderate-income families; and residents would have a continuing say in management.

Beyond the success of working out these fundamental programmatic and administrative principles, there are however some serious problems and inconsistencies in the Diamond & Myers scheme. These difficulties raise the critical issue of the role of the form of the project in influencing long-term liveability of the Dundas-Sherbourne project itself, and of the neighbourhood in which it is located.

Though the old houses keep a portion of their backyards, and new ground-floor apartments have some private garden space, the dimensions involved are much tighter than usual in similar Toronto neighbourhoods. The distances between the back windows of the old houses and the windows of the new apartments are 35 to 48 feet, in contrast to the usual minimum of about 80 feet. The only discernible attempt to take this compaction into account is the historicist gesture of making sloping mansard-style roofs for the new north buildings, presumably to somewhat minimize their five- and six-storey heights. In spite of this, the building will appear as a continuous large wall.

Another problem arises from the decision to keep the back lane as a back lane, and have the front doors of the new housing open towards the backs of the existing old houses along Sherbourne St. rather than onto the lane. Family dwelling units open onto a new mid-site "pedestrian spine" which runs between the backs of the old houses and the fronts of the new buildings the entire length of the project, passing underneath the seven-storey building for roomers and continuing to Dundas St. An alternative arrangement, and one which has been traditional in Toronto when new houses were built in the backyards of houses that had long lots, would have been for the new buildings to be reached by existing sidewalks between the old house. This would have, in the case of Dundas-Sherbourne, kept Sherbourne St. as everyone's front street, and as the front access to every part of the new building.

As it is, the new project "pedestrian spine" running mid-site means that residents of the new buildings "in behind" need not use Sherbourne Street very often as part of their daily routes. The spine is neither as formally public as an ordinary street nor as informal as a back lane. Its precedents can rather be found in the internal organization of housing "projects" which enforce rigorous car-pedestrian separation and create "project" public space which is quite different from the normal public spaces of Toronto streets.

The introduction of such an intra-project "spine" is a major departure from Diamond & Myers' earlier block renewal prototypes in which the use and primary symbolic importance of the existing streets and lanes as public space is reinforced without calling for "project" access systems and spaces.

The same criticism applies to the upper-level outdoor walkways in the new buildings which run the length of the new buildings at the third and fifth floor levels. The walkways serve relatively few people to make them worthwhile given alternative forms of walk-up arrangements. The fact that only old people and childless couples will live in the upper apartments means that the walkways are type-cast as new project "public" space. The idea of "streets-in-the-air" was originally proposed to sponsor contact between a wider variety of people in the way that the traditional street on the ground does. At Dundas-Sherbourne, the walkways are used to facilitate the segregation of inhabitants by user-type.

The rigorous segregation of occupants by social type within the Dundas-Sherbourne Project follows from conventional, current social planning theory and practice where, in spite of advocating an accommodation mix, each group within the mix is housed in its particular portion of the total project. Such segregation gives us a premonition of a city containing separate buildings or "blocks" for old people, for childless couples, for families with children, for roomers, and so on, and threatens the public character of access systems at any scale smaller than that of the street as we have traditionally known it. At Dundas-Sherbourne, roomers occupy a conventional seven-storey apartment building of their own at the south end of the site, even though the usual pattern of accommodation for roomers is to live scattered through a neighbourhood.

The Diamond & Myers design reflects a concern to provide the families who live on the ground with private yard space. However, there is no consistency about where front and back yards are placed. Some of the ground-level family apartments in the new building *front* onto the new mid-site project "spine" while others have their front doors on the existing back lane. In the renovated houses, some of the apartments have their back yards facing onto Sherbourne Street, an awkward arrangement which undermines its continuity as a public street serving the formal fronts of the houses. An early intention to include roof terraces was abandoned due to their cost. A more stage-wise strategy to meet such an objective would have been to provide in the first stage clearly visible stairways to the roofs so that a more ambitious use of them by residents could remain an open possibility.

The plans for individual apartments are mostly conventional. Generally the plans of the renovated apartments are more generous than those in the new units, which are equal to or slightly larger than conventional Toronto apartments in terms of floor area for rent though smaller in absolute size. However, it is clear from the plans that maximizing choices that allow occupants to decide for themselves how they will organize individual apartment is not innovatively pursued.

There are 32 mini-one-bedroom apartments, directly accessible from the upper-level outdoor walkways, which had rather peculiar plans in the original drawings. The bedroom was located next to the semi-public walkway, and you entered the apartment directly into the bedroom, then walked by a kitchen through a hallway to get to the living room at the "back" of the unit. This inversion of the usual front and back arrangement reduced the potential of the walkway to serve as a substitute balcony as an easy extension of the kitchen or living room space. In all the upper mini- and one-bedroom units, living rooms are fixed to get east light while bedrooms get west exposure, which is the opposite of what most people would probably want if they had the choice. In the working drawings stage for the project, however, several improvements have been made including the provision of private balconies for the dwelling units higher up in the buildings as well as revisions to the obviously awkward plans of some of the smaller one-bedroom units.

The degree of control that occupants can exercise over the use and interpretation of their dwellings is not simply the question of their power as tenants with respect to administrative organization. The appropriation of buildings by their users is also a question of form and material. Building configurations can be more or less adaptable and adhesive to the multifarious ways that inhabitants can actively attach personal meaning to places: painting, decorating, choosing where belongings and furnishings might go, being able to interpret and use the interior of a dwelling in other ways than conventionally planned, etc. Although Diamond & Myers have popularized the "infill" concept at the larger scale of city-building as their trademark, their buildings demonstrate limited intentions with respect to the process of infill at the scale of the day-to-day engagement between form and user.

Diamond & Myers played active supporting roles throughout the Dundas-Sherbourne struggle — at the O.M.B. hearing, during the April 1973 crisis. The design process that followed was limited by cost, time and by particular site constraints including the assumed density. Yet the "structural" consistency of their previous block renewal prototypes was abandoned in dealing with issues of the relationship between public and private spaces within the project, the clarity and comprehensibility of the order of fronts and backs of dwellings, and the relationship of the project to its surrounding urban fabric in terms of systems of access, patterns of use, association and symbolic image. The stylish vocabulary of forms, objects and industrial rhetoric that consistently characterizes their completed works is non-existent at Dundas-Sherbourne in a way that suggests that these may have limited applicability and appropriateness. Within the context of a "bare-bones" budget and conventional construction modes and materials, an appropriate vocabulary of building adaptable to the various ordinary but often subtle, complex circumstances of living-in architecture was not developed. Apart from general objectives, there was not a clearly worked-out set of qualitative but precise criteria for housing which could form a critical framework within which decisions could be made not only by the architects but also by the Project Team.

Dundas-Sherbourne is a vanguard project in terms of its politics and its program: saving the old houses, providing 75 per cent of the accommodation for limited income families, old people, couples and roomers, and placing administrative control of the project when built in the hands of residents. But in many of its planning and design aspects, there has been a serious failure to carry through the overall politics of the project, to develop the form of reform in the same innovative, in-depth and committed fashion as the reform politics that made the project possible.

THE CITY AND ITS REGION: PLANNING STUDIES

As well as their designed, single buildings and their schemes for projects like Dundas-Sherbourne, Diamond & Myers have had an opportunity to work on major issues of urban planning and growth through planning studies they have conducted. Two of these were underway simultaneously in the firm's office in the first half of 1974, and both involved projects with major implications concerning Toronto's growth and its role in the southern Ontario region. The first was a study of the Metro Centre project proposed by the CNR and CPR for the huge tract of railway lands which adjoin Toronto's downtown; the second was a study of the Pickering project which was to combine the federal government's second Toronto airport with a "new town" development planned by the Ontario government.

Both planning studies were commissioned by the "reform" Toronto city council elected in December 1972. In both instances, the city was faced with projects which it had little power to influence. In the case of Metro Centre, the city had given away most of its considerable bargaining power just before the 1972 election when the pro-development majority of city politicians had rushed to accommodate the developers' demands. In the case of Pickering, the project lies outside the city's boundaries, and in any case was being carried out by governments over which the city had little influence.

The occasion for the Pickering study came when the federal government, under fire for the lack of evidence of any need for a second Toronto airport and for the decision to locate the project east of Toronto on prime farmland, appointed an inquiry commission to review the airport. City politicians decided not to confine their presentation to the commission to its relatively narrow terms of reference, but to undertake an ambitious, broad review of the impact on the entire Toronto area of the airport and the adjoining new town.

The resulting Pickering Impact Study is a sophisticated analysis which effectively separates words from deeds concerning provincial and federal policy towards the Toronto region. It demonstrates clearly the conflict between provincial policy documents (like the Toronto-Centred Region Plan and its successor, the Central Ontario Lakeshore Urban Complex Task Force Report) which appear to call for decentralization of urban growth and the hard facts of provincial decisions regarding sewer, water and road developments. The provincial government's actions regarding these expensive urban services are effectively providing the infrastructure which is necessary for continued growth of suburban housing and industry on the outskirts of Toronto around a correspondingly specialized administrative, cultural and commercial city centre. The rhetoric of decentralization only disguises the continued provincial commitment towards growth of Toronto.

The implication of this real policy toward Toronto's growth, manifested by new infrastructure, is to rapidly undermine the kind of city Toronto has traditionally been. Its mixture of uses and its multi-centredness are quickly disappearing. Manufacturing jobs in the central city area are being eliminated in favour of white-collar, professional and service jobs. Moderate-cost family housing is being destroyed and replaced by apartment accommodation for young singles, couples, and senior citizens. When the physical fabric of the old city is preserved, as in residential neighbourhoods which are not subjected to high-rise redevelopment, the buildings themselves are being redeveloped one by one by the white-painting urban middle class who displace working-class families. This is a pattern which the hard-line reformers on Toronto's city council are opposed to; and even the moderate middle politicians, led by mayor David Crombie, are at the minimum committed to mitigating this trend.

At the same time as the Pickering Impact Study was underway, Diamond & Myers were also working on a study of the Metro Centre scheme. Like the Pickering airport and new town, Metro Centre was another major piece in the rapidly-growing specialized city which provincial (and to some extent, federal) policy advocates for Toronto. But the politics of Diamond & Myers' role in the Union Station Study are completely different from the Pickering situation. By implication, the Pickering Impact Study would see a much different role in the Region for Metro Centre and Union Station than the Union Station Study accepts.

The original Metro Centre project was to achieve two things. First, it involved a substantial expansion in transportation terminal facilities in downtown Toronto so as to increase the number of commuters who could travel from the outer suburbs into the downtown office towers. Second, it called for construction of an enormous additional quantity of downtown office space.

The developers in their plans tied these two elements together. The existing Union Station railway facility was to be demolished and replaced with a new terminal to the south, and railway tracks were to be moved southwards so they ran parallel and just to the north of the Gardiner expressway. By demolishing the old station and moving the tracks, the railways gained a huge buildable site on the "right side" of the railway tracks, adjacent to the existing Toronto downtown. The key to their scheme, and the most attractive portion of the

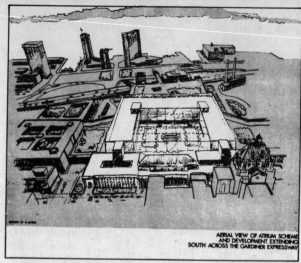

AERIAL VIEW OF ATRIUM SCHEME AND DEVELOPMENT EXTENDING SOUTH ACROSS THE GARDINER EXPRESSWAY

A sketch by Barton Myers showing the Union Plaza proposal developed by Diamond & Myers for Metro Centre. Note the decks shown over Bay Street (left) and the Gardiner expressway, and the broad walkways towards the Campeau Harbour Square development on the waterfront.

155-acre site, was the 12-acre piece of land — still owned by the City of Toronto — on which Union Station stands.

The Metro Centre scheme was approved by the 1971-72 Toronto city council just before the December 1972 civic elections. Their approval was appealed by a coalition of citizen groups to the Ontario Municipal Board, but the OMB gave the scheme further momentum by approving it with only minor changes. All that remained for implementation was a detailed development agreement between Metro Centre and the city. It was this requirement which gave reform aldermen their handle with which to fight for retaining Union Station and scaling down the project. The result was a consultants' study of the developer's proposal and of alternatives which would retain Union Station.

Wary of what might happen to the study in the hands of radical-minded consultants, the moderate politicians led by David Crombie insisted on prime consultants who had corporate credibility, and selected Peat Marwick and Partners, a large consulting firm with experience in the technology and personnel of railways. Diamond & Myers were included as subconsultants on the urban design section of the study team.

While the Pickering Impact Study was pointing out the damaging implications for Toronto of continued growth and specialization of functions within the city, the Union Station Study accepted without question the role of a downtown transportation terminal as a cornerstone for a regional transportation system which would permit that very specialization and growth. The study focuses on the complexities of accommodating the tracks,

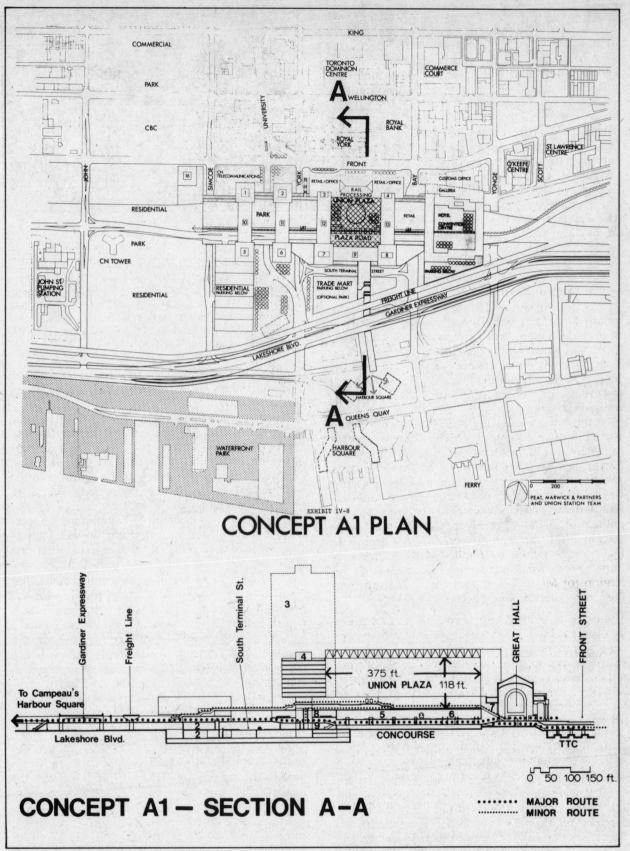

EXHIBIT IV-8

CONCEPT A1 PLAN

CONCEPT A1 – SECTION A-A

········ MAJOR ROUTE
········ MINOR ROUTE

Above, the plan for one of the Metro Centre alternative schemes developed by the consultants. Below, a north-south section through the plan which shows the relationship of Diamond & Myers' Union Plaza to the Great Hall of Union Station.

The original architect's sketch (1913-14) for Union Station. From *The Open Gate* (Peter Martin Associates, 1973).

VIEW TO WEST OF UNION PLAZA
AND ATRIUM BUILDING ABOVE RAIL CORRIDOR

Union Plaza, sketched by Jack Diamond. On the right are the escalators which would lead up to the plaza level from the Great Hall of Union Station. The relationship between the station and the new plaza can be seen in the section, and is numbered '7'.

platforms and service facilities required for a multi-mode transit facility. The only substantial difference between the study and the developer's scheme is that the city consultants succeed in showing how this could be done without demolishing Union Station.

As well as accepting the developer's transportation program, the study assumed that the developer had a right to the profit which would be earned on their original scheme. Without making this explicit, any alternative which substantially reduced the developer's potential profit was consi-

dered to be unfeasible. The study eventually identified six alternative arrangements, all of which allow for the construction of 8,000,000 square feet of new commercial and office space in the railway's land in the station area. They differ in the way the space is distributed over Metro Centre's site, ranging from concentrating the bulk of it over the tracks behind the retained Union Station to spreading it more evenly at street intersections along Front Street west from Yonge to Bathurst. This is as far along the road towards decentralization as this study goes, and clearly it is not far at all.

In developing their alternative schemes, the consultants accepted and worked with "the trip generation rates established by the consultants of Metro Centre Developments Ltd." As a result, they assumed vastly increased car traffic in the vicinity of the development, and were forced to devote tremendous amounts of space at grade level to roads for the movement of vehicles. To accommodate pedestrians, the consultants proposed to "extend the existing weather-protected pedestrian system now being implemented in the city core southward to the waterfront and east and west through the Metro Centre site." The result is to abandon both the traditional grid of streets and the usual combination of people, cars and other activities on city streets in favour of massive specialized sub-expressway road facilities and developer-controlled shopping malls.

Instead of reinforcing two potentially different routes formerly offered by Bay and York Streets, the new pedestrian spine allows one central route. It moves from below-grade to above-grade as it goes south because of the natural slope of the land down towards Lake Ontario. When this pedestrian level reaches Lake Ontario, it is 20 feet above grade, and requires a sharp descent by stair or ramp to reach the ground. In lieu of the historic visual corridors to the Lake down Bay and York, from which pedestrians can see approaching lakeside activity, the "spine" offers an axial view framed by the two future 40-storey office towers of Harbour Square, and terminated by its 6-storey parking structure.

Having established this entirely new primary level above grade, the consultants established yet another artificial grade level on the roof of the train shed behind Union Station. Here they applied at a grand scale Diamond & Myers' atrium courtyard prototype first seen at York Square, and named it "Union Plaza."

What gave rise to the Union Plaza idea was the need felt by Metro Centre's developers for an address for their new office buildings which was clearly on the right side of the tracks, and which was linked to and part of the existing Toronto downtown. By demolishing Union Station, the developers achieved a 12-acre site for development right along Front Street. Union Plaza was the consultants' attempt to do the same thing for the developer.

Located (in most of the study alternatives) 33 feet above the floor level of Union Station's Great Hall, Union Plaza is a huge square with an enormous U-shaped multi-storey office building on three sides, and Union Station on the north side. Union Plaza would be the address for the office buildings and retail facilities around its edges. It would be connected to the ground by escalators descending into the Great Hall, and on the south side by banks of elevators running down to a new east-west street, South Terminal Street.

The Union Plaza idea appears in all the consultants' alternative schemes, including a radical and expensive one to depress the railway tracks running into Union Station. It is seductively packaged, with most of Diamond & Myers' sketches devoted to it, and is shown with a free-span glassed roof which would give it both daylight and protection from the elements. It is described as "a meeting place on an upper level pedestrian route that could be a major feature of the north-south pedestrian way now being developed between Bay and York Streets connecting the city hall with the waterfront."

In the Union Plaza scheme, the problems of what constitutes a real public space which appear at York Square become an issue of first importance. Unlike Toronto's one successful recently-constructed civic square, City Hall Square, this interior plaza located above and behind the street would not be casually visible to the public from Front Street and other adjacent streets. This lack of connection between the plaza and ordinary street-level activity of passers-by on foot and in cars eliminates the spontaneous interplay that enhances publicness. Rather than adding to its urban context, Union Plaza more likely would be rather empty. Discontinuously supported by the morning-lunch-and-afternoon cycle of office workers, it would be dependent on programme conveners for life, especially after hours, much like the base plaza of Toronto's Toronto-Dominion Centre.

Implicitly these weaknesses are recognized by the consultants who attempt to give priority to the Union Plaza level by making it a major level of retail activity and the primary level of pedestrian movement west through Metro Centre and east to St. Lawrence. In addition, they propose that the adjacent train shed roof be made into "artificial grade" for parks.

However, there is already an urban outdoor public space where events both spontaneous and organized can easily occur in the area: the area just outside the Great Hall on Front Street. Instead of picking up on this potential and strengthening it, the consultants proposed to set up a competitive focus of activities.

Rather more serious is the way in which the Union Plaza proposal reduces Union Station's massive and impressive Great Hall into a kind of vestibule, through which people would pass on their way from the street to the planned extravaganza of Union Plaza. Its various functions and the many activities which it now accommodates would be diffused and undercut, leaving — no doubt — the space itself, but stripped of many of the events and possibilities which now belong to it.

The ease with which the Union Station Study's major, and in our minds, most dubious recommendation — Union Plaza — could be appropriated by the designers of Metro Centre as a palliative for their own terminal scheme is demonstrated in the last revised plan of Metro Centre's developer (before the railway abandoned the project, not because of public opposition but rather due to the collapse of the market for new office space in Toronto). It also retained the Great Hall (though not the wings of the station) and used it as an entrance to a large square which the developers called "Union Square." On the same level as the Great Hall, the square was to be ringed with new office towers, and the only substantial difference with the consultants' proposals was that the transportation terminal was still to be located on the south side of the project.

The Union Station Study report did succeed in demonstrating that Metro Centre's developer could retain the railway station in its present location and build all the office space the city permitted without significantly reducing his profits. But it did not address itself to the many problems created by large scale downtown commercial developments, and it had nothing whatever to say about the larger-scale implications of such an enormous addition to office space and commuter transportation facilities in downtown Toronto. Given the involvement of architects like Diamond & Myers with such an acute sense of political issues, the report is curiously muted — and in the end, compromised — by its faulty design judgment as much as its absence of political consciousness.

CONCLUSION

In late May 1975, the rumoured disagreements between Jack Diamond and Barton Myers about priorities with respect to the relationship between architecture and politics, and the remarkable differences of personal style came to rest. The partnership has been terminated. Jack Diamond has established an independent practice, and a newly-formed Barton Myers Associates has emerged. Speculation that Diamond was the partner with the developed sense of the politics of current urban issues who was opportune in offering professional comment and services, and that Myers was the skilful but temperamental designer, pragmatic and committed primarily to issues of architectural design, will be confirmed or disproved by the direction that they pursue from this juncture.

In any case, the body of their work — single buildings, infill housing projects and major planning studies — constitutes a prolific and relevant contribution to the Canadian scene of the late sixties and seventies. Its scope and intensity raises important issues and propositions: the notion of prototypes, the referential nature of post-modern architecture, the appropriate use of contemporary technologies in building, the appropriation of form in all its dimensions, the significance of city "fabric" and the nature and role of new public space in the city. As architects of reform, Diamond and Myers stand apart from other Canadian architects in their serious and consistent commitment to reformist and radical city politics as the context of architectural intervention.

Canada's urban experts:
Smoking out the liberals

James Lorimer

'Go out, then, and seize power.'

That advice came from a young, mild-mannered urban expert turned university professor, and it was directed at me and people like me. It was the culmination of a tough, sometimes nasty discussion on power and city government which shattered the atmosphere of fellowship and mutual sympathy at a conference—the only one of its kind in recent years—which brought together many of the analysts of city government in Canada.

The conference, held in Banff at the Banff School of Fine Arts in May, was organized by the Political Science Department at the University of Calgary. A dozen Canadian urban experts, professors, theoreticians and authors were present to give papers and commentaries. They included Thomas Plunkett, author of many municipal studies and government reports; Paul Tennant, UBC political scientist and a backroom organizer of TEAM, Vancouver's governing municipal political party; Lloyd Axworthy, the CMHC-funded urban researcher at the University of Winnipeg and now Liberal MLA in Manitoba; Dennis Cole, a man who looked like a retired British army sergeant and who turned out to be the effective city manager of Calgary; Allen O'Brien, one-time mayor of Halifax and now a professor at the University of Western Ontario; Stephen Clarkson, University of Toronto professor, editor of University League for Social Reform publications, and author of *City Lib*, a chronicle of his failure to get elected as mayor of Toronto in 1969, and Meyer Brownstone, lecturer at York University, consultant to NDP governments, and author of the unicity reorganization of Winnipeg city government.

It was an odd group, no doubt about that, but it is a good representation of the people who have made the field of urban studies in Canada.

What was significant about the conference—and what makes the event worth recording in some detail—was that it demonstrated that the breakdown of consensus politics and one-party government at city halls in many Canadian cities has finally been reflected in the intellectual world which surrounds city government. So long as municipal government was completely monopolized by the land investment and development industry, it was possible for the city planners, administrators, professors and consultants to ignore the real issues of power and money and concentrate on administrative issues and on debating alternative strategies for producing a smooth, trouble-free civic administration where the real estate industry could maximize its enormous profits and receive the greatest possible support from city hall. But that arrangement has broken down in city after city in the last five or six years as ordinary city residents, faced with civic policies and actions which posed a real and immediate threat to their security as home-owners, tenants and neighbourhood residents, have organized first to fight city hall on specific issues and then to organize electoral battles to wrest control from the hands of politicians representing the property industry.

Try as they might—and they tried hard at the Banff conference—the experts and professors cannot restore the old consensus, whip the members of their group into line and maintain one-party discipline.

THE UNANIMOUS 'WE'

The Banff conference had a mild beginning. It started with Paul Tennant of Vancouver explaining how the new citizen-based municipal political party, TEAM, got itself organized in 1968 and after running in civic elections in 1968 and 1970 had managed to take control of Vancouver's city council in December 1972 by electing the mayor and eight out of the 10 aldermen.

Were the radicals inside the gates? Tennant half-thought so, though his paper didn't make it sound quite that way. 'The nine TEAM members,' he wrote, 'are the cream of the cream. All of them are university graduates; eight of them have post-graduate degrees; and of these eight, four are UBC professors with Ph.Ds or equivalents. What is even more significant is that, with one or two partial exceptions, each of them is a professional expert in an area of direct concern to urban policy making.'

Vancouver, it seemed, had thrown out the real estate agents, small-time contractors, and developers to replace them with the urban experts themselves. And the experts, as the record since December 1972 shows, have operated much more smoothly and elegantly than did developer Tom Campbell's clumsy council. But there has been no overthrow of the policies which the property industry likes to see at city hall; what radical innovations there have been in Vancouver have come not from TEAM's administration but the NDP provincial government.

Tennant's complaint about TEAM, however, was that it has left behind its professed good intentions about 'citizen participation'. Now that the experts have power, and have it directly by occupying council seats, they are doing good ('An expert,' Tennant wrote only half in jest, 'by definition is one who knows what is good for others.') for the people without even consulting them.

What Tennant did in his opening paper was to define clearly the liberal option for city hall, government by the experts, smooth implementation of policies which protect the fundamental status quo but offer token accommodation to other interests.

Tennant's paper was followed by one by me which dealt with the city government-property industry connection. The paper summarized the view that city governments in Canada are strongly and directly tied to the property investment and land development industry, with the strongest link being the arrangement which puts a hard core of small-time property industry people like contractors, real estate agents, architects, developers and real estate lawyers onto city councils. These politicians with property industry connections form the centre of a majority voting bloc which implements policies protecting and promoting the interests of developers, property investors and other industry members. That these conflict with the interests of specific groups and communities and often the public in general is ignored.

Implied in this analysis is the notion that the alternative to property industry domination of city hall is a radical alliance of citizens' groups, tenant organizations and labour which could take over the powers of city government, promote the interests of the citizenry and end the exploitation of city residents and the city itself by the property industry. This is the radical option—civic government which would destroy the status quo and put an end to the arrangements which make the property industry such a powerful and wealthy interest.

Concluding the Banff conference's first morning of papers was Louise Quesnel-Ouellet's account of the implementation of regional government in Quebec. It was a familiar story, the abolition of traditional structures and jurisdictions in favour of larger metropolitan and regional governments whose only claimed advantage is efficiency and rationalization. The real implication of all this is of course the creation of authorities which can be more effectively controlled centrally by a provincial government and which can more easily implement policies suiting the interests of the large corporate developers, particularly when these conflict with the small-time local property interests which used to dominate the smaller, traditional local government authorities.

Quesnel-Ouellet's approach was descriptive, but her focus on structures was reinforced by later papers and discussions at the conference. It emerged as the red tory option, one which puts great faith in government institutions and structures, which holds that by altering these institutions it is possible to create new city governments that can serve the interests of various groups better, and which even (in the reddest tory version) creates a situation which can promote if not cause a takeover of city hall by the people.

Faced with papers which implied, when they did not explicitly assert, three quite different ideologies of city government, ideologies which strongly conflict with each other, the response of the conference-goers was extraordinary. The three of us who had delivered the papers resumed our seats amongst the group who were sitting in a U-shaped—almost a circular—formation. The chairman called for discussion. And the conversation proceeded.

What was most striking about it was the use by almost everyone of the collective, societal 'we', as in 'what can we do to promote change?' and 'What do we really want from city government?' and 'We obviously need new policies and structures at city hall.' Everyone made his contribution to the discussion, and the vast variety of backgrounds and experience present emerged clearly. There were undergraduates in political science from the University of Calgary; three aldermen from Saint Albert, Alberta, looking for hints about how to fight and beat a Syncrude development; young ambitious executive assistants to the Social Credit opposition caucus in Edmonton hunting for ways to hitch the urban revolution to the search for urban votes for their party; citizen activists from Calgary, and civic administrators and politicians. Everyone spoke at some length in the first morning's discussion, and everyone nodded wisely and referred politely to everyone else's contribution. Everyone's heart was in the right place, everyone's goals were the same, everyone had great respect for everyone else's point of view, and the world was one big 'We'.

It was a bit like church, and a bit like group therapy. The fact of three warring approaches to the problems and powers of city government became submerged in a sea of good feeling, which in itself demonstrated that there was no real conflict involved amongst the people present. The conference had re-achieved the situation where city politicians and city administrators together work for the good of the city as a whole, and where nobody questions their interests or objects to their policies.

BREAKING UP THE PARTY

The afternoon of the first day was devoted to a discussion of municipal government structure. Tom Plunkett began with an analysis of the structure of the typical Canadian city. He noted how many of its structural characteristics, like small councils and administrative departments working autonomously and answering directly to the city council, had been developed out of the notion that city government is not political but administrative. The important decisions to be made are non-political ones, about where to put the sewers and how best to allow traffic to move. These present structures, he suggested, do not allow for ideological conflict but rather militate against it.

It was an elaboration on the red tory approach which had been hinted at in the morning. Plunkett took the matter further by proposing a model very similar to Winnipeg's unicity structure as the arrangement which would make room for politics at city hall and which would permit a real struggle for political power.

Plunkett's advocacy of a Winnipeg-style structure led directly into Lloyd Axworthy's talk. Axworthy attacked Plunkett and the architects of Winnipeg's unicity, arguing that it is necessary to recognize the limitations of this 'structural engineering.' He catalogued what he considers to be the failures of the Winnipeg reform: the same level of civic services after as before amalgamation, in spite of promises that services would improve; no change in local government priorities as reflected in budgets and spending; instead of the promised 'better planning,' more 'red tape' and obstruction for new development. As a result there is (he claimed) no new serviced land for industrial development in Winnipeg and a shortage of residential land.

Axworthy considered his most serious charge against Winnipeg and structural engineering to be the way in which reorganization has affected the distribution of political power in the city. Suburbacity, not unicity, is what the Winnipeg reform should be called, he said, and he claimed that the new system has given predominance to what he called suburban interests and suburban politicians who outweigh city interests and city politicians on the new Winnipeg city council.

But Axworthy also had some kind words for the new Winnipeg system. He cited with approval the community committee and resident advisory group system, noting that in some cases they have attracted large numbers of city residents to participate in city government, and that they were generating reformers and candidates for the October 1974 Winnipeg elections.

Axworthy's position was really an elaboration on Tennant's definition of the liberal option from the morning. Analyzing a city government like Winnipeg's unicity which has protected and promoted the status quo, permitted a few major developers to gain control of the supply of new suburban land for residential developments, subsidized major developers like Trizec to build commercial developments downtown, and promoted major public works schemes which sacrifice the interests of neighbourhoods for roads, expressways and bridges which make both new suburban development and new downtown development profitable, Axworthy quarrelled about details and accepted the status quo without question. He would promote reforms which reduce the red tape obstructing developers; he would do away with a popularly-elected mayor; and he would try to introduce a little brotherhood between the politicians on the executive policy committee and the senior commissioners who, said Axworthy, now hate each other.

The Tennant-Axworthy liberal line was supported and extended in the discussion which followed. Criticizing the Plunkett position that new structures are required in order to make the politics involved in city government more explicit and open, Dalhousie professor Dave Cameron argued against any such major changes. 'Do we really want urban governments to govern?' he asked. Perhaps all there is to do, he said, is administration, low-level trivia, and for that what is needed is efficient administrators and politicians who steer clear of politics.

The argument was picked up by senior Calgary administrator Dennis Cole, perhaps the most unreconstructed advocate of the status quo at the conference. He argued that the powers of city hall really amount only to powers over trivia, and that in these circumstances the only safe thing to do is to maximize the power of the experts and administrators who have the best interests of the people and the city at heart. He related in Sunday-school terms a parable of the big sea and the little sea, telling us that city politicians only concern themselves with their wards and getting re-elected, the little sea, and it is bureaucrats like himself who are concerned about the big sea, the city as a whole, the long-term view, and possess a genuine concern for the public interest.

> . . . only bureacrats like himself, he said, are concerned about the big sea, the city as a whole, the long-term view, and possess a genuine concern for the public interest.

All of this was taking place in an atmosphere of great friendliness, of mutual jokes shared by everyone in the room, with people taking little digs at each other on the implicit understanding that there were still really no serious disputes amongst them, and no question on which reasonable men did not more or less agree with each other.

No one had been asked to present a radical viewpoint on the question of city government structure, and the few of us who shared that position found ourselves wallowing in a sea of good feeling, hypocrisy (witness Cole's absurd claims about the interests of city bureaucrats) and misrepresentation of reality (like Axworthy's claim that the fundamental division amongst Winnipeg politicians is based on the part of the city they represent).

I decided to try to tie some of the afternoon's discussion to the analysis which I had presented in my paper in the morning. The position I took was that the Axworthy position and its elaborations offered by Cole and Cameron amount to a defence of the status quo, to an apology for a system in which the property industry controls city hall and uses city government to promote its interests. Axworthy's description of Winnipeg completely ignores the central fact about the Winnipeg reform: that it established a single, centralized, powerful municipal government in the Winnipeg area and delivered that undiluted power into the hands of real estate and land development interests in Winnipeg. Axworthy's attempt to introduce the red herring of a suburban-city split distracts people from the fact that the property industry controlled and funded party, the Independent Civic Election Committee (ICEC), won 37 of the 51 seats on the Winnipeg council in the 1971 unicity election. Its members vote together, control the membership of all committees, and make all the decisions in Winnipeg's city council. The ICEC finds much of its electoral support in middle-class areas, both in the former City of Winnipeg and the suburbs, whereas the opposition group, NDP politicians with one Labour Election Committee man, finds its support in older, lower-income, working-class areas. But the policies of the ICEC are not to promote the interests of the ICEC constituents over those of the property industry and those of the constituents of NDP councillors; rather ICEC policies are the policies of Winnipeg's property industry. Axworthy's position implied that as long as there are more people living in the suburbs than in the former City of Winnipeg, politicians and policies like those which now dominate Winnipeg's city government are inevitable. That elegant distraction serves only to apologize for the Winnipeg status quo by suggesting to people that it is inevitable and nothing much can be done to change it.

Cameron and Cole's elaboration on the liberal position was less inventive than Axworthy's. Cameron's rhetorical question about whether we really want urban governments to govern was an apology for leaving things exactly as they are, leaving the politicians to worry in public about potholes and administrators to carry on with their property industry-oriented programs. Cole's position, and his apology for the power of senior administrators with their long-range vision and their wholehearted concern for the public, was a view that can be taken only in front of people who have never witnessed a city commissioner rushing to do the bidding of Eaton's or the CPR or Trizec or Campeau —a familiar sight in most Canadian cities, including of course Calgary.

That critique of the Axworthy-Cameron-Cole line broke down the unanimous 'we' at the conference, and defined the gulf between liberal apologies for the status quo and demands for a wholesale transformation of city government which would wrest power from the hands of the property industry and change completely the policies and programmes of city hall.

But what was remarkable was how, put in this situation where they were attacked and forced to declare themselves, one by one the liberals lined up to declare explicitly their allegiance to the status quo. A suburban alderman from Victoria, B.C. put it quite neatly, though he shifted responsibility for his political position from himself to his constituents: 'People understand Stop this freeway,' he said, 'but they won't buy Change the world.'

Cameron deplored the fact that citizen groups and neighbourhood organizations are always pressuring city hall for support, and for funds so they can organize more widely and develop their power. If they want to take power, they should try to do so. 'Go out, then, and seize power,' he said, 'take it at an election.' Gone was the polite talk about participation and about encouraging citizen involvement; when it came to the crunch, Cameron made it clear that he understands that citizen groups do not now have real power, and he also made it clear which side he'd be fighting on when these organizations mounted an electoral challenge to the status quo.

The session was coming to a close, and the chairman, an American political science professor at Calgary (the only Americans present were professors teaching at that Canadian university, where we were told that 10 of the 15 politics professors are from the U.S.), made one last unsuccessful attempt to restore harmony and unity in the group. He thought that the major dispute going on was over the power of civic bureaucrats, and he wanted us all to remember that the bureaucrats are human beings too. It is, he said, humanly impossible for them not to attempt to play a role in policy formation in city government. We should, he implied, all sympathize with them in that difficult situation. Of course some people did, but it was evident that the circle had been broken, harmony had disappeared, and there were some people present who foresaw the day when new city council majorities might take power away from the property industry and use that power to fire liberal administrators who think that the little seas belong to the politicians and the big sea, by right, belongs to them.

VARIATION ON THE THEME

The morning session on the second day of the Banff conference was identical in form to the previous afternoon, though the content was different. The subject for discussion was local government financing. The liberal viewpoint on this question was expressed in two papers, one by J. Johnson, the other by D. Sanders. It amounted to the view that city governments should be able to increase their revenues somewhat, and should have access to kinds of taxation which provoke less resistance from taxpayers than the property tax. This position leads to arguments that cities should be able to collect income taxes and sales taxes from their residents. The beauty of these sources of revenue, from the point of view of politicians, administrators, and their academic supporters, is that people would find them hard to resist and the invidious connection between city hall and the property tax would be broken.

None of the advocates of this approach paid much attention to the highly regressive nature of the present system of sales and personal income taxes in Canada, in spite of evidence which makes it quite clear that these taxes (like property taxes) are paid mainly by low- and middle-income people and not by the wealthy.

Plunkett, in a commentary on the subject, argued that the link between the property tax as the major source of municipal revenue and the regulation and servicing of property as the focus of the activities of civic governments created a structure which maximized the interest of the property industry in city

> . . . Cole's view was one that can be taken only in front of people who have never seen a city commissioner rushing to do the bidding of Eaton's or the CPR or Trizec or Campeau — a familiar sight in most Canadian cities, including of course Calgary

hall and the vested interest of city politicians and bureaucrats in the property industry. New development and increased property values which are so important to the property industry are, through the property tax system, also important to city hall because they increase the property tax base and the revenues which can be collected at a given mill rate. Breaking that link, he suggested, would help break the power of the property industry at city hall.

Several people developed the radical position on this matter. One person invoked Henry George and the single tax, and noted that in one corner of the U.S. there are several municipalities which finance themselves completely through an assessment on the increase in value of property in their jurisdiction. Someone else reported on a proposal by one Canadian city politician to tax property investors at the rate of 50 per cent of the capital gains they make on increases in the value of property, and to make the tax 100 per cent in cases where the property investor was also a municipal politician. Edmonton's mayor Ivor Dent claimed that Edmonton is already placing stiff taxes on developers and corporations, taking 45 per cent of the land in any new development. Asked how much revenue these measures raise, however, he was forced to admit that no money actually changes hands. Presumably the land extracted from developers goes for roads, lanes, sidewalks, school sites and parks to serve the developer's own development.

Other people commented on the substantial revenue possibilities of civic taxes on the wealth which city government generates through its activities, particularly taxes on the increases in value of land and buildings, and more flexible forms of property taxes such as substantial taxes on hotel rentals, on business rents, and property tax rates which vary as the value of the property owned increases. A further step in this direction is municipal ownership of land, which creates a situation in which city governments can develop a land policy

... the myth of non-political city government, of impartial administrators, had been shattered

which combines raising revenue through ground rents with a housing policy which keeps the cost of housing low by eliminating the profits now made through land ownership.

The pattern of this session was remarkably similar to that of the previous afternoon, and proved that the splitting up of the circle and the breakup of the group along ideological lines carried right through to the details of civic policy making and had been no accident. This second morning's discussion had started off very comfortably, with people nodding wisely as the liberal position that cities should have more money and a more comfortable way of raising it was spelled out. By the end, quiet talk about how to persuade the provinces and the federal government to let cities share a few percentage points of the personal income tax had disappeared. Again the liberals were smoked out. The morning ended with Dave Cameron, who said that he would rather have what we have now at city hall than to see the kind of taxation measures that had been raised implemented. The message was clear to everyone: there are real choices, real and fundamental disagreemets, and in the positions which people take their political ideology is clearly expressed. The myth of non-political city government, of impartial administrators, had been shattered.

THE THREE-CORNERED CIRCLE

The last afternoon of the conference was devoted to papers from two Toronto professors, Stephen Clarkson and Meyer Brownstone. Clarkson, said the session chairman, was to 'lead us into the future.' In fact he proposed an elaborate scheme for action research and participant-observer research on the activities of citizen groups, perhaps an understandable preoccupation for an academic but not of much direct help to anyone.

Meyer Brownstone was to sum up the two days of discussion. For a day and a half he had been sitting listening to the discussion, saying almost nothing, though he certainly muttered imprecations at Lloyd Axworthy when Axworthy was committing particularly obvious violence on the facts about Winnipeg and the unicity reorganization which Brownstone carried out.

It was Brownstone who laid out the lines of ideological position and conflict amongst conference participants. He called the radical position one which emphasizes the role of the city as a part of the state where corporate economic power in the form of the property industry translates itself into political power over matters touching the industry's realm of activity. The red tory position about the potential of city government structures taken by Plunkett (and one which seemed to come very close to Brownstone's own work in Winnipeg) he characterized as a position which views the city as a political system, where the nature of the system greatly influences content in the form of policies and programmes. Axworthy and Cameron (who by this time had departed) were identified as proponents of the standard liberal position, defending the status quo while advocating modest reforms which pose no challenge to the present power structure.

Brownstone argued that anyone involved in city government must make an explicit choice in this area of ideology, and that each of them forms the building base for new forms of local government and new programmes for city hall.

His example was the Winnipeg reorganization, and he argued that this was structural reform which had flowed from an explicitly stated ideology which combined elements of the liberal position —promoting greater efficiency and rationality in structure—with a more radical commitment to democracy at the local level which means breaking down the control by vested interests like the property industry in order to create local politicians who are elected and controlled by the people in the wards they represent. Brownstone admitted many flaws and weaknesses in the Winnipeg structure, and also agreed that a red tory position of placing faith in the power of institutions has yet to be confirmed by events in Winnipeg since the beginning of 1972. Nevertheless he made a convincing case that it was a major step towards intellectual clarification and to correct policy to make ideology explicit and open as in Winnipeg.

In place of the circle, Brownstone's analysis left the conference in three corners. Perhaps that was a surprise to the organizers, who might have expected Brownstone to draw everyone together instead of splitting them up. The conference had been organized so that people would rush to leave the moment Brownstone finished. No time was allowed for people to fight about this analysis. But it could also have been that his message was one which the liberals, who of course dominated the conference, didn't much want to hear and didn't know what to do about.

THE END OF THE PARTY

The Banff conference, odd event that it was, achieved one important result: it introduced, finally, the reality of what has been happening in city politics across Canada in the last seven or eight years into the mainstream of intellectual discussion about Canadian urban affairs. It upset the one-party system of administrators and academics who have pushed their liberal version of reality and pretended that it was no ideology at all. It clarified the fact that there is more than one kind of city politics, just as there is more than one kind of politics federally and provincially. There is also more than one kind of urban analysis, policies and programmes, and radical politicians and citizen groups need no longer find themselves imprisoned by the ideology and programmes of liberal administrators and intellectual strategists. The liberal consensus which has held the professors, the consultants, the planners, architects and bureaucrats together through the fifties and the sixties has broken down. City hall is the focus of a fight for power, and everyone involved in it has lined himself up on one side or another of the battle. In many cities the fight has been going on now for several years; in others, like Winnipeg, it has not really begun.

When Dave Cameron told the radicals 'Go out, then, and seize power,' he may have thought he was suggesting a novel and unheard-of idea, one which the radicals probably wouldn't take seriously but which would either shut them up or stop them consorting with the experts, professors, and administrators. The irony of the situation is that all around him people's organizations of various kinds, with their allies of politicians, planners, and intellectuals, are working towards power. Part of their fight is smoking people like him out, forcing them to take a stand, to declare themselves politically, to draw a line between themselves and those of us who want to push the property industry out of city hall and construct political organizations which can take power and see city government run in the interests of ordinary people. Cameron declared where he stands, and made it clear to everyone that there is a choice between being with him, Axworthy, Cole and Tennant and being where some of the rest of us are. It was one more step towards defining and changing the present realities of city government in Canada.

III Politics and politicians

Vancouver City Hall

The developers' TEAM: Vancouver's 'reform' party in power

Donald Gutstein

Urban reform came to Vancouver in a big way in 1972 when a young, progressive political party called TEAM swept out of office the pro-developer aldermen of the NPA, the party which had controlled Vancouver City Hall for 35 straight years.

Fed up with the constant assault on citizen interests mounted by the NPA politicans led by millionaire-developer mayor Tom Campbell, Vancouver's citizenry turned to the most visible, most publicized and least threatening alternative. It was called TEAM, for The Electors' Action Movement.

In spite of all the attention devoted to TEAM before and after it won the 1972 elections, little was done to investigate and publicize the party's roots to see whom it really represented. Now, with two years' experience of TEAM's version of municipal reform, its roots and background are of even more interest. For TEAM in office has proven to be a newer version of the same old kind of city politics, pro-developer, pro-business interests, unconcerned about proper citizen representation or legitimate citizen interests. And it turns out that this new party is directly connected to the same establishment business interests which previously ruled Vancouver through the NPA.

In this year's Vancouver elections, TEAM has been challenged by an informal alliance of the NDP, citizen-oriented groups and long-time political radicals. But the task of this opposition has been rendered very difficult by TEAM's success at appropriating the image of change at the same time as it staunchly refuses to adopt any policy—even policies it included in its 1972 election platform — which make fundamental changes in the civic status quo.

People in Vancouver seem to feel that TEAM is doing a good job. But the reality belies that feeling. In fact, it could be argued that Vancouver's citizens would have been better off if TEAM had never been elected, and if the reactionary NPA had remained in power.

To cite one example, as long as the NPA was in power, there was never any development of the Four Seasons site, at the entrance to Stanley Park. Granted, the NPA was going to give the developers everything they wanted. But the issue was clear to the citizens of Vancouver. They bitterly opposed the development at every stage, *and would have gone on opposing it for as long as necessary*. When TEAM came into power, the opposition let up. TEAM was going to give the people what they wanted. Very soon, TEAM became unclear and fuzzy on the issue. Various proposals were publicized. A referendum held on the question further confused the citizenry, who voted to buy the first block, but not the second. The net result was that there would be no development on the first block, but there would be fairly substantial development permitted on the next block, something that never would have occurred under the NPA. And the developers won again.

TEAM's record on other major issues has been just as doubtful.

*There still is no local area representation, no ward system on city council

*Downtown development is more rampant than ever, though slightly more spread out

*The CPR is getting everything it wants on its False Creek property, and will probably get the same for its extensive waterfront holdings

*The inner residential neighbourhoods are still being destroyed

*Although Vancouver will get some form of rapid transit, it is not clear who will benefit the most—the citizens or the downtown property owners.

While TEAM was in opposition, its policies had the ring of reform. Since coming into power, it has shifted far to the right. Alderman Walter Hardwick, TEAM's "guru of urban affairs" is the extreme example of the trend. Hardwick was first elected to council in 1968, the year TEAM was formed. He spent the next four years as a strong opposition spokesman. James Lorimer, in *A Citizens Guide to City Politics*, tabulated the Vancouver City Council voting record for 1971-72 and showed Hardwick, along with COPE Alderman Harry Rankin, to be the most consistent anti-development voice on council, with an almost perfect record of voting for the people's interests. A similar tabulation of council's voting record for 1974 shows that Hardwick had done a complete reversal in his voting pattern, now being one of the most consistent pro-development voices on council.

Who is TEAM and why are they doing this to Vancouver? For the answer to this question, we have to look at the party's origins in the collapse of the last political group to dominate city hall, the Non-Partisan Association (NPA).

THE FALL OF NPA AND THE RISE OF TEAM

The Civic Non-Partisan Association, formed by a group of wealthy Liberals and Conservatives in 1937 to keep the CCF out of power, dominated Vancouver City Hall for an unbroken 35 years. It was then the height of the depression, and the CCF had improved their civic electoral position to the point where they were likely to take control at the next civic election. In fact, a CCFer, Dr. Lyle Telford, had been elected Mayor.

The NPA won the first election it entered, and never looked back. With extensive funds provided by the membership and its sympathizers, the NPA was able to mount effective large-scale campaigns. At the same time, the NPA abolished the ward system that had existed in Vancouver, making it necessary for every aldermanic candidate to run on a city-wide basis, thus requiring more expensive campaigns that only the NPA-backed candidates could afford.

The NPA always supported real estate promoters and big business interests, believing that what was good for the real estate industry was good for Vancouver. Many NPA executive members were themselves real estate developers, property insurance agents, developer's lawyers or directors of large corporations. Many were members of the Vancouver Club, whose self-appointed task was to run the city. NPA members dominated the boards of governors of the universities, all the civic boards, and the cultural institutions. The NPA and its supporters ran Vancouver.

And yet, the NPA was demolished as a civic force in the 1972 election, probably never to recover from the blow. The apparent cause of the defeat was a blatant conflict of interest involving the NPA's mayoralty candidate, Bill Street.

Bill Street was Vancouver's pre-eminent developer's lawyer and paid lobbyist at city hall. Bill Street was also the fund-raiser for the NPA. He would collect the money from the developers to pay the election expenses of the NPA aldermen. He would then appear before those aldermen to plead the cause of those same developers. Bill Street served a two-year term on council in the early 60s, presumably to learn the ins and outs of city hall, and hence serve his clients better.

Every Vancouver developer deals with his own law firm on most matters. But whenever the developer had to go to city hall to get a rezoning, or a higher density for his development, or some other special consideration, he would retain Bill Street to do the job.

The shock raised by these revelations in the 1972 mayoralty campaign caused Street to resign from the race and left the NPA in a state of confusion.

But the NPA had been in trouble, even without the Street affair. Many longtime supporters were becoming dissatisfied with the NPA's performance. NPA had been in power for so long that it seemed to be losing touch with reality. The inanity of nominating Bill Street for mayoralty candidate was just one example.

Another was the secret deal made between NPA Mayor Tom Campbell and NPA President Peter Birks (also head of Bowell McLean Motors), which would have allowed Birks to build a high-rise office building on his property *after* Campbell had announced that the property would be acquired for open space. This infuriated many of the most powerful NPA supporters including BC Telephone president Ernie Richardson, who cut off his financial support of NPA.

Other city hall-promoted projects such as the Chinatown freeway, the Arbutus Shopping Centre and the Block 42/52 giveaway aroused strong hostility from many of NPA's middle-class supporters, and split the usually solid pro-NPA business

Vancouver's controversial Four Seasons site: After development was stymied by strong public opposition to an NPA-supported project, TEAM aldermen found a way of getting a major portion of the scheme approved.

Photo: Marian Penner Bancroft

community. These people, while entirely pro-development in outlook, felt that development should be carried out in an orderly way so that property owners and business interests could make their plans in a more stable investment environment.

Moreover, they feared that the NPA might be losing its popular base of support. At the rate they were going, it was not inconceivable that—horror of horrors—the NPA might lose out to the socialists or other progressive elements that had been successfully kept out of city hall for 35 years. It was time to set up a new civic political party to perpetuate control of city hall by the business establishment. That new political party was TEAM.

THE TEAM CONNECTION

TEAM is a younger, more vigorous and flexible group than the NPA but there is no question that *TEAM represents exactly the same interests as the NPA*, with two minor differences: TEAM is much more closely tied to the Liberal Party; and TEAM has a preponderance of professional and middle management types, whereas the NPA executive was top-heavy with the speculators and entrepreneurs

for whom the TEAM people work.

For example, *Bob Henderson*, Mayor Art Phillips' handpicked choice for 1974-75 TEAM president (he was narrowly defeated) is director of Management Information Services for BC Telephone, that bastion of NPA support. In 1972, five members of the board of directors of BC Telephone were active members of the NPA. For many years, BC Telephone was the main source of funding for the NPA.

Another active TEAM member is a supervisor for Crown Life Insurance Co. For many years, Crown Life was headed by Brenton Brown senior, one of the original founders of the NPA. Two of Brown's sons are still influential in the company.

The wives of middle management personnel are also active in TEAM. One TEAM executive member's husband is a vice-president, marketing for Cominco. Cominco president Gerald Hobbs, was an NPA vice-president, and Cominco was reputed to be the NPA's second largest source of funds. Elsje Armstrong, a member of Phillips' campaign committee and TEAM's "girl Friday", is wife of Bill Armstrong, UBC deputy president and front man for the NPA-loaded UBC Board of Governors. Former UBC Chancellor Allen McGavin was an NPA executive member, and his firm, McGavin Toastmaster, another large NPA funding source.

The pattern at UBC is that the board of governors

CORPORATE AND LAW FIRM CONNECTIONS: TEAM AND NPA

TEAM MEMBERS	CORPORATIONS AND LAW FIRMS	NPA MEMBERS	OTHER PROPERTY INDUSTRY CONNECTIONS

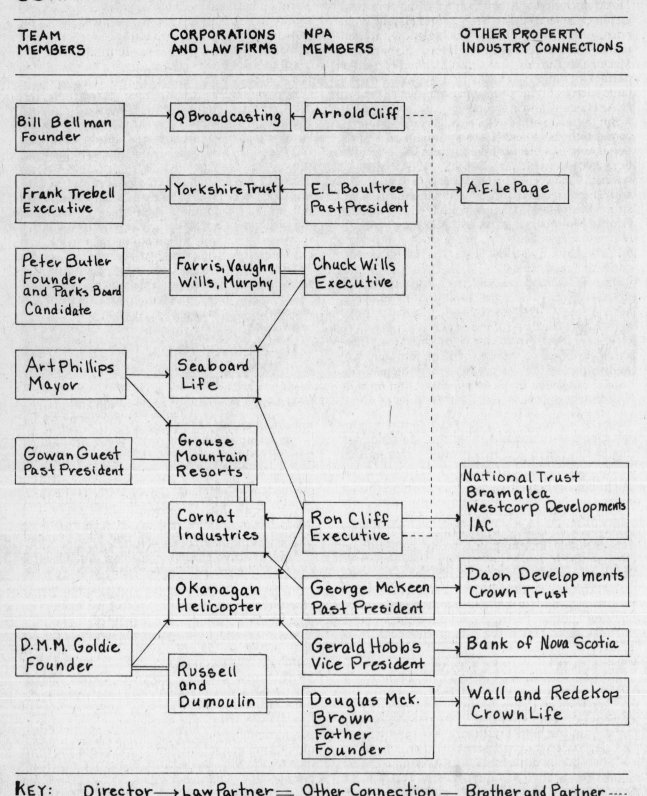

KEY: Director → Law Partner = Other Connection — Brother and Partner ----

represents the NPA, and the professors support TEAM. There were four UBC academics sitting for TEAM on the 1973-74 city council.

As well as the corporate and professorial types, TEAM included the consultants to big business, architects such as Geoff Massey and Harald Weinreich, engineers such as Tom Ingledow, accountants such as George Wiginton, manager for McDonald Currie, and J.C. Clapham, resident partner for Kates Peat Marwick, and finance consultants such as Phillips himself and Dennis Diebel of G.A. Higgens and Associates.

But there are other even stronger, more intimate connections between TEAM and the local and national business establishments, and these connections also often lead directly to the NPA. Many local law firms and corporate boards included both NPA and TEAM members. Mayor Phillips himself has strong business connections with the NPA through Grouse Mountain Resorts and his former association with Seaboard Life. Some of the significant NPA/TEAM connections are traced in the accompanying diagram.

Since TEAM and the NPA are so closely aligned the crossing of party lines should not be unusual. Jack Volrich, a 73-74 TEAM alderman and past president, was unsuccessful in his bid to get NPA endorsement as a Parks Board candidate in 1966. Harald Weinreich, another TEAM founder, had tried unsuccessfully to get NPA backing as a city council candidate in 1964. Theo DuMoulin, NPA Parks Board commissioner, 1960-66, tried to run as a TEAM candidate for council in 1972.

There is a clear merging of interests between TEAM and NPA, but TEAM is much more closely aligned with the Liberal Party. Mayor Art Phillips was onetime campaign manager for Jack Davis, his neighbour on Bowen Island. Phillips himself ran, and lost, as the Liberal candidate for West Point Grey in the 1963 provincial election. Alderman Jack Volrich is a law partner of Liberal MLA Garde Gardom. Another founding member of TEAM, Peter Oberlander, formerly head of the UBC School of Planning and after that Ron Basford's right-hand man at Urban Affairs in Ottawa, was an unsuccessful Liberal candidate in the 1974 federal election. Ed Lawson, another TEAM founder and president of the Teamsters' Union (he was always held up as TEAM's labour connection), is a Liberal Senator in Ottawa.

Stuart Clyne (son of J.V. Clyne), one of the original figures in the formation of TEAM, is a partner in the law firm of Campney and Murphy, one of Vancouver's staunchest Liberal Party strongholds. The firm has included among its partners; Ralph Campney, a Liberal MP 1949-57 and minister of national defense and one-time parliamentary assistant to MacKenzie King; and Walter Owen, Liberal Party organizer and currently Trudeau-appointed lieutenant-governor of B.C.

But the strongest Liberal Party/big business connection of all is through Haig Farris, the fund-raiser for Art Phillips' costly election campaign in 1972, and one of the originators of TEAM in 1968. Through his family and his business, venture capital financing, Farris has contact with many of the powerful political and corporate figures, and, presumably, access to the necessary funds.

All of the TEAM connections are epitomized in Art Phillips, and it is appropriate that he should be TEAM mayor. Phillips is a millionaire like the two NPA mayors, Campbell and Rathie, that preceded him. Phillips is a Liberal, as we have already noted. And Phillips' business activities ties him in directly to the centres of business power and indirectly to the NPA.

There were a number of conservative NDPers and liberal social workers associated with TEAM but these never formed more than a very small minority and their influence has declined further as they have gradually drifted out of the organization over the years. The main thrust of TEAM has been to replace the NPA as the business party that controls city hall. TEAM has been so tied in with business interests and through them to the NPA that it is impossible to separate the two.

THE TEAM RECORD

If this analysis of TEAM's background and connections is correct, we would expect the voting record of TEAM aldermen to reflect the dominant relationships—to vote more consistently in favour of business interests than in the interests of citizens — in spite of TEAM's image as a reform, pro-people government. To see if this is the case, TEAM's 1974 voting record was tabulated. The 1973 record has not been considered because TEAM aldermen argue that much of their effort that year had to be expended cleaning up the NPA legacy. A fairer pattern would thus emerge from 1974's voting.

The tabulated voting record verifies the view that TEAM is the NPA under a new label. TEAM is slightly more citizen-oriented than the NPA precursors, but only *slightly* more. On the great majority of issues, the TEAM-dominated council duplicated the record of the NPA.

Sixteen major issues came to a vote between January and August 1974. Pro-citizen interests received majority on four. Three of these were development and planning issues: down-zoning the high-rise areas of Kitsilano for one year; requiring hotel owner Ben Wosk to turn off his yellow night-time lights; asking the provincial government to buy the Birks Building. The fourth pro-people vote was on a tenant issue, limiting rent increases in city-owned Englesea Lodge to 9.3 per cent.

Haig Farris: Portrait of a TEAM fund-raiser

Perhaps the best way to determine in which direction a political party's interests lie is to find out who pays the bills or, if this is impossible, to find out who collects the cheques. In the case of the NPA, fund-raising was performed by lawyer Bill Street. In 1972, Art Phillips ran a very costly election campaign, relying heavily on expensive TV advertising to get his face and name known to the electorate by election day. His chief fund-raiser in that campaign was lawyer *Haig Farris*, a behind-the-scenes name associated with TEAM right from the beginning.

J. Haig deBeque Farris is a partner in the venture capital firm of Brown, Farris and Jefferson, who specialize in raising capital and assisting companies in mergers, takeovers and acquisitions. Haig is a third generation member of the powerful Farris family, a Liberal Party stronghold for over half a century. The family law firm, Farris, Vaughan, Wills & Murphy, is one of the largest and most influential firms in the province. It had been founded by Haig's grandfather, John Wallace deBeque Farris, boss of the Vancouver Liberal Party machine, one-time Attorney-General in the Provincial government, and a Liberal Senator for 32 years in Ottawa. Farris acted as Counsel for BC Electric, BC Telephone, and the Bank of Toronto.

The son, John Lauchlan Farris, inherited the father's connections and succeeded him as head of the law firm. He was a director of BC Telephone, Toronto-Dominion Bank, Sun Publishing, Kelly-Douglas (part of the Weston food empire) and Pacific Petroleum, before being appointed Chief Justice of the BC Court of Appeals by Pierre Elliott Trudeau in 1973.

The family included other notables: one a Chief Justice of the BC Supreme Court; another a director of MacMillan Bloedel Ltd. Haig's uncle Ralph, also a lawyer, was convicted of perjury in 1964 in connection with the Northern Ontario Natural Gas Pipeline scandal. When one of Ralph's daughters got married in 1968, it was Pierre Elliott Trudeau who proposed the toast to the bride.

Although lawyer Haig did not go into the family law firm, he did maintain the strong Liberal Party/big business connection. In 1973, the Brown, Farris, Jefferson firm became a wholly-owned subsidiary of Ventures West Capital Ltd. Ventures West in turn is a subsidiary of the Canada Development Corporation, and its operating arm in Western Canada. The CDC was set up by the Liberal government with the approval of big business. Its corporate task: to buy back selected parts of the Canadian economy from foreign-owned corporations.

There is no hint of the nationalization of Canada's resources. All CDC transactions take place through the private sector, so that the benefits will not be enjoyed by the general public, but rather by the capitalists—the banks and trust companies and other corporate interests who provide the financing, and the same Canadian interests who sold out in the first place.

Farris is president of the Ventures West subsidiary, of which the CDC owns 57 per cent. The remaining shares are held by individuals and corporations, not all of them Canadian. For example, the Bank of Tokyo has roughly a 10 per cent share. Farris' board of directors includes such powerful business figures as Albert E. Hall, chairman of the Bank of B.C. and H.E. McArthur, of Macaulay, Nicolls, Maitland, one of Vancouver's largest real estate companies, partially owned by the Hong Kong and Shanghai Banking Corporation.

Farris is thus tied in to some of the most powerful financial and economic institutions in Canada. On the one hand his family connections reach to the pinnacles of power in the old Vancouver establishment. On the other hand his business connections have national and international links to major financial resources. With the right family *and* business connections, Farris is indeed the ideal fundraiser for TEAM.

Art Phillips: Portrait of a millionaire mayor

In 1972, just after Art Phillips had been elected mayor, Bill Fletcher, business columnist for the Vancouver Sun, wrote the following: "Some people have voiced doubts that Phillips has the qualifications to run a city the size of Vancouver. Well, all I can say is that a 42-year old who became a millionaire before he was 40 shouldn't have too much trouble with the job." Being a millionaire seems to be the one essential requirement for being mayor of Vancouver, as both NPA mayors Tom Campbell and Bill Rathie had been before Phillips.

Phillips got his start as an investment manager for Capital Management Ltd., at that time controlled by the Power Corp. of Canada. Although based in Quebec, Power Corp. has always been important on the Vancouver scene. Power Corp., for example, owned BC Electric before it was nationalized by Wacky Bennett in 1961.

In 1964, Power Corp. transferred its mutual fund operations to Montreal. Phillips stayed in Vancouver, although he remained a director and vice-president of Capital Management for several years.

In 1965 Phillips and several associates from Capital Management set up their own firm of investment counsellors, Phillips, Hager & North. The firm has assets under management of over $100 million. These include the NW group of mutual funds whose board includes such notables as Einar Gunderson, Socred Premier Wacky Bennett's chief henchman, and Jacques Barbeau, NPA school trustee.

In the past Phillips has been a director of Seaboard Life Insurance Co. His fellow directors included Ron Cliff and Chuck Wills, two NPA executive members.

Phillips most recent corporation connection was as director and shareholder of Grouse Mountain Resorts Ltd., owner of the Grouse Mountain Skyride and skiing facilities on Grouse Mountain, just north of Vancouver. Controlling shareholder in Grouse Mountain Resorts, before control passed to a large eastern developer this year, was Peter

Paul Saunders, a partner along with Power Corp., in the Four Seasons development proposal. Power Corp. was also part owner of Harbour Park Developments Ltd., which was attempting to put a high density highrise development on the Four Seasons site during the time that Phillips worked for Capital Management.

Grouse Mountain Resorts is strongly interlocked with Cornat Industries Ltd., a mini-conglomerate controlled by Saunders. Cornat, in turn, is strongly interlocked with Daon Developments Ltd., the owner of the Four Seasons property before the city-held referendum in 1973, and still planning a development on the second block of land.

Two of Phillips co-directors on Grouse Mountain Board are directors of the Greater Vancouver Visitors and Convention Bureau, and one of these, along with Phillips, is a member of Garibaldi Olympic Developments Ltd. Phillips has spent a great deal of time lobbying for the 1980 Winter Olympics. Clearly, Phillips personally stands to gain if Vancouver gets the Winter Olympics.

Another Phillips business interest is his family holding company, Beaumont Enterprises Ltd., which holds Phillips' shares in the Phillips, Hager, North firm. It was also involved in some minor business dealings such as buying a 'Pinky Coin Laundry' in West Vancouver in 1970. Lawyers for Beaumont were Russell and DuMoulin, who were top-heavy with NPA connections.

So, although he is a TEAM mayor, we see that many of Phillips business connections are rather NPA-ish and Socredish. Phillips may do his mayoring from city hall, where the differences between TEAM and NPA are carefully elaborated, but he does his investment counselling from his office in the Guiness Tower on Vancouver's waterfront, where business is business and the only thing that really counts is a profit-and-loss statement.

VANCOUVER CITY COUNCIL: VOTING RECORD, JAN.—JULY, 1974

	1 Landmark lighting	2 Stop Sands expansion	3 Down-zone Kitsilano	4 Buy Birks Building	5 Stop hotel addition	6 Stop highrise	7 Limit rent increases	8 Mediate rent dispute	9 Limit rent increases	10 Stop demolitions	11 Pay $275 to citizen group	12 Cut NSA grant	13 Down-zone Kitsilano	14 Stop speculation	15 Disclosures Act	16 Limit vending
GOVERNMENT GROUP																
Hard-line																
Fritz Bowers	●	●	○	●	●	●	●	●	●	●	●	●		●		●
Art Phillips	●	●	○	●	●	●	●	●	●	●	●	−		●	●	●
Walter Hardwick	●	●	●	●	●	●	●	○	●		−			●	●	●
Marianne Linnell	●	●	○	○	●	●	●	●	○		−			●	●	●
John Volrich	●	●	○	○	●	●	●	●	●	○	●	○	○	●	●	●
Setty Pendakur	○	●	−	○	●	●	−	−	○	●	●	○	○	●	●	−
Soft-line																
Geoff Massey	○	○	○	○	○	●		●		●	●		○	●	●	
Bill Gibson	○	●	○	○	○	●	−	○	○	○	−	○	−	●	●	●
Michael Harcourt	○	●	○	○	●	●			●	●	○		●	●	○	○
OPPOSITION GROUP																
Harry Rankin	○	○	○	○	○	○	○	○	○	○	○	○	○	○	○	○
Darlene Marzari	○	○	○	○	○	○	○	○	○	○	○	○	○	○	○	○

THE VOTING RECORD: HOW THE SCORING WAS DONE

The voting record was compiled by reviewing city council minutes for the period January to July, 1974, noting the formal recorded votes. Over 90 per cent of these were discarded since they dealt with the routine business of city hall: hiring staff, dealing with local improvements, receiving reports, listening to delegations, amending by-laws. The remainder, 16 in all, were considered relevant to the issue of whether the TEAM-dominated council was 'reform-oriented' or still spoke for the developers and other business interests. The 16 votes were placed in four categories: planning and development issues, tenants' issues, citizen involvement issues, and relations with the development industry.

On each vote there was clearly a pro-development side and pro-community side. For example, on tenants' issues, the development/business interest lay in opposing initiatives which would limit the right of landlords to make as much profit as they could.

In the *detailed tabulations*, a black spot (●) means that the vote favoured the developers; a white spot (○) means that it favoured the community; a (−) means that no vote was cast. In the *summary tabulations*, the record is given for each of the four groups of votes, and the total vote record, with the community-favouring vote first, the pro-developer vote second. The issues on which the votes were taken are recorded in the *issues table*.

VANCOUVER VOTING RECORD:

THE ISSUES

Development & planning issues

1. Requiring Ben Wosk, owner of the Sheraton Landmark Hotel, to turn off his outside yellow night-time lights, as they did not conform with the terms of the development permit and were upsetting many people (Jan. 15/74).

2. Negotiating a compromise design solution with United Equities Ltd., who were proposing a 23-storey addition to their West End Sands Motor Hotel (Jan. 15/74).

3. Down-zoning the highrise areas of Kitsilano to a 3-storey maximum for a one year period (Jan. 31/74).

4. Asking the provincial government to buy the Birks Building since the Vancouver City Council lacked the power to prevent the demolition of any historical building (March 19/74).

5. Allowing Ben Wosk to put an addition on his Sheraton 500 Hotel over the objections of neighbouring residents (approval in principle (July 23/74).

6. Allowing the Canadian Legion to change its funding arrangements with CMHC, so that it could go ahead with a high rise for senior citizens over the objections of the residents of the area (March 12/74).

Tenants' issues

7. Urging the provincial government to tie rent increases to the cost of living index for the previous year (Jan. 22/74).

8. Asking Block Bros. to agree to mediation of a dispute with Century House Tenants' Association who organized after Block Bros. raised their rents from 20-30 per cent (Feb. 5/74).

9. Limiting rent increases in city-owned Englesea Lodge to 9.3% (March 12/74).

10. Passing a by-law which would give the city discretionary power to prevent the demolition of housing which was affording accommodation for low income tenants (June 25/74).

Citizen Involvement

11. Reimbursing the West Broadway Citizens' Committee $275 for expenses incurred in publicizing the down-zoning of Kitsilano hearing after the director of Planning had noted that the West Broadway Citizens activities "contributed significantly to the high degree of community involvement" (April 23/74).

12. Chopping 1/3 from a grant request by the Community Development Unit of Neighbourhood Services Association for funds to pay its community development workers (April 9/74).

13. Agreeing to a request for a further down-zoning of Kitsilano made by the Kitsilano Planning Committee, representing the citizens of Kitsilano (July 9/74).

Relations with property industry

14. Setting up a committee to examine the problem of the speculative buying of buildings, rent raising and remortgaging which was driving up rentals and housing prices (April 9/74).

15. Asking the provincial government to water down its Public Officials and Employees Disclosure Act so that information on only a portion of an official's holdings would be available to the public (May 28/74).

16. In a by-law to regulate street vending, leaving to city hall control so that "incompatible goods and displays in poor taste would not be detrimental to adjacent property owners" (June 11/74).

VANCOUVER CITY COUNCIL

VOTING RECORD SUMMARY

JAN.—JULY, 1974

	Planning and Development	Tenants	Citizen power	Relations with property industry	TOTAL
GOVERNMENT GROUP					
Hard-line					
Fritz Bowers TEAM	1-5	0-4	0-3	0-2	1-14
Art Phillips TEAM	1-5	0-3	0-3	0-3	1-14
Walter Hardwick TEAM	1-5	1-2	0-3	0-3	2-13
Marianne Linnell NPA	2-4	1-3	0-3	0-1	3-11
John Volrich TEAM	2-4	0-4	2-1	0-3	4-12
Setty Pendakur TEAM	2-3	1-1	1-2	0-2	4-8
Soft-line					
Geoff Massey TEAM	6-0	0-4	1-2	0-3	7-9
Bill Gibson TEAM	4-2	2-0	1-1	1-2	8-5
Michael Harcourt TEAM	4-2	2-2	3-0	2-1	11-5
OPPOSITION GROUP					
Harry Rankin COPE	6-0	4-0	3-0	3-0	16-0
Darlene Marzari TEAM	6-0	4-0	3-0	3-0	16-0

Of the remaining 12 votes, 11 went against the people and in favour of developers and business interests. The twelfth issue, on cutting the grant to the Community Development Unit of the Neighbourhood Services Association, had a pro-developer outcome because even though a majority of aldermen voted *not* to cut the grant, a two-thirds majority of council was required to approve the funds.

The TEAM council voted against citizen involvement on all three issues which came up during the period; and voted for the property industry on all occasions.

Council members have been placed into three groups depending on their records: a hard-line government group, a soft-line group, and an opposition group. The core hard-line group, Bowers, Mayor Phillips, Hardwick and Linnell, voted consistently for property industry interests and against the community in 1974. Interestingly, of this group, Marianne Linnell, the lone NPA member, had the best record. Volrich scored well on citizen involvement issues but was hard-line in every other category. This is understandable since Volrich is chairman of the community development committee and rode into office on his reputation as a champion of community interests.

Pendakur did have a scattering of pro-community votes, and it was difficult to place him in hard-line or soft-line groups. Pendakur was also the most frequently absent alderman.

A disturbing fact about the hard-line group is that it contains the four most powerful council figures: the Mayor, Alderman Bowers, head of the finance and administration committee, Alderman Hardwick, head of the civic development committee, and Alderman Volrich, head of the community development committee.

The soft-line group consists of three TEAM aldermen who consistently support neither the developers nor the citizens. But each one has his own peculiar voting pattern. Architect Geoff Massey voted consistently pro-community on planning and development issues, but was the hardest of hard-line in every other category. Gibson's performance was surprising, coming out well above 50 per cent pro-community overall, and in every category except relations with the property industry. Alderman Harcourt almost made it into the ranks of the opposition, with nearly three-quarters of his votes being cast for community interests. His only lapse was on tenants' issues; this is surprising considering that he is chairman of council's housing committee.

Finally, the opposition group, Rankin and Marzari, were consistently and uniformly pro-community.

TEAM AND THE ISSUES

Given the strong business links of TEAM, and its distinctly pro-developer voting record, it would not be surprising to find that TEAM aldermen have not really lived up to their campaign promises on the key issues affecting Vancouver over the next few years. What were TEAM'S promises? What, in fact, have they done? And what should we expect from another TEAM council?

PUBLIC PARTICIPATION IN DECISION MAKING

Vancouver is one of the few remaining cities in North America without some form of area representation. The people of Vancouver are better represented at the provincial and federal levels than they are at their own city hall. It was TEAM's official policy, and one of their election campaign promises, to institute a full ward system. And indeed, TEAM did hold a referendum on the issue in October, 1973. However, by the time of the referendum, the TEAM council had split on the issue, some aldermen, a minority, wanting a full ward system, and others wanting a partial ward, partial at-large system.

The public became confused. Mayor Phillips who commanded the greatest access to the media was surprisingly silent on the issue, coming out neither in favour nor against. But both Vancouver newspapers were vehemently against wards of any kind, suggesting that wards automatically equalled corruption and local bossism, and referred to what happened to the city of Boston in 1910! *TEAM did nothing to counter this propaganda*, preferring to spend its money on getting a TEAM member elected to the school board in a by-election occurring at the same time as the referendum.

The real issue was that a ward system, whether partial or full, would mean that the east side of the city, the strongly working class areas, would have some representation in city hall for the first time in 35 years—since NPA came to power: the reality of the NPA's long reign being directly tied to the abolition of wards in 1937. It was clear to TEAM that they, like the NPA before them, represented only the west side of the city, and a ward system would loosen their grip on city hall power. With a silent TEAM and two foaming-at-the-mouth newspapers, the outcome was a foregone conclusion —defeat for the ward system.

Another official TEAM policy was to decentralize planning, which for too long had occurred behind closed doors at city hall, where the planners were only too susceptible to pressures from real estate interests that swarmed over the place. Phillips hoped to assign community planners to neighbourhoods to work with local groups. "This would enable citizens to say what happens in their neighbourhoods," he explained to an interviewer in 1972.

Indeed, once in power one of TEAM's first actions was to sack city hall czar Sutton Brown, and his lackey, chief planner Bill Graham, the symbols of the developers' control of city hall. TEAM brought in Ray Spaxman from Toronto, whose specialty was local area planning.

Spaxman set to work in earnest, setting up programmes in several parts of the city. At this point TEAM began to back-pedal furiously. Local people *were* getting involved and were coming up with recommendations that the council did not want to hear: controlling growth, down-zoning, local control over development. One of council's objections was that local area planning was presenting only local views, but that was the purpose of the exercise. The newspapers characterized the citizen groups that became involved in planning as power hungry maniacs just grinding their own axes. TEAM cut back. The head of the West End planning team quit in frustration. The very first recommendation that came from the Kitsilano Citizens' Planning Committee to council — to down-zone the RM-3A areas of Kitsilano until a plan for the area had been completed—was slapped down by council. TEAM had a well-publicized "showdown" with Spaxman, at which his plans for local area planning were trimmed. And at a TEAM policy meeting held in August 1974, the notion of citizen participation in planning decisions was severely emasculated.

It is in the miscellaneous, less significant areas of public participation that TEAM has had its greatest "success". Phillips promised to set up an information booth in the city hall lobby, to tell people where to go with their problems, and in fact, he did set up an information booth.

Phillips promised to hold council meetings in the evenings when the major issues would be discussed, so that the working public would have greater access to council, and in fact he did hold evening council meetings. Another reason for the evening council meetings was to make it easier for working people to run for office. How the working man was to get elected in the first place was something to which Phillips did not address himself.

It is clear that TEAM views public involvement much as corporations do—as promotion and public relations: to explain city hall's decisions to the masses, and to detect if the consumers of city hall services are disgruntled. The city's social planning department was the chosen instrument for this job. A P.R. man from the world of New York corporate advertising was hired to head "information and communications projects". That a major function of the Social Planning Department was to promote city hall's plans was demonstrated clearly in the False Creek project, where Alderman Hardwick was ram-rodding his plans for the area through the ranks of the citizen groups who were unhappy with his ideas.

A False Creek information centre had been funded by Local Initiatives and the city. Its real job was to sell the city's plans to the public. It gave the illusion of accepting public reaction to those plans, but in reality there was nowhere for the public input to go. There were no issues for the staff to focus on. They could merely direct the public to the "proper channels." There was no connection with the strong citizen groups in the area who were concerned with many aspects of the city's plans. A worker, hired by the city to deal with those citizen groups, was sacked when she attempted to get a real citizen input to the process. Meanwhile, the Social Planning Department has flourished.

It has flourished because it has become a willing tool for political manipulation, promoting the politicians' pet projects and attacking the politicians' enemies. It became the promotional agency for Mayor Phillips' chief re-election campaign goodie, the Granville Mall. And it acted as hatchet man in attacking community development workers who were organizing citizens into effective groups to get their demands met.

GROWTH AND DEVELOPMENT

The key issue in TEAM's ascendancy to power was growth, and how to manage it. The NPA attitude has been that what was good for the developer was good for the city as a whole. Phillips, however, was going to adopt a "selective approach" toward development, adding "I'm not one of those who believes that all growth is good."

However, what Phillips meant by his statement was not what we might expect. He wasn't against high-rises; he simply wanted them to be more attractive and more spread out. But high-rises there would be. As Phillips told the Downtown Business Association: "Downtown is the executive centre of Western Canada. There is a great deal of room for expansion in the core area. But I believe basic densities should be reduced."

TEAM did indeed down-zone the downtown commercial areas, decreasing the allowable density of development. This in no way slowed down the pace of development which was the main issue. It merely spread the development out. Before TEAM, development was concentrated in one or two "superblocks." After TEAM, it was being strung out, especially along Georgia Street. If anything, the pace of development and projections for future development has increased considerably. City

planners have had to dramatically revise upward their estimates of how many people would be working in the downtown core.

There were two reasons for this. The mere fact that TEAM was in power rather than the NPA was reassuring to the pro-business interests which had become disenchanted with the way the NPA had been running things over the past few years.

The more important reason was the TEAM policy for rapid transit in the downtown core. Even before TEAM came into power, downtown business interests had seen the wisdom of rapid transit access to downtown rather than a spaghetti maze of freeways with half of the core area given over to parking. A rapid transit system would make downtown more accessible to more people, make the limited supply of downtown land more desirable for development, and hence further increase its already inflated value.

The real issue for downtown was how to control the total growth of population and the continuing concentration of office workers. TEAM did not deal with this issue. Instead, they preoccupied themselves with the motherhood issue of improving the downtown environment, "to make the pedestrian king" as Phillips quaintly put it. However, when the needs of the "king pedestrian" came into conflict with the desires of private property owners you can be sure which side Phillips supported.

One expression of the so-called "pedestrian king" approach is the Granville Mall. It isn't really a mall at all, but a widened sidewalk with vehicular traffic restricted to buses. But Phillips wanted the widened sidewalk to serve business interests. No public benches were provided. The only place for the public to sit was supposed to be in the "sidewalk restaurants", which, of course, cost money. Police patrols were doubled on Granville Street to control the more "undesirable" elements that might make shopping less attractive. The TEAM council was allowing street vendors to sell their wares on the widened sidewalk, but council was retaining control of what would be allowed, so that, "incompatible goods and displays in poor taste would not be detrimental to adjacent property owners."

TEAM did nothing to slow down the unrestrained growth of the downtown area, their only action being to spread out the growth rather than concentrate it in a small area. Rather, by drawing attention to the pedestrian environment with projects such as the Granville Mall, TEAM diverted the public's attention from the still unresolved issue of how large the downtown area should be.

Granville Mall during construction: construction workers used trained guard dogs to keep people from writing in newly-laid concrete.

City-owned property in False Creek, scheduled for development under a plan being promoted by TEAM alderman Walter Hardwick.

THE FALSE CREEK REDEVELOPMENT PROJECT

False Creek is really a bay that separates the downtown Vancouver peninsula from the inner residential neighbourhoods. For over 80 years, False Creek has been designated for heavy industrial uses. The bulk of the land was owned by the CPR which leased its property to those industries that generated the most traffic for the railway. During the mid-sixties, the CPR decided that it would be far more profitable to develop its extensive inner urban land holdings for high density residential and commercial uses. The City of Vancouver—that is, the NPA-dominated council—following its long-standing policy of giving the CPR everything it wanted, designated the False Creek area for residential-commercial-recreational uses.

Following a series of complex land swaps, the CPR ended up owning the north side of the creek, and the city 85 acres on the south side. Early in 1972, as a gesture to the TEAM minority on council, Mayor Tom Campbell set up a special False Creek committee under Walter Hardwick to oversee the

total False Creek development, and to specifically plan the city's 85 acres of land. False Creek has been Hardwick's baby ever since.

Hardwick has ram-rodded his plans through all opposition—past the Parks Board and citizen groups who wanted to see an extensive regional park, past the residents' groups who wanted to see low-income housing on the city-owned land, even past his own fellow aldermen, going ahead with his own plans before council had established any policy for the False Creek development.

He hired a private developer, E.D. Sutcliffe, from Dominion Construction Ltd., to manage the city's part of the development. (Sutcliffe had been hired even before the city had decided to build housing on their land.) Sutcliffe's job is to act as a liaison with private developers and set up controls to ensure a quality development. This would be a difficult task under any conditions and requires a man dedicated to protecting the public's interest. Sutcliffe, a developer with a reputation for block-busting residential neighbourhoods, is hardly the man for that job.

Public input in the project was a sham. Whenever real issues emerged, Hardwick acted quickly to nip them in the bud. One such issue was the preservation of the old VIEW (Vancouver Iron and

Engineering Works) buildings on the city's property. An exciting concept was proposed to Hardwick to turn the building into a farmer's market and craft centre. This would have brought many people down to the creek, something Hardwick had been trying to promote. Hardwick acted quickly and decisively to prevent the idea from taking hold. It would have gotten in the way of his plans.

Attempts by the Fairview slopes residents — those who would be most affected by development — to participate in planning have been consistently diverted. When the residents found out that the city was almost finished with its detailed plans — the residents had not been consulted — they set up an organization of all the concerned groups in Fairview. Hardwick, in a typical city hall move, questioned the validity of this organization and refused to deal with it. As a token gesture however, he did set up a series of meetings between city planners and area residents to inform the residents of the city's plans. There was no channel back to city hall for the citizens' reactions.

As a further gesture, the city hired a community worker, Pat Canning, to promote the city's plans. She saw her job as getting real citizen input. Consequently, she was quickly sacked, and the programme fell apart.

Hardwick then set up two advisory committees on housing and open space for False Creek, but these committees in no way represented the citizens concerned. They were composed of developers, academics and professionals. Yet even these committees came up with recommendations that Hardwick found unacceptable, so he scrapped them.

At this point, one of the city hall planners working on the False Creek development quit in frustration. He charged that Hardwick's proposed development was a blunder of classic proportions, and that the critical facts about the city-owned land had never been honestly presented to the public. He accused Hardwick of outright deception, and of intervening time and time again in the internal operations of the planning department to influence planning decisions for political reasons. Hardwick merely denied the charges, and council accepted Hardwick's denial without further investigation.

Hardwick forged ahead with his plans. When federal government winter works funds became available, Hardwick set to work building a seawall around the creek, thus fixing the shoreline for all time, without having decided what was to occur behind the seawall.

On the two basic False Creek issues, parkland and housing, Hardwick rejected the voice of all those who spoke for the citizens and adopted a strict pro-developer stance. The amount of parkland to be included in the total development had never been satisfactorily determined. The Parks

The False Creek seawall, built with federal government winter works money.

Board was still pushing for a large regional park comprising all of the city's land. Hardwick was totally against this. He came up with a formula of 5.81 acres per 1000 people. This formula however applied only to new population in the False Creek basin. The area south of False Creek is the most deprived part of the city in terms of open space. In a 100 block area, from Granville to Cambie, and from False Creek to 16th Ave. (after the West End, the densest area in Vancouver), there are no parks whatsoever. Hardwick ignored the needs of these people, perhaps because they are mainly tenants. If he had considered their needs perhaps the whole False Creek area would have been open space.

If there is to be housing on the south side of the creek, the next issue is the mix of housing that should occur. Originally there had been talk about providing housing for low-income families, those with the greatest housing need. The CPR, on its side of the creek wasn't going to provide this kind of housing, so it was the city's responsibility to do so. But these ideas gradually disappeared from the discussions between politicians and planners.

TEAM now argues that the land has become too valuable for subsidized low-income housing, and besides, the poor do not need to be near downtown.

Both of these arguments are of course ridiculous. It was council's action in the first place—by designating the False Creek area for redevelopment — that made the land valuable. Therefore, council could take further action and make the land suitable for low-income housing, if it so desired. The truth is that TEAM does not want low-income housing in the False Creek area, and is using the argument that the land is too valuable as a convenient excuse. The second argument, that the poor do not need to be near downtown, borders on discrimination.

TEAM finally decided that a third of the housing should be for families with incomes below $9,600, and the other two-thirds for those over $9,600, hardly a mix favouring the poor. On the other side of the creek, the CPR is engineering one of the greatest swindles in Vancouver's history with an unparalleled high-rise, high-density development —at least 21 buildings over 15 storeys—on land that it got for free in the first place and that has been consistently undertaxed ever since. Walter Hardwick subsequently gave the go-ahead to CPR.

In effect, TEAM has abdicated its responsibilities towards those who elected them in favour of the developers and downtown business interests. The Board of Trade was against "family" or subsidized housing around the creek and wanted only executive-type accommodation to house the hordes of junior executives necessary to man all those downtown high-rise office buildings. Three TEAM aldermen are members of the Board of Trade.

In 1976, Vancouver will be host for the United Nations Conference on Human Settlement. Experts and professionals from all over the world will be in attendance. The TEAM showpiece will be the False Creek redevelopment project. It *must* be finished by then. And it must be a fancy, slick "urban village" that will appeal to all those experts. This was the decision made by Hardwick a number of years ago, and he has stuck to his decision ever since. But it was not a decision in which the citizens of Vancouver played the slightest role.

The False Creek redevelopment project clearly illustrates the reality of TEAM in power, running roughshod over the needs and wishes of the citizens for the personal glory of a few elected officials. Council's actions have dispelled any lingering hopes that TEAM holds the interests of Vancouver's citizens at heart. TEAM is seen for what it really is, the old business establishment with a new face.

six years earlier, Mayor Phillips didn't even bother to campaign. With the reform and progressive groups still in disarray, the 1974 election saw TEAM returned with a bare majority along with some of the oldest of the tired old NPA faces, and COPE alderman Harry Rankin. In 1972 the standings had been: TEAM — 9; NPA — 1; COPE — 1. After the 1974 election the standings were TEAM—6; NPA— 4; COPE — 1.

Although the party standings changed, the voting pattern remained exactly as before. There were still six hard-line pro-developer votes, three TEAM: Phillips, Bowers and Volrich, and three NPA: Warnett Kennedy, Hugh Bird and Ed Sweeney. There were three moderate pro-developer votes, TEAM aldermen Harcourt and Art Cowie, and NPA alderman Helen Boyce. And the same two opposition aldermen: Marzari and Rankin.

As council stumbled its way through 1975, TEAM continued its decline. Cracks began to show between the moderate/opposition group and the developer group, but it was the issue of medium-density housing in the affluent west side single-family areas that finally split the party wide apart.

In June, 1975, Phillips and Volrich joined with the NPA aldermen to defeat a rezoning application to allow 26 units of cooperative housing on a 1.2 acre site in the Dunbar area. That brought alderman Marzari to tears and angry responses from the remaining liberal TEAM members.

Within three months Marzari had resigned from TEAM and was sitting in council as an independent. Shortly after, Phillips announced that he would not be running municipally again. And Harcourt, looking for greener pastures elsewhere, threw his hat into the provincial political arena as a New Democratic Party candidate in the December election. He lost, but has since been looking for a politically viable way to move out of TEAM.

By early 1976, TEAM had come full circle. It was a poorly kept secret that alderman Volrich, TEAM's most conservative council member, planned to run for mayor, either for TEAM, the NPA or both. In 1966 Volrich had tried unsuccessfully to get NPA endorsation as a parks board candidate. In between, during TEAM's more prosperous days, he was the party's president. Volrich's move back to the NPA is the signal for the curtain to fall on TEAM's reform act. The developers realize that there is no longer any need for two pro-development parties in Vancouver's civic politics.

The False Creek caper was TEAM's finest moment. After that it was downhill all the way. Three TEAM aldermen, Hardwick, Massey and Gibson, decided not to run in the 1974 election. A fourth, Bowers, was persuaded to stand only after enormous backroom pressure was applied. Not seeming to care much for the party he was instrumental in forming

Reform politics in Winnipeg: Opening things up

The editors

The City of Winnipeg must appear like a rest haven for the property development industry threatened (if not overwhelmed) by strong reform movements in other Canadian cities. The election of October 23, 1974, on the surface would appear to have confirmed Winnipeg's status in this respect. Stephen Juba, Winnipeg's maverick, populist but decidedly pro-developer mayor, was easily re-elected with about 95 per cent of the vote over four nuisance candidates. The Independent Citizen's Election Committee (ICEC), a conservative municipal political party which has dominated Winnipeg civic government since 1919, retained its majority on city council winning 29 of the 50 seats, thereby ensuring that the council's enthusiasm for developers' high rises, shopping centres and freeways (now politely called 'thoroughfares'), would continue unabated. But the election produced some hints that change is coming. The victory of Civic Reform Coalition candidate Evelyne Reese in Winakwa Ward plus the election of a couple of other reform-minded councillors seems to have begun a new era of sharp conflict in Winnipeg civic politics unmatched since the post-Strike election of 1919 and the bitterness of the Depression.

Unlike most Canadian cities Winnipeg has had class-based party politics at the civic level since 1919. Explicit partisan conflict grew directly out of the General Strike. The Citizen's League of Winnipeg fought with Labour for control of city council in order, they said, to prevent the 'Bolshevik Reds'

from launching a revolution. Labour, on the other hand, offered a social democratic programme which called for such things as exempting all houses valued at less than $3,500 from property tax. The Citizen's League, with a little help from a plural voting system based on property, eked out a narrow win. But with the exception of two years in the thirties, they and their successors have held civic majorities ever since.

Without an obvious revolution to oppose in civic elections, the Civic Election Committee (successor to the Citizen's League) has always attempted to disguise its role as the defender of business and property interests by alleging that it existed only to keep party politics out of civic elections. In earlier years the CEC clashed bitterly with first Labour, then the CCF over many issues, most notably the question of municipal ownership of privately held public utilities and the rights of labour. One particular dispute concerned the elimination of conductors from buses and streetcars.

During the late 1950s and 1960s, there ceased to be any serious difference in political perspective between the CEC and the NDP. In effect, the kind of one-party dominance prevalent elsewhere, which accepted without question the programme of the real estate interests for urban development, was just as much the case in Winnipeg. In an article on city hall in the 1960s, former NDP alderman Lloyd Stinson recently recalled the major debates of that decade as being on an NDP resolution calling on the

A memorial to the good old days of Winnipeg city politics: modelled after the old Winnipeg City Hall, a cake which was constructed as part of 1974's celebrations of the City of Winnipeg's centennial.

... The new City of Winnipeg has yet to endorse WATS as official civic policy, while simultaneously proceeding with its detailed implementation. They have also found other names for freeways, such as 'major thoroughfares', 'river crossings' and 'corridors'.

federal government to bring in a Medicare programme, on an argument about whether or not Mayor Juba should receive a chain of office from the Chamber of Commerce and on an unsuccessful proposal to change the City of Winnipeg motto ('Commerce, Prudence, Industry') to something more in keeping with the times.

Municipal reorganization seemed to be the central issue of the sixties. The Roblin administration created a second tier Metro government in 1960. Just a decade later the NDP provincial government, with its 'unicity' legislation of 1971, amalgamated all the municipalities composing Greater Winnipeg.

The ICEC won an overwhelming victory in the unicity election of 1971, taking 37 of the 50 seats. The win was partly based on a successful appeal by the ICEC to the suburbs on the 'party politics has no place in civic government' issue. To opponents it seemed remarkable in light of the fact that many ICEC candidates were prominent, active members of the Liberal and Conservative parties. The ICEC seems in this respect to be simply a municipal coalition of the two parties. But while the belief in anti-partyism might seem bizarrely irrational in light of the partisan characteristics traditionally displayed by the ICEC and its predecessors, given that there was a consensus about the appropriate direction of city government, it is quite reasonable to say that there is no point in having political parties clash bitterly over seemingly trivial items.

But 1971 marked the beginning of the end of traditional politics in Winnipeg. Immediately following the election the ICEC wrecked its non-partisan reputation by packing the council's standing committees exclusively with its own people and holding regular, well-publicized pre-council caucuses. Anti-partyism lingered on in 1974, but it had been drastically muted as a consequence of the ICEC's betrayal of its 'ideals.'

Further damage was done when, shortly after the 1971 election, council approved a new and controversial convention centre, apartment, office and hotel complex. (The centre itself is scheduled to have a perpetual deficit.) A couple of months later the ICEC put through council a pay raise measure—but only for members of the standing committees.

By 1971 the pace and pressures of urban development had noticeably begun to accelerate. This can be illustrated in a statistical sense by looking at apartment unit starts. For most of the 1960s they were under 2,000 per year for the province of Manitoba. But in 1969 they took a quantum leap, soaring to over 7,000, and they stayed high, ranging from 4,000 to 6,000 starts through 1974.

WATS IN A NAME?

One of the principal activities of the bureaucracy attached to the Metro government in the sixties had been the authoring of studies of Winnipeg's future growth and development. This included a Downtown Development Plan which envisioned filling up Winnipeg's downtown with high-rise office and apartment blocks, all of which was to be made possible by publicly financed parking towers.

Metro also sponsored the Winnipeg Area Transportation Study (WATS), the central feature of which was a proposal for a spaghetti-like sprawl of freeways. One proposed freeway, the Northern, calls for the destruction of some 20 blocks of older low-income houses in Winnipeg's north end. The Metro government in its last days and subsequently the new City of Winnipeg began implementation of both these schemes. In the spring of 1974, city council approved a $61-million capital works budget, which included for the first time some of the major bridges and freeway components of the WATS plan. But this council has learned some lessons from the hard times experienced by freeway advocates elsewhere. It has yet to endorse WATS as official civic policy, while simultaneously proceeding with its detailed implementation. They have also found other names for freeways, such as 'major thoroughfares', 'river crossings' and 'corridors'; another favourite is 'needed public works.' 'needed public works.'

What started out as an apparent problem for the WATS enthusiasts has become a bonus. While WATS was endorsed by Metro council, a few members of which are now on Winnipeg city council, the new unicity council has never endorsed WATS. The City's administration, which absorbed the transportation planners who drew up the WATS scheme, has nevertheless simply proceeded to implement the plan. They have been supported in this by the ICEC leadership, including former Metro councillor Bernie Wolfe. It seems clear that these politicians and bureaucrats are afraid to ask for public approval for these plans.

The City has constructed a whole series of road widenings, major street extensions and inter-

The beginnings of Winnipeg's expressway system: the perimeter highway which circles the city just outside the built-up areas.

changes, hoping that the traffic generated will create sufficient congestion to allow the WATS advocates to rush forward as saviours of the public good by laying down their freeways.

While the minor street widenings usually get approved without too much flack, things do get a little stickier whenever the City buys or expropriates some land clearly intended to be used as part of this or that WATS freeway. Questions are asked, and an occasional eyebrow raised, but with the argument that if the land is not purchased now it will cost more later, approval is usually forthcoming.

The $61-million capital works budget mentioned earlier includes two major stretches of the WATS plan's inner beltway, but the City is still trying to get away with calling them bridges. Whether or not the province approves its 50 per cent of this budget should have a major impact on the future of WATS. An internal bureaucratic struggle at the provincial level on this point has yet to be resolved.

Subsequent to the WATS plans being drawn up, a study of relocating the railways in the Winnipeg area was published. The study arose out of discussion of a new bridge over the CPR freight yards. The study was carefully supervised by a number of the WATS principals, including Bernie Wolfe and City of Winnipeg transportation head, H.F. Burns. It is not surprising, therefore, that one of the major recommendations of the study is that the rail lines be removed and replaced by, among other things, freeways. Removal of the rail lines is also expected to free up large amounts of downtown land for high-rise redevelopment. Finally, the CPR wants to move its freight yards because the present ones are inefficient, and they would likely regard a huge government subsidy in exchange for their land with considerable favour. But controversy has developed over the Winnipeg railway study because some of the new lines would, alas, plough through some existing suburban housing. The study has thus joined WATS on the sidelines, waiting no doubt for the people to come to their senses.

The most incredible sellout of the 1971-74 council had to be the agreement between the City and Trizec Corporation for a high-rise office development at the corner of Portage and Main. The terms of the agreement amount to a huge subsidy to one of the richest developers in Canada for a real estate development at the one location in the city where such an investment is guaranteed not to fail. Trizec will lease the air rights to almost a square block of land once the City has built a 1000 car parking garage. The City therefore undertakes to provide Trizec tenants with parking space, thus enhancing the development's profitability. But the most outrageous subsidy is in the lease terms. Trizec will pay 7 per cent of half the cost (which seems like a fancy way of saying $3^1/_2$ per cent of the full cost) of acquiring the land, which is to be carried out by the City, plus 7 per cent of the cost of the strengthening of the parking garage necessary to support the Trizec tower. It is as if the City were buying a savings bond with an interest rate of $3^1/_2$ per cent. While developers elsewhere scream about rent control, Trizec has in its lease the kind of rent control ordinary people will just have to dream about. Trizec will pay the same rent for the first 40 years of the 99-year agreement. At that time the land will be revalued, as it will be again after 65 and 90 years. Defenders of the deal note that the City gets title to the building at the end of the 99-year agreement. Detractors note that the buildings being demolished for the project are about 80 years old.

As if all this largesse were not enough, in its original memorandum of agreement with the City Trizec included a clause granting it the right to back out of the deal whenever it so pleased. This leaves open the possibility that Winnipeg may one day be the owner of the strongest parking garage in the world.

Approval of the project was rushed through council in a matter of weeks in 1972. It has come under heavy criticism ever since from environmentalists, planners and the Civic Reform Coalition. It has been the subject of a couple of lawsuits, one initiated by a travel agency being expropriated for the project and the other launched by the Environmental Advisory Office against the City for not

Buildings on the Trizec site at the corner of Portage and Main, now being demolished by the City of Winnipeg, which agreed to lease the land to Trizec for a rent fixed at $3^1/_2$ per cent of the cost of the expropriation for 40 years.

having prepared an environmental impact statement in accordance with the City of Winnipeg Act. This latter suit was important because it is now clear that the 1000 cars being dumped at the corner of Portage and Main during rush hour are likely to create considerable chaos.

FROM RAGS TO URBAN REFORM

In the past few years Winnipeg has experienced an explosion of the urban issues that have produced an enraged citizenry elsewhere in Canada. Aside from the controversial freeways, there has been a whole series of other development issues cropping up.

A major fight erupted during the life of the 1971-74 council, one reminiscent of the battles to defend the rights of workers in the thirties. When the city was unified the question arose of who should provide certain civic services, specifically road and sewer construction and garbage collection. The former inner City of Winnipeg had a large public works and engineering division which provided these services directly. The suburbs contracted them out to private corporations. The ICEC, apparently seeing a golden opportunity to do their private enterprise friends a favour, immediately com-

missioned the consulting firm of Urwick-Currie to do a study of alleged inefficiencies in the City's public works operations. The consultants naturally concluded that the only thing to do was to contract out these civic services to private firms.

The publication of the consultants' report immediately occasioned a strong counter-campaign by CUPE, the union representing civic employees. The climax came at a stormy council meeting in March, 1973 with a crowd of more than 2,000 demonstrating outside. Council voted narrowly to refer the report back for further study and nothing more has been heard of contracting out from that day to this.

A proposed *winter* racetrack (in Winnipeg, believe it or not) for the Windsor Park-Southdale area of the city has provoked considerable citizen unrest over the past few years. The prime mover of the Southdale Raceway has been Winnipeg's current deputy mayor, Bernie Wolfe, acting with his real-estate-developer hat on. Despite strong support from the two councillors for the area, Ed Kotowich and Michael Dennehy, the suburban residents were enraged, mainly about the noise and air pollution, increased traffic, etc. the proposed project would create, and over a thousand quickly signed a petition of protest. Later, the developers proposed moving the location to a prime piece of riverbank land in south St. Vital which was suitable for park development. The people in nearby Fort Garry

127

didn't much like this either and said so loudly. So, despite their friends in high places, the Southdale Raceway developers are still looking for a home.

Despite these latter two successes at curbing some of the more outrageous zeal of the development industry, citizen participation has not particularly been a roaring success in Winnipeg.

A unique feature of the 1971 City of Winnipeg Act was the provision for institutionalized citizen participation in the form of local Resident Advisory Groups (RAG groups as they have come to be called). The RAG's were included because the consultants from Toronto recommended them and not because there was a demand for them in Winnipeg.

The Resident Advisory Groups have to date largely failed to provide an effective and direct means for ordinary people to influence civic government. The RAG's were a bureaucratic creation to begin with. They were given no independent authority under the unicity legislation. And the present council has both ignored them and given them almost no financial support. Attempting to establish institutions of this nature in a society largely characterized by authoritarian hierarchies in schools, universities, governments, corporations and unions, all of which encourage passivity and deference, might logically be expected to be difficult. The RAG's, while they still exist, are now much smaller and less active than they were originally and are composed principally of people fascinated by the enormous amount of trivia generated within municipal government.

Only on a couple of occasions did RAG's prove to be at all useful in struggles over municipal issues. The Fort Rouge RAG organized an articulate, well documented and popular opposition to a rezoning application by Safeway which, in order to expand a shopping centre in the area, wanted to knock down some old, architecturally interesting houses occupied by low-income roomers. The RAG group on its own initiative conducted a traffic study of the affected area, organized public hearings where various experts, local citizens, architects and environmentalists voiced their opinions. The Fort Rouge RAG unanimously opposed the zoning variance, but just as unanimously the five councillors constituting the Fort Rouge Community Committee supported the variance, and so the rezoning was approved. It remains possible, however, that in the future the RAG's could prove to be useful instruments in the fight for urban reform.

A COALITION IS BORN

It was within this context of growth pressures and a reactionary council that various people began to be interested in developing a reform alternative for 1974. There were several reasons why the existing

> ... a proposed winter racetrack for the Windsor Park-Southdale area has provoked considerable citizen unrest. The prime mover has been Winnipeg's current deputy mayor, Bernie Wolfe, acting with his real-estate-developer hat on.

NDP opposition was considered unsuitable. For the most part the sitting NDP councillors were inarticulate and ineffectual and often enough supported the ICEC majority. The most effective and persistent critic of the ICEC from a reform perspective was Joe Zuken, a Labour Election Committee (Communist) member of council since 1962. The idea of a 'coalition' drew some strength from the fact that the ICEC won at least two seats in Winnipeg's north end in the 1971 election as a result of the NDP and the Communists splitting the vote. It was also supported by those who were interested in civic reform but who had no attachment to the NDP. It was thought that antagonism to the provincial or federal wings of the NDP would distract some people from the reform platform that was the central focus of those seeking a change. Indeed among those interested in a reform coalition were people who supported other provincial or federal parties and still others, without partisan affiliation, who were hostile to the federal or provincial NDP. These feelings merely underlined the disregard reformers felt for the sitting NDP caucus.

Early in 1974 two small discussion groups were organized to explore informally the possibilities of building a new alternative for the 1974 election. One group included a number of dissident New Democrats, a couple of Liberals frustrated by the present council's antagonism to the RAG's, and Joe Zuken. One member of this group was Brian Corrin, a city solicitor with an insider's view of the effects of ICEC control at city hall, who later was to be elected as an NDP councillor (with CRC endorsement) in Sargent Park Ward.

Another group, composed of environmentalists, social workers and community organizers, was also meeting independently. After a member of this group discovered that an acquaintance belonged to the other, a joint meeting was held and the Civic Reform Coalition was born.

'We cannot support their expensive or destructive tastes any longer . . . '

Two public meetings were held in the spring and summer to generate interest and support. A formal structure and membership was adopted and plans were laid for a policy convention and the nomination of candidates for the fall elections. Links were established to various citizen groups and self-help groups actively involved in civic issues. The most fortuitous connection turned out to be that with the Southdale Raceway adjacent to Windsor Park. Support also came from people with the Council of Self-Help Groups, particularly as a result of the callous attitude of the ICEC to the inner-city poor.

At a policy convention held in early September, the CRC adopted an election platform. Resolutions were passed calling for an end to conflict of interest on the part of members of city council, for support for the RAG's and for greater citizen participation, for measures to discourage land speculation and for a comprehensive public transportation policy; other resolutions were passed criticizing Trizec and the Raceway. The resolutions in general, recognized that the policies generated by the existing council clearly had their roots in the economic interests tied to the ICEC. Collectively, the resolutions were a defensive response aimed at halting the real harm the ICEC was beginning to inflict on Winnipeg. As CRC spokesman Pete Hudson put it, 'We cannot support their (the ICEC's) expensive or destructive tastes any longer.'

To some extent, however, the resolutions reflected a somewhat naive faith in the ability of a reform council to overcome what is a fundamental social conflict. In one resolution on citizen participation the CRC pledged to 'respect the spirit as well as the letter of the City of Winnipeg Act.' The CRC-ICEC confrontation, however, is another example of social contradictions inevitable under a competitive economic system. Profit maximization by the few frequently is done directly at the expense of the general populace. The activities of developers are perhaps one of the best illustrations of this. The changes needed to resolve the problems of Winnipeg or any city go beyond respecting the 'spirit' of provincial legislation.

The CRC subsequently began the task of finding candidates and fighting an election. It proved to be an onerous one for an organization new to politics, still small in membership and limited in resources. Moreover, the CRC did not supplant any of the existing municipal parties. Indeed, in addition to the CRC, the NDP, the ICEC and the Labour Election Committee, for the first time Social Credit ran candidates in a Winnipeg civic election. The NDP's election effort this time was a pale shadow of its 1971 presence. Despite all the issues that had come up during the previous few years, the CRC was and is a relatively weak organization and its election effort was in some ways rather limited.

The CRC ended up nominating 10 candidates and endorsing another 11 who were running for other parties (except the ICEC), or as independents. These endorsements included several members of the sitting council who had shown some inclination towards reform in terms of their voting records. While all eleven had indicated some interest in getting an endorsement from the CRC, only NDP candidate Brian Corrin and LEC candidate Joe Zuken had been active participants in the CRC. One candidate, Boyd Kramble, welcomed the endorsement publicly, but disavowed any connection to the CRC. Nevertheless, Mr. Kramble, who ran against ICEC heavy, Bernie Wolfe, said the issue in the campaign was 'whether the ward's councillor is to represent the community or real estate development.'

That some CRC activists chose for tactical reasons to run under traditional party banners reflects the persistence of the old partisan routine and the embryonic nature of the reform debate in Winnipeg. Because in this election the NDP and the LEC had platforms of a broadly similar nature to the CRC there was no contradiction involved in following this strategy — although there ought to be at some point in the future.

The ICEC initially attempted to disarm the CRC. ICEC spokesman Norm Turner issued a policy paper calling for various measures to increase citizen participation, including for example, the establishment of citizen groups to advise the ICEC caucus. Mr. Turner claimed that the CRC and the ICEC had the same goal; the CRC, he said, just wanted power. In announcing the platform he declared that any ICEC candidates who didn't measure up to the new standards would not be endorsed by the central caucus. A close scrutiny of these measures reveals that they do not mention the RAG's or previous efforts aimed at greater citizen participation. It may fairly be said that the ICEC platform offered citizen participation every sort of assistance short of actual help.

But apparently even this platform seemed to be too much for the ICEC to handle. A reporter for the *Winnipeg Tribune* investigated and discovered that no one in the ICEC caucus had heard of this programme. ICEC chairman William Palk labelled Turner's antics as 'flying kites.' It turned out, in fact, that the paper Turner referred to was done for another organization and was critical of a number of ICEC councillors; hence the empty threat to veto endorsements. Mr. Palk added that the ICEC central caucus spent most of its time finding candidates and perhaps 2 per cent discussing policy. The reporter labelled the whole episode, quite appropriately, as 'dirty tricks.'

The CRC concentrated its fire during the campaign on the cost and destructive impact of the freeways, the Trizec sellout and the conflict of interest that permeated the ICEC. The campaign was, nevertheless, fairly quiet. There were 10 acclamations to council and no serious challengers emerged to run against Mayor Juba. Many of the policies that concerned the CRC, such as freeways and the Raceway had yet to be implemented, thus muting more generalized conflict.

The CRC climaxed its campaign five days before the election with a press conference held to detail and to criticize alleged conflicts of interest on the part of ICEC councillors Abe Yanofsky, Bernie Wolfe and Lorne Leech.

Wolfe was criticized for conflict of interest in his role as a promoter of the Southdale Raceway. Yanofsky, who was chairman of the environment committee of council, had a former law partner who acted for a person selling land to the developers of a shopping center in west Winnipeg. It was Yanofsky's committee that approved the rezoning for the development. The most serious allegations were reserved for Lorne Leech. He was accused of having been part-owner of some land near Maple Grove Park in St. Vital slated for hotel development which was now being expropriated for the city's land banking programme. It was alleged that he had been involved as a Metro councillor in drafting an area plan for St. Vital which stated that there should be no further development for 15 or 20 years. Leech allegedly acquired the land for the hotel while it was designated for the development.

All three heatedly denied the charges. Leech counter-attacked, accusing Ermano Barone, his CRC opponent, of conflict of interest for being a teacher who was involved in the local teachers' society salary negotiations.

The results of the election indicate that the CRC attack had some positive effect. Bernie Wolfe only won his election by 17 votes over CRC-endorsed Boyd Kramble and faced a recount. Lorne Leech was badly scared by CRC candidate Ermano Barone in a ward he might have expected to be safe.

... Mr. Park added that the ICEC caucus spent most of its time finding candidates and perhaps 2 per cent discussing policy.

PROSPECTS FOR REFORM

The most interesting race in this election, from a reform perspective, was in Winakwa Ward where Evelyne Reese, a CRC-nominated candidate, toppled ICEC'er Michael Dennehy. Winakwa Ward was the centre of opposition to the Southdale Raceway. Mrs. Reese put together a strong, well organized campaign and had a large number of workers. She attacked Dennehy for his strong and unequivocal support of the Raceway developers. During the campaign, Ladco, the development company that had built the suburb of Southdale, which was within Winakwa Ward, donated 13 acres of land to the city for a park. This land was located next to the Seine River in the last remaining area of Southdale under development. Councillor Dennehy praised the developer while Evelyne Reese denounced the gift as 'woefully inadequate' to meet the recreational needs of the area, and noted that the land given was subject to spring flooding from the Seine River and therefore unsuitable for housing in any case.

The success in Winakwa Ward of a reform campaign based on real issues with a significant perceived local impact amply illustrates the potential for the reform movement throughout Winnipeg. And the pressures from the ICEC's transportation and redevelopment plans will be far greater over the course of the next three years than they have been until now.

Therefore, while the results of the election might appear unfavourable to the CRC, they did produce a solid caucus of three (Reese, Corrin and Zuken), with some prospects for growth within the present council and real hope for the future.

The election also significantly weakened the ICEC, who dropped from 37 to 29, while the NDP increased its strength from 7 to 9 and the number of independents rose from 5 to 10. A week after the election, the ICEC also lost one caucus member, Morris Kaufman, who resigned protesting the ICEC's allocation of standing committee memberships. Mr. Kaufman complained that the ICEC had divided places on the executive policy committee so as to balance representation of Liberals and Progressive Conservatives, but ignored striking a balance between inner-city and suburban councillors (a distinction of no interest to reformers except for its effect of dividing the enemy).

After the election it took about three weeks for controversy to return to city politics. It came when Vic Krepart, president of Metropolitan Properties, admitted to having offered funds to defray expenses to councillors who were acclaimed in the recent election, as well as donating to those candidates in contested wards who, in his words, 'we as a corporation felt merited our support.' This touched off a lengthy squabble about the conflict of interest inherent in developers' donations to civic election campaigns.

Robert Steen, the only councillor to admit having accepted the offer of funds, said he saw nothing wrong with it. He indicated some companies would probably try and use a campaign contribution as a lever, but he did not think that Metropolitan would. Despite this and the assurances of other councillors who admitted to having received donations from developers, Joe Zuken (LEC-Cathedral) demanded rules requiring full disclosure of such funds and Brian Corrin (NDP-Sargent Park) wanted provincial funding of civic elections. The day after Krepart admitted his offer, he was reported to have said he probably made a mistake in sending out the letter. The *Winnipeg Tribune* quoted him as saying. 'I don't feel apologetic nor do I feel I have done any thing improper. It is unfortunate I PUT THE OFFER IN WRITING, THAT'S ALL. (sic)'

He went on to say that he was 'flabbergasted' at all the attention the media was giving the issue. Indeed he ought to have been, for the Winnipeg press, with a rare zeal for investigation, sought out information from all councillors on their sources of funds.

Even as this scandal was breaking, Mayor Juba was announcing that BACM, a huge foreign-owned construction conglomerate, and the Royal Bank would sponsor a dinner for former city councillors, reeves and mayors at the Holiday Inn at a cost of $5,000. At the same time it was revealed that Ladco, another local developer, had given a reception for the new council just prior to its inaugural meeting. Coincidentally, the City of Winnipeg had earlier in 1974 switched its banking from the Bank of Montreal to the Royal Bank.

The ICEC strived mightily to sweep the issue under the carpet, but the controversy persisted. When the ICEC-dominated environment committee shouted down Councillor Corrin, who was insisting that its chairman, Ken Galanchuk, resign until he named the source of over $500 in election funds he had received from three developers, the story hit the front pages of the newspapers the next day.

Then someone discovered corporate contribu-tions were a violation of the Local Authorities Election Act. It then took some very fast talking by Manitoba attorney-general Howard Pawley to avoid his having to begin criminal prosecution of a fair number of city councillors.

The scandal did not eventually amount to much except as a rather clear indication early in the term of the new council of just what the reformers had been talking about. No doubt there is more to come.

City council continued its pro-developer ways throughout 1975. A clear priority was placed on roads when at a cost of several hundred thousand dollars a sharp curve was straightened in Wellington Crescent so that ICEC heavy Bill Norrie could make it to work a few seconds earlier each morning. The road project was more expensive than usual because the provincial government had refused to cost share it. It incidentally involved knocking down four older but still solid rooming houses. Giveaways Trizec-style were the order of the day when council approved the high-rise Centennial Gardens development in downtown Winnipeg. The City was to pay for the cost of the development's park while at the same time the developers bought a City-owned building for one dollar.

However, Centennial Gardens and the Trizec project have become embarrassments for council as tight money and an office market glut (at a time of housing shortage) have forced delays. In addition, a report leaked to the press, written by federal, provincial and city planners, strongly criticized the Trizec project and suggested construction of a federal office building and a public plaza as an alternative.

As a reward to themselves for their good works the NDP and the ICEC colluded in ramming a substantial pay increase for themselves through council at one sitting. Only Brian Corrin, Joe Zuken and Evelyn Reese opposed the measure which partly demonstrated that with the exception of Corrin the NDP caucus is as reactionary on urban issues as the ICEC.

Despite the articulation of a reform critique within city council since the 1974 election, particularly by Brian Corrin, the CRC has been dormant. Its existence might perhaps have been forgotten were it not for a dispute about the status of NDP members of the organization within the NDP. Issues which might spark controversy remain in abeyance. Pressure to redevelop East Fort Rouge has not yet emerged. The provincial government continues to procrastinate on funding the City's freeways but won't reject them. A polarization is needed but has yet to emerge.

Nanaimo:
Pirate in office

Grant Anderson

What, you've never heard of Nanaimo? The "Hub City of Vancouver Island?" "Home of the Boxing Day Polar Bear Swim?" "The Bathtub Racing Capital of the World?" The base of operations for fabulous Frank Ney, entrepreneur par excellence?

A booming little metropolis on the east coast of Vancouver Island, Nanaimo is unfamiliar with the ideas of ecology, historic preservation, slow-growth and no-growth. Rather, the city thrives on a turn-of-the-century civic boosterism aimed at "putting the city on the map" — and putting money in the pockets of local land barons in the process. The champion of this booster approach is Frank J. Ney, 57-year-old Mayor of Nanaimo, Admiral of the Bathtub Navy, ex-M.L.A. in W.A.C. Bennetts's former Social Credit government and, oh yes, President of Great National Land and Investment Corporation Limited. There's no such thing as a conflict of interest in Nanaimo, where what's good for Nanaimo Realty is good for everybody.

In recent years, Mayor Ney has taken to staging grandiose publicity stunts, like the annual Nanaimo to Vancouver bathtub race. He presides over these events in his crimson pirate's suit, brandishing a cutlass and posturing on the deck of his cabin cruiser. The voters love it — Ney has been returned to office five successive times. The local press records every move he makes. And between stunts, Ney continues to run the city with one hand and his private holdings with the other.

The extent of these holdings is well known to the voters, through B.C.'s Public Officials Disclosure Act, and appears to be a source of admiration. In real estate alone, Ney has interests in Great National Land & Investments, Sunnyslope Estates, Gabriola Sands Resorts, Ocean Village Developments, Ocean Village Holdings, Great Western Land & Investments, White Sands Estates, BBC Realty Investors, Frontier Land & Investments, Shoreline Park Estates, Protection Island Resorts, Protection Island Estates, Nanaimo Properties, Cortez Properties, Thunderbird Homes, Old Dutch Farms, Decourcey Properties, Sunrise Beach Properties, Reef Apartments, Sugarloaf Mountain Properties, Driftwood Island Resorts, Metropolitan Land Corporation, Pirate's Beach Properties, Departure Bay Highlands Ltd., Channel Estates, Nanaimo Industrial Developments, Nanaimo Industrial Sites, Blackjack Developments, Denco Properties, Daon Developments Ltd., Lancashire Estates, Ruxton Island Resorts, Yellow Point Park Estates, Homestead Enterprises, Sonora Island Estates, Whaling Station Bay Estates, Denman Developments, Five Acre Lands, and Nanaimo Realty. Not included are about twenty building lots in the city and numerous holdings in large corporations.

One cannot deny Ney's effectiveness in his role as head cheerleader for the real-estate culture of Nanaimo. Since his arrival in the late 1940's, he has seen the city grow from a humble coal-mining town of 5000 into a sprawling city of 45,000. Each year 5000 more residents arrive, part of an 11 per cent growth rate that's a subdivider's dream; all made possible by a fortunate combination of promotion, expansionary sewer and water policies, the natural beauty and resources of Vancouver Island, and a city council with the old booster spirit.

In early 1975, when the Chamber of Commerce complained that planning decisions were taking too long — "costing Nanaimo industry, housing and business" — Ney struck a committee of city bureaucrats and development interests to "work courageously and vigourously to strengthen our tax base." Meanwhile, mining-era housing along the Island Highway is being ripped down at a frantic pace to make way for a ten-mile strip of drive-ins, motels and gas stations that one planner has christened "Little Los Angeles."

Despite his track record, it's difficult to be totally

OFFICE OF THE MAYOR

NANAIMO, B.C.

September 25, 1975

Mrs. Evelyn Ross
City Magazine
35 Britain Street
Toronto, Ontario
M5B 1R7

Dear Evelyn:

Norma Sevcov advised me that you would like a picture
of myself in Bathtub regalia. I am very happy to enclose
two pictures herewith as well as a Bathtub Program which
gives you a little background on the race.

Happy Bathtubbing.

Sincerely,

Frank J. Ney
Mayor

FJN/sh
Enclosure

A letter from Nanaimo's Mayor Frank Ney which came
with the accompanying photo of the mayor in Bathtub
regalia.

cynical about Frank Ney. The man believes in what
he's doing, and in himself as a friend of the people.
When this year's Bathtub Race celebrations turned
into a late-night riot, Ney rushed downtown to the
police barricades, still dressed in his pirate outfit.
True, his attempts to calm the mob resulted in a
barrage of rocks and bottles, and an automotive
charge through the barricade by some particularly
enthusiastic riff-raff, but the incident demonstrates Ney's sincerity as well as as his capacity for
grandstanding.

In all likelihood, Nanaimo will keep booming for
as long as Ney wants it to. People don't seem too
concerned that the city has a drug problem, a vandalism problem, a culture problem, a social services problem, a civic administration problem, and
a general quality of life problem. There's money to
be made, and if you choose to do it dressed up in a
pirate suit, who can complain?

Timmins:
Company town politics

Brian Wilkes

In December of 1974 Texasgulf Canada Limited announced plans for a major expansion of its mineral extraction and processing operations in Timmins, Ontario. Estimates indicated that the cost of the expansion might exceed $500-million, and this amount was displayed in an enormous red headline on the front page of the Timmins Daily Press. It seemed reasonable to me that a project of this magnitude, to be carried out in an essentially mining city and necessarily involving a major impact on the environment, would prompt almost limitless graft and wheeling and dealing between Texasgulf executives and city officials and the Chamber of Commerce. Payoffs for land assembly, tax concessions, sub-contracting deals, material purchases and tenders and a host of other possibles also seemed likely, so I went to Timmins to investigate. What I found follows.

The news of the expansion was greeted by most of the Timmins citizenry with such blind enthusiasm, and by city council and local businessmen with such a burst of fawning, it became obvious that corruption between Texasgulf and the city simply was not necessary. I could find no unsavoury dealings between the two, and this was at least in part because there did not have to be. The people were prepared to grant Texasgulf *carte blanche*, believing that whatever is good for the company would also be good for them.

Manifestations of this kind of posture on the part of the people and institutions in Timmins is common throughout Canada. Cobalt, The Pas, Sudbury, Noranda, Labrador City all owe their existence to some industry and at the same time reflect a remarkably obsequious attitude toward that industry. Somehow in the process of development, these single industry communities have transformed themselves into great social failures of our civilization. They are often regarded as backwaters or the "end of the earth" by the plump and pretentious occupants of comfortable Toronto or fashionable Vancouver. They are often badly planned, or unplanned, often with self-serving or outright incompetent local governments. But why do the people in mine towns *act* like people in mine towns? Why does a mine town mentality block effective local social development?

Timmins has always had an economy based on mining, first for gold in the days of "the Porcupine" in the early 1900s, and now more recently for base metals. It is a city of 43,000. The pervasive presence of mining in Timmins appears to have generated a heavy psychological dependence on that industry. Financial dependence is one thing, but this psychological dependence, manifest by general feelings of security when the mines are making money, is an even more destructive component in the city's own social structure. The people hold enormous faith in the ability of the mines to hold their society together, largely because there appears to be no other choice. As well there exists a pervasive fatalism about their existence and rejection of futuristic thought about the community.

With such a mentality in place, planning just becomes nonsense, and politics begs community exploitation. It makes the fawning posture of the citizens inevitable *and* an imperative. It guarantees that mayors and aldermen will be boomers of the gross national product, for to be consistent with the mentality, only such individuals would be appealing. Finally, it engenders an enormous fear of losing anything, and yet actually precludes finding satisfaction in life, for such a mentality has as its base and as its result, the total preoccupation with mere survival, and nothing more.

The prominent example of this mentality in Timmins is the mayor, Leo Del Villano. Del Villano has been involved in city affairs for a long time, first as a councillor, then off and on as mayor since 1956. He brags about being fired from every job he ever held before he made the office of mayor a full time position. He is proud of his employment history, claiming that he would have to be fired from the mayor's post too. He has also stated that if not elected he would have to go on welfare.

Policy-wise, the mayor's philosophy is founded on the notion that what the city really needs is more assessment — period. Matters of environmental quality are snorted at if they threaten jobs or enlargement of the tax base. On municipal waste water treatment matters, Del Villano once said in Windsor: "The bears don't care what we send them down the river." In February of this year, a Johns-Manville asbestos mine and mill west of Timmins closed down due to dangerously high dust levels. Del Villano was quoted to say on this: "If you ask me, this environment stuff is going too far," and that the health hazard of asbestos dust is "a lot of nonsense and not worth a thing."

The mayor dominates the city council which is reflected in council's procedures. At bi-weekly council meetings, the committee of the whole meets about 5 p.m., and only after matters have been dealt with in camera does the meeting open to the public at 7 p.m. The "public" part of the meetings is purely perfunctory, preserving perhaps the spirit but not the intent of the democratic process.

The first order of business, as the council goes "public", is the suspension of the rules of procedure which allows the mayor to enter into all debate and the passage of bylaws through all three readings in one night. As one alderman has said, "since no public notice of the content of these meetings is available to the public prior to the meeting in most instances, there is no opportunity for the public to be present."

In 1974, Al Pope, a young Timmins lawyer, opposed the suspension of procedures on the grounds that the "public has a right to some input into council discussions prior to the passage of a bylaw." For this he was labelled a "radical", and this, in part, led to his resignation from council. After he quit the council, his papers which had been located in a private filing cabinet in city hall, were burned in "a mistake committed by the janitorial staff." City officials admitted that the incident was an unfortunate one.

This kind of operating style for a city government is a clear manifestation of a community avoiding itself and its responsibility. The mayor and his council are the spearhead of reaction against meaningful social change. The council generally has an anti-planning orientation, and will cheerfully ignore zoning bylaws to grant building permits for incompatible land uses. Perhaps they know better and perhaps they don't, but these councillors' operating style is deeply rooted in the mine-town mentality, which is further reinforced by the single priority of the survival and maintenance of what their limited consciousness defines as their city.

Some examples illustrate what is meant. According to Dr. Killingbeck, the Timmins Health Officer, the incidence of tuberculosis in the city is second

Leo Del Villano, Mayor of Timmins.

only to Toronto in the province. This high incidence is attributable to overcrowding in substandard housing, much of which is owned by absentee landlords who could not care less about the tenants. In the last two years there have been about 900 housing starts in the city, but the population size is unchanged. This raises speculation that many people have been and still are doubled up or living in attics and basements.

Lack of housing is one thing; low quality housing and high density is another. Timmins residents would be eligible for federal and provincial home improvement assistance if the city had a maintenance and occupancy bylaw in effect. Alone the city would be eligible for about $130,000 in assistance from the Ontario Home Improvement Program. An attempt was made last fall to pass a maintenance and occupancy bylaw, but some landlords feared the consequences, and the bylaw became an election issue. A public meeting was held at which vested real estate interests argued that tenants who otherwise qualified for assistance would have to countenance the "demeaning" process of having an inspector look over their dwellings. Invasion of privacy and lose of human dignity were terms that swayed public opinion against the bylaw. The low level of consciousness in city council will probably ensure the maintenance of this problem. While the city debates over neighbourhood fence heights and the placement of stop signs, some people in Timmins are coughing to death in run-down drafty hovels.

Timmins' main street.

Timmins' attitude to shopping malls also illustrates the town's survival mentality. Retail sales in Timmins for 1974 amounted to between $67- and $75-million. The Texasgulf expansion is seen to promise some growth and vitality to the retail sector of Timmins, and there has been a great deal of pressure from various developers to expand retail space in the form of shopping malls.

A retail needs study of Timmins was undertaken in 1973 by Canadian Real Estate Research Corporation as part of the preparations for an official plan for the city. The study concluded that given the outside limit of population growth in the city by 1981, only 100,000 square feet of additional retail space could be accommodated without seriously draining the vitality of the downtown retail core.

The figure is probably accurate. Despite the Texasgulf expansion, and the original Texasgulf development in 1967, the population of Timmins has remained static for about twenty years. In fact, between 1966 to 1971, there was a net decrease in population of about 800. But it is reasonable to suspect that despite the stable population, purchasing power may increase, so that by 1981 or beyond, the addition of 100,000 square feet of retail space would be sufficient.

The form of this additional space was visualized as a suburban shopping mall, and applications for building permits came in from developers. One was for a 411,000 square foot facility in Mountjoy township well west of downtown. Another was proposed for the old Hollinger townsite (a potential historic monument); and a mall was proposed along the Schumacher highway east of the downtown area. The city approved all three applications, flying in the very face of all reason or empirical evidence.

The downtown merchants were horrified; the Mountjoy township development alone was four times larger than recommended by the retail needs study. Understandably, some opposition from them erupted. Opposition from the downtown merchants led to a hearing by Ontario Municipal Board officials to settle matters.

The OMB's mission was to decide which mall site or sites would be best. Alas, the Mountjoy project could not be touched by the OMB decision because it was protected by township bylaws existing prior to January 1973. (This is a complex matter, but the result is that Timmins is stuck with the huge mall regardless of the OMB's decision on the location of the others). So the OMB had to decide between the site on the Schumacher highway and the site on the old Hollinger townsite. The developers, Texmalls Limited and Canadian Jamieson, fought it out before the OMB in January 1975, and its decision was in favour of the Hollinger townsite.

The implication here is that the city itself, by willy-nilly approving of all three applications, is incapable of doing its own planning or decision making. This has to be a consequence of a small-minded consciousness and predilection for financial aggrandizement regardless of the consequences.

Timmins itself is only one of a very long list of company cities and towns in Canada's "resource frontier", communities whose survival is based on the presence of a resource extraction industry. Paradoxically, the industry itself needs the ore for its survival, and cannot do otherwise but develop near the resource. This suggests that rather than assume an obsequious posture, people in these cities should place equal demands upon industry as the industry does upon them.

Can all the blame for the exploitive consciousness fall on the residents of Timmins? Unfortunately, external forces assume that exploitation is the rule for resource towns. The federal government talks about a national urban policy which really means let's help Toronto, Montreal and Vancouver and more or less ignore the rest. The Ontario government talks about decentralization and acts to centralize. Texasgulf is now under control of the Canadian Development Corporation but acts in the exploitive style of a private corporation. In effect these government and industry policies are destructive to the human condition in Canadian resource towns, and therein lie the fundamental causes of the resource town problem.

David Crombie's housing policy:

Making Toronto safe – once more – for the developers

Jon Caulfield

David Crombie is the best-known and most visible of the wave of moderate reformist city politicians who rose to sudden prominence in cities like Victoria, Vancouver and Toronto in 1972. After two years in office, David Crombie still has an excellent image amongst Toronto residents who think that he has brought real change to city hall. And his reputation amongst politicians and planners across Canada is, if it is possible, even better.

Jon Caulfield in his book The Tiny Perfect Mayor *examines for the first time the real content of David Crombie's reform politics. The publication of the book was timed to coincide with Toronto's 1974 municipal election campaign and in fact, as the Globe and Mail commented, Caulfield's book was David Crombie's only serious opponent in the mayoralty race.*

What follows is a shortened version of Caulfield's account of housing policy in Toronto as it evolved during the two years of Mayor Crombie's first term in office.

When David Crombie won his surprise victory in the 1972 mayoralty race in Toronto, everyone thought it was a victory for citizen activism and for a saner approach to urban development.

Was it? Many Torontonians think things have changed at city hall since Crombie's election, and this is an impression which the media has helped to promote.

Perhaps the most important key to understanding Toronto City Hall today, centres around understanding Mayor David Crombie. When one gets straight the kind of politician he is and the directions in which he has led or failed to lead council, many other pieces of the puzzle fall into place. Getting Crombie straight is not easy because, of all the false images about city hall, those concerning him seem most widespread and least accurate. One sees images of a strong, decisive figure whose first term as mayor has been marked by bold programs and innovative policies—the personality whom *Time* magazine recently ranked among the world's 150 leaders of tomorrow. The reality, however, is a mayor whose grasp of politics is often shallow and geared to public relations impact, whose programs and policies have been largely flaccid and inconsequential, and who has abdicated leadership on several critical issues.

Nowhere is this reality clearer than in the record of Crombie's council on housing policy.

HOUSING: THE BACKGROUND

Toronto's housing crisis is in part only a local version of a national pattern of shortage and rapidly inflating costs, but has also been badly aggravated by more than two decades of municipal neglect, decades during which the high-rise industry had been given *carte blanche* and other forms of housing had been ignored. During those years, many people had been squeezed out of the city, forced into increasingly expensive housing or left to the mercy of slumlords as a direct result of city hall policies.

Historically, the housing industry (particularly high-rise developers) did not lack friends at city hall. During the fifties and sixties, almost every application for a higher-density rezoning received by city council throughout those years was approved. In the case of the 1969-72 council, not a single major development application was rejected. In fact, by then, developers had been given a hunting licence in the form of a document called the City's *Official Plan* which was passed by the 1966-69 council in 1969. The plan indicated certain areas in which high-density development would be "encouraged", and developers were virtually assured that high-rise proposals for sites in those areas would be rubber-stamped by council. By some remarkable coincidence, many of the areas in which the plan "encouraged" high density were districts in which developers like Cadillac, Greenwin and Meridian already owned large assemblies. For example, developers had been assembling land in the Quebec-Gothic neighbourhood throughout much of the sixties. By a stroke of good fortune, city council chose to designate precisely that area, a pleasant district full of fine old houses which was, for all practical purposes, wholly indistinguishable from many other west-end neighbourhoods, as one in which higher-density redevelopment would be "encouraged." Similarly, council happened to "encourage" high-density development in areas south and west of St. Jamestown in which the Meridian Corporation had been busy assembling land, a lucky break for the enterprising company. The developers did, indeed, have good friends at city hall.

However, with the 1972 election of Crombie as Mayor of Toronto and an assortment of "reformist" candidates to council, it was anticipated that this new "majority" would repudiate the earlier years of developer-favoured council policies.

EARLY INITIATIVES

David Crombie played a key role in determining the way in which the new council would deal with housing, for council's approach to housing became tightly interlaced with the new mayor's view of his office and his politics. Crombie the candidate had vowed to be an activist mayor criticizing the city's traditional weak mayorality in which the chief executive was little more than a figurehead. Crombie said that, if elected, he would take a strong role in shaping the direction of council. Housing was one field in which Crombie promised dramatic action. "Toronto should get back into the housing business," he had said repeatedly.

Crombie hoped also to take a strong role in policy-making, and not to leave the initiative in the hands of reform aldermen like Sewell and Jaffary. (A second key to the puzzle of Toronto City Hall politics are the eleven aldermen who are identified —for the most part, by the media—as "reformists". There are two fundamental facts to get straight about the reformists. First, they are a minority of council and have not dominated city hall decisions since taking office in January 1973. Second, the reformists are not a strong, cohesive bloc which agrees on a philosophy of how Toronto should be run and a clear program of how to carry this out. They are a loose unco-ordinated alliance which is cleaved down the middle by critical political differences, and which strikes common positions only on occasion and less frequently as time goes by.)

To strengthen his role in policy formulation, Crombie sought two advisors. He hired both Susan Fish and Michael Dennis, authors of *Programs in Search of a Policy*, the suppressed federal housing study. Dennis's job was to advise the mayor on housing and development.

But right from the start, the initiative on housing action did not come from Crombie. The Dundas-Sherbourne issue was a prototype of the new council's housing politics. In that instance, the City became involved because of pressure from local residents. Crombie's response was to negotiate cosmetic changes to the original, but to leave the developer with his high-rise—and his profit. Only a group of early morning picketers, preventing wreckers from demolishing a block of houses, forced him to renegotiate that deal for one more satisfactory to the local citizens and concerned aldermen. But even the changes did not hurt the developer, for he still made his substantial profit by selling the assembled site.

Even though the mayor and his assistant Dennis had done the negotiating, Crombie indicated by his criticism of the aldermen and citizens who made the

Early-morning picketers in front of the Enoch Turner house in the Sherbourne-Dundas area, after wreckers had destroyed the front porch and demonstrators had responded by tearing down the construction fence to stop work on the demolition.

deal possible that it was not the kind of housing initiative he would take on his own. He had done it only under pressure.

The next round of council decisions and actions in housing also came not from initiatives from Crombie and his staff but rather from reform aldermen and citizen groups. Protests by Annex residents about a developer's (Annex Developments) plan to demolish nine houses on Huron Street and Madison Avenue as a blockbusting tactic to pressure for an apartment-hotel led council to buy the houses. Non-profit groups went to city hall to get some help in funding their purchases of moderate priced houses which they repaired and rented to low income and working-class households. After pressure from west-end Toronto aldermen and residents, six run-down houses in Parkdale were purchased for renovation as senior citizen and family housing. Because of reformist initiatives, the city's housing rehabilitation loan program for lower-income home-owners was expanded. After protests by area residents about a plan by Metro

Toronto and the policy to demolish houses in Grange Park for a new police station, council traded a city-owned parking lot with Metro for the houses. Metro agreed to build the police station on the parking lot land instead. On the initiative of local aldermen John Sewell and Dan Heap, the city took over management of a row of downtown rooming houses on Shuter Street which had been slated for demolition by the federal government to make way for a parking lot. In the course of these deals and decisions, the council majority which approved them also strengthened local working committees and planning task forces whenever it could.

It sounded like a busy, fruitful time, but in fact it was nothing better than last-minute crisis management, dealing with issues as they surfaced, and trying to find ways of softening the most damaging development projects when there was opportunity for some bargaining. Adding all these projects up, they did not amount to very much, and did almost nothing in the way of providing new housing.

Responding to initiatives from citizens and some

aldermen, David Crombie was looking for solutions which followed a course which he had outlined in his inaugural speech—"approaches so that the haves don't have less and the have-nots have more." As it turned out in practice, this meant not interfering with the normal business of the housing industry except in a few instances. In the minds of Heap, Sewell, Jaffary and some of the others, on the other hand, the people Crombie termed the "haves" had too much, and were getting it at the expense of the tenants in the housing they were demolishing and in their high-rent new buildings. But Crombie was not interested in a head-on challenge with the housing industry.

Crombie's fellow Tories at Queen's Park had much the same attitude. In 1973 they turned down a request by the City for demolition control, a measure which would have meant some interference in the developers' normal way of doing things. Crombie called demolition control "the most important piece of legislation ever sought by the City of Toronto." But a cabinet minister dismissed it as "an intrusion on the rights of property owners", and that was that.

As it turned out, the failure of the request for demolition control in 1973 may have been a result of Crombie's refusal to push hard for it. "The theory was," Karl Jaffary wrote later, "that the partisan minded members of the city executive committee would all nail down our respective members of the Private Bills Committee (the committee of the legislature dealing with the City's request). I was to deal with the NDP, Kilbourn with the Liberals, and Crombie with the Conservatives. It is pretty clear that somebody had gotten to the government, and that somebody was not His Worship."

The city's more successful experience with demolition control in 1974 testified to the power of the strong pressuring, public and private, which Crombie had failed to launch in 1973. This time aldermen did not rely on Crombie to win over the Tory government. Sewell, in particular, took an active role in rallying support for demolition control. He organized a telegram campaign and went to Queen's Park himself to hand around photographs of several dozen houses which were about to be demolished by Cadillac, Greenwin and Meridian. The government responded with a bill which enabled the city to block demolition, though it did not require property owners to keep their buildings up to city standards once they had applied for a demolition permit.

THE LIVING ROOM REPORT

As 1973 wore on, council's activities in housing seemed passive and increasingly paltry responses only to crises and to the demands of citizen groups. *Living Room: An Approach to Home Banking and Land*

Banking for the City of Toronto was the report of council's housing task force formed shortly after the new council took office. The task force had been at work throughout 1973. The motif of its thinking had been set out by Alderman Mike Goldrick, a task force member, in a preliminary report to council in May. "The City is presently deeply involved in housing. In fact, the provision of adequate shelter is probably the most important function of municipal government. But heretofore the City largely has been restricted to a role of responding to initiatives from the private development industry; of acting as a referee between builders and communities; of producing generalized land use plans; of maintaining minimum housing standards. Clearly such a benign and regulatory role is no longer acceptable. If the residents of Toronto are to be adequately housed at prices they can afford to pay, a start must be made not only to plan the distribution of new housing produced within the city but also to take an active role in seeing that such housing is actually provided."

The *Living Room* report, written principally by Dennis, was conceived not only as a housing report but as a political proposal, written as a motion, 112 pages long, which council could debate, amend and pass as legislation. The policy, which it set out emphasized the development of moderate and low-cost housing; preservation of the city's existing structure; and integration of new development with the physical and social context of existing neighbourhoods. It called for "co-ordination of all housing development, both private and assisted, in accordance with (council) objectives," and it stressed the role which local non-profit co-ops could play. According to *Living Room*, the city itself would enter the housing industry and adopt as a target for 1974 and 1975 the production or acquisition of 4,000 units, including 2,000 moderate-cost units and 2,000 low-cost units; 1,000 of which would be family-sized.

But the report accepted the Crombie approach to housing by suggesting that public initiatives should not challenge developers directly. There was no reference to issues like rent control or to correcting the most serious inadequacies in the already existing housing market. It was the approach of leaving the "haves" with everything they had managed to acquire, while attempting some marginal improvements financed by the taxpayer for a few—very few—of the many "have-nots."

Council passed *Living Room* without amendment in mid-December 1973 by a 17 to 5 vote. Also in December 1973 Michael Dennis left Crombie's staff to work as consultant to the housing task force, and in March 1974 he became housing commissioner heading up the new City Housing Department which had been established by *Living Room*. While by mid-1974, the new housing department was administering five housing projects and had three more, including the huge St. Lawrence project on the drawing board, there was little change in the pace of the city's progress in housing. Most of the concrete positive initiatives being taken by the city were still coming, not from Crombie or his staff or from Dennis, but from residents' groups, non-profit housing organizations, tenants and reform politicians.

There were, for instance two low-rent, low-rise projects in Ward Seven which were both threatened with conversion into fancy, high-rent apartments. The projects, the Spruce Court Apartments and Bain Avenue Apartments, had been built in the 1910's and 1920's by a unique non-profit housing company formed by philanthropic businessmen who lent money on low-interest bonds to build some decent housing for the city's working poor. They had since passed into private ownership. When the tenants of the 338 apartments saw, in early in 1974, that the projects were about to be renovated and rents jacked up beyond their reach, they worked with Sewell to purchase the buildings, using Central Mortgage and Housing Corporation mortgage money, and to covert them into tenant-owned co-ops. Their success, however, brought no addition to the supply of low-cost housing in the city. It was only a protective move to save 338 low-cost units that were about to be converted into expensive accommodation. It was not so much a victory as a successful avoidance of defeat.

Besides the Bain Avenue and Spruce Court apartment projects, the housing department was working on the Dundas-Sherbourne development which would eventually provide 381 housing units; there were also the 11 houses which the city had acquired in a police station land swap, which would provide 40 units; and the Parkdale houses, which would provide 26 units. All told, these five projects amounted to a meager 785 units of housing, of which more than half were not new construction, but were converted or rehabilitated houses and apartments.

In June 1974 the department announced its ambitious plans for the St. Lawrence site, 44 acres of parking lots, vacant land and industrial sites east of the downtown area close to the St. Lawrence Market. To be developed over ten years the St. Lawrence site would, according to Dennis, eventually provide low-density, moderate and low-cost, non-profit housing for 7,000 to 9,000 residents. The site, south of Front Street between Yonge and Parliament Streets, had been chosen because much of it was already owned by governments and other public bodies, and hence would cost less to assemble than private land. The city planning staff endorsed the project in part because it could help stabilize the area and protect it from wholesale demolition and change.

Further, the housing department was considering two other projects both involving properties which the city was to acquire from the Meridian company as part of the June 1974 settlement of the South St. Jamestown question. In 27 houses which the city might purchase in the Wellesley-Parliament district, 200 low-cost rooms for roomers could be provided, and on property which the city could buy in the Pembroke-Dundas area, 200 further rooming units and 70 low-cost family units could be developed.

Put beside the overall statistics of Toronto's housing crisis, these initiatives were so small as to make not even a modest dent in an increasingly bad situation.

Besides its minimal scale *Living Room* had other shortcomings. One of these was its complete failure to deal with a mushrooming trend which was badly exacerbating Toronto's housing crisis during 1973 and 1974. The development industry had been slowed to a near-halt by the hostility of the new council to its old style high-rises, by an increasingly tight mortgage market and by a natural tapering off of building after a decade of galloping growth. But a new line of attack against neighbourhoods and low-cost housing was taking up where the high-rise left off: town-housing.

Unwilling to tackle the town-housing problem, Crombie and the city's housing department could not even provide accurate statistics on the extent to which it was eating up the city's low-cost housing stock. But there were inroads made by summer 1974 in virtually every older working-class neighbourhood, and some areas, like Don Vale, had been almost completely taken over by the new middle class. *Living Room* offered no tools for controlling this process of change. In short, *Living Room* is at best a very small scale program.

The chief author of the *Living Room* report and now the man responsible for implementing Toronto's housing policy, Michael Dennis, admits that the goals of the city's policy are very modest in view of the needs. In his view, the approach is an exemplary model, a small-scale version of what can be done in Toronto and across Canada, and he emphasizes the novel fact of city involvement and not the scale of its work. "What the city does under the program," Dennis said in an interview, "in itself isn't very important. It's something—maybe we'll produce 4,000 units a year—but it's not much. It's hard to have an impact on the quality of housing or the quality of life at that rate." What, then, is the point of getting involved at such a small-scale level? Dennis's best rationalization is that Toronto can serve as a good example, to itself and to the rest of the country. "In terms of the country, what Toronto is doing in housing is pretty important because it's setting an example to other municipalities. We have people calling up here all the time from other cities wanting to know what we're doing and how we're doing it."

Demolition in the South St. Jamestown area

LIVING ROOM
AND THE CROMBIE STRATEGY

David Crombie, in contrast, sees it differently. He has called the *Living Room* report and the housing actions of the 1973/74 Council "a great program," a "wonderful program," and "the most creative and ambitious program which Toronto could undertake." He has presented *Living Room* as the answer to Toronto's housing problems and has used it as a reason for doing nothing tougher and more comprehensive about housing, and as a reason for allowing developers to carry on their housing business as usual, with no interference from city hall, as, for example, in the case of Hazelton Lanes. Hazelton Lanes, a proposed luxury apartment development in the Yorkville area, required exemption from the 45-foot height by-law which council imposed in 1973. The exemption was opposed by

Thomas and Sewell; Sewell argued that, since the project did absolutely nothing to help solve Toronto's housing problems, it should not be approved. Crombie, echoed by several aldermen, responded that it did not matter that Hazelton Lanes did nothing for the city's housing crisis because council had its *Living Room* housing policy. "We're meeting our policy on low-cost housing," Crombie told council during the Hazelton Lanes debates; he failed to mention that the policy sets out so small an annual quota of low-income housing as to be nearly negligible.

An even more dramatic case of Crombie's using *Living Room* to protect a developer was in his defence of the deal he negotiated with Meridian, the developer of St. Jamestown and of West St. Jamestown (which Crombie had in the past termed "obscene"), and now the assembler and blockbuster of the area known as South St. Jamestown, between Wellesley and Carlton Streets, west of Parliament.

Meridian had originally planned South St. Jamestown as a simple extension southward of St.

One of the tactics used by Meridian in South St. Jamestown was to knock out a single house in the middle of a row.

Photos: Myfanwy Phillips

Jamestown. But in 1969 home-owners and tenants in the houses to be demolished began organizing, and their resistance to Meridian was tough enough to make South St. Jamestown a protracted struggle for the company. With the help of John Sewell and other organizers, and with support from activities in other parts of the city, many of the people of South St. Jamestown hung onto their homes till the bitter end, forcing Meridian to send in sheriffs and security guards to throw them out on the street. By the time the new council was in office, Meridian had managed to wreck only one block of its South St. Jamestown holdings; and now the company was stale-mated. It could, if it chose, try to continue the painful blockbusting process of eviction and demolition, but it had no chance of winning a rezoning from the new council for another St. Jamestown. The impasse continued for a year; until the spring of 1974, when a fire in a dilapidated Meridian rooming house which killed five people and subsequent damning publicity, resulting from the discovery of additional housing standards violations in Meri-

dian owned houses, shifted the balance of power.

In late April, 1974, Crombie chose to get involved with this developer who was under attack, and he began a series of closed-door meetings with Meridian president Philip Roth to negotiate a South St. Jamestown settlement. Here again, Michael Dennis was a key personality. During May the negotiators haggled back and forth about aspects of proposed deals, and on May 29 agreement was finally reached after a long session at which Crombie, Dennis, and Bill Marshall, a Crombie assistant, represented the city. Also drawn into the negotiations were Ward Seven alderman Karl Jaffary and city planning official Howard Cohen. The other Ward Seven alderman, John Sewell had been briefly involved at an early stage but dropped out. On May 30 Crombie announced a "memorandum of understanding," whose terms were:

1. Meridian would be given a rezoning allowing it to build a profitable high-density development on the razed block. The development could include high-rise towers and some lower buildings; it

would offer 739 luxury-cost units, 252 senior citizen units, to be subsidized by the province, and 185 subsidized "average income" ($11,000 to $14,000 yearly) family units.

2. The city would buy 27 of the 68 houses owned by Meridian elsewhere in the South St. Jamestown district and a Meridian land assembly in the Dundas-Pembroke area; for these properties, the city would pay approximately market value, yielding Meridian a substantial profit.

3. Meridian would give 90 days notice, rather than 30 days, as required by law, before evicting the roughly 300 people living in the remaining 40 South St. Jamestown houses; the Company indicated that it planned to renovate these houses and sell them as expensive townhousing.

For the city and for the area's residents, it was disaster. The development would provide a total of zero low-income family units. It would provide about 250 rooming units for senior citizens, but it would also result in the destruction of more than 250 rooming units—albeit badly substandard units in houses Meridian had allowed to run down. Hence it offered no net gain in low-cost rooming units. The deal's merit was only that it ended Meridian's blockbusting and slumlording in the Don district. For Meridian, it was a major victory. The company won a profitable new development involving concessions which would cost it little, and the moderate-and-low-cost housing would be publicly subsidized.

When the deal came before council, Sewell argued that council should send the negotiators back to bargain for a better settlement—one which included low-cost family and rooming units for people besides senior citizens; seven other aldermen supported him. But Crombie argued that the city had gotten the best deal it could hope for and that further bargaining was futile. The settlement, said Crombie, "provided about as good a private development as this council has seen." He had apparently forgotten his pledge, made after the Queen's Park decision to allow West St. Jamestown, that "as long as I am mayor there will be no high-rise built in South St. Jamestown." Then the mayor once again cited *Living Room*, saying that the deal with Meridian yielded 41 per cent subsidized housing and that, while this included no low-cost family housing or rooming units, the city was meeting its commitment to provide these units elsewhere in its *Living Room* program.

And so, *Living Room*, which had been described as a minimal housing program by its author, Dennis, served at times as a public relations gimmick for David Crombie to justify not taking a stronger line in encounters with developers.

THE REAL DAVID CROMBIE

In retrospect, it is clear that it has been the hard-line reformists who have pushed for solid, aggressive action to take possession of land from developers; to protect low-cost housing from demolition and from conversion to high-cost units; and to expand rapidly the role of non-profit housing operations including the city's own tenant co-operatives and non-profit companies. They have worked alongside residents' and tenants' groups and other citizens involved in the housing problem in efforts to persuade city council to act to support their initiatives, and to help squeeze funding out of reluctant provincial and federal officials.

Resisting these pressures, even when they had to respond to them, were David Crombie and some of the "moderate" aldermen. With the help of city planners and his new housing commissioner, David Crombie searched for deals which left the developers no worse off than they had been under an explicitly pro-development council. A few projects for public ownership, non-profit companies and tenants' co-operatives went ahead with the support of these politicians, but the measures were small enough to pose no serious threat to the development industry's control of housing— and too small to make any substantial impact on Toronto's housing problems. Crombie's rhetoric allowed him to embrace these initiatives, to make a lot of the deals he put together like South St. Jamestown, and to praise and vote for fancy high-profit schemes like Hazelton Lanes. As progress in adding to the supply of low-cost housing in Toronto, it was not nothing, but it was certainly nothing much.

For the development industry Crombie's approach was proving excellent camouflage. The developers could get approval from Crombie and a city hall majority for high density schemes like Hazelton Lanes, and South St. Jamestown, while Crombie argued that these schemes were all part of a wonderful new approach to housing in the city. That was the difference between David Crombie's city hall and earlier administrations. Both would govern to protect the long-range interests of the industry by scotching any efforts to restrict free trade in urban property. But while previous city hall administrators did so blindly, finding ways of granting virtually any request the industry chose to make, David Crombie seemed to act thoughfully, with a constant eye to conflicts and crises which the developers were creating. He attempted to cool down these conflicts, or to appear to do so, in order to prevent them from erupting into pressure for real reform.

TORONTO CITY COUNCIL VOTING RECORD

		Quebec-Gothic	West St. Jamestown	Huron-Madison	Living Room	Hazelton Lanes	High-rise rooming house	South St. Jamestown
		1	2	3	4	5	6	7
the old guard	Archer	■	■	■	■	■	■	■
	Beavis	■	■	a	■	■	■	■
	Ben	■	■	a	■	a	a	■
	Boytchuk	c	■	■	□	a	■	■
	Clifford	■	■	■	a	■	a	a
	Negridge	■	■	□	□	a	■	■
	Piccininni	■	■	■	■	■	a	■
	Pickett	■	■	a	■	a	■	■
"moderates"	Crombie	■	■	■	□	■	■	■
	Eggleton	■	■	■	□	■	■	■
	Scott	■	■	a	□	■	■	■
	Smith	■	■	a	□	■	■	■
"soft-line" reformists	Chisholm	□	□	■	□	■	■	□
	Eayrs	□	□	■	□	■	■	■
	Hope	□	□	■	□	■	■	□
	Kilbourn	□	□	■	□	a	■	□
	Vaughan	□	□	■	□	■	■	□
"hard-line" reformists	Goldrick	□	□	■	□	■	□	■
	Heap	□	□	■	□	a	□	□
	Jaffary	□	□	■	□	■	□	■
	Johnston	□	□	■	□	■	■	□
	Sewell	□	□	□	□	□	□	□
	Thomas	□	□	□	□	□	□	□

The real estate industry today remains nearly as powerful, perhaps more so, as it was when the 1973/74 council was elected. The only difference is that city hall has, in effect, unwittingly rigged a sturdy line of defence for the industry by pretending to itself and the public that drastic action has been taken to challenge and control it. The central figure in this protective approach to the development industry has been Mayor Crombie.

In short, David Crombie has not only failed to initiate positive change or firm action at city hall; he has often resisted it.

With a majority of councillors taking a strong approach to housing, there might be moves to impose tough regulations on developers and to wrest the city's housing stock out of the hands of profiteering owners and put it in the control of home-owners, tenants' co-ops and non-profit companies. Officials like Michael Dennis might gladly adapt to a more aggressive approach which directly confronted the housing industry. Some politicians and citizen groups were exerting pressure to try and bring this about in 1973 and 1974. David Crombie was not part of this pressure; he, in fact, resisted it. Toronto had, as he had promised, re-entered the housing business, but it had done so in a way which took the heat off the Meridians, Cadillacs, Greenwins and other corporate vandals who had sacked the city in the sixties. So long as Crombie and the "moderates" remained in control of council, the heat would stay off.

HOUSING ISSUES

(1) *Quebec-Gothic* (February 1973): This indicates the positions of councillors on repeal of the Quebec-Gothic development by-law. Only Crombie, however, actually voted against repeal. The remaining anti-repeal members walked out in an unsuccessful effort to break quorum. In March, Negridge, Archer, Ben, Clifford and Beavis successfully broke quorum and forced council to adjourn during a subsequent discussion of Quebec-Gothic.

(2) *West St. Jamestown* (March 1973): This time the old guard stayed in their seats and, under Mayor Crombie's leadership, defeated repeal of the by-law 12 to 11.

(3) *Huron-Madison* (May 1973): Sewell and Thomas, with the unlikely support of Negridge, opposed the other reformists and the rest of council on the question of whether the city should pay a real estate speculator $800,000 for nine houses in order to save the houses from demolition. Sewell and Thomas argued the price was too high. Within a couple of months, other reformist aldermen, including Goldrick and Heap, decided they should have opposed the deal too.

(4) *Living Room* (December 1973): The reformists and "moderates" united to pass the *Living Room* housing policy.

(5) *Hazelton Lanes* (February 1974): With Heap absent, Sewell and Thomas again stood alone, this time in opposition to allowing an exemption from the 45-foot holding by-law for a swank Yorkville district apartment project. They wanted council to consider the economic and social implications of Hazelton Lanes.

(6) *High-rise rooming-house* (May 1974): Council voted 16 to 5 to let a developer build a 13-storey rooming house in Parkdale in spite of the facts that a similar high-rise in Ward Seven was bitterly criticized by its tenants and that the developer offered no economic feasibility research to prove that his building had to be high-rise.

(7) *South St. Jamestown* (June 1974): This 14 to 8 vote was on Sewell's motion that Mayor Crombie be sent back to negotiate a better deal with Meridian for South St. Jamestown. The mayor's original deal yielded to net gain in low-cost rooming accommodation or family housing in the neighbourhood. Unlike the Dundas-Sherbourne deal, Crombie stuck by his initial South St. Jamestown settlement and pushed it through council with the unlikely support of Jaffary and Goldrick.

How to run and win

Irene Harris

In the wake of growing public interest in urban issues and city politics, people who have been active in citizen groups across Canada are deciding to run as 'reform' candidates to defeat pro-development city aldermen. It's always a big step for people who are involved in fighting city hall on specific issues to decide to take on the politicians, especially because the politicians so often taunt their critics by calling them self-elected, unrepresentative spokesmen for vocal minorities. But in the cities where it's already happened, the presence of a few politicians with a citizen-group background at city hall has proved to be an invaluable asset in the long-term campaign to wrest control of city government out of the hands of the development industry.

For many people, running election campaigns and winning is a mysterious process. So the editors of *City Magazine* decided to commission this article, describing how one reform politician ran his campaign to keep the seat he'd first won in 1972 in a west end, working-class, mainly Italian Toronto ward.

As a middle-class Anglo-Saxon non-resident university professor, Mike Goldrick is probably the last person you would expect to be able to run and win in Toronto's Ward 3. But he's done it twice, and his campaign in 1974 is a textbook example of the way in which citizen candidates run and win.

This article, written by Goldrick's campaign manager, explains exactly how he did it — and, hopefully, how many more such candidates can do it elsewhere in Canada.

The municipal elections in Toronto on December 2, 1974 returned four reform aldermen to office and elected two new ones. Three of those aldermen came first in their wards and so hold seats on Metro council. In Ward 3, Michael Darcy Goldrick held his position as the senior alderman. This was the aim of the Goldrick campaign: not only to have Goldrick re-elected, but to make sure he came in first. As senior alderman he represents the ward on both city and Metro councils.

Ward 3 has a population of 65,000. Approximately 25,000 of those are eligible voters. The two most prominent language groups are English and Italian. There are also a number of Greek and Portuguese people. Before Goldrick's election in 1972, Ward 3 was represented by Hugh Bruce, a pro-development alderman who was accused of having a conflict of interest when he voted at council on some major developments, and Joe Piccininni, who was also a pro-development, 'old guard' alderman. Before running for alderman, Goldrick had worked with residents in the ward on neighbourhood issues and had set up two projects: an Assistance-Information Centre and a service for senior citizens. In his first campaign the majority of workers were people who lived outside of the ward, including a large number of students. The initial campaign was long and difficult, since it had to raise the issues, as well as make Goldrick's name known in the ward. Goldrick was elected then because he was a strong candidate with a well-organized campaign. That campaign lasted for seven months and during that time literature was distributed door-to-door and all voters were canvassed three times. Significantly, all of the literature stressed this point: 'You have two votes for alderman, make one vote for Darcy Goldrick.' That strategy worked and Goldrick came in first, topping Piccininni by a close 500 votes.

Since the 1972 election, six residents' associations have been organized through the efforts of Goldrick and ward residents. They have worked together to obtain a new six-acre park for the ward, convert two acres of vacant Hydro lands into park space; obtain neighbourhood planners and site offices in five neighbourhoods, and implement traffic control proposals in three neighbourhoods. As alderman, Goldrick also assisted approximately 2,000 people with problems. Consequently, the majority of people who worked to re-elect Goldrick in 1974 were residents of the ward—people who knew and had worked on issues with the alderman they wanted re-elected.

KNOW THY ENEMY AND THYSELF

In organizing the campaign, a number of factors had to be considered. To begin with, this election was a race between Goldrick and Piccininni for first place, since both were assured re-election. Piccininni had represented Ward 3 on city council for 14 years as the junior alderman and was still trying for the senior seat. The five other candidates were unknown and did not run full-scale campaigns. This meant that our campaign had to reach strong Goldrick supporters and encourage them to vote only once, for Goldrick. Second, it was acknowledged that more ward residents recognized the name Piccininni than Goldrick. This conclusion was reached on the basis that Piccininni had been on city council for 14 years, has an Italian name in a predominantly Italian area, and has a name which is easy to remember. However, not all who know the name support Piccininni the candidate. It was expected that the people who knew the name Goldrick also supported him. Third, many of the people involved with the organizational aspect of the campaign did not have previous experience in running a campaign. As well, most of the canvassers had never canvassed before. Finally, our campaign was to be run on a low budget. We expected to produce eight pieces of literature, maintain an office, and put up 3,500 signs on a budget of $5,000.

Piccininni, who has a lot of support from the business sector, was expected to spend at least three times our budget. As it turned out, he distributed pens, sewing kits, emery boards, stickers, note pads, matches, a glossy calendar and two pieces of literature. All, naturally, carried the Piccininni name. As well, he had what seemed to be an endless number of signs which were put up by paid sign crews. He purchased large ads in the Italian

Alderman Darcy Goldrick

City Hall Report	Rapporto Municipale

DEAR RESIDENTS OF WARD 3

As the Senior Alderman, I have four different responsibilities: to assist individual residents with personal problems; to provide services to Ward 3 as a whole; to deal with City-wide matters; and to represent the City of Toronto on the Metropolitan Toronto Council.
Over the past year, I have received more than 2000 telephone calls and letters asking for help with such things as parking and traffic matters, unemployment insurance, daycare, snow removal, tax rebates, building permits and housing for senior citizens. All of these calls have received the close attention of my office.

PRINTED BY VOLUNTEER LABOUR
PAID BY ALDERMAN M.D'ARCY GOLDRICK

CARI RESIDENTI DEL RIONE NUMERO 3:

Come Consigliere Municipale Superiore, ho quattro differenti responsabilita' : aiutare ogni residente con problemi personali, provvedere servizi a tutto il Rione numero 3, occuparmi di problemi che effettuano tutta la citta'e di rappresentare la Citta' di Toronto nel Consiglio Metropolitano di Toronto. Nell'anno 1973, ho ricevuto piu' di 2000 telefonate e lettere riguardanti l'assistenza per: parcheggio, traffico, disoccupazione, asili infantili, rimozione della neve,ribasso delle tasse, assistenza sociale, permessi per costruzioni ed alloggi per gli anziani.

STAMPATO DA LAVORO VOLUNTARIO
E PAGATO DA M.D'ARCY GOLDRICK

The Goldrick newsletter, dropped door-to-door to launch the campaign.

papers, rented three billboards and had three days of commercials on the most popular Italian radio station. It was his standard campaign and we had expected it.

Given all of this, we began to organize our campaign at the end of August. The organization was divided into eight parts: canvass committee, literature committee, sign committee, fund raising, publicity, office organization, Goldrick's canvass, and the election day organization. Each committee was given set responsibilities. A timetable was developed which staged each event in the campaign. It was crucial that each part of the campaign produce at the date set. When one group is behind, the whole campaign falls behind.

The work and responsibilities were linked and followed a logical progression. What I have tried to do here is describe the steps taken by each committee and to discuss some of the specific problems with which these committees had to deal during the campaign.

PUBLISH OR PERISH

Eight pieces of literature were produced by the literature committee: a newsletter; three pamphlets used in the canvasses; a one-page piece which was dropped at each house; a card telling voters where their polling station was; a 'candidate's calling

149

AN ALDERMAN MUST LISTEN TO PEOPLE BEFORE HE ACTS

KEEP HIM WORKING FOR YOU

RE-ELECT DARCY GOLDRICK YOUR SENIOR ALDERMAN

The piece of campaign literature used in the first canvass. Left is back cover, right is front cover.

card', which was used by Goldrick and his wife, Penny, on their canvass, and a card left by scrutineers on election day. To produce each piece, six steps were involved:

1. Collect raw material for each piece.
2. Write content in final form.
3. Have content translated into Italian.
4. Photography and selection of pictures.
5. Layout.
6. Have plates made and delivered to the printer.

In preparing this literature we were not so much concerned with getting Goldrick's name known as with refreshing voters' memories about him, with raising the issues and with letting the voters know what kinds of things Goldrick was worried about.

In writing the literature, we concentrated on establishing the fact that Goldrick was the senior alderman and should remain in first place. Slogans developed for the literature were straightforward and simple: 'Re-elect Darcy Goldrick, your Senior Alderman' and 'Keep Him Working for You.' On each piece we used two crests, one representing city council and the other representing Metro council.

There were three pieces of literature developed for use in the three canvasses that were planned for the campaign. We decided that these should cover everything from city-wide to neighbourhood issues. The first piece was general and discussed city-wide issues which related to the ward: hous-

ing, transportation and community services. The second piece concentrated on ward-wide issues and accomplishments under the headings of parks, traffic and transportation, community services and industry in the neighbourhood. The third piece was on individual neighbourhood issues and accomplishments. This piece was very special. We divided the ward into seven areas. Each area had its own piece which included a map of that area, a description of what Goldrick had accomplished for that area, and what he would do in the future. The content was written simply and precisely. We attempted to use the least number of words possible, while pointing out the stands on issues Goldrick had made in the past two years and would continue to make.

A special 'calling card' was designed for use of the candidate in his canvass of the ward. This included a biography, committees on which Goldrick sat at city hall, and boards and groups in the ward that Goldrick worked with.

A newsletter covering Goldrick's first term on city council (with both English and Italian texts) was dropped door-to-door and a final piece delivered had a letter to constituents and newspaper clippings written about Goldrick over the past two years. Then there was the 'vote-at-card' telling where the polling stations were. This carried the Goldrick campaign logo (a red house and a green tree) as well as the two slogans and was personally addressed to each voter. The final card produced

The inside two pages of the literature for the first canvass.

was used on election day. It reminded people to get out and vote and that the polls closed at 8 p.m. This card was dropped off by scrutineers at homes of our positive supporters. (Because there was some thought that voters would not be aware that distributing campaign literature on election day is quite permissible we included the number of the statute under which this practice is allowed in Ontario.) Scrutineers found it useful and reassuring to be able to leave such a reminder behind.

The photographs for the campaign literature were also taken and chosen deliberately. All of the photographs depicted Goldrick interacting with people, as opposed to the usual smiling, posed picture of the candidate. The content of the photographs always complemented the content of the canvass literature. The first piece (on city-wide issues) had a picture of Goldrick walking from city hall. Inside there was a picture of Goldrick and a resident talking at city hall. This was beside the section on Community Services. Another picture beside the section on Transportation showed Goldrick standing beside a bus which travels the new route he got for the ward.

The second piece (on ward-wide issues) had a cover picture of Goldrick and his family shopping in the ward. The inside showed a picture of Goldrick with members of a senior citizens' club; under 'Parkland' there was a picture of him with members of the residents' association in front of the site of the new six-acre park; and under 'Industry in the Neighbourhood' a bleak picture of industry in the ward. Below the industry picture we discussed the work that Goldrick, ward residents and city council had done to pressure the Conservative provincial government to enforce its laws on pollution.

On the cover of the third piece (on neighbourhood issues) there was a photograph of Goldrick walking with two residents. Inside, the map of the neighbourhood had drawings of key buildings in that area at their locations. Each piece carried the same 'portrait' of Goldrick on the back cover. The candidate's calling card, vote-at-card, sign, letterhead (on the final drop piece), store signs and lawn signs all carried our house and tree logo. Many residents commented on this consistency, saying they knew whose literature it was before they read the name. The continued use of the logo, slogans and portrait picture also simplified the designing of the literature.

All of our literature was produced in both English and Italian. This was essential because a large number of the residents are Italian-speaking and we wanted to familiarize them with the issues as well as Goldrick's name. There are also some Portuguese- and Greek-speaking people in the ward. To have produced the literature four times in each language was considered too cumbersome, both for the canvassers and our time constraints. To compensate for this, with the third canvass piece we distributed one sheet in Portuguese summarizing the main points expressed in all of the literature.

INDUSTRY IN THE NEIGHBOURHOOD

KEEP HIM
WORKING FOR YOU

DECEMBER 2, 1974

Re-elect Darcy Goldrick

SENIOR ALDERMAN

DARCY GOLDRICK and the residents of Ward 3 are working to reduce the noise and air pollution caused by industry.

While industries are necessary to provide jobs for residents of Ward 3 DARCY GOLDRICK believes that they must keep up their property just as homeowners must.

DARCY GOLDRICK is Chairman of the City Committee which has passed a By-law setting factory standards.

DARCY GOLDRICK continues to demand tougher pollution control laws from the Ontario government.

DARCY GOLDRICK is pressing the City for regular factory inspection and enforcement of established standards controlling pollution.

Re-elect Darcy Goldrick

Campaign Office

The Galleria
Dufferin & Dupont
532-2831

CITY OF TORONTO   METROPOLITAN TORONTO

The outside three panels of the literature used in the second canvass.

We had an energetic Macedonian woman send a personal letter and summary in Greek to all the Greek people living in the ward.

TO THE STREETS

The canvass committee had the major workload. This committee contacted all potential canvassers by letter and phone, organized meetings with canvassers, put together the canvassers' kits, kept track of the canvassing, assigned canvassers to polls, and kept a master list of the results of all the canvasses.

The first piece distributed across the ward was the newsletter. It was expected that this distribution would give an indication of the number of people we could rely on to canvass. Once the newsletter was produced by the literature committee, the canvass committee folded and collated the piece. They then made 87 bundles, one for each poll. Each bundle included a map outlining the boundaries of the poll. The next step was to recruit canvassers. Two hundred and fifty letters were sent out asking people for their support in the campaign. Five people then phoned those 250 people to find out who would help and to inform them of a canvass meeting. At the first canvass meeting, which was held on October 2, we described what the campaign would consist of, and emphasized that the objective

was to keep Goldrick in first place. The canvassers picked up their bundle of newsletters at that meeting (which was on a Wednesday), or over the next two days and spent the next two weeks dropping one in each home across the ward. At this meeting, 100 people turned out to volunteer their help on a variety of tasks. About 70 of these worked as canvassers. Fifty-five people canvassed one poll each on a regular basis while the others came and went, canvassing when they could.

Three full canvasses were done. For each canvass, canvassers received a letter and phone call informing them about the next meeting. Again, the literature was folded and bundled. The bundling of the literature for the canvassers required more work than the drop. Each bundle, or 'canvassers' kit' contained a clipboard, sheet of instructions, voters list for that poll, one bag with literature in English and a second bag with literature in Italian. The two bags were taped to the back of the clipboards. The front of the clipboard had the voters list and instruction sheet. This made a neat, easy-to-carry bundle. Canvassers were asked to go to each door in their poll. They added names of those left off the voters lists; crossed off names of those who were on the voters list but were not citizens or had moved; and indicated how each voter responded. A check mark indicated a positive supporter, a 'P' a possible supporter, a '?' for undecided, and an 'X' for hostile. The canvassers were phoned during the canvass to see if there were any problems, to ascertain whether they were going to complete their canvass

COMMUNITY SERVICES

During DARCY GOLDRICK'S first two years at City Hall:

- He received and acted on over 2,000 telephone calls and letters from Ward 3 residents with problems about building permits, day care, unemployment insurance, traffic and parking.

- He requested and received a local District Tax Office to assist elderly residents with their annual tax rebate.

- He works closely with residents to: (a) increase the number of day-care centres in Ward 3 and (b) establish Community Centres the Ward urgently requires.

PARKS

In 1972, Ward 3 had less parkland than any other Ward in Toronto. Since DARCY GOLDRICK was elected:

- Hydro land has been converted to park use.

- TTC land is now used for parkettes.

- 6.2 acres of obsolete warehousing is being demolished to make way for a new park at Dufferin and Dupont.

TRAFFIC AND TRANSPORTATION

During the past two years DARCY GOLDRICK worked actively to solve traffic and transportation problems in Ward 3:

- In 1973 and 1974 the City spent $579,730 improving street surfaces and lanes in Ward 3.

- There is now a $30 fine for all illegally parked heavy trucks in residential areas.

- This year a Caledonia/Davenport bus service was introduced.

DARCY GOLDRICK continues to oppose through traffic on residential streets.

The inside three panels of the second canvass leaflet.

and to remind them of the deadlines. To keep track of the canvassing we made charts which were put up in the office. These had spaces for each of the 87 polls and a column for each drop and canvass. The squares were coloured in as each canvasser returned his canvass sheets. We were then able to tell at a glance where we stood with our literature distribution.

The dropping of the newsletter on a door-to-door basis was done in two weeks. This was a warm-up for the canvassers. The first canvass was completed in three weeks (October 16 to November 6), the second canvass in two weeks (November 6 to 20), and the third canvass in one week (November 20 to 27). Another drop was done in the final week of the campaign and the 'vote-at-cards' were delivered by canvassers and scrutineers in two hours, the day before the election. We found it useful to start each new phase in the canvassing by a meeting on Wednesday. People could come, exchange notes, ask questions, gain a feeling of working together, and pick up their next bundle of literature. For those who were unable to come on Wednesday we would arrange for pick-up over the next two days. This way we knew that by the weekend (especially Saturday), the new canvass would be off to a good start.

The first canvass was really a warm-up for both the canvasser and the voter. The canvassers were given copies of the voters list from the 1972 election (a new list of voters is provided each candidate by the city clerk when his nomination is registered, but

these weren't ready for the first canvass), and asked to visit each address on their sheet. They were just letting people know that an election was coming up, that Goldrick would be running again and that they would be coming around again in a few weeks with some more literature. At this point the most important job for the canvassers was to make a note of people who had moved away from the area and people who had moved in since the last election. If anyone requested a sign the canvasser passed on this information as well.

For the second canvass the information gathered before was transferred to the new voters list. The emphasis in this canvass was to gain an impression of voter reaction to the candidate. Canvassers only indicated a positive reaction if the person expressed his support very firmly. Otherwise, the question mark was indicated. Canvassers never asked the voters directly if they were going to vote for Goldrick. They used the line, 'Hope we can count on your support' very often and then waited to see what the reaction might be. Information from the second canvass was transferred to fresh lists for the third canvass. Ideally, there would have been two people canvassing in each poll area, one English-speaking and one Italian-speaking. We did not have enough people for this and as a rule assigned one person to each poll. If a person felt very nervous about canvassing we would send out a companion to help him out.

As well, a separate canvass was done throughout the campaign by Goldrick and his wife, Penny.

Together they canvassed 45 polls (about half the ward). Because it wasn't possible for them to canvass each poll, we devised a list of priority polls. This list was based on the principle of concentrating on our strong areas. The polls chosen were those with which Goldrick had had a lot of contact over the past two years. In October, polls which we won in the last campaign by a low margin were canvassed. During November, they canvassed polls that were won by a wide margin. This way, our stronger areas were canvassed close to election day. Goldrick and his wife gave out the candidate's calling-card on their canvass. Before they did a poll, we contacted the regular canvasser, who could then go out with them. This co-ordination was necessary in order to prevent having someone's door knocked on two nights in a row. If there was no canvasser for a poll Goldrick and his wife were about to canvass, they gave out the literature with their cards. This proved useful in the third canvass, which had to be completed in a week.

The candidate's personal canvass is extremely important to an election campaign. Voters want a chance to meet the candidate and to ask questions, make comments and bring up problems. In the 1972 campaign, Goldrick had spent every spare moment knocking on doors in the ward. But this time his duties as an alderman curtailed his ability to give as much time to his canvass. We found that voters complained if he spent too much time away from city hall. To save time Goldrick and his wife would canvass separately; he would take one side of the street while she took the other. And if anyone speaking with Penny had a particularly vehement complaint or worry she would say, 'Well, he's just across the street. Shall I call him over so you can tell him?'

In addition, Goldrick had spent all his spare time in September meeting with the various groups and organizations in the ward. He would set up appointments to meet and talk with senior citizens' groups, with priests, with clubs and service organizations, basically to remind them that there was an election coming up and to let them know that he would be running again.

WHY IT WORKED

The spacing of our literature and the large number of pieces distributed ensured that each home had our literature and that the name 'Darcy Goldrick' was before the voters a number of times during the campaign. As well, through the canvassers, we knew exactly where our supporters were and what the outcome in total votes would be.

Our canvass committee was organized in a way that differs from other campaigns. The usual procedure is to divide the ward into x number of areas.

The front cover of the leaflet used in the third canvass. This, like the other leaflets used in the campaign, was produced in English and Italian.

Each area is then given an 'area captain' who informs canvassers of meetings and keeps track of the canvassing. We rejected this system at the start of the campaign for a number of reasons. We felt it would have been difficult to find the seven people who had enough time to keep track of whole neighbourhoods. Those seven people would be more productive canvassing a poll each. Moreover, if any of the area captains prove to be unreliable, it is difficult to replace them at a later stage in the campaign. This system also creates another organizational layer. In a campaign it is crucial to keep the organizers down to a bare minimum. While organizers are needed, it is the canvassers who identify and win support. Within our canvass committee, one person kept track of the results of the canvasses, one person made sure letters to canvassers went out on time and kept track of the results of the phoning, and three others helped with the folding and bundling of the literature.

MEANWHILE, BACK IN THE OFFICE . . .

The organization of the campaign office developed during the first part of the campaign. We found that

The inside two pages of the third canvass leaflet. A separate map and list of achievements and continuing problems was produced for each part of the ward.

locating and setting up the office meant more than renting a room and throwing in some tables and chairs. It took us two weeks to find an office. In the ward, key store-front locations are very expensive. We concluded that to pay $600 a month for a large store-front on the main street would look too expensive, and instead took a fairly large office in a local shopping plaza for a reasonable price. We had two large work tables, two desks and shelves for literature (it's a good idea to keep all the literature in one accessible place). One desk and phone were kept in a back room (originally designed as a storage area and fire-exit). This left one quiet space for meetings. One man acted as office-manager and book-keeper. He recruited people to help in the office folding letters, stamping cards and doing the various odds and ends that make the difference if you want everything to run smoothly. The main important in-office job was personally addressing vote-at-cards to the 25,000 voters. Each card then had its polling station address stamped on it. This took hours of work with about 20 people over the space of four weeks.

While canvassers and office people were doing their part, sign crews were organized and out covering the ward with signs. In any campaign, there are a number of steps involved in putting up signs:

designing and making the signs; deciding when the signs should go up, which streets should be covered; organizing sign crews; and finding staples, staple-guns, stakes and hammers.

Our campaign had one person who organized all of this. We used the same design which was used in the last campaign. Our sign had a white background, a red border and DARCY GOLDRICK in large black letters. In the upper righthand corner we had our house and tree logo. The sign was large, simple and easy to read. We began putting up our signs a month before election day. This date was decided on for three very practical reasons. By that time people realized an election was on and were more likely to put a sign on their house, we had more people working on the campaign, and it gave less time for the opposition to tear down our signs. Many of the residents who were canvassing also helped put up signs. A number of people switched over from canvassing, and others brought out their sons, friends and relatives. In the end, anyone who could spare any extra time took out a pile of signs and covered as many streets as possible.

Given that we only had a month to cover the ward, we had to decide which streets should be done first. The choice was between doing the main streets or the side streets. Piccininni was quickly

RE-ELECT
DARCY GOLDRICK
DARCY GOLDRICK
DARCY GOLDRICK
DARCY GOLDRICK
YOUR CITY ALDERMAN
MICHAEL DARCY GOLDRICK

Dear Constituent:

During this election campaign, I have done two things. First, I have given you an accounting of my work as your Senior Alderman. Second, I have tried to place the issues -- Ward, City and Metro -- before you.

In my two years as Senior Alderman for Ward 3, I have accomplished many of the things that I promised in 1972. I am proud of the eight acres of new parkland in the Ward and two new public transit routes we now have. Because you elected me as Senior Alderman, I was able to fight successfully at Metro Council against a T.T.C. fare increase and for the establishment of the City's new housing programme.

Many things remain to be done. I have brought energy and leadership to Ward 3 during the past two years ... and I think it has been to the benefit of all residents. Your vote for me on December 2 will assure that Ward 3 will continue to be represented by a full-time Alderman who can produce results, both on City and Metro Councils.

Yours truly,

Michael D'Arcy Goldrick

Michael D'Arcy Goldrick
Alderman - Ward 3

MONDAY DECEMBER 2
RE-ELECT

2 MICHAEL **DARCY GOLDRICK** ⊗
Professor

WHAT THE NEWSPAPERS SAY...

The Toronto Star

Alderman Goldrick seeks plan that will 'pay off' for people

"City government, local bureaucracy, call it what you will, has in the past simply not paid off for ordinary people," says Alderman Michael D'Arcy Goldrick.

It was this belief that first motivated him to run for City Council last year, and that now has him putting in long hours every week as chairman of a council-appointed work group to devise a housing policy for the city.

"The provision of adequate shelter" for citizens ought to be "the most important function of municipal government," Goldrick told his council colleagues a few months after the task force got under way.

"It's only when you speak to the people who are affected by these decisions that you learn their full implications. In fact all municipal services benefit some people and penalize others. It's up to us as politicians to help citizens realize these implications."

Goldrick's long hours spent on constituent and ward issues, coupled with his heavy workload on the housing work group, make him one of City Hall's most hard-working aldermen—a fact that's sometimes overlooked because he's not the public attention-getter at meetings that, say, John Sewell is.

'Someone must pull it all together'

"And he really is working at it—he's always talking to city staff, digging up information from other levels of government, seeking out technical expertise—it's tremendously time-consuming.

"There are good people on the housing work group, from planning and development and the city legal department and so on; but they've all got their own jobs to do, and most of the burden of the work falls to the chairman. I's partly because there's no sense of responsibility for housing under the present city system; no housing commissioner or department, to pull it all together. So someone has to do that, and it happens that it has been Mike Goldrick."

The Globe and Mail

Goldrick: modest PhD in politics

By LOREN LIND

Michael Goldrick seldom lets it show that he did his doctoral thesis on the transportation system of Greater London.

Nor does he mention very often his 15 years of dealing with urban affairs, his tenure as assistant to Mayor Charlotte Whitton of Ottawa around 1960, his editing of an anthology on urban politics, his chairmanship of the graduate political science program at York University, his directing of the Bureau of Municipal Research in Toronto back in 1963.

When first elected in working-class Ward 3, his goal was to take two years "to help that community sort itself out," and this included helping resident groups get together, answering local complaints, keeping the people informed. He hired assistant David Langer with $5,000 of his council salary and put out a mid-term fact sheet and questionnaire in English and Italian.

His way of helping residents was illustrated on Somerset Avenue, where cars were cutting south to avoid the light at Ossington and Davenport, endangering children on the narrow residential avenue. Mr. Goldrick's office called a street meeting where the residents agreed to make the avenue one way north, whereupon Mr. Goldrick pushed the measure through council.

.....he and Housing Commissioner Michael Dennis piloted City Council in major new initiatives through a policy worked out in the housing work group, of which Mr. Goldrick was chairman. The group did its behind-the-scenes homework all last year and finally put the city in the housing business with a policy outlined in a report called Living Room.

One noteworthy result is the St. Lawrence landbank, a plan for homes for 9,000 people in a downtown factory district.

It takes a lot of pushing to get federal and provincial bureaucracies to yield the promised benefits of the National Housing Act.

"You have to turn an awful lot of heads around to effect change," Mr. Goldrick says.

But Toronto has done relatively well because it has an explicit policy to back up its requests. This housing policy stands as a model that has hardly been equalled by the fruits of the reformers in areas such as health and transportation.

The Globe and Mail

You might be interested to know how these worthies rate in Ron Haggart's Highly Opinionated Poll, an annual assessment that now runs in Toronto Life, rating aldermen on how they voted on 15 issues that Haggart considers significant.

In the other wards where plumbing might be the decisive factor, Haggart would pick Goldrick by a wide margin over Piccininni; Eggleton by as wide a margin over Ben; Clifford by a narrow margin over Beavis (both are very low in his ratings).

The Toronto Star

District tax offices set up for aged

Senior citizens who find it difficult to travel downtown to City Hall to apply for their property tax rebate will be able to apply at special district tax offices set up in the next few weeks.

Alderman Michael D'Arcy Goldrick yesterday asked City Executive Committee to authorize $6,000 to Batchelor to set up district tax offices conveniently located around the city for elderly persons who may find it too difficult to go downtown.

...ABOUT DARCY GOLDRICK

The last appeal, distributed with a 'vote-at-card' just before election day.

The calling card used by Mike Goldrick and his wife in their personal canvass of the ward which reached about half the polls.

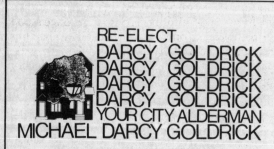

RE-ELECT
DARCY GOLDRICK
DARCY GOLDRICK
DARCY GOLDRICK
DARCY GOLDRICK
YOUR CITY ALDERMAN
MICHAEL DARCY GOLDRICK

RE-ELECT
DARCY GOLDRICK
DARCY GOLDRICK
DARCY GOLDRICK
DARCY GOLDRICK
YOUR CITY ALDERMAN
DARCY GOLDRICK

Biography
- Born in Vancouver in 1933 • Married to Penelope in 1958
- Children: Chris 13 and Tim 11
- Education: Bachelor of Commerce and Public Administration · Masters in Political Science · Doctor of Philosophy in Political Science

Professional Background
- Executive Assistant to Mayor, City of Ottawa, 1959-61
- Director, Toronto Bureau of Municipal Research, 1961-64
- Current Positions: Professor of City Government, York University, 1967-74 · Co-editor: 'The Government and Politics of Urban Canada'

Community Involvement
- Advisor: West Metro Senior Citizens Services · Bloor Youth Centre · Dovercourt Boys' Club
- Director: Social Planning Council of Metro Toronto
- City Hall: Senior Alderman, Ward 3 · Chairman: Fire, Housing and Neighbourhoods Committee · Mayor's Committee on Housing · Member: Public Works Committee, Social Services and Housing Committee

ALDERMAN M. DARCY GOLDRICK
CAMPAIGN OFFICE.
IN THE GALLERIA
1245 Dupont St., Toronto
TEL. 533-2691

156

plastering the main streets and at a glance looked very prominent and popular. We decided that the side streets should be done first. This was based on our feeling that people liked to see signs on their homes, that their neighbours would see our signs, that Ward 3 voters spent more time on their own streets than on the main streets, and that there are more voters in homes than on bridges, public fences and vacant buildings. The ward divides into seven neighbourhoods and we rated each area according to our strength. We covered the neighbourhoods in which we were stronger first, and then covered the others. Our sign crews 'blitzed' streets in the evening and on weekends. They went to each door, showed residents our sign and then asked if we could put up the sign. This was in sharp contrast to the usual method of hammering up signs without asking. During the day, we did homes where a sign was requested, either through the canvassers or calls to the office. At the office, we had a huge land-use map. These maps outline all the buildings and streets. We coloured in the houses that had our signs, a method which helped us keep track of where our signs were. This proved useful when replacing signs that were torn down. Two days before the election we put up signs on houses surrounding the polling stations — the idea being that our sign would be the last thing people would see when they went in to vote. As well, one man put signs in almost every store on the ward's main street. In the end, all of the streets in the ward were covered, including three of the main streets.

MONEY PROBLEMS

Another event that occurred simultaneously with the other parts of the campaign was fund raising. In total, we spent about $6,500. Raising money is always difficult and it turned out to be much harder than in the last campaign. Most of the reform candidates in Toronto ran into this problem. We did two things to raise money. Letters were sent to people who had contributed to the last campaign and to people who we knew supported Goldrick, but did not have time to work on the campaign. As well, five residents organized a fund-raising party about four weeks before the election. At that party we raised about $700. Through the letters we raised about $2,100. The campaign is still in debt by about $3,500. We now are thinking of organizing another fund-raising party in the ward to help cover this debt, and we will look for some other ways to raise whatever is still missing. We find that if we put our minds to it there are a lot of things we can do — in the last campaign we raised money by selling portfolios by Canadian artists.

In retrospect, though, we feel that we should have had a committee for fund raising who would be concerned only with that task, rather than leaving it to one man to do along with a number of other things in the campaign office.

USING LOCAL MEDIA

Publicity in our case was token. In the last campaign $1,000 was spent on ads on the Italian radio station which is the most popular in the ward. It is practically impossible to evaluate the effect it had at that time. For this campaign, we budgeted $250. At most this would have bought five 30-second ads. Our choices were to buy those five ads on radio, or buy space in the local papers, or up our budget to accommodate a full-scale ad campaign on radio, or in papers or both. Since we had already gone well over our original budget of $5,000, we decided we could not afford to spend more on advertisements. Instead, we used the money budgeted for ads in two local Italian newspapers. This meant that a large number of people would be reminded that there was an election and that Darcy Goldrick was running for re-election. It was token in the respect that, by this time, the ward had already been covered a number of times with a lot of information. However, it did give our support to the two local papers, which we felt was important.

ELECTION DAY

The final work of the campaign was to organize the activities for election day. All of the work done throughout the campaign led up to that day in terms of providing information on where we stood, which were our strongest and weakest areas, and the number of people we could rely on to make everything come together. The aim of the election day organization was to pull our vote, to make sure that all of our positive supporters went to the polls and voted.

Organizing and preparing for election day took about two weeks. The first step was to recruit scrutineers. People who had worked on all parts of the campaign worked on election day. In addition, we had students and people outside the ward volunteer their time. We then had at least one person for every poll, as well as a group of twelve people who organized the day's activities.

The election day organization consisted of seven area co-ordinators, one driver, three overall co-ordinators and a back-up person. Once we knew who was available to scrutineer, we began to assign people to polls. We rated our polls according to strength. This information came from our canvassers, who had their marked voters lists. Those polls which had been thoroughly canvassed and had the greatest number of positive supporters were considered our strongest polls. In those polls we assigned people who were available for the whole day. Polls that had a large number of positive supporters, but were not well canvassed, had people who were available from the middle of the afternoon until the polls closed. Our weak polls—those poorly canvassed and with the least amount of positive supporters — had people who were available for a few hours before the closing of the polls. Some of our stronger polls were given two people, one who was there for the full day, and one to help pull votes in the evening.

Two preparatory steps were involved the day before the election: delivering the cards telling people where to vote, and giving scrutineers instructions. We sent letters and phoned our scrutineers a week before, asking them to come to the campaign office at 1 p.m. the day before the election. As they came in, they were given a bundle of vote-at-cards which they then went out and delivered in that poll. Again, each bundle had a map outlining the location of the poll. Two hours later, all of the cards had been delivered door-to-door. Everyone came back to the office for the instruction meeting. At that meeting, each scrutineer was given a kit. This kit included information on counting the ballots, a summary of election rules, a form authorizing them to be in the poll, a clipboard, a voters list and a small stack of cards. The voters list had check marks beside the people we knew were our positive supporters. The scrutineers were asked to be at the poll early, and inspect the ballot box to make sure it was empty. They stayed in the polls until 1 p.m., marking off on their list those who had voted. At that time they went to the homes of our positive supporters, asking them to come out and vote. If there was no one home, the scrutineer left our card, which was a reminder that the polls closed at 8 p.m. and to vote for Darcy Goldrick. The scrutineer went back to the polls and went out again in the evening to encourage our supporters to vote. While in the polls, our scrutineers challenged people who came to vote but were not, in fact, eligible voters. These included people who were on the voters list, but were not citizens, or used the name of a person who had died. Again, we had this information as a result of our three canvasses.

Throughout the day, our seven area coordinators visited each poll at least twice. We had one co-ordinator in each of the seven neighbourhoods. These people visited each poll, kept track of the number of people who had voted, helped the scrutineers with any problems they had, helped to pull the vote and give voters rides to the polls. Our area co-ordinators phoned the campaign office after each of their rounds to let us know of any problems and what the turnout was. This way, we knew exactly what was happening in each poll. After the

Rita Ferrari
1877 Dufferin St.

KEEP HIM WORKING FOR YOU

RE-ELECT
DARCY
GOLDRICK

AT: 91 CLOVERLAWN AVE

Monday, Dec. 2nd
11:00 a.m. - 8:00 p.m.

For Information call: Campaign Office
The Galleria
Dufferin & Dupont KEEP
532-2831 THIS CARD

The 'vote-at-card', one of which was addressed by hand to every voter in the ward and distributed just before election day.

SORRY YOU WERE OUT
I HOPE THAT YOU WILL TAKE A MINUTE
ON THIS BUSY DAY TO VOTE FOR ME.

Yours sincerely,

M. Darcy Goldrick

M. DARCY GOLDRICK
SENIOR ALDERMAN, WARD 3
PLEASE REMEMBER THAT THE POLLS CLOSE AT 8 p.m.
pamphlets permitted election day by R.O.S. 1974 C 65

The reminder card, used on election day and dropped off at the homes of Goldrick supporters who did not vote early in the day.

polls closed and the ballots were counted in each poll, the scrutineer phoned in the results to the campaign office for tabulation.

SUMMING UP

In the end, Goldrick retained his position at city hall as senior alderman for Ward 3. In fact, he received more votes in the ward than David Crombie, who regained the mayoralty for a second term in the face of what can only be called non-existent competition. As Graham Fraser pointed out in the *Globe and Mail*, Goldrick was the only alderman to top Crombie's vote for a particular ward.

The most compelling reason for this success must be the canvassing done on Goldrick's behalf by his many supporters in the ward. During his past term in office, he had worked continuously with residents, helping them to organize, to overcome neighbourhood problems and to improve city services in the ward. We were able to bring these people together to work on the election because they were now used to being organized and acting politically. The most important factors contributing to the success of this campaign were the canvass and the literature prepared for it, the candidate's personal canvass and the efforts of the scrutineers on election day to pull the vote.

While signs are considered by most people to be the most important element in an election campaign, we are inclined to suggest that their usefulness is over-emphasized. They are expensive (the cost has doubled in the last two years), and posting them is a time-consuming business. What we would stress is a good, simple campaign organization, careful design of campaign literature, and the personal contact of door-to-door canvassing. With this kind of campaign, and a candidate who has demonstrated his willingness to work with people and to protect local interests against developers and their friends at city hall, we've learned you can beat a smooth, heavily financed pro-development candidate.

IV Case studies in urban development

Saving Montreal

Dida Berku

On January 7, 1975, for the second time in three weeks a demolition crew working without a permit resumed the wrecking of three historical houses on Montreal's Drummond Street. Drummond was once one of the most elegant streets in the city, but is now increasingly given over to high-rise apartment buildings. In the 20 minutes before the police arrived to stop them, the wreckers half-demolished the Queen Anne style mansions. Built in 1904, on the southern slope of Mount Royal, these houses belonged to George H. Smithers, a former president of the Montreal Stock Exchange.

By this illegal demolition Montrealers lost more than just some fine, old buildings; they lost 65 medium- and low-cost housing units, to be replaced by 10 storeys of high cost condominiums.

The developer, Jean Talon Fashion Inc., by the swift commando-like action, bypassed the city's new authority to withhold demolition permits for historical buildings. Only since the beginning of 1975 has Montreal had this power, granted by recently-approved provincial legislation. Before that the city issued demolition permits routinely to any and every applicant for a five dollar fee. The recent amendment to the city charter gives

Montreal the power to prohibit for up to a year the demolition of any building constituting a "cultural property" within the meaning of the Cultural Property Act (1972). This Act has been selectively used to classify only eight Montreal landmarks in the past year. However, increasing pressure from preservation groups has encouraged the expansion of the programme both at the municipal and provincial levels. Because one of the three houses was deserving of historical classification and because they were near the Mount Royal Club, whose recent classification put the houses into its 500-foot radius of protection, the demolition permit for the Drummond Street mansions was refused. Special permission from the minister of cultural affairs is required to tear down any structure within 500 feet of a classified property.

A public outcry and strong pressure from the new municipal opposition party led the city to act promptly, for the first time, to check the defiant action of the developer. Even though by-laws provided for only an insignificant $500 fine against illegal demolition, the city successfully requested an injunction to prohibit further wrecking, and then placed the ruins under police surveillance.

Drummond Street houses demolished without a permit in late 1974. Photo: Garth Pritchard

Though developers have a freer hand in Montreal than in most cities no one had so spectacularly flouted the law before.

In an effort to assure everyone that he meant business, Michel Coté, the city's lawyer, called the reckless destruction "anarchy." His statements and the city's actions seem to represent a change in the casual attitude of the Drapeau administration towards the issue of wanton and unrestricted demolition. However this small change should not be seen as anything more than what it is. The city, with the aid of the province, will now protect a few "heritage" buildings, which are imminently threatened. Since the law provides for a very narrow power of protection, it changes little with regard to the demolition of so-called "ordinary" buildings and neighbourhoods.

The municipal government of Montreal is still not prepared to address itself to solving the basic development issues which are plaguing the city: uncontrolled high-rise development downtown; the low-cost housing shortage; and the destruction of viable inner-city neighbourhoods by private and public super projects such as Place Radio Canada, the east-west autoroute, Complex Concordia, and the federal public works Guy Favreau project in Chinatown. In fact, most Montreal residents understand that the administration's policies and outright collaboration with developers is largely responsible for these problems.

MONTREAL INVESTMENT MECCA

In an effort to raise development capital, Mayor Jean Drapeau last summer told a meeting of German businessmen that "there would never be a mousetrap for investors in Montreal." Quoted in the October 21, 1974 edition of *Der Spiegel* magazine in an article entitled Montreal Investment Mecca, the mayor was probably referring to the Ontario land speculation tax and the restrictive zoning of Vancouver and Toronto, suggested the magazine.

In the last year alone over 30 major multi-storey commercial and residential complexes, covering some 500,000 square feet and representing $500-million of investment, were under construction in downtown Montreal. (This area, bounded by

163

The George Hampton Smithers mansion, built in 1904, and half-demolished in early 1975 by Jean Talon Fashions Inc.

Atwater, St. Denis, the Mountain and Craig Street, covers approximately five square miles.) During the same year and in the same area, demolition permits were issued for 245 buildings, on 100 different sites, covering about 1200 dwelling units. The majority of these demolished houses offered rental units for families with low and moderate incomes; none of the buildings under construction do so. The new residential high-rises have smaller, more expensive units.

Between 1967 and 1974, 15,041 units were demolished in the entire city, including and surrounding the expanding city core. The majority of these were also low cost: 778 dwellings were demolished for Place Radio Canada; 3000 dwellings were demolished for the east-west autoroute; and hundreds of homes were lost to the Concordia Complex, a luxury hotel and residential project in the heart of the Milton Park district (a mixed, poor, working-class and student community). Here, four large city blocks have been taken over by an American developer with little concern for the surrounding milieu. The major concern of the project planners seems to be how it will look from atop Mount Royal. In Chinatown, the federal Public Works Department, after having levelled hundreds of homes

and ravaged an entire community already struggling for survival, has now indefinitely suspended the Guy Favreau project. The city still has no comprehensive plan to accommodate for the loss of housing.

Since the federally-funded programme of "Habitations à Loyers Modiques" (H.L.M.) began operating in Montreal in 1967, the city has built a total of 5,067 low-cost houses. (This represents only one-third of the houses lost since then. No attempt has been made to replace the communities destroyed. The city builds houses, not neighbourhoods.) Rising costs have forced severe cutbacks in the construction of low-rental units, and the renovation programme in Montreal is still largely ineffective. More than 22,000 of the 27,000 housing units inspected by the Montreal housing and planning department since 1970 failed to meet the standards of the city's Housing and Building Code. With many of these homes facing virtual obsolescence in the next five years, the housing situation in Montreal looks bleak.

This depressing pattern of redevelopment has culminated in the present scramble for "developable" land in the downtown area. Working against a double deadline, the speculators have rushed into the mixed commercial and residential "core." They have to make their profits quickly before the new construction market is saturated and before the anti-development lobby effectively organizes to drive them out.

In the past two years alone in the 18 blocks of the western residential sector of the downtown between Atwater and Guy Streets, hundreds of homes were demolished to make way for 11 23-storey high-rises. This has increased the population in the area from 6,000 in 1966 to 10,000 in 1975, and has replaced family units by more expensive, smaller bachelor apartments.

On the southern slope of Mount Royal, 10 turn-of-the-century converted mansions were demolished to make way for high cost condominiums. These did not substantially increase the stock of housing, but instead increased its cost.

In the core zone of the bistro and boutique quarter, every street is owned by a handful of developers whose plans to raze and rebuild have been temporarily dampened by new zoning and height restrictions. However this has not prevented demolition in order to produce illegal parking lots; nor has it prevented conversion from residential to commercial office space.

In fact in these three subzones of residential downtown Montreal, where the demolition pressure has been greatest in the past two years, it is hard to find a single block among the 50 or so which is not ravaged by demolition or construction.

The reasons for the rampant demolition and full scale redevelopment are many. The combination of apparent stabilization of provincial politics and the tightening of development restrictions in other Canadian cities, especially Toronto, has made Montreal a relatively open and inviting building haven. Big-time foreign and local developers have taken advantage of the open land market and the few zoning restrictions.

Without a master plan, although many have been drafted and shelved, with zoning laws as old as 30 years, Montreal has exercised little control over growth. Buildings on the major downtown arteries of Sherbrooke and Dorchester streets are restricted by height minimums of 60 feet, and on St. Catherine Street by 38 feet. The Floor Area Ratio (F.A.R.) of the downtown up until a year ago was 12:1. This means that buildings were allowed a size equal to 12 times the area of their lot.

In an effort to control the height and density of downtown residential buildings, last February the city council reduced the F.A.R. to six times the area of the lot. And in September 1974, in response to the imminent danger of losing the charming bistro quarter to a canyon of high-rises, it established a height freeze on the 18 downtown blocks between Stanley, Guy, Sherbrooke and 150 feet north of Dorchester. The height ceilings in this area are 40, 80, and 120 feet depending on the specific street.

On the right, Windsor Station, built in the 1860s. On the left, the Chateau Champlain.   Photo: Steve Jensen

Both measures offer certain safeguards but have their drawbacks. The F.A.R. reduction is not applicable to offices and hotels and is likely to discourage the construction of downtown housing which Montreal desperately needs.

The height restriction in the short term did not prevent demolition. Permits for houses in the area continue to be issued, and while parking lots were prohibited, two prominent developers are operating illegal lots instead of building under the height restrictions.

In the long term such spot-zoning can only result in a spill-over effect of development to the north and west of the boundaries, into areas which are already overtaxed by construction.

Finally, a study plan made known to the citizens of downtown as an election promise before the November 10 civic elections, has been shelved. This plan would have extended the height restrictions to the west of the present boundaries into the area of the 23-storey high-rises — Guy to Atwater, Sherbrooke to St. Catherine.

Another important factor promoting development is a municipal property tax system which discourages rather than encourages the maintenance of low-rise structures. First, part of the tax is based

The demolition of the Van Horne Mansion in 1973, an event which helped touch off the formation of a broadly-based anti-development political force in Montreal.

on an assessment of the value of the building on a piece of land. Consequently should a landlord renovate, the city reassesses his property and raises the tax. However the greater pressure comes from the assessment of the land. Because it is valued at the highest potential economic usage, when the property is zoned for high density it is taxed accordingly. The landlord who suddenly finds himself surrounded by 16-storey high-rises will find that the value of his land and his taxes have risen dramatically. This makes selling out for redevelopment almost an economic necessity.

The lack of control over development is aggravated by the ease with which demolition permits are obtained. Save for the exceptions introduced by the new law with respect to historical buildings, there are no criteria for the issuance of demolition permits. Nor does the city have the right to withhold permits. Neither the usefulness of the building nor its relationship with the neighbourhood is considered. A permit can be issued on a tenanted building and without an application for construction on the site; more often than not this is what happens. The advantage to developers who blockbust is obvious. They can demolish their property and force the devaluation of surrounding buildings, while a parking lot reaps profit and taxes are paid only on the land.

SMALL SUCCESSES

The chief inhibitor of unrestricted growth in Montreal has not been municipal policy but rather the result of the efforts of tenant associations and city-wide action groups.

Since its isolated beginnings—in such groups as the Milton-Park Stop Concordia Committee of the late 1960s, the various tenant associations against the east-west autoroute, the unsuccessful organizations dedicated to saving the Van Horne Mansion (demolished in '73)—the anti-development lobby has by now built a strong political base in Montreal. The lobby was partly responsible for the recent election of 18 new opposition councillors to city hall. These Montreal Citizens' Movement councillors, who occupy almost one-third of the 57 seats in council, give unprecedented political support to the anti-development stance.

The focus of the present fight is on three downtown city-core zones where 450 tenants were put under the imminent threat of eviction and demolition in the past year alone. Since January 1974, demolition permits were issued for 27 buildings on 11 different sites in this inner downtown sector.

Photos: Don McKay

The buildings on five sites have been demolished; the rest have been temporarily saved by the efforts of the tenants. All the buildings were structurally sound and all were beautiful examples of turn-of-the-century architecture. The magnificent mansions had been converted to moderate-rent apartments. The luxury apartment buildings from the 1920s still offered reasonable downtown rentals and had become over the years cornerstones of their particular neighbourhoods. The fact that these stand at the corner of major cross-streets probably adds to the potential profitability of their land.

All structures offered a fast disappearing kind of apartment-lifestyle. There were spacious rooms with high-beamed ceilings, stained glass and leaded windows, magnificent interior staircases, marble fireplaces, fine oak panelling and all the elaborate decorative detail so important to the housing of the turn-of-the-century bourgeoisie.

The two recourses open to the tenants of "heritage" buildings who want to resist eviction and demolition are: first, an appeal to the rental board for an extension of lease; second, a request for classification under the Cultural Property Act. Also, as more church properties and historically valuable structures are coming onto the market, preservation groups and tenants are organizing to buy the buildings under the co-operative schemes offered by the CMHC. With the advantage of working with funds at preferential interest rates, co-operatives might very well become the real alternative to speculative private development.

At the Bishop Court Apartments—a 70-year-old, elegant Scottish ballast structure—five of 25 original tenants have been holding up demolition for a year. They went to the rental board and got their leases extended (for a year) until June 1975. Their landlord, Yale Property, headed by the Mashaal family, has turned off the heat, suspended janitorial services, thus increasing the risk of fire and vandalism. Recently Yale began demolishing the vacant apartments. The tenants have held firm and have been granted a court injunction ordering the landlord to stop. Following the example of the illegal demolition of the Drummond Street mansions, developers are scrambling to do as much damage as possible before their buildings get classified.

At the Royal View Apartments, an elaborate and spacious four-storey building, 28 tenants resisted a February 1 eviction notice by getting an extension of their leases. But of course not all tenants are so determined. At the Drummond Street mansions the tenants chose the path of least resistance. Although the eviction of two of the tenants with leases was illegal, these tenants never got to the rental

167

Dorchester Blvd. at St. Matthew. These houses were demolished in 1973-74. Photo: Steve Jensen

board. The day before their hearing, the landlord came and paid them off.

In four McGregor Street mansions, 80 tenants successfully avoided eviction and demolition by appealing to the rental board and by lobbying the minister of cultural affairs for the classification of their buildings. McGregor Street like Drummond was once an elegant way lined by Victorian and neo-classical mansions. On the southern slope of Mount Royal it was a major artery of the Golden Square Mile, the residential district of the rich in the nineteenth century. Later, McGregor became known as Consulate Row, when the foreign offices moved into the mansions. Today most of the consulates have moved into high-rises, and this street, like the rest of the Golden Square Mile, is quickly losing its low-rise character, its charm and its history. Only 80 mansions remain, and these are disappearing at a rate of 15 per cent a year. The house on McGregor that was classified was built in 1904 for J.N. Greenshields, a lawyer who once defended Louis Riel.

At the Somerset Apartments, built in 1929 as part of a 12-building complex around an interior courtyard, the tenants saved their corner block by successfully pressuring for the classification of the Sulpician Towers (1694) across the street. By this indirect method their building has been saved because it falls within 500 feet of the classified property, which is a "protected area." The owner has responded with an action against the city to try to force it to issue a demolition permit.

Added to the small successes of the tenant groups have been the efforts of preservation organizations led by Save Montreal. Their historic inventory was adopted by the planning department, they were instrumental in the original 10-day-delay by-law which allowed the city to withhold demolition permits for that short period, and their efforts surely led to the most recent charter change. However this new protection is not enough.

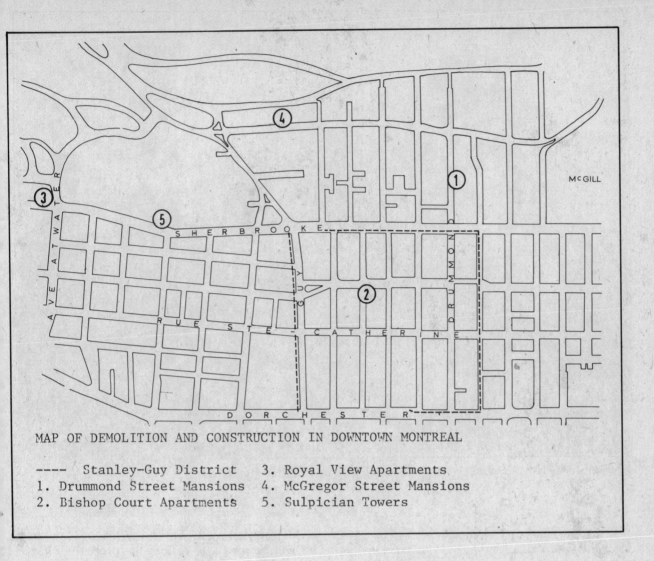

MAP OF DEMOLITION AND CONSTRUCTION IN DOWNTOWN MONTREAL

```
----   Stanley-Guy District      3. Royal View Apartments
1. Drummond Street Mansions      4. McGregor Street Mansions
2. Bishop Court Apartments       5. Sulpician Towers
```

SAVE MONTREAL

A recent study by Save Montreal has outlined some far reaching measures which would alter the present pattern of development. The study points out that one-fifth of downtown land is vacant; that is, not being used for buildings, roads or parks (mainly it is used for parking lots or rail yards). If new development was limited to this empty land, Montreal would still have room for 192 years of "progress" at the present rate of growth. The suggestion is not that all existing buildings be preserved, only that they could be. Downtown development is going in the wrong direction, the study suggests. Most of the "heritage" buildings in downtown Montreal lie north of the existing core, on the Mountain slope and to the east, while most of the empty land lies to the south. Instead of the present northerly pattern, the alternative suggested is that growth of the core be directed towards the south and west, onto empty land. This would result in the preservation of the mature buildings and communities, while it would also bring new activity closer to Old Montreal and the waterfront area.

Also required for Montreal is a major innovative housing policy. Houses must be renovated to meet maintenance standards. In this regard a rent subsidy system might be necessary and complementary. Second, the system of tax assessments must be changed so that increased tax assessments don't wipe out the benefits of renovation. Also, there should be tax incentives for the maintenance of low-rises instead of high density and costlier higher buildings. Third, in recognition of the fact that there are whole areas to be saved as preservation districts, zoning changes should provide for a reduction of the permissible size of the buildings.

These measures are simple ones which have been

Another demolition carried out without a building permit, on Drummond Street.

used in other cities and which have been debated in Montreal for the past few years. Perhaps more important than any of these measures is the necessity for citizen participation in any revision of existing demolition and tax structures or adoption of a master plan. While many planners state that they would not want the responsibility of creating a master plan without neighbourhood co-operation, no such means of participation exists in Montreal. The proposal of the Montreal Citizens Movement is to have "neighbourhood councils" which would determine at the local level the direction that development should take.

The issue of demolition of historical buildings cannot be separated from the low-cost housing shortage: the effects of concentrated high-rises are not separate from the problems of the preservation of viable neighbourhoods. Certainly we need adequate protection for historical buildings, but we also need many other changes if those houses are to survive in an urban context which can give them meaning.

Ideas about progress are slowly changing in Montreal. By his flagrant violation of the law the developer of the Drummond St. mansions shocked many Montrealers into understanding the truly reckless attitude of developers in this city. Whether he will be forced to restore the property will be decided by the court; in the meantime, the positive political fallout of the case is that finally a public debate has begun on alternative ways of development. If Montreal is to retain a continuity with the past, if it is to restore to the urban fabric the elegance and charm for which the city is famous, if it is to provide adequate housing and green spaces for its growing population, then it must make far-reaching policy changes and respond to the needs of the people, not to the needs of uncompromising development interests.

Halifax: Spitting into the wind on Quinpool Road

Dave Reynolds

A group of Halifax residents have come up with what could be a first for Atlantic Canada in neighbourhood planning. They have devised—in conjunction with some professors and students from the Nova Scotia Technical College School of Architecture—a proposal for the development of a fifteen acre site on Quinpool Road in the centre of the Halifax Peninsula. The proposal is for a largely residential, mixed use project to rival a high rise apartment-hotel-commercial-office-shopping complex planned by a Halifax developer for the same site. The resident's proposal, called QR2, was unveiled in February, 1974 after protests from citizen groups delayed for more than a year the developer's initial high-rise, high-density scheme.

Paul Brodie and S.L. Richards, residents of the Quinpool Road area, filed a writ with the Nova Scotia Supreme Court claiming that a resolution passed in May 1973, to allow the developer to build his project, was illegal. The writ was filed after a long legal battle over an identical appeal by the Halifax Ecology Action Centre before the province's Planning Appeal Board was lost in September of 1973. The residents hope, by their legal action, to get City Council to take a second look at the project they have approved. This time, however, when the developer's scheme comes before council and the public, there will be an alternative: a medium density, low rise residential community with a limited amount of commercial services, a scheme which fits in well with existing neighbourhoods and is acceptable to their inhabitants and with the overall aims of the city as expressed in its draft plans to date.

BACKGROUND

The land in question is in a primarily residential area of the city, formerly owned by three Roman Catholic religious orders, and occupied by a monastery, a convent, and an orphanage. It is abutted on the south by Quinpool Road, a major east-west artery, on the east by St. Patricks High School and St. Vincent Guest House, and on the north and west by residential neighbourhoods.

The controversy began late in 1972, when Halifax developer Ralph Medjuck, principal of Centennial Properties Ltd., approached the city with a scheme to develop the land, which is zoned 'park and institutional'. The scheme called for the construction of three 30-storey apartment towers, a 17-storey office building, a 9-storey hotel, and a shopping mall housing 260 thousand square feet of retail and commercial space. Also to be included were a service station and three levels of parking facilities for 2300 vehicles. The nearby residential areas were neither impoverished nor extremely well-to-do, with a density of about 50 people per acre. The residents consisted of both tenants and home-owners.

After the city had looked over the idea—at least the general idea of a mixed use development on the site—and privately given it the nod, Medjuck called a meeting of people who owned property nearby. This meeting was called in order to sell the idea to those whose financial interest might be affected. Only homeowners were invited. The homeowners asked questions about the project, but didn't learn very much. The daily newspaper was on hand, and reported the residents the following day as having been more or less favourable toward the project. This was disputed by at least one person who had been in attendance, in the form of a letter to the editor.

Still, the meeting gave Centennial Properties the chance to reap the benefits of media coverage by appearing concerned about 'citizen input', and getting people committed publicly.

When Centennial went to the City with its formal

proposal, the City scheduled its own public hearing on the matter for January 16, 1973. The following description of that hearing, and of the next regular council meeting, is taken from the brief that was later filed by the Ecology Action Centre with the province's Planning Appeal Board:

At the public hearing six persons spoke 'in favour' of the project and nine persons spoke 'against' the project. The minutes show that two of those speaking 'in favour' of the project favoured it because they felt it would reduce the tax burden on homeowners. The others speaking 'in favour' of the project favoured it in a general way but had specific complaints, i.e. that it was 'poorly planned' and that the buildings were too high. One person felt that Quinpool Road was a beautiful street and 'should be developed.' Mr. Medjuck also spoke at some length in favour of the project. He described the proposal and said it would provide tax benefits to the city.

Nine persons spoke 'against' the development. The questions they raised included lack of planning on the part of the city, poor urban design (blocking of sunlight), undesirable effects on the downtown, conflicts with the draft Municipal Development Plan, social problems, and eventual costs to the city that would be greater than the economic benefits of the project.

At the council meeting held January 25, there was some discussion about the project. A staff report over the signature of Mr. Henderson (the City Manager) asked for more time for the various departments to complete the studies that had been begun as a result of the January 16 meeting. Some aldermen wished to give the developer some sort of approval immediately so that he could begin to look for financing. Council withdrew and met in camera for slightly less than one hour and emerged with a resolution approving the project in principle with certain restrictions.

These 'restrictions' consisted primarily of a reduction in the size of the office building by 50,000 square feet, and the donation to the city of whatever lands the city deemed necessary in order to make traffic improvements which the design of the project would necessitate.

Shortly after this hearing, the Ecology Action Centre got involved. People had begun to contact the EAC for information on the Quinpool Road Project or to suggest that the Centre take some action against it. Working through the Centre's urban team, a Halifax architect put together a short leaflet describing some of the effects that a development of this type was likely to have on the neighbourhood and the city as a whole. These were distributed in the neighbourhood, and, while they seemed to be well received—most people were glad to get some information on the subject—there was no strong response. There was, in fact, little to respond to by this time. After the January 25 meeting, the developer had claimed that council's restrictions were too heavy to allow the project to continue. He had more or less threatened to pick up his marbles and go home; and, to all appearances, that was precisely what he had done.

Meanwhile, the EAC and other groups were busy trying to lobby for a Municipal Development Plan for the city. Halifax has been working toward this goal now for several decades, without success. Each new council has been increasingly reluctant to place restrictions on developers. The inevitable effect of this is that the city now sprawls in several directions simultaneously; it is without adequate sewer and water service in much of its area; it is scarred by ugly strip development; it is subject twice daily to traffic jams that are ridiculous for a city of 120,000; and its historic downtown area is, at best, twitching spasmodically after its untimely demise a dozen years ago.

Two or three years ago, in an apparent attempt to comply with the requirements of the Provincial Planning Act, the Halifax Planning Department put together all local plans and documents on which it was then working, bound them in one volume, and called it the 'Master Plan'! This was sent to council for approval and/or comment; but, as it was in the vicinity of 200 pages in length, council predictably sent the monster back with orders to come up with something more manageable. By the end of 1972, (just about the same time the Centennial project was to be made public), the new plan arrived in council chambers. It had been boiled down considerably, as it now totalled four pages in length, plus a lone map. It was mostly nebulous 'policy' statements designed to comply—minimally—with the ministerial order to produce a plan.

One thing the plan did do was to make it fairly clear that major new developments of stores, offices, hotels, or theatres and entertainment were to go in the downtown area. The idea behind this was to bring the downtown back to life. Some particularly alert alderman realized at this point that Medjuck's project, which was not to be built downtown, contained every one of the things specifically mentioned in the plan to be located only in the downtown. Council quickly tried to remedy the discrepancy between the Centennial scheme and the proposed plan, by adding a clause which provided that, on any site of over five acres, council could grant a special development permit to allow a mixed use project, regardless of plans or zoning. The City Manager's staff report on the subject made it clear that the amendment was inserted specifically for Centennial Properties.

This showed how blatantly unconcerned council members were about planning issues. They wanted to pass the most ludicrous of plans, and were willing at a moment's notice to change even that to suit a developer's wishes.

The public hearings on the draft municipal development plan and the Centennial Quinpool Road project were held less than a week apart in January of 1973. If the reception received by the Quinpool Road development was less than enthusiastic, the response to the proposed municipal development plan was downright belligerent. About 500 people, appalled that the future of Halifax was summed up by 4 pages and a map, jammed the Queen Elizabeth High School gymnasium and confronted the mayor and aldermen. One after another, citizens got up and spoke against the vagueness and lack of teeth in the plan. There was still a little pressure from within City Hall to adopt the plan, 'as a beginning'—notably from

... Council quickly tried to remedy the discrepancy between the Centennial scheme and the draft plan by adding a special 'development permit' clause.

... 'what if they had a public hearing and people opposed the roadway. Then what would they do? Better not to hold a hearing at all.'

... despite citizens' groups from all over the city calling for a strong municipal development plan, Council was blithely ignoring every plan and principle so far established.

City Manager Cyril Henderson. But even if Mayor Fitzgerald had not been forced into publicly claiming that the city had no intention of adopting this flimsy statement as *the* municipal development plan, the matter would have been settled shortly thereafter, when the province informed the city in no uncertain terms that the plan under consideration failed entirely to fulfill provincial requirements.

In May of 1973, Centennial Properties, which had been negotiating privately with the Halifax Development Department for the past four months, made a second formal proposal to the City Council. The new scheme called for four 22-storey apartment buildings with a housing capacity of 3300 persons instead of the original three 30-storey towers; the office building was reduced to nine storeys; the hotel was changed to a 208 unit 'apartment-hotel'; and the retail-commercial space was increased to 283,000 square feet (some of this space had been removed from the hotel in the initial scheme, and so the developer could claim a net decrease in retail-commercial space).

On May 17 a resolution was passed by council outlining these changes and authorizing the mayor to grant a development permit allowing Centennial to build the project. The development permit was to be granted under Section 538 A of the City Charter, which had nothing to do with the Planning Act. This section does not change the formal zoning on a piece of land, it simply allows council and the developer to ignore the zoning by-law.

A second resolution 'solved' the anticipated traffic problems by linking Vernon Street and Windsor

Centennial's Proposed Development

Street at an intersection on the east end of the complex. Because the alterations in the traffic patterns were so major, there was some thought given to the idea of a second public hearing. But Council members decided against another hearing. The first had been bad enough, and since Council members weren't in the habit of listening to what was said anyhow, it didn't make much difference. As Alderman Sullivan had the candor to point out—what if they held a public hearing and people opposed the roadway? Then what would they do? Better not to hold a hearing at all.

This was too much even for the Halifax *Mail-Star*, and a few articles were printed criticizing Council for taking this drastic step without public approval. The traffic scheme would turn Vernon Street, a residential street, into a major collector. The high school would be surrounded on three sides by major four lane arteries passing within six feet of the building itself. The new road would also pass within a few feet of the St. Vincent Guest House, whose residents are old people, and whose board of governors strongly opposed the roadway. The pleas of the Guest House and the School Board did little to dissuade council from its decision, and the public criticism did less. It was apparent that no amount of petitioning or lobbying could change council's mind.

The situation, then, was this:

One of the largest developments ever contemp-

lated in Halifax had been approved by City Council without involving the residential area which would be seriously affected by it. Although every plan so far discussed in Halifax had named the downtown as the place for major commercial developments, this was well outside the Central Business District. Although the zoning by-law limits residential density in the area to 125 persons per acre, this development had a density of 250 persons per acre. Although Quinpool Road was already among the most congested areas in the city, this development would generate an additional 25,000 cars per day. Although low and middle income family housing is needed most in Halifax, the scheme contained almost no family-sized units. Although Halifax was far below its own standards for recreation land, the project, while eating up fifteen acres of park and institutional land, provided little or no open space.

The list was endless. Worst of all, perhaps, was the fact that despite citizen groups from all over the city calling for a strong municipal development plan, council was blithely ignoring every plan, draft plan and principle so far established.

THE HEARING

On June 7, the Ecology Action Centre filed notice of appeal with the Provincial Planning Appeal Board.

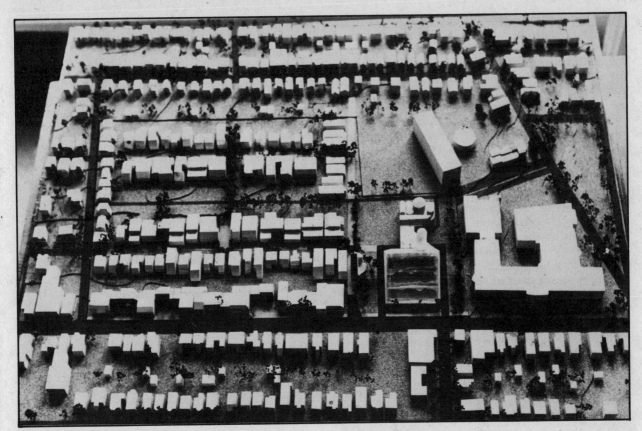

QR II—the Alternative to Centennial's Highrises

One question in everyone's mind at this point was whether or not the Board would agree to hear the appeal. The Planning Act gave the Board power to hear appeals from re-zonings, but the decision under appeal by the EAC was simply a council decision which had managed to circumvent the Planning Act. However, if the Board did not have the power to hear it, it would mean that the Planning Act was virtually useless, as it would be unable to protect communities against unconcerned, incompetent or misled City Councils. Let it be said here that the purpose of the Centre's appeal was not to harass the developer. It is not the duty of the developer to be scrupulous, to have a 'social conscience', to worry about City plans. It is the job of the City Council to insure optimum utilization of the city's resources, and guarantee the best possible environment to all the residents of the city. In this case, they had failed miserably. So it was the city that the EAC was calling to task, not the developer.

Although the City was the respondent in the appeal (that is, it was officially billed as Ecology Action Centre vs. the City of Halifax), the Planning Act states that any interested person may appear and give evidence. Centennial Properties apparently considering itself interested, hired a team of lawyers from one of the largest and best known firms in Halifax. The City then sat back and kept its mouth shut for the most part, letting the gentlemen from Centennial take over the presentation of evi-

dence and the cross-examination of EAC witnesses. One could not help getting the impression that the lawyer from the City Solicitor's office was not quite certain what the proceedings were all about.

The hearing began on July 31, 1973 with arguments on whether the Board had jurisdiction to hear the case. The City and the developer pointed out that no amendment to the zoning by-law had been passed; therefore none could be appealed. The EAC pointed out that the land had been zoned 'park and institutional', but would be used for stores and offices. If that wasn't re-zoning, what was?

The real question, of course, hinged on the definition of the word 'amend'. Stan Makuch (a law professor at Dalhousie, and an expert in planning law), cited case law and argued to the effect that the decision under appeal constituted in fact and in law an amendment, and could therefore be appealed. The Board upheld this view and agreed to hear the appeal. In doing so, they closed one of the larger loopholes in Nova Scotia planning law. In future, any permits granted under section 538 A of the City Charter (these tend to be among the worst developments in the city) may be appealed.

After this decision was made, the hearing began in earnest. The EAC raised nine major objections to the Centennial scheme through the testimony of nineteen witnesses. The witnesses pointed out that:

While the power behind Halifax Developments Ltd., Trizec, and other development firms lies somewhat concealed behind boardroom doors, Centennial Properties is, for all intents and purposes, Ralph Medjuck. A home town boy, not yet forty, he is responsible for a growing number of developments in and around Halifax (he claims $100 million worth). None of his enterprises have been particularly brilliant or imaginative, and the only previous one to ignite anything resembling controversy was his 500-unit Cowie Hill housing project. Financed extensively by CMHC, the development was singled out by the Charney report—a forerunner of the Dennis-Fish report—as an example of poor housing. Mr. Medjuck makes no bones about the fact that he is out to maximize his profits, and doesn't put forth a lot of piffle about community concern as do so many other developers these days. As the successful businessman that he is, he receives—and deserves, by all standards presently in use—the respect of the community at large.

1 The development permit granted by the city was so vague and open-ended that Medjuck was free to put up whatever kind of development he wished. City Council had abdicated any control over the development by issuing such a permit;

2 The development would have a disastrous effect on the Quinpool Road neighbourhood;

3 The proposed complex was in defiance of the Draft Municipal Plan on numerous key points;

4 The residential density was too high;

5 There was not enough open space in the project, and the developer had not agreed to donate open space elsewhere in the city;

6 Traffic generated by the project would be too heavy for the neighbourhood, the school, and the old people's home. The cost of traffic improvements would be excessive, if in fact such improvements could be made at all;

7 The development would not improve the city's tax base;

8 The retail and commercial elements of the development would detract from the viability of the downtown. (This was a strong argument in Halifax. The only time the Board had reversed a Halifax re-zoning was in a case fought on the ground that a hotel proposed by Medjuck, for a site not far from the one in question here, would detract from growth in the downtown);

9 A development of this magnitude would eliminate so many options for the future development of the city that it should not be carried out until a municipal development plan could be achieved. Halifax had been doing its planning by default for decades. This was another in a long string of decisions which produced major changes in the community (new roads, new schools, and deteriorating neighbourhoods)—changes which were unplanned and unthought-of at the time the developments were approved.

Stan Makuch, Dalhousie planning and expert in law and Dimitri Procos, architect and planner at the School of Architecture, both took the stand to point out how nebulous the development permit was, giving none of the details (such as landscaping, fountains, number of bedrooms in units, facings of buildings, etc.) which were usually included, and that the project included a number of specific failures to meet standards which the city would correct with a more stringent agreement. Procos also pointed out that, by permitting a project of this size, Council was allowing the development itself, rather than the people, to determine the direction of Halifax's future growth.

Guillio Maffinini, (planner for a private firm, and one of the authors of the newly-completed Halifax-Dartmouth Regional plan) agreed with this, adding that the size of the commercial space allotted in Centennial's plan would compete with the downtown area, and would probably result in further strip development along Quinpool Road as well as competing to their detriment with retail outlets in the downtown.

Another professor from the School of Architecture, Tony Jackson, drew attention to studies done on the density of apartment buildings, (one of which was built by Centennial) which indicated that buildings exceeded the maximum densities of the original design by 25 to 43%. The Centennial complex, which was already double the usual 150 persons per acre, might eventually be crammed with 5,000 people.

The City's Social Planning Director, Harold Crowell testified that he not only agreed with Jackson, but had already made his opinions known to the City Manager. Opposing the development, however, was like 'spitting into the wind'.

He also pointed out that some of the so-called 'amenities' being provided by the developer, (two tennis courts, drop-in centres for teenagers and older people, and a day care centre for fifty children) would probably be inadequate for three thousand people. Moreover, the developer would provide no personnel to operate the communal facilities and the day care centre was to be run as a commercial operation. So, as it turned out, all the developer was really providing was a few empty rooms—and small ones at that (300 square feet for the senior citizens' drop-in centre).

Centennial had flown in a market analyst from Larry Smith Research Ltd. of Toronto. This 'expert' had done a study indicating that after the project was completed there would still be room for commercial development in the downtown. Under cross-examination, however, it was made clear that the study made no predictions of the effects of the Centennial project; only that there would be enough residual buying power in the metropolitan area to support a large department store somewhere. (Interestingly, the study—still incomplete—had not been started until July, weeks after EAC had filed its appeal.)

Centennial also called Hugh Porter, a local planner, who attempted to defend Centennial by declaiming that 'the retail sector must operate within a framework of competition', and that the downtown ought not to be protected.

By far the most overwhelming issue that arose was the destruction of the neighbourhood by the increased traffic. The high school and the Guest House could both expect to suffer greatly from the increased traffic. Art Donahue, a lawyer and member of the Board of Governors of St. Vincent Guest House testified that the noise from the roadway would interfere with the operation of the Guest House, and could even force relocation. Arthur Conrad, from the Board of Education, opposed the road development because it would cause excessive noise on three sides of the school and restrict access to such a degree that fire regulations would become impossible to follow. The head girl from the high school spoke against the project, because of the traffic aspects. And a resident of Allen Street charged that the development would adversely affect the neighbourhood.

Centennial's witness responded that property values would not go down as a result of the project and that, therefore, no one had a right to complain about neighbourhood deterioration, blatantly ignoring the fact that many of the neighbourhood residents are tenants and many others are retired on fixed incomes. These people are far more concerned about keeping their homes than making (or seeing their landlords make) a profit on the land at the expense of the neighbourhood.

Centennial then attempted to explain away the traffic problem. A traffic expert from the Toronto firm of consulting engineers, Damas and Smith, said that the project could generate 25,000 cars per day or 2,500 at peak hour. However, under the traffic scheme his firm had worked out with the city, he explained that the traffic situation after the project was constructed would be about the same or at least no worse. The traffic plan was premised on five changes to be made in the traffic pattern, changes, he said, the city intended to make anyway.

Mr. Smith, the traffic expert, also said that his firm had some experience with the problem of traffic noise. In the case of the school, he suggested, noise was already a problem which would be increased minimally by the project; the whole prob-

Little can be said about the ten-member council to give a clear understanding of why they function the way they do. In fairness, it must be said that two aldermen, Dave MacKeen and Lou Moir, opposed the Centennial scheme consistently, if not vehemently, since its conception, and are generally on the more radical and losing side of the touchier issues. The remaining eight range from long-time homeowners from the oldest Halifax families to up-and-coming real estate brokers and insurance agents starting out on that long political road in hopes of being future mayors or premiers. While they may argue for several hours over granting permission to an individual for an addition to a house on an undersize lot, they seldom reflect for as many minutes over encouraging one developer or another to annihilate a block or two of housing. As to whether this is owing to naivete or knavery, one only has opinions, but it is clear that Council functions on all the old axioms of reducing property tax by expanding development, etc. In short, it is the kind of council that veritably cries out to be replaced.

lem could be solved by putting double glazed windows on the school. Of course, Mr. Medjuck would not agree to pay for this, nor for the air-conditioning which double glazing would necessitate. As for the Guest House, Mr. Smith compared it to a hospital and said 'absolute peace and quiet is not necessary or desirable in a hospital; it could be just as much a problem as a lot of noise.'

Dexter Kaulbach, a traffic engineer who had worked on the regional plan, was called by EAC as a rebuttal witness. He agreed that it was possible for the scheme to work as Mr. Smith had described it, but that the evidence demanded further interpretation. The improvements upon which the scheme is premised had already been planned by the city because the situation was already very bad at the intersection in question—and indeed over the whole length of Quinpool Road. The scheme was premised not only on the five changes mentioned, but on several other improvements already planned, such as the Northwest Arm Bridge, costing a total of millions upon millions of dollars. If the Centennial scheme were accepted, all the millions of dollars worth of improvements would be wasted since the end result, as the Centennial witness had pointed out, would be a traffic situation the same or no better. Any benefits to be gained in the Quinpool Road area by the planned public expenditure of millions of dollars in traffic improvements would be entirely eaten up by the traffic generated by the Centennial scheme.

Planning in Halifax operates like a group of archers shooting arrows into a wall and then painting targets around them.

One reason that developments of the nature of Centennial's proposal for Quinpool Road are so hastily and easily approved is that the City of Halifax has not one planning department, but four. The actual Planning Department has only one responsibility—producing plans. It apparently matters not in the least that these plans are consistently disregarded by everyone outside the department. The Planning Department's only contribution to the Centennial issue was a memo opposing the project, sent from Planning Director Ed Babb to City Manager Cyril Henderson. This opinion never reached council and council never asked for it.

The real staff input is from the Development Department, whose director during the time of the controversy was Bob Grant. He said the Development Department had spent a good many man-hours figuring out how to cram the complex onto the site. It didn't seem to matter much that this use didn't match up with the picture the Planning Department was producing down the hall (they wanted to build a school). Mr. Grant couldn't for the life of him figure out what all this hubbub was about. After all, if the project turned out not to conform to the plan, the plan could always be changed.

Mr. Kaulbach also noted that in the scheme 3,000 cars would go through the single intersection behind the school in peak hour. This was too many to allow for safe turning and pedestrian crossing. Unless a way could be found of adding another access route to the project, the traffic scheme was unacceptable.

The City Manager testified that it was unlikely another access route could be found.

APPEAL REJECTED

As the hearing moved along through August and into September, more people began to show concern over the project. The press reported some of the testimony, and as the list of witnesses who opposed the project grew, the whole idea of opposition gained credibility. Little or no attempt had been made by EAC—or any one else for that matter—to organize the residents in the neighbourhood, but by the time the parade of witnesses was over, a group of citizens had begun circulating flyers saying that should the appeal be lost, an

organization would be formed to continue the fight.

On September 17 the Board dismissed the appeal. In its decision, the Board cited the evidence of Cyril Henderson and development director Bob Grant that there had been, and would be further, detailed negotiations with the developer and that it was still possible to develop an alternate traffic routing. Apparently the Board ignored Professor Makuch's point in this regard, that Council had already given up control of the permit and that any negotiations that did take place would not be subject to approval from Council.

The Board also said that since few residents from the area had come to oppose the project, there was no reason to believe it would have an adverse effect on the neighbourhood. The EAC found this to be a peculiar basis for the decision, largely because of the Board's own stand that 'the best interest of the municipality is to be interpreted in the light of planning considerations and that main guidance is to be obtained from professional qualified planners in various fields such as Urban Economics, Urban Design, City Planning, etc.' This principle had been stated once by the Board (Lord Nelson decision, Vol. I of *Planning Appeal Decisions*, p. 31), and reiterated in at least one later decision (Blakely and Pacey vs. City of Halifax).

Whether the members of the Board actually believed there was no opposition, or whether this was simply the 'out' needed to make the politically necessary decision, the neighbourhood residents were not satisfied.

TRYING AGAIN

Within a few weeks, a petition opposing the heavy traffic which would result from the project was presented to Halifax City Council. The petition was signed by 1100 neighbourhood residents. It was accompanied by the traffic diagrams prepared by EAC appeal witnesses. When Council was confronted with the statistics of tens of thousands of cars passing through the single intersection between the school and the Guest House, as well as the hundreds of additional cars which would use surrounding residential streets, they were visibly surprised. Not a single member of Council had shown up at any of the appeal hearings. They had not been shown by their own traffic experts how drastic the effects would be. But still they did nothing to alter the project.

A few weeks later the Ward 2 Residents Council was formed and a ward four group also began to organize (Quinpool Road is the common boundary of these two wards). Next, two residents, Brodie and Richards, filed the writ mentioned earlier. Their legal argument is a technical one, that rezonings must be done by by-law rather than by resolution. If the citizens win on this point, council will have to go through proper rezoning procedure, including another public hearing. Council will still have the final say, and Halifax aldermen are not known for their ability to learn by experience, but the residents' hopes are high.

Meanwhile, the two ward groups have cooperated with a number of professors and students from the School of Architecture to produce an alternate scheme for the site. The result of this is the QR 2 proposal, which embodies all the residents would like to see on the site. At the time of writing, several public meetings have been held, and more scheduled, to discuss QR2 with people all over the city. So far it has met with great success.

The QR 2 project is medium density, 100 to 125 persons per acre. The buildings range from one and a half to three and a half storeys high. Existing roads have been continued through the site; but as walkways, open only to emergency traffic. QR 2 will help fulfil Halifax's greatest need: family housing. It will be owned and operated co-operatively, and seems economically viable if the land can be obtained at a reasonable price. The citizens' presentation is impressive, and sure to win financial backing. Unlike the Centennial project which would place four 22 storey buildings virtually in the back yards of two and three storey dwellings, QR 2 is a continuous adjunct to the neighbourhood. And unlike the Centennial scale model, which conveniently omitted all the homes which would abut the scheme, the QR 2 model shows the project in relation to the neighbourhood. The ward groups are bringing facts to the public rather than obscuring them.

The biggest problem remaining is that Centennial owns one two-acre lot outright and still holds options on the remaining land—options it will not likely give up unless the original project is denied approval.

The residents opposing the development, their number increasing daily, are using every legal means available to make sure approval is withheld. They have at last forced City Council to agree to a public hearing on the roadway issue. Although Council claims to have made an irreversible decision to allow the project, development hinges critically on the new access road, from which Council may still withhold approval.

Even if Council does not reverse plans for the new road, it cannot be built without expropriation of school property. At a recent meeting of the Halifax Board of School Commissioners, the Board voted to oppose expropriation. The only negative votes came from the two school commissioners who are also aldermen, Margaret Stanbury and Dennis Connoly.

As it turns out, no sale of school property can be completed without approval of the Province. Once this was discovered, residents escalated the matter

```
                                              City Planning Committee
                                              December 20, 1972

To:         His Worship the Mayor
            and Members of City Council

From:       C. McC. Henderson, City Manager

Date:       December 19, 1972

Subject:    Possible Amendments to
            Proposed Municipal Development Plan
```

As a result of the submission made by Centennial Properties Limited re comprehensive development permit on fifteen acres, more or less, adjacent to Quinpool Road, Council members have asked staff for a recommendation as to how best the Municipal Development Plan might be amended in order to allow approval under Section 538 (a) of the City Charter of a comprehensive development scheme involving inter-related mixed uses in any area of the City for which comprehensive development is best suited.

It is suggested that the following paragraph might be included on page 1:

"On sites in excess of five acres located in areas designated on the overall Development Policy Plan for particular uses (e.g. "residential development" or "industrial, defence and Port-related facilities, inter-related mixed uses may be sanctioned in accordance with specific comprehensive development schemes when approved by Council, after due notice and Public Hearing."

There may be some discussion as to the necessity for including the last six words in that paragraph. Their inclusion is deemed desirable and appropriate, as in staff's view deviations from precise Zoning regulations or from a literal interpretation of the Municipal Development Plan should not be instituted without a prior Public Hearing - no matter how desirable they may be.

In discussions last week, it was suggested that a provision of this nature should be approved by Council for inclusion in the draft Municipal Development Plan before the Public Hearing on January 10th, which would require formal action by Council - not by the Committee of the Whole - on, say, the afternoon of Wednesday, December 20th.

It has been suggested that embodiment of such a provision should be proposed by parties other than staff or members of Council, and that the proposal should be introduced during the January 10th Public Hearing.

The other view, which is also the view of the undersigned, is that it would be preferable for Council to recognize in advance the deficiency, if that is what it is considered to be, and introduce an appropriate modification before the Public Hearing on January 10th, and in sufficient time for the change to be embodied into the material which is to receive wide publicity before that Hearing.

                                      C. McC. Henderson
                                      City Manager

CMcCH/H

to an issue in the provincial election. Upon being questioned by the electors, some candidates indicated they opposed the development; others didn't wait to be asked. National N.D.P. leader David Lewis brought the matter up in the House of Commons. His earlier condemnation of Medjuck's Cowie Hill project apparently still fresh in his mind, he referred to the Halifax developer's firm as 'disreputable' (for which he later apologized, while maintaining the Centennial scheme was not right for the site), and suggested to Urban Affairs Minister Ron Basford that CMHC might do well to find funds for proposals like QR 2.

The Quinpool Road controversy is far from being resolved. Aside from being the focus of continued legal manoeuvring by both the developer and the City of Halifax, the proposed project also became the topic of political debate during the recent Nova Scotia provincial election. Meanwhile opposition to Centennial's plans appears to be snowballing.

Clearly, the final resolution of the conflict cannot be forecast at this time, but it is evident that Quinpool no longer represents only neighbourhood residents responding to an isolated development issue. The intended development has escalated

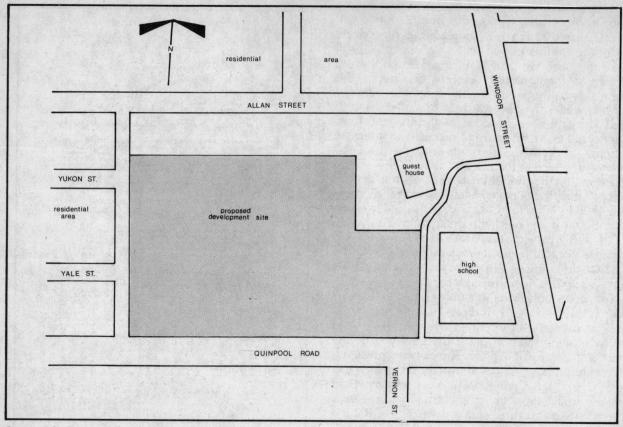

Centennial's Proposed Development Site

Proposed Roadway Realignment

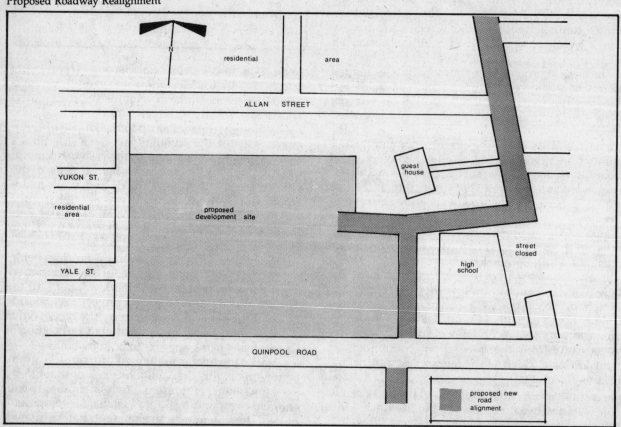

The Neighbourhood—Low Rise, Backyards and Trees   Photos by Fat Chance Photography Cooperative, Halifax

citizen interest to the point where the entire municipal planning and political processes are undergoing intense public scrutiny. The heightened public awareness and new vigilance of local political activity resulting from Quinpool augers well for those citizens concerned about how and for whom their city is governed.

Since this article was written, many new events have transpired in the continuing and convoluted tale of Quinpool Road. Briefly: the citizens lost their appeal which ended in the Supreme Court of Canada; the QR II idea evolved into an organization called Quinpool Community Development Council (QCDC) with a development plan for the site combined with rehab and renovation in the surrounding neighbourhood; the City of Halifax purchased the site from the developer at a cost of $5.3 million (this was only a few months after the developer had completed the purchase himself for just over $4 million) when the developer was reluctant to continue with his original scheme. QCDC's ideas failed to gain the approval of CMHC regional director Calder Hart, who still favoured high-rise development of the site; hence City Council refused to back the residents in their attempts to get financial support from Ottawa for QCDC.

Council members — and Mayor Edmund Morris

in particular — thus found themselves in a somewhat embarrassing position: when the City purchased the land, the mayor had insisted that its price was compatible with low-rise, moderate-income family housing; yet council rejected the QCDC proposal for precisely this type of housing to be constructed on a non-profit basis, because it was claimed that the plan would require too much subsidy—all this at a time when Mr. Medjuck was said to be wearing "a million dollar smile".

The City came up with its own set of criteria for the development of the site, designed to cut the city's losses and placate the still-anxious citizenry. This scheme, billed as a "compromise solution", aimed to persuade the Province to buy one-third of the site for a new school for the blind; the rest of the site would be devoted to a commercial/apartment complex of somewhat smaller proportions than the original Centennial scheme, but still, in the opinion of QCDC, out of proportion with the surrounding neighbourhood. The City called for proposals based on the new criteria, but received no response.

Subsequently the criteria were broadened and the city has apparently received two serious comprehensive proposals. One of these is from Century Twenty-One, a company responsible for urban core redevelopments in several Canadian cities; the other is from a consortium including Interfaith Housing Corporation (a non-profit housing corporation) and two private firms. The consortium proposal seems to satisfy many — though not all — of the demands made by citizens during the past several years. It would share amenity space with the school for the blind; it would provide some non-profit housing; except for a seven-storey commercial apartment strip fronting on Quinpool Road, it would not exceed three and a half storeys. The City is under considerable pressure to do something with the land, since the interest payments are over $1200 per day. Actually the City owns much more valuable pieces of land which have been neglected for decades, but the publicity over the Quinpool site has made the whole issue quite sensitive.

Meanwhile, part of the QCDC scheme has gone ahead in a modified form: some residents have formed a non-profit housing co-op (Nova Scotia's first) and begun to buy and renovate homes in the area. It is hoped that this will have a stabilizing effect on the neighbourhood, and mitigate any adverse effects of whatever development finally appears.

Friendly games: Edmonton's Olympic alternative

Batya Chivers

The Commonwealth Games have been called the "friendly games" because of their emphasis on non-competitiveness, hospitality, and low-cost facilities. These aspects clearly differentiate them from the expensive and elaborate Olympic Games. The next set of Commonwealth Games will be held in Edmonton in August 1978, but as far as residents of that city are concerned the games are bringing more dissension than friendship to the city and are costing citizens more in lost housing, broken communities and higher taxes than they can afford to pay.

Perhaps the single most important issue arises from the way Edmonton residents and other Commonwealth countries have been consistently misled about the cost of the games and the grandeur of the facilities which are to be constructed for them.

When Edmonton City Council first decided to bid for the games in November 1971, the total cost of needed facilities was estimated to be $9,750,000. This included $3.5-million for a stadium $3.5-million for an Olympic swimming pool, $500,000 for a cycling track, $250,000 for a shooting range and $2-million for upgrading various existing facilities.

But the same council meeting outlined a strategy for deceiving the public and using the games as a lever to get approval of public funding for elaborate new sports facilities which the electorate was not prepared to approve.

The city politicians knew at the time that this facility was not required for the games. Indeed, in the same meeting, the mayor said he was concerned about bidding for the games on a budget which included such a structure, as games facilities are supposed to be modest. However, he stated, "once we have gotten the games, the organization would accept the change." But, a bylaw to borrow money for an Omniplex had been defeated several years previously. Council accordingly changed the name Omniplex to multi-purpose structure, to prepare the bid for the games based on the minimal cost, and to later change it after the bid was accepted.

Accordingly, Edmonton's "Invitation Bid" presented in Munich and the attached covering letter of progress and amendment dated August 1972, seemed still to refer to the minimal capital budget totalling less than $10,000,000. All the news coverage at this time reinforced this message that facilities would total $9,750,000, perhaps with no cost to the city.

Edmonton is going full tilt to plan and build the 9.75-million dollar facilities it will require for the 1978 British Commonwealth Games.

Hal Pawson, interim executive director, said today the Edmonton Games Foundation was hopeful almost all the finances – as well as 2 million dollars operating costs – would be covered by federal and provincial grants, donations, and some financial schemes such as lotteries; "and that it is not necessary any money come from the city." – Edmonton Journal, 25 August 1972 p. 1

The cost of the games facilities became a public issue in late 1973. By this time, the capital expenditure budget had soared to more than four times the original cost ($44,611,000), and included $12,463,000 for an artificial ice rink coliseum. This is mostly a hockey facility, and is only sometimes considered to be a games facility — e.g. for federal and provincial funding purposes. But when the costs are presented to the public, it is not considered to be a games facility. By this time, the $3.5-million for a minimal stadium had been replaced by $23.6-million for a multi-purpose structure, in accordance with the strategy outlined in council in November of 1971.

Moreover, it became obvious that earlier statements that no cost would be incurred by the city were incorrect. Edmonton would have to contribute approximately one-third of the cost in order to get federal aid. The Province had already committed itself to $11.6-million, $3.7-million of it allocated towards the coliseum.

The city proposed to raise its share of the cost through debentures. At that time, council refused to clarify whether or not a plebiscite would be held. When it became apparent that a plebiscite would be held only if council was petitioned by the electorate, a petition was organized and the necessary number of 14,000 signatures was gathered in three weeks. The plebiscite was rescheduled at the request of the promoters, who launched a massive and misleading campaign, which resulted in a "yes" vote.

After the municipal elections in October 1974, new projected costs for the facilities were announced. This raised the total by another five to ten million dollars, and was still prior to official bidding or the beginning of construction of facilities (other than the coliseum). In May 1975, a revised estimate (pre-tender) of the cost of the pool was

released. The cost had climbed by another $500,000 and is now expected to be about $8-million.

Nor do these figures include all the direct costs to the city of the facilities being constructed for the games. For example, the city is donating some parkland as sites for the facilities and building a number of expensive roads to service the facilities. After the games, a stadium roof, a physical fitness centre under the stadium stand and artificial turf will all be added to the city's expenses.

This story of rising costs and hidden costs as it unfolds in Edmonton, is reminiscent of an article in *Fortune* magazine in March 1973 explaining how such projects are usually sold to the public:

The taxpayer rarely understands what he is in for when a stadium project is first announced. To drum up public support, the advocates of a stadium generally understate the probable cost, which invariably balloons as construction proceeds. They also overstate probable revenues by anticipating multiple use for the structure – rock concerts, races, fireworks displays, and conventions – that in actuality dwindle to a few. The stadium's recurring deficits prove to be much higher than promised, and the taxpayer discovers that civic pride has been compromised by special interests, blind boosterism and inept planning. Tainted with deception, the "can do" spirit becomes vitiated by a lingering bitterness that can undercut a city's ability to finance other and perhaps more important projects.

Cost for almost every super-stadium undertaken in North America surveyed by *Fortune* more than tripled from original estimates. In New Orleans, voters approved a bond issue of $35-million (total cost) for a covered stadium. The final cost was $150-million. In Edmonton, the original estimate in 1972 was $3.5-million for the stadium; by 1974 it was $23-million, this estimate still being in pre-bidding or construction stages. Considering the rate of escalation in estimated costs, the stadium in Edmonton might cost as much as $100-million by 1978.

THE PROMOTERS

The promoters of the games are representatives of the sports elite, professional sports, business, the city politician and the administration of the city. The 36 games directors are mainly representatives of large corporations, (e.g. Simpsons-Sears and Air Canada), financial institutions, the sports elite and political representatives from municipal and provincial bodies.

The foundation operates under some unusual bylaws. Directors can vote on business with their own companies (sec.33); directors are appointed for the life of the foundation (sec. 36); directors may grant free tickets, or complimentary reservations and bookings (sec. 50); and finally, directors can claim any personal loss or damage suffered as a result of their service, against the foundation (sec. 52)*. Such provisions are highly unusual.

The XI British Commonwealth Games, Canada (1978) Foundation was officially formed on August 16, 1972. The initial four members were Mayor Ivor Dent, Hal Pawson, J. G. Kuchinski, and Ian Archibald. Being the original subscribers to the Foundation's Memorandum of Association, these four were given the exclusive power of choosing the other 32 directors of the Foundation (sec. 5). Besides the mayor, four other members of council became directors (Aldermen Fallow, Ward, Mac-Lean and Hayter) as did Commissioner G. S. Hughes. Alderman Fallow became the executive director of the Foundation following the plebiscite vote. Three provincial Cabinet Ministers, Horst Schmidt, Fred Peacock and Robert Dowling, are directors as well.

The provincial Municipal Affairs Minister, Dave Russell, felt compelled to revise the Municipal Government Act especially to allow the mayor and aldermen to sit on the Foundation. Had the act not been revised, there might have been question of conflict of interest when elected municipal officials sat on the board of directors of a private corporation (the Foundation) which is funded by council but not answerable to it. They could be seen as voting taxpayers' money to themselves, especially since they could vote as Foundation directors to give contracts to themselves or their own profit-making companies. On two occasions council was voted to give money to the Foundation.

Considering these facts, it is not surprising that city council and Foundation interests are both in the front line defending the importance of the games and the benefits for the citizens and Edmonton. The campaign for the games in the March 1974 plebiscite was headed by the mayor (who threatened to resign if the plebiscite was defeated), some aldermen, other individual Foundation members and a newly formed organization named "Facilities for the Future."

"Facilities for the Future" was spearheaded by G. Lyall Rofer, who was one of the Foundation's directors. It was basically a front organization, an attempt to take the heat away from the city council and Hal Pawson, the executive director of the Foundation, and to create an illusion of citizens' support for the games. In reality, it was the same promoters wearing a different hat.

They ran a massive media campaign which was characterized by free-time allotments to the programme's spokesmen and little coverage or news for any opposition. Most TV and newspaper sports columns and many commentators during sports programmes emphasized the bargain the city was getting in building the "needed" facilities.

"Facilities for the Future" organized speakers to speak in public forums in support of the games, and distributed a leaflet called *Facilities for the Future and the 1978 Commonwealth Games*. The leaflet purported to ask and answer questions about the games. Some of the information was misleading and erroneous, as it left the impression that the facilities were already designed (questions 21 and 22), and that the city would only have to contribute $11.6-million toward the games.

The promoters did not discuss the experiences of other cities in North America with rising costs on similar projects or the likelihood that the city could well have to pay the unforeseen costs by contributions from general revenues or proposing another bylaw authorizing another borrowing, nor did they discuss the costs of related road construction and maintenance costs of the facilities in the years to come.

Opponents of the facilities prepared a publication: *The Games Council Plays: an inquiry into certain aspects of the XI British Commonwealth Games*, which did not get any coverage in the local newspaper, radio stations or television. It seems that the promoters learned their political lesson when they failed to get public support for the earlier Omniplex scheme, and this time they mounted a massive organizational campaign, overpowering the public.

The pro-development groups were very well-prepared and organized. They put the necessary work and money into ensuring that the citizens of Edmonton understood the issue from the promoters' point of view. By contrast, the group questioning the city's need for expensive "sports palaces" were badly disorganized. Disorganization, together with lack of experience and money, ensured their inability to open a debate on the question of facilities or to define the issues in terms of improving the average citizen's access to recreation facilities.

The results of the plebiscite, three-to-one in favour of the debenture, reflected the relative organization and energy of the opposing groups.

IMPACT STUDIES

A new group, Action Edmonton, got going right after the plebiscite result to oppose the stadium and to pressure city council to reconsider the proposed site. This marked a shift in focus from costs to location. The locations of the two major facilities were both debated. The proposed swimming pool location in the Saskatchewan river valley was fought — unsuccessfully — by city-wide groups (labour, environmental and valley watchdogs) concerned about the amount of recreation land to be lost to the pool and about the effects of access road construction. Most public debate, however, has

*The Games Council Plays - An inquiry into certain aspects of the XI British Commonwealth Games - Written by Winston Gereluk

FACILITIES For The FUTURE
And The
1978
COMMONWEALTH GAMES

1. WHAT ARE FACILITIES FOR THE FUTURE?

FACILITY	ESTIMATED COST	CITY'S SHARE
Stadium Complex	$22,835,000	$ 8,240,000
Aquatic Centre	$ 4,500,000	$ 1,624,000
Cycling Track	$ 660,000	$ 238,000
Shooting Range	$ 630,000	$ 227,000
Lawn Bowling Centre	$ 200,000	$ 72,000
Land Requirements	$ 1,800,000	$ 650,000
Facilities Upgrading	$ 1,520,000	$ 549,000
TOTALS	$32,145,000	$11,600,000

2. IS THE COLISEUM NOT PART OF THAT PROGRAM?
The 16,000-seat Coliseum now under construction by the Edmonton Exhibition Association is being financed separately by contributions from the Province of Alberta, the Government of Canada, the City of Edmonton (land only, approximately $1,000,000) and the Edmonton Exhibition Association.

3. WILL EXISTING FACILITIES BE USED FOR THE GAMES?
The Jubilee Auditorium will be the site for the weightlifting. Badminton will be staged at the Kinsmen Fieldhouse. Amateur Wrestling is scheduled for the Varsity Arena.

4. WHY ARE FUNDS NEEDED FOR FACILITIES UPGRADING?
The major portion of these funds will be used to bring such recreational facilities as Coronation Park,

the Jasper Place Arena, the South Side Athletic grounds and other grounds up to standards adequate for practice venues for the 2,500 athletes expected for the Games.

5. WHAT DOES THE BYLAW ASK?
Through the plebiscite to be held on March 20th, City Council is asking its taxpayers for approval to borrow by debentures up to a maximum of $11.6 million to pay its share of the facilities needed for the Games. It does not mean the City must spend that money.

6. WHAT IS THE CITY'S SHARE?
Up to one third of the total cost. The Province of Alberta has already agreed to contribute $11.6 million. The Government of Canada — through the Minister of Health, the Hon. Marc Lalonde — has said it will provide assistance, too, but has not committed itself to a figure expected to be at least one third.

7. HAS THE GAMES FOUNDATION ANY FINANCIAL RESPONSIBILITY?
Yes. It is the responsibility of the Foundation, a non-profit, volunteer group of citizens, to raise all capital funds required over and above the monies provided by The City, The Province and the Federal Government.

8. WHAT IS THE FOUNDATION?
All World Games are so constituted internationally that their operation cannot be in the control of any political body. Formation of such a group for the 1978 Games was approved by City Council on January 24th, 1972. It adheres to City Council's recommendation that it provide the necessary governmental representations and a wide cross-section of the community on its 36-chair board of directors.

9. HOW WILL THE FOUNDATION RAISE ITS FUNDS?
Lotteries, the sale of Games products such as pins, badges, mementos, clothing, the logo, coins, etc., corporate appeals and donations, television, concessions, programs, and tickets.

10. IF THE FOUNDATION EARNS A PROFIT, WHO GETS IT?
Any surplus realized by the Foundation will be applied against the capital costs as spelled out in a legal agreement between the City of Edmonton and the Foundation.

11. IF CONSTRUCTION COSTS EXCEED ESTIMATES, WHO PAYS THE DIFFERENCE?
Any deficit encountered in the construction of facilities must be met by the Foundation. By law, the City can not borrow more than the $11.6 million authorized by its taxpayers.

12. WHAT WILL THE BYLAW COST US?
The owner of a home with a market value of $30,000 - $35 000 will pay up to a maximum of $6.48 (or .71 mills) annually in City taxes for 25 years. That rate will not only pay off the loan and the interest, but will also meet the estimated maintenance and operating costs of the facilities.

13. WHAT ABOUT ALTERNATIVE FINANCING?
Once the plebiscite is passed, there is nothing to prevent the city from adopting short-term financing to pay back the funds over a five-year period. In that case, the cost to the taxpayer would be just under $12 a year over a five-year period as opposed to $6.48 for 25 years. However, if the plebiscite is defeated, this alternative does not exist as Edmontonians will have stated that they do not wish to pay their one-third share.

14. WHY CAN'T THE FUNDS BE RAISED BY LOTTERIES?
A major lottery will be held and it's estimated that the Foundation will raise $4,000,000 from it over the next four years. This and other Games revenue will exceed $7,000,000. That is $2,500,000 more than the total needed to operate the Games. This remainder — by legal agreement with the City — will be applied to the capital costs of the facilities.

15. WHAT ABOUT A COIN SALE?
Coins produced by Finland to finance the 1952 Olympics are now worth 32 times their face value. Coins issued for the summer and winter Olympics in Japan are 12 and 13 times their face value. And coins issued for the Munich Olympics in 1972 are three and one-half times their face value. Japan raised almost $200 million from the sale of its two Olympic coins; Munich $332 million. Montreal estimates that it will raise $250 million. Edmonton also is hopeful that the Federal Government will allow the Royal Mint to issue a coin in support of the 1978 Games. If permission is granted revenues from that coin sale will be applied against the

capital costs, and will finance all Games costs, capital and operating, without requiring tax money from any level of government.

16. IN VIEW OF THE POSSIBLE COIN SALE AND LOTTERY, WHY DO WE NEED TO PASS THE MONEY BYLAW?
The Government of Canada will not commit funds to the 1978 Games or consider the coin-financing option, until the citizens of Edmonton agree to contribute to the costs, on grounds that City Council asked for the Games and made promises up to $40,000,000. It therefore must show good faith by committing itself. As well, the Province of Alberta—which has already committed $11.6 million to the Games facilities—has indicated it will withdraw that support unless the City is prepared to commit itself to a share of the costs. The senior levels of government are not saying Edmonton must spend $11.6 million, but only that it must be prepared to spend up to that amount, if necessary.

17. WHO DECIDES WHERE THE FACILITIES ARE BUILT?
The legal agreement between the City of Edmonton and the Foundation states that the City shall determine the locations for the facilities.

18. WHO CONTROLS THE DESIGN AND CONSTRUCTION OF THE FACILITIES?
The same agreement states that this responsibility belongs to the City of Edmonton. The only string is that the facilities must provide international sports standards, for the Games sports.

19. WHO DETERMINES THOSE STANDARDS?
These are set by the international bodies governing each of the amateur sports. Each will send representatives to Edmonton during the next four and one-half years to ensure that their regulations are being met. The Foundation has no power in this matter, nor has the City.

20. WHO WILL USE THE FACILITIES AFTER THE GAMES?
As owner of the facilities, the City of Edmonton is the landlord and will determine the policies

covering the uses of them, and the rental fees that will apply to these new additions to the Edmonton Parks and Recreation inventory of City-owned facilities.

21. HOW WILL THE INDOOR/OUTDOOR STADIUM COMPLEX SERVE THE PUBLIC?
The most popular concept calls for a horseshoe-type stadium with a multi-purpose indoor structure or module enclosing the bottom of the horseshoe. The stadium will have from 30,000 to 40,000 seats, and will be large enough to accommodate a 400-metre international athletic track, permanently surfaced. The infield will consist of, natural turf, but funds are included in the budget to convert that to artificial turf after the Games to provide the City with an all-weather facility that can be used by all individuals and groups, both amateur and professional.

22. WHAT FACILITIES WILL BE INCLUDED IN THE INDOOR STRUCTURE OR MODULE?
The concept of the complex is dedicated to multi-use made possible in modern planning and construction technology. The indoor module will be designed to include an indoor track, courts for racquet-ball, squash, badminton and handball; rooms for gymnastics, amateur wrestling, weightlifting and boxing. Add to that, support facilities such as steam rooms, saunas, showers, change rooms, and medical/health rooms. Uncommited areas beneath the stands allow wide use by sports requiring lengthy space.

23. WHAT IS AN AQUATIC CENTRE?
The facility planned for the 1978 Commonwealth Games was selected after an exhaustive study of other similar centres across Canada. It will house a 50-metre competitive pool. A separate diving tank will also serve as a competitive area for such sports as water polo and synchronizing swimming. The centre is designed to attract the experienced and competitive swimmers, opening up more time in the district pools for neighborhood use.

24. IS THE AQUATIC CENTRE ONLY DESIGNED FOR THE ELITE?
The facility also includes two warm-up pools, one which will fulfill a general community use after the Games, the other which will serve pre-school and paraplegic swimming programs.

25. WHAT ADVANTAGE IS THERE TO BUILDING THESE FACILITIES NOW?
Most people will agree that as the City of Edmonton grows, a new stadium and an aquatic centre will be required — if not two or three years from now, then five or six years down the road. The City's Parks and Recreation department has already had pressure from amateur sports groups to provide an Aquatic Centre, an expanded lawn bowling facility with a clubhouse which could also serve local cricket clubs, and an all-round unit to serve all types of shooting clubs. At a later date — and without the Games — the City will be required to build such facilities at the full cost to the taxpayers and without senior government assistance.

26. CAN THE SITES ALREADY PROPOSED BE CHANGED?
The plebiscite does not dictate where the facilities must be built. City Council is not bound to any location and is free to change any site it has already accepted in principle. These include the area north of Clarke Stadium for the indoor/outdoor stadium complex, Kinsmen Park for the aquatic centre and Coronation Park for the lawn bowling green. The sites for the cycling track and the shooting range have not been selected.

27. WHO CAN VOTE?
Any person, renter or property owner, 18 years of age or over, who is a Canadian citizen or British subject and who has been a resident of the City of Edmonton for one year prior to 1974.

28. WHAT DAY DO YOU VOTE?
March 20th, with polls open from 10 a.m. until 8 p.m.

Advance Polls:
March 13th and 14th, 5 p.m. to 9 p.m.
March 15th and 16th, 1 p.m. to 9 p.m.
Main Floor, City Hall

We Want Facilities For The Future —
VOTE YES

For factual information phone Facilities for the Future — 488-4831.

The Facilities for the Future pamphlet, used by a front organization (established to create the illusion of citizen support for Edmonton's Commonwealth Games) to persuade voters to vote yes.

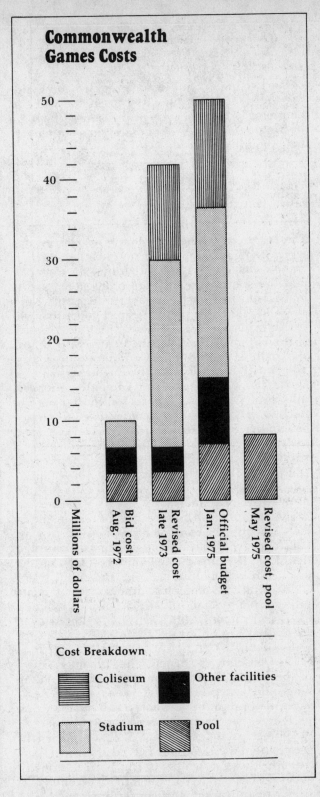

Commonwealth Games Costs

Millions of dollars

- 50
- 40
- 30
- 20
- 10
- 0

Bid cost
Aug. 1972

Revised cost
late 1973

Official budget
Jan. 1975

Revised cost, pool
May 1975

Cost Breakdown

Coliseum   Other facilities

Stadium   Pool

centred on the proposed site of the stadium.

In June 1974, Action Edmonton presented to council a petition signed by 1,600 people opposing the site. The neighbouring older residential areas are relatively low-cost ones, accommodating high percentages of older people and low-income families, and include Edmonton's Chinese resi-dential area and an Italian neighbourhood. In September 1974, council asked the Commission Board to advise as to whether it was necessary to have a social impact study as requested by the citizens. The Commission Board waited two months to report and gave their negative report to a newly elected council at their first meeting. (The Commission Board strongly supported the games; Commissioner Hughes is one of the directors of the Foundation. Some suggest they sat on the recommendation for two reasons: (1) the longer they waited, the less likelihood there would be for any reversal of plans, and (2) it was thought to be less likely that a new council would oppose the Commission Board Recommendations.)

However, council disregarded the Commission Board's recommendation not to have a social impact study and granted $4,000 to Action Edmonton and $10,000 and $15,000 to another consultant, L. J. D'Amore and Associates. It is interesting to note that the frame of reference to D'Amore's study was not to evaluate alternative stadium sites but to present recommendations of ways to minimize its negative social impact.

The two studies were due in February 1975. But in January 1975, without waiting for the reports, the council decided to reconfirm the Clark Stadium site without the information gathered by the two studies. The decision to uphold the Clark Stadium produced an even split in council.

According to the stadium impact report commissioned by Action Edmonton, municipal investments in the area will create the climate and infrastructure which will make further private redevelopment profitable. This redevelopment will largely transform the nature and character of the area, replacing the present human-scale communities with intensive high-density housing. Some of the consequences of locating on the proposed site were identified as:

1. increasing traffic densities substantially in the area and lead to pressures for further roadway expansions in addition to those already planned;
2. creating substantially increased parking congestion;
3. increasing noise, air and visual pollution;
4. increasing traffic danger to pedestrians, especially children and senior citizens;
5. reducing low-density and single-family housing stocks;
6. reducing the already short supply of lower-income housing available within the area and city, creating considerable financial difficulties for low-income persons who cannot afford to move to higher-priced area and accommodation;
7. up-zoning of many properties;
8. displacing a large proportion of present residents from the area with a very low probability

TOTAL DEPLETION BY NEIGHBOURHOOD

AREA	HOUSES	APARTMENTS	OTHER
McCauley	45	—	4
Norwood			
Parkdale	186-214	8	31
Cromdale	189	800	1
Eastwood	190	—	2
Bellevue	157	—	1
TOTAL	767-795	808	39

Total housing units lost: 1575-1603

NOTE:

This table was recalculated from information presented in tables on pages 153-156 of the impact study done by L. J. D'Amore & Associates Ltd. The report's tables lack internal consistency and do not agree with one another. The above table is a fair representation of the report's information, and is neither the highest nor lowest total presented.

of their return to the area after redevelopment has occurred. The elderly, ethnic groups and others with low income would be particularly affected;

9. increasing stress and withdrawal for individuals;

10. increase municipal expenditures for roadway expansions, welfare, police protection, public housing and social service costs;

11. cause ethnic cultures and communities in the area to become disorganized and "fragmented";

12. reduce the diversity presently available within the area and the benefit this diversity contributes to Edmonton's urban life:

The D'Amore study calculates the number of housing units to be demolished to accommodate the development of the stadium and other municipal investments.

The D'Amore study continued:

With an average of approximately 4 persons per dwelling, as indicated in the 1971 census, this means that some 6,000 persons will be dislocated.

Someone might argue that there would be a balancing or possibly even a net gain by the high density residential units which are developed on 112 and 118 Avenue. However, the problem for the displaced families will not be resolved by this type of development. They will not be able to afford the rents, nor will the apartment units be large enough to accommodate many of the families displaced.

This study concluded that cumulative primary impacts will destroy or change the character of several communities:

Cromdale will cease to exist as an identifiable community. The Parkdale community will undergo substantial change and it is questionable whether its identity will be retained.

There will be increased migration into McCauley of persons whose values, life styles and behaviour are not compatible with the values, life styles and behaviour of the predominantly immigrant population of McCauley.

The two impact studies are in agreement: building the stadium on the city-chosen site will add enormously to development pressures which are destroying several of Edmonton's inner-city neighbourhoods.

WHO BENEFITS?

The promoters of the games represent the groups which benefit the most from the facilities and their spinoff effects. It is not surprising, for example, that the sports elite and the professional sports lobby launched such a heavy propaganda campaign in selling the public a bag of goods that will basically be used for their own interests.

The Kinsman Park Aquatic Centre, which consists of three pools built to Olympic requirements, will benefit mostly competitive swimmers and the University of Alberta. The Edmonton proposal calls for an Olympic pool of six feet constant depth. Such a pool cannot accommodate children's swimming or swimming lessons. New Zealand built an Olympic pool for the games which has a varying depth, and can be used by the public generally. In spite of this option, the $4.5-million Edmonton pool will be designed to service just the competitive swimmers.

The stadium will benefit mostly the businessmen who own the Edmonton Eskimos. Norm Kimball, manager of the Edmonton Eskimos, has stated that if the Eskimos did not get their stadium, the organization would have to fold. The public sector is financing a $23-million stadium to accommodate professional football under the guise of building for the Commonwealth Games — without even presenting the option of a minimal stadium for $3.5-million.

The Coliseum also benefits the Edmonton Oilers of the World Hockey Association. The shooting range and lawn bowling will be operated on a private club basis after the games, and by definition will serve their own members.

Another group of promoters that will benefit greatly from the games are city businessmen, particularly those downtown. The tourist industry needs special services in the form of accommodation, restaurants and entertainment. The Foundation's public relations release estimates that $50 million will be spent in Edmonton because of, and during, the 21-day training and games period. This will most directly benefit hotels, restaurants and downtown stores, but presumably there will be spinoff benefits to others in the city as well. Whether these one-shot benefits to others will outweigh the on-going costs of maintaining and paying for the games facilities has never been analysed.

The construction industry may also benefit, but this case is not so clear. It would benefit as much if the same money were spent on other public facilites, and there are already shortages of skilled labour in the local construction industry, before the start of construction of the facilities for the games. It is possible, though, that the games' construction projects could be unusually profitable for their contractors. It has been rumoured that the stadium contract, for instance will not be tendered.

WHO LOSES?

The people of Edmonton are the real losers from the Commonwealth Games. They lose in the price that must be paid for facilities most of them will not be able to use. The citizens of Edmonton pay far more than the alleged $11.6-million city share of the games. Provincial and federal grants are not, in the final analysis, free money. The city also is donating parkland for games facilities and has committed itself to the finishing of the structures with more facilities after the games.

The residents of Edmonton also lose because other services will be under-financed due to this massive expenditure. Money is in limited supply, and when sports palaces get priority over, say, small-scale decentralized sports facilities, it is unlikely that the others will be built. Moreover, when citizens in the future discover the extent of the deception in the games financing, the "can do" spirit will, as *Fortune* predicts, likely become undermined by bitterness and mistrust, undercutting

the city's ability to finance other more important projects — such as extending the rapid transit system.

The taxpayers of Edmonton are also likely to lose because of long-term commitments to the maintenance of the facilities and the probability of a deficit. If past experience is any guide, the rent the Edmonton Eskimos contribute will not even pay for the maintenance of the stadium. Both the coliseum and the stadium are expected to incur continuing deficits.

More direct losers in these games are the residents of the Boyle Street, McCauley, Norwood, Parkdale, Cromdale, Eastwood, and Bellevue communities, which are adjacent to the stadium and the nearby coliseum. These communities are already threatened by the expansion of downtown, rapid transit stations and the modification and expansion of roadways. The addition of the major stadium can only make their future even more uncertain.

With decision-making at city hall in the hands of spokesmen for business interests, and with the powerful combination of the sports and commercial elites who have so much to gain, it is hardly surprising that Edmonton's Commonwealth Games should turn out to sacrifice the interests of ordinary Edmonton residents. This may not reflect the non-competitive, low-cost tradition of the games, but it accurately portrays how things are traditionally done in Edmonton's city hall.

V Urban policy

Saskatoon robs the bank

John Piper

Saskatoon's municipal land bank has always been held up as a shining example of how government involvement in land assembly can be a practical and effective means of reducing housing costs. In the nineteen sixties, the Hellyer Task Force on Housing cited Saskatoon as a 'positive instance' where 'municipal government has been able to provide land for private development at reasonable prices while at the same time planning the development pattern in a comprehensive sense.' As land prices and housing costs have skyrocketed across Canada in the last few years, the Saskatoon example has been cited time and time again both by urban experts and by the media. Writes Boyce Richardson, for instance, in his book *The Future of Canadian Cities*: 'Undoubtedly municipal land development in Saskatoon has been as sophisticated as in many parts of Europe.'

Saskatoon has revelled in its national notoriety. In 1971 the City planning department paid Don Ravis to write an eulogy to the scheme (reviewed in the preview issue of *City Magazine*). And in July 1974 the City sent Bert Wellman, its director of planning and development, to the TPIC convention in Quebec to reiterate Ravis' views. Recently a full-page story in the Saskatoon *Star-Phoenix* has hurled more accolades at the City land bank, 'the best and most successful in Canada.'

But a close examination of the way Saskatoon's land bank functions reveals that most of the claims made for it simply don't hold up. Housing costs are not reduced; land prices are not lower than in comparable cities where speculation and the private market function unhindered; developers' profits do not seem to be reduced and may even be enhanced by the operation of the land bank; and city planners do not use their planning powers to produce a different pattern of urban growth.

SASKATOON COMPARED

The evidence usually used to support the argument that Saskatoon's land policy is the 'best' is a comparison of land prices in Saskatoon to those in Re-

gina, Winnipeg, Toronto and other metropolitan areas, all of which have higher land prices than Saskatoon. But such a comparison is like comparing an acorn to an oak. Of the 22 census metropolitan areas in Canada, Saskatoon is third smallest (with a population of 126,000 in 1971) and has the fourth lowest rate of growth (with a 9 per cent increase in population between 1966 and 1971).

If land prices in Saskatoon are compared to land prices in smaller cities as well as those in larger metropolitan areas, then the myth of Saskatoon's progressive policies is shattered. For example, within Saskatchewan, Moose Jaw, Prince Albert and all the other smaller cities have land prices lower than Saskatoon. To compare the prices of land in different cities without reference to their sizes, rates of growth, and economics, is to ignore the very factors which determine land prices.

The price of a lot is determined by (1) the cost of servicing, (2) the degree of monopoly or competition in the land market, and (3) the demand for land. These three factors are all subject to variation from one region to another. For example, it costs more to service a lot in Sudbury on the shield than in Saskatoon on the prairie. There can be quantum jumps in the level of demand from region to region due to differences in income levels and because of variation in the age of towns which in turn affects the mix of first and second generation house building.

Within a region, e.g. the Canadian west, the cost of servicing and the degree of monopoly in the land market are probably similar from one town to the next. The demand for lots, however, will vary with the size, rate of growth, and general level of economic activity of different cities. Other things being equal, the number of housing starts is probably a fair indicator of the pressure of demand.

CMHC data for Canadian cities serves to support this analysis. In the accompanying graph, the average cost of lots and the number of housing starts in each of seven western Canadian cities are plotted. The seven cities—Moose Jaw, Saskatoon, Regina, Winnipeg, Edmonton, Calgary, and Vancouver —all have similar market structures and costs for servicing lots; but demand varies radically between the cities, primarily due to differences in their sizes. The graph shows a clear relationship between the demand for lots, as expressed by the number of housing starts, and the cost of lots for these western Canadian cities. Saskatoon is not exceptional; it merely has a lower demand for lots than do other metropolitan areas.

The conclusion is obvious: Saskatoon's land policy does not lower the cost of lots to the consumer. Further scrutiny of the land policy shows why Saskatoon does not have lower lot costs. Almost all developed lots in the City are privately owned so City land policy has minimal influence over the purchase price of old houses. As for new houses, Saskatoon's land policy forces most people to buy undeveloped lots from private firms. Of the 1150 lots sold in 1973, only 750 came from the City land bank and of those 750 lots, 625 were sold to private developers or contractors. In other words only 125, or 11 per cent of all lots bought in Saskatoon were sold by the City directly to individuals. Accordingly the City set the final price on only a small proportion of the lots sold, too few to set the general price of land.

DEVELOPERS' BANK

Ravis points out that the City makes no attempt to exercise a monopoly power; 'expropriation powers have never been used by the municipality to acquire assembled land; all land acquired to date has been purchased in the competitive land market by officials representing the municipality.' The private developers in Saskatoon are mostly small-time indigenous capitalists, Lou Churchill of Centre Developments, Harry Koehn of Plainsman Developments, Mike Boychuk of Boychuck Construction (Sask.) Ltd. Some larger Canadian and foreign corporations, Embassy, Trizec, Canway, Canarama, are also active though usually on a single development basis. For these developers who choose to speculate on land, the City will offer little opposition, and it may openly assist developers in acquiring land.

In July 1974, Mayor Bert Sears acknowledged that the City frequently pays local real estate firms substantial commissions for negotiating land purchases for the City. The City's latest land acquisition, 427 acres for residential development to the north of the City beside the South Saskatchewan River, was negotiated by Plainsman Developments Ltd. Plainsman is a small development firm owned by Harry Koehn and Walter Botting through their corporate identities Rycon and Land Ltd. and WAB Holdings. During the summer, after Plainsman had negotiated the purchase of 503 acres from Mrs. F. Lawson of Vancouver, Harry Koehn approached the City's planning and development committee to

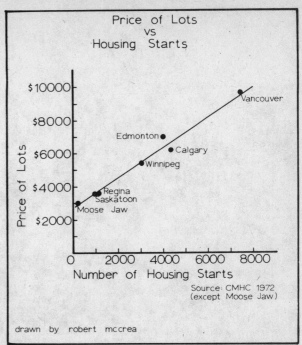

Price of Lots vs Housing Starts

Source: CMHC 1972 (except Moose Jaw)

drawn by robert mccrea

'avoid competition.' Plainsman arranged for the City to purchase 85 per cent of the 503 acres, and they the remaining 15 per cent of 76 acres, at a price of $1425 per acre. In addition the City agreed to pay a 6 per cent commission, $36,000, to Plainsman.

As the result of the deal Plainsman has hit the big time. Without making any cash outlay, Plainsman's commission will pay their share of the down payment and any interest charges on the remainder. As well Plainsman has secured enough land for 300 lots and the guaranteed co-operation of the City.

By far the largest private developer in the City is Mike Boychuk. Boychuk, his wife, or his company own over 1300 acres in the Rural Municipality of Corman Park which surrounds Saskatoon. One official in the City assessor's department recently commented: 'Mr. Boychuk is buying land so fast on the fringes of the City it isn't funny. Soon he'll have enough to control the price.' Most remarkably a large portion of his holdings are within the areas scheduled for immediate development by the Community Planning Scheme of 1966 as can be seen on the map. Boychuk, like the other developers, had early access to the community plan and used his knowledge to make astute land purchases.

Although Boychuk is heavily into land, many local construction and development firms have chosen to stay out of the land speculation business. Even Cairns Homes (1972), one of the largest builders in Saskatoon and probably the largest speculator in Regina, owns almost no land around Saskatoon. By default the City does control about 65 per cent of the land held for development in the foreseeable future. The reason for the inactivity of most private speculators is that the City land bank is admirably suited to the needs and profits of developers.

Saskatoon's land bank has been consciously used as a method of segregating people by income. Above: houses in the Confederation Park development on the west side of the city, where lot frontages vary from 37 to 42 feet. On the opposite page: houses in the College Park development on the east side of Saskatoon, with frontages of 55 to 60 feet.

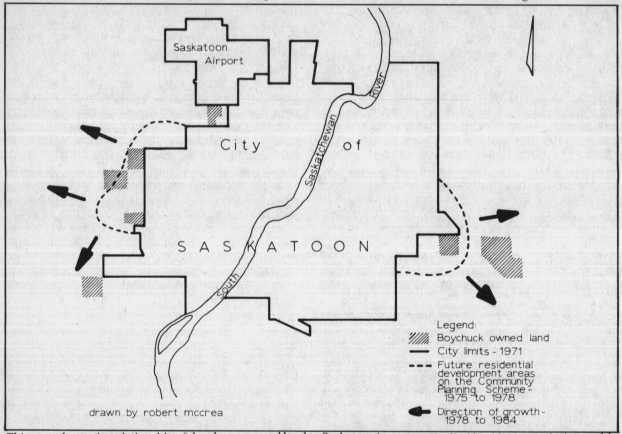

Legend:
////// Boychuck owned land
——— City limits - 1971
- - - Future residential development areas on the Community Planning Scheme - 1975 to 1978
➤ Direction of growth - 1978 to 1984

drawn by robert mccrea

This map shows the relationship of developer-owned land to Saskatoon's present city limits and to areas designated for future residential growth by city planners.

The land bank has always been set up to operate in the interests of developers. During the late nineteen forties contractors were offered land for one half the listed price 'to encourage large scale development.' Now the City offers favourable credit terms which allow up to eight months to pay and low interest charges. Most important the City exercises no control over the resale of land to house buyers.

Private building firms account for the majority, 83 per cent in 1973, of City land bank sales. Each year local builders are advised of the lots available and then given the opportunity to apply for them. The planning and development committee of council then makes an 'equitable division' of the land, in the same way that taxi licences are distributed. The biggest contractors are given the most lots, and the smallest are given the fewest.

The allocation system works against individual house buyers. In 1973 the City had only 125 lots on sale to the public. During much of 1974 there was a waiting list for land. In March of that year only one lot was up for sale, in August no lots. In Saskatoon the land raffle has become part of the adventure of house buying. People who are unsuccessful at the raffle have no choice but to go to a private building firm to buy a lot. Then of course they have a very very narrow choice of contractors.

Because the City doesn't control the resale price of lots (or the final price of houses) house builders charge the regular market price for land and pocket the windfall profits. A developer once challenged on local radio about the large mark-up in the price of a lot quipped, 'Then we can charge less for the house.' Needless to say, developers know how to shift profits as well as how to extract them.

Ravis argues that 'land purchase is a useful technique for plan implementation and planning is a useful technique in the acquisition process.' He omitted to say that given the fraternal relationship of city hall planners and local developers, the Saskatoon policy is more useful to private developers than the public. City land purchases assist developers to make the big time as in the case of Plainsman. City purchases save developers the cost of land investment by performing this function as a service to them. And public planning identifies the areas for future development as a guide to speculative purchases as seen with Boychuk.

THE SIDE EFFECTS

In much of the land bank's publicity, especially in Sidney Buckwold's article in *Habitat*, many side benefits have been attributed to it (e.g. eliminating leap-frog developments, allowing large replotting schemes, facilitating low-cost housing). Most of these claims are entirely spurious. Admittedly ownership provides a straightforward access to control, but in the absence of an innovative council or planning department, ownership has not been used to accomplish anything normally outside the reach of planning and subdivision regulations. There are, however, two real side effects to the land bank which have not received any attention. Firstly, the City has consciously used the land bank as a means of segregating rich and poor. Over the past five years the City has developed two areas simultaneously, College Park in the east and Confederation Park in the west. From Ravis comes the comment that College Park was intended to 'provide land for those people wishing to build more expensive dwellings in a somewhat exclusive neighbourhood.' Confederation Park was developed for low- and middle-income families. In College Park, land prices were $25 per foot frontage, and lots were 50 to 55 feet wide. In Confederation Park prices were $15 per foot frontage, and lots were 40 to 50 feet wide. The system works well. Time has shown that College Park has been kept a preserve for the rich.

The same process takes place in a laissez-faire manner in all Canadian cities. What makes Saskatoon unique is the large scale concerted effort by the municipality through which segregation is achieved.

Secondly, there are convincing arguments that the land bank improves the profitability of local development firms. The City profiteers through land speculation, but it is restrained profiteering since the City does sell land at below the market price. Consequently, developers who get lots from the City are then able to charge the full market price and collect the 'profit slack.' While the absolute profits of the developers are not as high as if they held the land from start to finish, the length of their investment is shortened and hence their rate of profit rises dramatically.

As a hypothetical example with a basis in fact, suppose the City purchases land now for $2,000 per acre, i.e. $10 per front foot, which is the going price for land five to six years from development. Five years hence, ignoring interest and inflation which should cancel out, the City will sell the land for $25 per foot frontage, realizing a profit of 150 per cent over five years, or *20 per cent* per year compounded. Again ignoring interest and inflation, a developer who buys land from the City and constructs a house over the period of a year will be able to resell the land for the market price of $40 per front foot, realizing an impressive profit of *60 per cent* per year. By comparison if, instead of the City, the private developer bought the land for $10 per foot frontage, held it for six years, and sold for $40, the developer's rate of profit would have been only 26 per cent per year. Clearly, by restraining public speculation, the City can allow superprofits to accrue to developers.

The best testament to the compatibility of the land bank with the interests of developers is given by the developers themselves. Stories in the Saskatoon *Star-Phoenix* testify to the fact that the City's three largest land developers have always 'welcomed city council's move to purchase more land.' The City land bank is like profits held in trust for the developers.

WHAT THEN?

What is needed to really control land prices and land use is a comprehensive policy of public ownership by the City of all urban land. Such a policy would immediately put an end to land speculation and profiteering, reduce the capital cost of housing, provide a powerful planning tool, ensure that any rents accrue collectively to the people of Saskatoon, and provide an additional tool for the redistribution and equalization of income.

How should public land ownership be brought in? There are many options open, and which one is the best is debatable. One possibility is the following: in place of titles, all land-holders could be given a long term lease from the city, existing owners would pay zero rent and new owners would pay a rent determined by the use of the land and the income of the lessee. All leases would only be transferable to or from the City, and any leaseholder leaving the city before his lease had expired would be reimbursed according to the portion of the lease outstanding. Under this scheme, home-owners would continue to own their own homes and have the security of a long term lease on the land, but individuals and corporations would no longer be able to accumulate land with a view to making a speculative profit. In the meantime, a duplication of Saskatoon's land bank policy offers no solution to the supply or cost of urban land. Over the past 10 years Saskatoon, Hellyer and Co. have done a good job of putting on the con, but the current Saskatoon evidence shows the land bank for the sham it is.

The OMB:
Citizens as losers

Bruce McKenna

For citizen groups all across Ontario, there is always one last consolation when a strong, well-based, carefully-argued, and fundamentally just objection has been ignored by a local council intent on expressway building, demolition, sale of the city hall to Eaton's, rezoning for a local developer, or any of the other major decisions which city politicians are continually making in spite of public protests. Their consolation is the OMB. The Ontario Municipal Board, a quasi-judicial body appointed by the Ontario government to review the decisions of local governments involving planning, zoning, capital expenditures and a number of other matters, is the losing citizens' second chance. In spite of the difficulties and often the high costs involved in finding a lawyer to take their case to the OMB, many citizen groups are convinced enough of the justice of their case or anxious enough to have a delay to go to the OMB. In other provinces with similar review boards, the same route is often used.

What are their chances of success? How fair a hearing can they expect? What are the principles which determine the outcome of OMB hearings?

Thanks mainly to the strong public image and occasional anti-establishment decision, crusty old Joe Kennedy, OMB chairman for many years until his retirement in October 1972, gave the OMB a good reputation among citizen groups. Under Kennedy's regime they certainly didn't always win; but they didn't always lose. With hard-line right-wing developers' pals in office in city halls across the province, the occasional OMB victory — and some of them were very important — looked good to many people.

It seemed clear that the Ontario cabinet and their many friends in the land development industry wanted a somewhat different approach from Kennedy's successor. They selected William H. Palmer, a former deputy minister of municipal affairs, to take over. Palmer's personal politics were presumably well known to his political-mentors, and he knew exactly what the province's overall policies towards planning and local politics were. When Palmer arrived, he made it clear that he planned a change from Kennedy's approach of openly challenging some municipal decisions. Palmer had been appointed, reported the *Globe and Mail*, "to pull the Board back from open combat with civic politicians."

What that amounted to, and what the real politics of the OMB are, can be seen in an analysis of all the cases heard by the board in 1973. There were about 480 in all, of which 135 dealt with issues which pitted citizen groups against developers or city councils or both. Each of the decisions was read; and cases involving citizens and citizen groups identified. Based on the facts of the case as reported in the written decisions, a subjective determination was made about where the citizen interest lay and who emerged as the victor. A careful evaluation of these 135 cases indicates clearly that the OMB is a tool of provincial policy, and that in spite of its semi-judicial atmosphere and its practices of taking evidence which seem to resemble an impartial court of law, it is performing the job of keeping citizens in their place and implementing the pro-development, pro-developer, pro-centralization policies of the Ontario government.

The success rate of citizens in cases before the OMB gives a clear indication of this tendency. Of the 135 cases analyzed, the overall success rate of citizen groups was 40 per cent. Breaking down the cases by their importance, however, a very clear pattern emerges. On cases of very minor importance, 23 in 1973, citizens won 16, or 69 per cent. And in the 29 cases of major municipality-wide importance, citizens won only six, a success rate of

The OMB's political principles

Reviewing the 135 cases involving citizens before the OMB in 1973, ten leading principles which are constantly used to justify the OMB's decisions emerge. These, better than anything else, give an indication of the board's basic attitude towards development, planning and citizen groups. And they are helpful for predicting the outcome of an OMB case.

(1) *Narrow the issue.* When J. A. Kennedy was OMB chairman, he often seemed to encourage a broad view of the issues which came before the board, and was prepared to hear evidence on every aspect and implication of the matter the board was to decide. W. H. Palmer's attitude to this approach can be seen in his complaint that when he took the job "he found board members listening to 'days and days of stuff' over which the board has no jurisdiction. Now the board is constantly trying to narrow down the issue it has before it, to limit it as much as possible."

Thus for instance in a case involving a Brantford bylaw which eliminated a setback requirement for a downtown development occupying a full city block to which there were fundamental planning objections, the board focussed entirely on the setback matter and ignored the larger issues about the development itself (*re Brantford Restricted Area Bylaw 55-73*). In another case involving a storage building in a scrap yard, the board did not face the question of whether the yard should be allowed to replace its building and hence continue indefinitely. They narrowed down their attention to the neat legal question of whether the storage building was a physical extension of the yard or a variation from the previously-existing non-conforming use (*re Ricco et al*). This approach of narrowing and limiting the issue speeds up OMB hearings and makes it easier to ignore fundamental objections raised by citizen groups.

(2) *Decide on technicalities.* Another way of achieving this same result of speeding things up and avoiding major issues is to allow the outcome of hearings to be determined by technicalities. The best example of this is a Toronto ratepayers' group objection to a developer which the developer challenged by arguing that the association, as an unincorporated body, was not a legal "person" and thus had no standing to appeal to the board. Not only was this argument upheld; the board went on to refuse to allow officers of the group to add themselves as individuals to their objection because it

W. H. Palmer, Chairman of the OMB.

OMB members decision record, 1973

Member	Decides		Assists		Total		
	W	L	W	L	W	L	%
Jamieson	9	4	1	2	10	6	63%
Blake	8	5	1	2	9	7	56%
Speigel	5	4	4	4	9	8	53%
Van Every	4	3	1	2	5	5	50%
Arrell	5	6	-	1	5	7	42%
Roberts	1	3	1	-	2	3	40%
Smith	5	8	2	3	7	11	39%
McCrae	6	9	-	1	6	10	38%
Shrives	4	6	1	3	5	9	36%
Colbourne	3	12	3	3	6	15	29%
Shub	1	5	1	1	2	6	25%
McGuire	1	6	1	-	2	6	25%
Lancaster	3	7	1	5	4	12	25%
Thompson	-	2	-	1	-	3	0%

W - citizen wins   L - citizen losses
% - percentage citizen wins
Decides - Author of deciding opinion
Assists - Concurring in deciding opinion

The old city hall in Brantford, torn down for a downtown development following OMB approval.   Photo: The Brantford Expositor.

The site of Brantford' old city hall, now a parking lot.   Photo: The Brantford Expositor.

"cannot amend a nullity by permitting a new application." (*Bedford Park Homeowners Association v Davmark Developments*). While offering developers and municipal councils a nice way to avoid citizen groups in some situations, the board's willingness to decide matters on technicalities has occasionally been used by citizens and their lawyers (*Sussex-Ulster Residents' Association v General Investments*).

(3) *Reliance on experts.* The board often uses the testimony of experts as justification for its decisions. This works against citizen groups in a number of ways. First, it means that when people raise ordinary common-sense objections to projects up for board approval, their evidence and analysis may well be ignored unless it is supported by expensive and hard-to-get expert advice (*re Kincardine Restricted Area Bylaw 2242*). Second, when citizen groups do have experts they often cannot afford to pay for the same kind of time as experts on the other side would devote to learning about the case. In a Vaughan Township case involving a new subdivision, for example, the citizen group's planner had his evidence discounted because he had not had an opportunity to survey the site, no doubt because the group couldn't afford to pay for both the hearing and such investigation (*re Vaughan Restricted Area Bylaw S2-73*).

The third problem about relying on expert testimony is the obvious one that experts in the pay of wealthier parties like municipalities and developers can be expected to bend their expertise in the direction their employers wish. A classic example of this was the Metro Toronto council decision on routes for the Spadina subway. Many of the transit experts had argued for a route different from the one along the Spadina expressway right-of-way which Metro council selected, but changed their opinion soon enough to testify in favour of the Metro route and against routes they had previously supported. Turning this expert about-face into a curious virtue, the board in its decision said: "The board is satisfied that their evidence is quite to the point in this regard and their changed position merely substantiates the need and expediency of the subject application which it reinforces" (*re Spadina Subway*).

(4) *Support for provincial government policies and decisions.* As a creation of the provincial government, and with a former deputy minister of municipal affairs at its head, the OMB might be expected to fall quickly in line with provincial policies and to expedite matters in which the province has an interest. The province is a shadowy figure behind many OMB matters (like the controversial decisions on the Spadina subway and expressway, for example) but sometimes its involvement is clearly seen and explicit, as for instance with municipal

West St. James Town in Toronto. Photo: Charlotte Sykes.

plans for sewage and water works which are in fact prepared by the Ministry of the Environment. Explicit involvement appears to lead the board to approve what the province wants, and provincial commitments to controversial projects are often used as justifications for OMB decisions in favour of them. This came up, for instance, in a decision about a Thunder Bay downtown urban renewal project where land designated as a parking lot became a two-storey parking structure on top of which a private developer was being allowed to develop a shopping mall. There were many strong objections from a citizens' association which argued that the developer had been improperly chosen, and that other business interests were being prejudiced by the city's close relationship and support for this developer (*re Thunder Bay Parking Structure; re Thunder Bay Redevelopment Plan*). In its decision the board emphasized that all three levels of government had approved this scheme as part of an urban renewal plan.

(5) *Faith in the good government of municipal councils.* As the body which gets to review hundreds of municipal council decisions every year which citizens object to, the OMB might be expected to have a realistic sense of how local governments operate, how they bend to development

interests, and how they often ignore legitimate citizen interests to do favours for their friends. But there is not a hint of this in OMB decisions; and in fact the board often uses its professed faith in the wisdom and representativeness of local government as an excuse for overriding a citizen objection which has demonstrated the absence of those qualities.

In an annexation case, for example, cottagers of Loon Lake objected to a takeover by the Township of Shuniah on the grounds that they had successfully protected the lake against "undesirable" development and pollution. The board accepted the cottagers' achievement but allowed the township to annex the area, on the grounds that this was necessary in order to allow "proper" planning and controls (re Township of Shuniah Application for Annexation).

In another case involving the town of Richmond Hill north of Toronto, the municipality sought approval for a bylaw which dropped the height restriction along Yonge Street which had been in the previous bylaw. A citizen protester got the board to agree that the height control was essential to the preservation of the character of the town, but rather than requiring that the existing maximum be included in the new bylaw the board told the council that they had to include a height restriction — but the only specification laid down was that it could not be *lower* than the previously-imposed limit. It could be as high as the council wanted. And this was laid down to a council which had already expressed a desire to remove the height restrictions entirely (re Richmond Hill Restricted Area Bylaw 66-71).

(6) *Hostility to citizen groups.* The board's expressed faith in local councils is paralleled by its lack of faith in citizen groups. One astonishing example of this involves a new sewer system proposed for the town of Ancaster. The ratepayers group had a membership of 1,000 in a township with a total population of 11,600. The group showed a remarkable sense of realism when it decided that the effective way of preventing development is prevention of the installation of a sewage system that would make development possible. In its decision the board was flowery in its praise of the group. "The formation and perfection of an organization of about 1,000 members (in a township of 11,600) in less than one year, so constituted that the association was able to introduce the finest of expertise available, is testimony to the strength of a popular movement that could help substantially to shape the future of the municipality." But instead of permitting this to happen by refusing to approve the sewage system, or by calling for a referendum on the matter, the board approved the sewage system and told the citizen group that it would be able to

participate in the planning process. "It would seem incredible if the ratepayers would not play a prominent role in any future planning." But of course with the sewage system installed the real planning decisions were taken, a fact everyone involved no doubt understood very well (re Township of Ancaster Sewerage Application).

The board had no hesitation in expressing its hostility to organized citizens in a decision of the very controversial West St. Jamestown high-rise apartment redevelopment project in Toronto. The group of residents and former residents of the low-rent housing located on the site was attacked and contrasted with the 10,000 residents of the next-door high-rise complex who the board ingenuously described as "those people most directly affected." Correspondence from these tenants in favour of an extension of their project was cited favourably, and contrasted with the "widespread dissemination by vociferous and active groups of their position in opposition to this application." The residents' group opposing the project was criticized for its community organizer who, said the decision, "appeared to the board to be not only the motivating force behind the opposition by this organization, but it could almost be said that he was the organization itself."

Also opposing the project was CORRA, the city-wide organization of Toronto residents and ratepayers groups. CORRA was also attacked in the decision. Interestingly enough, one of the two board members on this hearing was W. J. H. Thompson whose 1973 record was limited to three hearings but who decided against citizen groups in all three cases (re Toronto Restricted Area Bylaw 258-71).

(7) *Give developers and municipalities a second chance.* If a developer loses at the OMB, nothing prevents him from making a few changes in his project, getting municipal approval for the new project, and taking it to the OMB again. This was recognized as undesirable in one case in 1973 (re Kitchener Restricted Area Bylaw 7474) but during the year there were many instances where municipalities were given a second chance by the OMB, often being sent away to gather enough evidence so that the board would have grounds to approve their request. When residents of the village of Alfred objected to a sewage system on the grounds that it was expensive and unnecessary, the municipality was sent away to prepare documentation to answer these objections, and when the documentation was received the project was approved (re Village of Alfred and Ministry of Environment). When property owners on a Belleville street complained to the board about a major reconstruction of their street on grounds of cost, amenities and safety hazards, the town justified

need using a traffic count taken while a parallel major road was blocked for construction. Rather than rejecting the application, the board merely delayed its approval until other counts were taken so that "residents can be better assured that the projections rest on substantial foundations" (re Belleville Street Construction). Similar leeway was not given to citizens in any of the 135 cases surveyed.

(8). *Support for urban growth.* Running through OMB decisions are the terminology and arguments that are always used by pro-growth, pro-development planners and politicians. All the cliches are evident in a decision regarding Scarborough's official plan which dismissed objections by saying that the area was "ripe for redevelopment," that it is not economically feasible to construct anything but high-density residential projects, and traffic increases are inevitable as a result of such projects (re Borough of Scarborough Official Plan).

(9). *A few must suffer.* The fact that individuals or groups can demonstrate that their interests will be harmed by a developer or municipal proposal does not lead the OMB to reject the project. It embraces the comforting view that all progress requires a few people to suffer for the greater good. This is stated neatly in a case where agricultural land was being rezoned to permit a private harness racing track. The board admitted the project would cause problems but said "this type of irritation to a few local ratepayers must be considered in relation to the benefits which may accrue from such a development to the municipality as a whole" (re Township of West Flamborough Official Plan).

(10) *Selective reliance on official plans.* The final leading principle in OMB decisions is a one-sided reliance on official plans. If an application for a rezoning is consistent with a previously-approved municipal official plan, this is usually conclusive grounds for OMB approval and the merits of the specific case are not dealt with (re London Restricted Area Bylaw C.P.-315(en)-109 and re London Restricted Area Bylaw C.P.-374(dq)-134). But if a project is not consistent with an official plan, an official plan amendment making it consistent is usually passed by the municipality and forwarded with the specific zoning bylaw permitting the project at the same time. Though it helps if a project was contrary to the official plan before its amendment, this is by no means taken as conclusive evidence that a project should be rejected. Official plan arguments, in other words, can occasionally be successfully used by citizen groups but only in the special case where there is a contradiction between a project and the official plan or where the plan is being amended; but official plan consistency with a project is certain trouble for a citizen group objecting to it.

Individuals and citizen groups success rates: a comparison

Importance rating	Organizations			Individuals		
	W	L	%	W	L	%
Major	-	11	0%	6	12	33%
Local	9	9	50%	23	42	39%
Minor	1	1	50%	15	6	71%
TOTAL	10	21	32%	44	60	42%

W - wins L-losses % - percentage wins

Citizen victories and issue importance

Importance rating	Municipality			Citizens			Total cases
	W	L	%	W	L	%	
Major	21	2	91%	6	23	21%	29
Local	50	23	69%	32	51	39%	83
Minor	6	4	60%	16	7	69%	23
TOTAL	77	29	73%	54	81	%	135

W - wins L-losses % - percentage wins

Types of issues and citizen success rates

Issue type	Municipality			Citizens			Total cases
	W	L	%	W	L	%	
Down-zoning	2	-	100%	2	-	100%	2
Comm. of Adjustment	5	1	83%	16	4	80%	20
Non-conforming uses	3	1	75%	5	3	63%	8
Annexation	3	-	100%	3	2	60%	5
Development: misc.	6	5	55%	5	6	46%	11
Development: indus.	2	2	50%	3	4	43%	7
Development: comm.	6	5	54%	4	7	36%	11
Development: res.	24	13	65%	13	27	33%	40
Public works	25	2	93%	3	26	10%	29
Legal issues	1	-	100%	-	2	0%	2

W - wins L-losses % - percentage wins

21 per cent. Even this low figure is misleading, however, because of the six, three were annexation hearings, a special kind of matter where citizens often get what they want, two merely resulted in delays for the municipalities opposed, and one involved the rare situation where a municipality was alongside a citizen group fighting another municipality.

In contrast municipalities do extremely well at the OMB. Their overall success rate in the 106 cases where they took a firm stand one way or another was 73 per cent. And the success rate of municipalities rose as the importance of the matter increased; it was 60 per cent on minor matters, 68 per cent on local matters, and 91 per cent on major questions.

Perhaps even more surprising is the fact that, on the whole, individuals appearing to object before the board do better than organized citizen groups. The overall success rate of individuals in the 104 cases in which they were involved was 42 per cent; but citizen groups won only 32 per cent of the the 31 cases in which they were involved. The success rate of both types of objectors declined as the importance of the case increased, but on the 18 major cases where individuals were involved their success rate was fully 33 per cent, whereas citizen groups lost *all 11* major cases they were involved in.

Citizen success rates varied considerably depending on the kind of issue they were fighting. On cases involving appeals from committee of adjustment decisions, for instance, where property owners were given permission for a major violation of a city zoning or building bylaw, complaining neighbours or residents' associations succeeded in 80 per cent of the cases. On new commercial, industrial and residential development projects, however, citizen success rates were 32 per cent, 36 per cent and 43 per cent respectively. The lowest success rate was on major municipal public works projects. There were 29 cases of this kind in 1973, and citizens won just three of them — a 10 per cent success rate.

Behind these overall statistics are remarkable differences in the success rates of citizens in front of different OMB members. In 1973 there were 14 OMB members who heard the 135 analyzed cases, and the success rate of citizens before these members ranged from 0 to 63 per cent. The most pro-citizen decisions that year came from D. Jamieson, the member of longest standing on the board. A former municipal planner, Jamieson heard thirteen cases on his own and citizens won nine of them. In three other decisions he combined with other board members who wrote the judgments; and of these three citizens won one. Two other board members, F. G. Blake and S. S. Speigel, both accountants, decided in favour of citizens more than half the time. At the other end of the scale is lawyer W. H.J. Thompson who heard three cases and decided against citizens in all three.

In spite of this great range, there is little use that citizens can make of these figures even though they may influence the decisions of the board's chairman, W. H. Palmer, on which board member is assigned to important cases. The member who is to hear a case is not revealed in advance. A request for an adjournment may or may not yield another board member, and the bulk of the board members fall within the 25-40 per cent citizen success rate range.

By determining the type of issue involved and by applying to it relevant leading principles of OMB decisions, it ought to be possible for citizen groups to make a very good guess about their chances of success in an OMB hearing. It is the kind of case, and the kind of challenge which citizens pose to the policies of the provincial government at Queen's Park and the local politicians and planners — and not the strength of the citizens' objections — that seems most important in their chances of success. Objecting to a committee of adjustment decision in favour of a small-time developer on a matter of purely local importance, a citizen group can be reasonably confident of success, although it may be better for individuals to go as individuals rather than as an organization. But fighting a private developer who has the municipality on his side is a chancy business at best. And fighting a public developer, or some public works project like a new library, a new expressway or a new swimming pool, is about as close to a lost cause as citizens can get. The main benefit of forcing an OMB hearing is the benefit of delay, of playing for time in case there is a local election or enough pressure that forces politicians to change their mind.

As for the province, the OMB seems a perfectly-tuned policy institution. It gives angry citizens a second chance to fight when they lose, it gives them the appearance (though often not, as the statistics indicate, the substance) of a fair and impartial hearing, and it siphons off anger and political energy that might otherwise be devoted to organizing local election campaigns or fighting for real local government reform. The citizens can be allowed to win quite a few small issues when no big interests are at stake, but not many big ones. The province can be sure that its interests, its policies, and its basic commitments to growth, to development and to the land development industry are respected and promoted. Developers may get upset when they lose the occasional case, and municipal politicians may not always appreciate having to live under the benevolent provincial thumb. But the system works well for everyone on the winning side, and the losers win just often enough to keep on playing fair.

Neighbourhood improvement: What it means in Calgary, Vancouver and Toronto

This article has been prepared by the editors of City Magazine with the help of Donald Gutstein (Vancouver), Jack Long (Calgary) and Dorothy McIntosh (Toronto).

Early in 1973, the Liberal government unveiled the Neighbourhood Improvement Program (NIP), billing it a dynamic and sensitive approach to the rehabilitation of older, lower-income, residential neighbourhoods. Concurrent with NIP was the Residential Rehabilitation Assistance Program (RRAP) which offered loans and grants varying with income to owners of residential buildings for rehabilitation purposes.

The new stress on rehabilitation was in response to a complex set of economic, social and political forces at work in urban Canada beginning in the mid- and late sixties. For one thing, the Central Mortgage and Housing Corporation (CMHC), the principal funder of urban renewal, began to recognize that renewal costs were escalating at a phenomenal rate in the late sixties. Huge financial commitments had been made into the 1970s.

More apparent was the strong and vocal public dissatisfaction with the existing urban renewal programmes, which ostensibly were designed to revitalize rundown urban areas but in the process destroyed long-time, primarily working-class communities. The designation of areas for urban renewal heralded, without fail, the disintegration and demoralization of entire communities as owners and landlords recognized their temporary status and ceased to maintain and improve their properties. Even more damaging was the wholesale expropriation and destruction in urban renewal areas of significant stocks of housing owned and occupied by low-income families, many of whom being unable to compete in the private market, were then forced to seek rental accommodation in public housing.

The utter failure of urban renewal in Canada finally came to a political head in the late sixties when the Hellyer Task Force on Housing and Urban Development succeeded in putting a freeze on urban renewal in the autumn of 1968 which was reconfirmed by the federal government the following year.

At about the same time as these events were occurring, strong citizen groups were emerging in several parts of Canada as a reaction against the arbitrary destructiveness of government-initiated urban renewal schemes. In Vancouver, the Strathcona Property Owners and Tenants Association (SPOTA) was instrumental in halting further destruction of a community in which one-third of the homes had already been demolished. Instead, a programme for rehabilitation was demanded which led, after a year of foot-dragging by city council, to the establishment of a Strathcona Working Committee composed of SPOTA members and representatives of all three levels of government. The committee came up with a programme emphasizing rehabilitation and the upgrading of existing facilities. This programme, completed in the spring of 1974, resulted in an amazing physical and psychological transformation of the area, although in the process it drove up land values to the point where many of the original inhabitants could no longer afford to live there.

In Toronto, citizen groups had succeeded in becoming involved, despite city council reservations, in the planning of three inner city neighbourhoods designated as urban renewal areas — Kensington, Don Vale and Trefann Court. Unlike the traditional plans produced by city hall planners, the involvement of residents created plans intended to conserve and improve existing neighbourhoods instead of destroying them. They dealt with the residential neighbourhood in a comprehensive manner, developing policies not only related to the repair and renovation of houses but also dealing with public works such as roads and lanes, services such as garbage collection and police, and community facilities such as recreation centres and schools. The Trefann Court experience has been thoroughly documented in Graham Fraser's book, *Fighting Back.*

In Calgary, the primarily working-class community of Inglewood emerged as a model for subsequent funding programmes such as NIP and RRAP. Citizens of Calgary refer to this area, the oldest in the city, as East Calgary and the term is synonymous with slum, despite the natural beauty of the area. Within the community's boundaries are quiet neighbourhoods, a variety of light and heavy industries, old retail and commercial enterprises, an almost impossible web of railway trackage, and some of the city's first old sandstone schools. Continual expansion of industrial uses since the Second World War coupled with the planning of a major freeway system through the area in more recent years has meant continuing neighbourhood deterioration and erosion of the residential community. Beginning in the late 1960s, however, the community had developed a growing awareness that it needed to gather its forces if it was to survive. A local voluntary resource group was formed to foster a community participation process and to produce a community plan. The process was very much a departure from the traditional planning model especially, in that it was designed to remove the old-style approach of the "professional planning for the people" and instead successfully substituted a philosophy of "everyman a planner".

Through the early 1970s, the Inglewood community was involved in a number of successful projects including a two-year community-oriented, experimental pre-school programme; a joint effort with the city to integrate as sensitively as possible a freeway through the community; Local Initiatives Program grants obtained to assist in carrying out the planning programme; a three-day community summer festival that reaffirmed the community's desire to plan for and ensure its own future; a community participation programme with Mount Royal College and the University of Calgary.

There were several enduring results from all these activities. First, the Inglewood community was creating a new shared interest in its future Second, it was learning to work effectively with resource people and government. Third, it began to understand a whole range of political, psychological and economic issues — the meaning and necessity for persistence, the value of strategy, the need for a plan, the cost factors involved in projects, the commitments required, when to fight, when to apply pressure, and when to compromise. Fourth, it proved to itself and to others that community people with intimate local knowledge can contribute to the resolution of planning problems, that citizens possess a very close identity to their community because of a deep, emotional commitment. All that was required was a process whereby this commitment could be harnessed as positive and creative energy for the community.

Near the end of 1972, CMHC, after refusing earlier requests for financial assistance, finally came through with funds to assist the community in preparation of a plan. The plan included a resolution to existing traffic problems, land use controls, housing objectives, etc. — all the usual ingredients of a local plan. However, what set it apart was the continuing emphasis on the human element and community values. These prevailed throughout the entire plan. In short, it was a legitimate grass roots effort that produced a plan which was officially approved by the city in the summer of 1973. The community now had a shared perception of what its future should be and how such a desired future could be achieved.

As these events were occurring, the federal Liberal government saw the new trend towards rehabilitation of inner city neighbourhoods as an opportunity for building their waning political strength in Canada's urban areas. For example, in Vancouver, much of the Strathcona area lies in the riding of Liberal M.P. Ron Basford, who as Minister of Urban Affairs was responsible for setting up the Neighbourhood Improvement Program. With support declining in other parts of his constituency, Basford relied more heavily on the middle-class Chinese community. He could see that, as a result of local improvement, the original inhabitants, often supporters of the New Democratic Party, were being replaced by more affluent voters likely to support the Liberal party. The same kind of programme would be desirable in other parts of his constituency and in other threatened or potential Liberal ridings.

The Strathcona experience also had implications at the municipal level. The visibly successful results made the city hall planners and politicians believe that they had become experts on the subject and knew what was needed in other parts of Vancouver to improve housing conditions. The planners did not have any of the doubts or difficulties that might have plagued other cities about improvement. They simply used the planning studies done during the old urban renewal days and updated them for NIP. Thus they felt prepared to jump in and give Vancouverites what they really needed.

NIP: FROM CONCEPTION TO POLICY

The failure of old-style urban renewal combined with the rise of vocal, action-oriented citizen groups forced public officials at all levels of government to reevaluate their policies and programmes. This was especially true of the Central Mortgage and Housing Corporation, the principal funder of the programmes. Initially, the staff members at CMHC responsible for developing a new approach to urban renewal supported a trend towards neighbourhood or community assistance and a movement away from simply revamping the old urban renewal approach. The objective of the community assistance approach, as originally envisaged by OMHC staff, was to centre on the need for neighbourhood stabilization — to reduce the social disruption often associated with urban renewal, to strategically intervene so as to break the cycle of events which normally leads to neighbourhood deterioration, to encourage community participation in the larger municipal planning process and to promote the preservation of historically interesting neighbourhoods in terms of their diverse cultures, age groupings and so on.

Accordingly, the elements necessary to achieve these kinds of objectives placed an emphasis on (a) planning at the neighbourhood level; (b) rehabilitation as opposed to razing; (c) basic infrastructure needs, and (d) community facilities and services. The mood of the early authors of the proposed neighbourhood improvement legislation in the now-defunct Policy Planning Division of CMHC was bold and imaginative, with little emphasis on cumbersome delivery mechanisms, bureaucratic checks and balances and administrative red tape. In short, the early pre-programme bias seems to have been getting funds to neighbourhoods in need, as quickly and as directly as possible, so that the community might develop its own planning process and articulate its own objectives and aspirations.

Given these laudable principles and objectives, it is difficult to account for the changes which transformed the elements of a potentially exciting idea in 1971 into the cumbersome, frustrating and watered-down programme which was launched in 1973. In fact, however, this transformation serves to illustrate how powerful senior bureaucrats and economists within CMHC and elsewhere in the federal government, can pervert a programme concept into a programme destined to make only conservative career public servants and Liberal Party supporters happy. The need to negotiate provincial-federal master agreements, the neighbourhood designation process required to be conducted by the municipality, the subsequent delay of governments at all levels in mobilizing themselves to deliver the programme to the neighbourhood and the complex, multi-stage approval process — all the current elements of the programme — are time-consuming and frustrating to local residents. As well, the rather cavalier view of most CMHC and municipal officials as to what constitutes citizen participation and a satisfactory neighbourhood planning process also tends to cast serious doubt on just how vigorously these principles are being promoted through the legislation. Questions have also been raised which suggest that many municipalities merely use NIP funds to substitute for municipal funds already ear-marked for the improvement of neighbourhood infrastructure, community services and facilities, etc. This tends to bastardize the intention of the CMHC legislation — namely to provide federal aid above and beyond existing municipal or provincial programmes or budgets in an attempt to stabilize and revitalize urban neighbourhoods.

The clearest indicator of real federal interest in this matter is the relatively insignificant sum of money allocated by CMHC for this programme. Specific funding figures for NIP across Canada are left purposefully vague with the excuse that this programme is an experimental one which should remain flexible, not fixed and definitive. What is clear, however, is that NIP spending is considerably less than for the previous urban renewal programme. For example, $17-million was allocated to Ontario in 1973 and $13-million for 1974 and 1975 respectively. Given that this was to be shared by about 27 municipalities, the funds available were paltry indeed. Compare this to the approximately $6-million given to Trefann Court, an area of only a few blocks, in the late sixties under urban renewal.

Compounding the uncertainty regarding the impact and utility of NIP and RRAP is CMHC's determined unwillingness to participate in a comprehensive, multi-dimensional evaluation of these two new programmes. Consequently, with the ex-

While residents of Vancouver's Kitsilano area worried about how to use $1.2-million in NIP funds to preserve their neighbourhood, developers like Daon Developments were demolishing houses like these.

ception of the crudest of CMHC-developed indicators, no one in Canada, and most certainly no one at CMHC, is capable of commenting on the real social, political and economic effects of these programmes let alone how they could be improved.

In sur ary, the NIP legislation, despite the idealistic intentions of its early designers, does not appear to be a significant response to a crucial urban problem. This is the experience of three cities — Vancouver, Calgary and Toronto — whose NIP projects we examine here.

THE VANCOUVER EXPERIENCE

In February, 1974, the Vancouver City Planning Department produced its report, "Neighbourhood Improvement in Vancouver," which designated eight inner residential areas as potential candidates for NIP. Three million dollars was requested from the senior governments for 1974, and this was received in mid-March.

Up to this point Vancouver citizens had no idea this money existed, let alone have any say in deciding what should be done with it. Nor were citizens any more involved in selecting from amongst the eight originally proposed areas the one or two that would receive funding for 1974. That was done by the city planners and politicians to suit their own needs. They selected the entire area of Kitsilano and a portion of Cedar Cottage to receive respectively $1.2-million and $1.8-million.

Why was an area such as Kitsilano designated for NIP? If the purpose of NIP was to preserve stable areas then Kitsilano should never have been selected, because it is not stable (i.e. undesirable for private redevelopment). As Vancouver continues to grow at a phenomenal rate, to expand its retailing activities and office functions, great pressure has been put on inner areas such as Kitsilano for accommodation to suit downtown-oriented people. The traditional residents of the area, working-class and lower middle-class families, are being rapidly displaced by the more affluent singles and childless couples who can live in smaller bachelor and one-bedroom units and who can afford to pay much more for that accommodation. Thus developers see many opportunities for profitable redevelopment. In fact, large parts of Kitsilano were, by 1974, already lost to bulldozers, even though the majority of houses are only 50 to 60 years old.

If, on the other hand, the purpose of the programme was to prevent unstable areas from deteriorating further and to bring a degree of stability to an area, then Kitsilano should not have been selected either, because areas such as Fairview, on the slopes above False Creek, were in much greater danger than Kitsilano. In fact, the Fairview Residents Association and Community Action Society (FRACAS), the major citizen group in Fairview, pleaded with city hall to designate Fairview as a NIP area immediately, because it was in such great danger of imminent redevelopment. In addition, FRACAS wanted a freeze on development and a downzoning to preserve the many older houses

And replacing them with small, high-priced condominiums like the building which actually went up on this site.

that were succumbing to the bulldozer. However, city council and its TEAM majority turned its back on the Fairview slopes (where TEAM alderman Geoff Massey, TEAM Parks Board Chairman Art Cowie and TEAM fund raiser Rand Iredale were property owners), thereby condemning the older houses to demolition and high-priced redevelopment.

Instead, the city planners chose Kitsilano. Could this have been because the city planner who wrote the report on Neighbourhood Improvement in Vancouver was the same planner who was to be assigned to Kitsilano as its local area planner? Over the previous year the city has been engaged in pushing its Local Area Planning programme (LAP) as a means of bringing public participation into the planning process. The local citizens' committees that were set up had no decision-making power. That remained where it always had, in the hands of city council. City council and the planners saw it was a good idea to tie NIP to LAP. It was well known that nothing turns off the average citizen more than interminable meetings discussing abstract planning issues. The NIP money could be used as bait to get more citizens out to meetings. Thus NIP was used to help LAP work. And because a structure for "citizen participation" had already been set up, LAP was used to help NIP work.

Cedar Cottage, the other 1974 NIP area, was selected for different reasons. It was stable — that is to say, developers were not interested in redeveloping the area. It did not have a local area planning programme underway. But it had been the subject of city planning studies for many years. As

one city planning assistant said: "We already knew the problems in the area." Here too, the planners could expect to achieve good results with NIP. And achieving good results was important if the city expected to receive more NIP funds.

With the area selected and the money allocated, the citizen input stage worked smoothly in both areas with few hitches. A volunteer committee was established in Cedar Cottage which began to meet in July 1974. In Kitsilano, a citizen planning committee had already been set up under LAP and it too began considering how to spend the NIP money at about the same time. In both areas the committees met weekly for a number of months. Public meetings were called from time to time, for wider community pariticipation, but it was mainly the committee members themselves who put forward the NIP suggestions. Some bitter infighting developed in the Kitsilano committee over the spending of the money. The more conservative ratepayer groups' representatives wanted the money to go to the community centre which they dominated. The moderate and progressive groups represented on the committee wanted all the money to go into low-income housing and daycare facilities. The ratepayers' groups themselves opposed both of these because (a) they feared low income housing would attract people on welfare and hence lower their property values and (b) they believed that all mothers should stay at home with their children. Although the moderate and progressive elements commanded a majority on the committee, the planners and politicians made it clear that they would not approve a recommenda-

This senior citizens' housing was promoted by the Kitsilano Area Resources Association, and the seniors were involved in planning and designing the building right from the beginning.

These frame houses are typical of those in the duplex and conversion transition zone of Kitsilano where city zoning policy contradicts the preservation orientation of the NIP project.

tion that all the NIP money go into daycare facilities and low-income housing. Thus a compromise was fashioned in which 70 per cent would go for housing and daycare and 30 per cent to the community centre and for mini-parks.

The Cedar Cottage committee did not exhibit the same polarization of concern, but its final recommendations were surprisingly similar to those of the Kitsilano committee: slightly less than one-third for housing for seniors and physically handicapped, about one-third for parks and beautification, about one-third to the Grandview centre and a small amount toward traffic improvements.

The recommendations from both groups were finalized and endorsed by Vancouver city council unchanged at the end of October 1974. They next went to the province and from there to CMHC. In both Cedar Cottage and Kitsilano, subcommittees were set up to deal with the various areas of funding. Some of the smaller projects in the Cedar Cottage area are now already close to being implemented: improving the traffic situation, beautification, park and playground projects. Housing subcommittees have been working closely with the city planners in the site selection process. The city has been acquiring potential sites which it will then make available to non-profit and co-operative groups at a cost in some cases of 50 per cent of what the city paid.

Given the well-known inflexibility of government bureaucracies, there does appear to have been a genuine attempt to involve the residents of designated areas in selecting projects which they felt would improve their communities. But what does NIP really offer to the citizens of Vancouver? In all the controversy swirling around the programme, one fact seems to have been lost. There was so little money available for the programme that it could not have any serious effect in improving neighbourhoods. One of the participants in the Kitsilano programme called it "tease" money. "NIP raised your hopes about the future of your community, but what could you really accomplish, for example, with $584,000 for housing, when the average selling price of a house in Kitsilano was $50,000-$75,000, and when the city was keeping tight reins over what properties would be bought?"

True, the Residential Rehabilitation Assistance Program (RRAP) was providing grants and loans up to $5,000 for home improvements in NIP areas, and this was having some effect in Kitsilano. Little effort was being made, however, to ensure that landlords who used RRAP money did not raise their rents after renovating their buildings. And, of course, housing prices were bound to escalate even further. Clearly, NIP would not prolong the life of a community if it was seen as desirable for redevelopment by the private sector. And, indeed, small-scale redevelopment has been occurring at

> ...' At least in urban renewal we had the bulldozer to organize around. Now they've even taken that away from us.'

an increasingly rapid pace in Kitsilano.

Is the Neighbourhood Improvement Program in Vancouver an improvement over the old urban renewal days? Most city hall planners and politicians answer with an unqualified yes. They feel that NIP is more selective and flexible. And they are very happy with the public participation. But one resident of Fairview who had been involved in the unsuccessful attempt to have Fairview designated for NIP feels that the programme has a more insidious side to it. As she put it: "At least in urban renewal we had the bulldozer to organize around. Now they've even taken that away from us."

CALGARY'S
INGLEWOOD-RAMSAY PROJECT

"The Neighbourhood Improvement Program purports to respond to community needs, but it can't deliver; federal, provincial and municipal governments' perceptions of community needs are not the real community needs." So comments an early and knowledgeable participant in the Inglewood-Ramsay NIP experience. This was not stated as an indictment of government, but a plea for a more sensitive response to a badly needed programme.

As outlined earlier, Inglewood had been involved in a serious grass roots effort for five years prior to NIP. It had succeeded in reversing a process destined to exterminate the community. This, in turn, brought a new dimension of perception to the residents in which they felt some control over their own destiny. They had organized, with the assistance of a locally based resource group, an innovative planning process that was having substantial success. It was a community ready for, needing and meeting the perceived substance of the new legislation.

In anticipation of the NIP and RRAP programmes and their apparent usefulness in fulfilling the aspirations of the Inglewood community, the local residents and their resource group sought the city's

On this page: houses in Calgary's Inglewood-Ramsay NIP area.

official support in designating their neighbourhood in advance of the legislation's passage. The administration was reluctant to make such a move; procedurely it was not in order as the legislation did not yet officially exist. City council decided otherwise, because there was a need irrespective of a programme. They approved the Inglewood designation in advance of the legislation and advised Ottawa of their move.

Alberta was the first province to negotiate a NIP and RRAP master agreement with the federal government. The signing of this agreement resulted in the designation of one NIP neighbourhood in Edmonton and one in Calgary — Inglewood-Ramsay. The budget for the latter was $1,500,000.

Ramsay, a neighbouring community, was named as a joint recipient of the grant despite the fact that it had never been a part of the neighbourhood planning process carried out by Inglewood citizens. In fact, Ramsay was way behind in terms of community organization and development and at that point in time nothing in that community could be seriously equated with the community participation and organization of Inglewood.

The 'piggy-back' involvement of Ramsay held up the process of organizing and planning in Inglewood considerably. Fortunately, these problems have now been overcome for the most part. However, this did not start to happen until both parties realized that all three levels of government

were waiting for them to get their houses in order. In fact, this was an excuse for bureaucratic delay — certainly there was no assistance forthcoming to help resolve a delicate situation.

There were no significant problems with the federal legislation itself, as it was presented, from the community's point of view. It would reinforce the kind of programme already initiated in Inglewood which would breathe new life into an older inner-city neighbourhood. But it was soon clear that the awareness of the value of the new legislation was only understood at the neighbourhood level — not the three levels of government responsible for administering the programme.

This was one of the major problems for the local area. Indeed it would not have been too difficult to rectify if there had been an honest effort to make the programme succeed and if the three levels of government had given the programme a genuine community focus. In other words, the approach could have been to get behind the local community and reverse the normal process of administrating from the 'top-down'. This perhaps would also have been the only way to lessen the parrying and dissension that presently exists between Calgary and the province, and between Alberta and Ottawa over 'ownership' of the programme.

While governments frequently tend to react to new programmes with the creation of new bureaucratic empires, this has not happened to any great degree in Calgary. Rather, the municipal government has been reluctant to spend money on staff as opposed to capital projects in the communities. Yet even with this attitude it is apparent that in Calgary a few individuals within the structure have made the programme work. But the committed group is all too small.

In any event, it seemed that no level of government was prepared to deliver these new programmes despite the obvious indication that they were coming. CMHC's local office appeared to be the most poorly equipped to handle enquiries — a bizarre circumstance inasmuch as CMHC was the programmes' creator. The city, despite its pre-legislation designation of Inglewood for NIP support, was also incapable of establishing a smooth delivery mechanism for the movement of NIP funds to the neighbourhood. With respect to the Alberta government, an Inglewood participant perhaps best summed up the situation when he stated that, "Alberta may have been the first to sign a NIP agreement but they are the last to understand the programme."

This general lack of understanding or sensitivity toward the goals of the NIP programmes was best exemplified by both CMHC and the Alberta Housing Corporation when it told the Inglewood - Ramsay Community (after they had been designated to receive NIP and RRAP funds) that they could not approve public housing sites, despite the fact that the neighbourhood had specifically requested them, because both agencies felt that the neighbourhood's future was in jeopardy. The same agencies which gave the neighbourhood $1,500,000, to improve and stabilize the neighbourhood, refused public housing units because of the community's questionable future.

While NIP funds are now being employed by the joint Inglewood-Ramsay Redevelopment Centre to assist in the revitalization of both communities, their influence has been perverse and perhaps counter-productive. Ardent supporters of the legislation point to communities such as Inglewood-Ramsay or the Kingston, Ontario, experience (see *City Magazine*, Preview issue, Summer 1974) and stress its important role in assisting community organization and the fostering of local participation in neighbourhood planning. However, the Inglewood-Ramsay case would suggest precisely the opposite impact. In this case a neighbourhood that was already well organized, and functionally prepared to employ the NIP and RRAP programme to further its priorities, found itself subjected to immense bureaucratic stumbling. Where NIP should have responded to existing and well articulated community aspirations, the community instead had to accommodate NIP.

An Inglewood-Ramsay NIP participant summarizes the existing situation as follows: "The renewal of neighbourhoods in any Canadian city

should be a priority. However, NIP is a weak-kneed response to a desperate social need. And, in Calgary, the NIP programme is bottom drawer stuff."

TORONTO SOUTH OF CARLTON

The first Neighbourhood Improvement Program in Canada was created by the City of Toronto in September, 1971. The city's NIP was a response to a total absence of any intergovernmental programmes following the freeze on urban renewal funds in 1969. The main objectives of the programme were:
• ultimate municipal responsibility
• elimination of gaps and lags between planning and implementation
• continuity
• flexibility — providing both social and physical facilities
• meaningful participation of affected residents
• independent municipal funding

By the spring of 1973, three areas had been designated by city officials and programmes drawn up for housing rehabilitation, service lane improvements and the development of a variety of local facilities including a park, community health care centre and a daycare facility.

When Ottawa announced amendments to the National Housing Act which provided for a new tri-level NIP, it appeared at the time that this new programme would complement the funding and enlarge upon Toronto's own Neighbourhood Improvement Program. This seemed especially true given that emphasis was to be placed on the local municipality's role in selecting, developing and implementing neighbourhood plans. After the federal and provincial governments entered into a master agreement in December 1973, the Ontario Ministry of Housing issued an "Administrative Guide" for NIP, outlining the three-stage process of approval — neighbourhood selection, neighbourhood planning and neighbourhood implementation. Eight months later the Ministry outlined additional procedures required for NIP under the *Planning Act*, namely, that Council must designate each NIP area as a Redevelopment Area and prior to obtaining funds, a Redevelopment Plan must

---

The following list indicates the necessary approval process required for each NIP area in Ontario.

NIP as per Federal/Provincial Agreement

A. Submission of neighbourhood selection application.
    1. Provincial and Federal approvals required.
    2. Signing of Municipal/Provincial agreement.

B. Submission of neighbourhood programme planning application.
    3. Provincial and Federal approval required.
    4. Signing of Municipal/Provincial agreement.

C. Submission of neighbourhood implementation application.
    5. Provincial and Federal approval required.
    6. Signing of Municipal/Provincial agreement.

NIP as per Planning Act of Ontario.

A. Designation of Redevelopment Area
    7. Provincial approval required.

B. Adoption of Redvelopment Plan (requires a public hearing).
    8. Provincial approval required (possible referral to the Ontario Municipal Board.)

---

be submitted and approved by the Minister. In all eight approvals are required for any one NIP area (see box). A brief critical of NIP which was adopted by Toronto city council in September1974, bluntly summed up the existing situation: "It is self-evident that any programme which requires such an elaborate approval process is bound to suffocate in red tape, incur great losses of time and eventually grind to a halt."

Eleven applications for Neighbourhood Improvement in Toronto were formally submitted to the Ministry of Housing in July 1974. To date, because of lengthy approval procedures as well as Ottawa's refusal in some cases to recognize neighbourhood priorities as determined by local residents, *no funds* have so far been spent in Toronto other than the portion allotted for the city's own Improvement Program.

A specific case study of local frustration with the tri-level Improvement Program is South of Carlton, a densely populated community skirting Toronto's downtown core. Once the home of the wealthy, its attractive, turn-of-the-century houses are now a major source of accommodation for people on low incomes. A high proportion of tenant households exists, including many single parent families. South of Carlton is also associated with the skid-row population — missions, flophouses and hotels in the area serve single men with few resources.

By far the most serious problem facing South of Carlton residents, however, is the increasing disappearance of the community's low-income housing stock. Several years ago, residents became concerned about the increasing number of high-rise projects in their area. Housing in good condition was demolished to make way for high rental buildings which threatened the old cohesive neighbourhood. In addition, prices for existing housing throughout the city have risen dramatically. In South of Carlton, this trend has been aggravated by townhousing — a process whereby real estate companies and other entrepreneurial interests buy older houses, evict the existing low-income tenants and renovate to townhouses which sell for as much as $60,000 to $80,000.

In response to these threats to the neighbourhood, an intensive planning study was initiated by the City of Toronto Planning Board, with planners assigned to work with a local citizens' committee. Among the study's major aims were (a) to ensure that future redevelopment fit in with the neighbourhood and (b) to retain South of Carlton primarily as a community for existing residents on low to moderate incomes.

Now nearing completion, the planning study will go a long way towards implementing the first objective. Realization of the second goal, however, has become virtually impossible. Ironically, the study, having acted to stabilize South of Carlton primarily as a low-density residential area, has in-

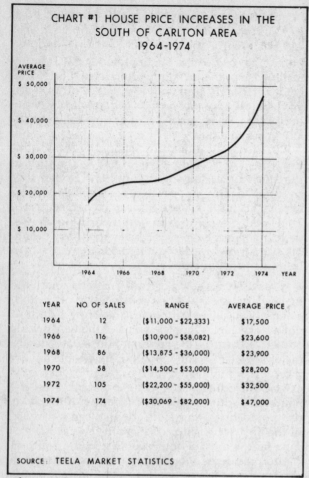

CHART #1 HOUSE PRICE INCREASES IN THE
SOUTH OF CARLTON AREA
1964-1974

YEAR	NO. OF SALES	RANGE	AVERAGE PRICE
1964	12	($11,000 - $22,333)	$17,500
1966	116	($10,900 - $58,082)	$23,600
1968	86	($13,875 - $36,000)	$23,900
1970	58	($14,500 - $53,000)	$28,200
1972	105	($22,200 - $55,000)	$32,500
1974	174	($30,069 - $82,000)	$47,000

SOURCE: TEELA MARKET STATISTICS

advertently encouraged the rise in land values.

For local residents, there has been only one solution to preserving the neighbourhood's existing population — direct intervention in the housing market. Since very little vacant land remains in the community, the sole alternative is to purchase as many of the existing houses as possible. A start in this direction has already been made. Don West Neighbours and the City of Toronto Housing Corporation, both non-profit organizations, have provided housing for South of Carlton tenants. Later efforts, however, have met with serious obstacles.

Like other inner city areas of Toronto, house prices in South of Carlton have simply risen too high to meet present requirements of the National Housing Act for subsidy of non-profit housing ventures. For example, under NHA standards, the maximum allowance for acquisition and renovation of a house containing one three-bedroom unit and one one-bedroom unit would be $50,000. Comparable costs in South of Carlton would be $60,000. It was obvious that unless extra subsidies were granted, it would be impossible under existing NHA regulations to obtain low-income housing in South of Carlton. NIP appeared to be an ideal vehicle for these subsidies since it was geared to fund such low-income residential communities.

With this issue in the forefront, South of Carlton

residents called a public meeting in May 1974 to discuss neighbourhood improvement. After an energetic and, at times, tense three-hour discussion, people overwhelmingly voted to spend most of the NIP funds to secure low-income housing. Soon after, local residents, ward aldermen and city planning staff got together to come up with an innovative proposal for South of Carlton's NIP. The programme was to use funds to lower the acquisition costs of local housing purchased by non-profit groups. At this lower cost, the non-profit groups could then bring in rents at a level most local tenants could afford.

Using NIP funds in this fashion would also avoid the antagonisms inherent in previous urban renewal ventures where valuable housing was demolished — this appeared to be just what the federal government was looking for. Accordingly, Toronto city council strongly supported the South of Carlton proposal and in July 1974 submitted it to the senior levels of government for approval.

After some months of frustration and amid rumours that Ottawa "was not happy" with the South of Carlton plans, the proposal was flatly refused. This, despite the fact that a similar proposal in Vancouver was accepted. Barney Danson, the current Minister for Urban Affairs, stated: "I cannot agree that NIP funds should be used in the manner you suggest, for I am sure you will appreciate that the end result would have the effect of using NIP funds for housing subsidies. I believe it is most important to *preserve the integrity of NIP* and to use allocated funds for the primary purpose of improving deteriorated neighbourhoods."

The South of Carlton community was astounded to learn that the retention of its low income housing stock was not regarded as an improvement! The residents' initial skepticism was confirmed. Pressing local needs identified by residents were to be ignored by Ottawa. It brought to light the fact that the federal government's perception of citizen involvement and determination of the future of their neighbourhood only went so far as the plans met with Ottawa's perception of the needs of a local area. Moreover, Ottawa insisted that the South of Carlton proposal was unnecessary since existing NHA programmes were adequate.

On March 1st, 1975, a delegation of South of Carlton residents and the area aldermen met with Urban Affairs Minister Danson in an attempt to persuade him to reconsider his decision. The Minister at that time said he agreed with the objectives of the group to preserve the housing in South of Carlton for the long-time residents of the area. He also indicated that he shared the group's frustrations in achieving these objectives.

But no firm commitment was made at the meeting. In response, area residents organized a telegram campaign from sympathetic groups across the city to apply further pressure on the govern-

While residents of Toronto's South of Carlton area were discussing NIP plans for their area, developers and high-income middle-class families were redeveloping relatively low-cost family housing into tarted-up extremely-expensive renovated "townhouses" like this one. Townhouse prices in the area are $60,000-$80,000 for houses of this kind. Federal housing minister Barney Danson has refused local residents' requests to use NIP funds to buy up unrenovated houses to keep them for moderate-income working-class families.   Photo by Bruce Kuwabara.

More developer-renovated town houses in the South of Carlton area.

ment. The response to this campaign was overwhelmingly sympathetic.

A firm and final answer was received from the Minister a month later. The Minister wrote: "I remain convinced that NIP funds cannot be used to write down the cost of property acquisition for non-profit groups." There has been some speculation that the Conservative member of the provincial legislature for a neighbouring riding, M.P.P. Margaret Scrivener, a strong opponent of local non-profit proposals for housing and health care, was instrumental in the decision to refuse funding for the acquisition of low-income housing in South of Carlton.

At a recent meeting, the Working Committee decided that to use NIP funds for area beautification would only further increase property values and displace more long-term, low-income residents of the neighbourhood. Consequently, it decided to pull out of the NIP programme altogether.

The group plans to go ahead and use city money to acquire houses in South of Carlton without the help of the other two levels of government. The experience with NIP has convinced South of Carlton residents that Ottawa and the province are not genuinely committed to effectively assisting and preserving low-income housing areas from predatory private-market prices, but rather are engaged in carrying out token, band-aid measures.

CONCLUSION

The experiences of three Canadian cities with Neighbourhood Improvement clearly reveal similar patterns. The most prominent one is that of government bureaucrats orchestrating, directing and using the programme as best suits their purpose and convenience. This has been apparent since the inception of the programme when senior management of CMHC redefined the direction of the programme in order to protect their own interest. Subsequently, local citizen groups have experienced the difficulties of dealing with bureaucracies at a number of levels. In Vancouver, this has been felt most strongly at the municipal level; in Toronto, the frustrations have primarily been concentrated at the provincial and federal level; in Calgary, all three levels have contributed to an equal degree.

Inherent in this priority for bureaucrats' interests is the fact that while funds may be poured into developing a process whereby citizen groups are encouraged to spend considerable time deciding on what their neighbourhood priorities should be, this by no means suggests that these priorities are the ones that will be implemented. That, of course, depends on the extent to which they fall within the definition of neighbourhood improvement as defined separately and, on occasion, in contradiction, by various federal, provincial and municipal administrations.

Undoubtedly, the root of the problem goes back to the original reasons for setting up Neighbourhood Improvement. The "social disruption" caused by urban renewal as vigorously voiced by community groups, coupled with the huge financial commitments made to urban renewal, called for a new programme that would appease local neighbourhoods yet at the same time cause a considerably smaller dent in CMHC's profit margin. Thus what emerges is the sense that local communities are indeed being bought off with "tease money" at the same time as governments give a semblance of being concerned with inner-city problems. In short, NIP is a government programme designed to pacify social unrest at the least possible financial cost.

Where does the involvement of local citizens come into all this? Much was made of involving local citizens in the publicity surrounding the introduction of the programme, yet little appears about it in the legislation itself. Subsequently, the experience of Canadian communities has been that this involvement occurs when the government so desires and follows the procedures that it lays down. The concept of grass roots planning as exemplified in the initial Inglewood, Calgary experience has nowhere been met. This is really not surprising given the politically potent implications inherent in such a concept, namely, of people organizing themselves and running their own neighbourhoods. (The claim of government bureaucrats that they must be there to settle intra-community differences, as have occurred in Vancouver, smacks of paternalism and only serves to consolidate their own power.)

However, the result of such a tightly-reined programme is that the flexibility required to deal with the unique problems in a particular municipality and in a particular neighbourhood is greatly decreased. As the City of Toronto brief stated: "The fundamental problem of tri-level involvement in NIP seems to be that the original concept of a flexible, responsive, municipally based programme has been lost. The major cornerstone upon which the Neighbourhood Improvement Program was to be built now seem precariously close to toppling." The Neighbourhood Improvement Program has also brought in even sharper focus a dilemma that cannot readily be resolved without strong public initiatives. This relates to the escalation of property values that follows the process of upgrading an area. As has happened in Strathcona, Kitsilano and South of Carlton, the commitment to preserve neighbourhoods through the rehabilitation of property and the upgrading of existing facilities has been partially responsible for land values so high that many working-class families can no longer afford to live there. Instead, the areas have become increasingly attractive to middle- and upper-income persons desiring to live close to downtown. Development interests, too, have gained considerably since these areas have become even more attractive for redevelopment. In the old days, urban renewal assisted developers on a massive scale; today, neighbourhood improvement continues to aid developers on a smaller, yet still significant scale. Thus, the Neighbourhood Improvement Program continues to support establishment interests while at the same time buying off certain inner city problems.

NIP costs less than the old urban renewal, and provokes less citizen resistance. That, it turns out, is what the federal Liberals meant when they announced their dynamic, sensitive approach to the rehabilitation of older low-income residential neighbourhoods.

VI Sources

Canadian urban studies: a selected bibliography

Kent Gerecke

Until recently Canadian city planning, and land policy generally, have avoided fundamental questions about the development process and have merely sought after more order. In the past few years there has emerged a new consciousness over land and planning which recognizes the political realities of city hall. This selected bibliography identifies the major Canadian books in city planning and city politics with an emphasis on this new approach.

T. Adams. *Outline of Town and City Planning*, Russell Sage, New York, 1935.
Canada's "first" city planner provides a comprehensive manual of how to plan with examples from around the world.

H. B. Ames. *City Below the Hill*, University of Toronto Press, Toronto, 1972.
A classic early study of poverty in Montreal, 1897, reprinted with an introduction by Paul Rutherford.

F. J. Artibise. *Winnipeg: A Social History of Urban Growth 1874-1914*, McGill-Queen's University Press, Montreal, 1975.
A comprehensive and sensitive urban history which shows the strong heritage of economic power in running city hall.

L. Axworthy and J. M. Gillies (eds). *The City: Canada's Prospects, Canada's Problems*, Butterworths, Toronto, 1973.
Government-academic views of urban problems which identify problems and fall short of cohesive solutions.

G. Barker, J. Penny, and W. Seccombe. *Highrise and Superprofits*, Dumont Press Graphix, Kitchener, 1973.
Using Marxist analysis this book offers the best account of Canadian housing to date.

H. Blumenfeld, *The Modern Metropolis*, Harvest House, Montreal, 1967.
Canada's foremost planning theorist writes on many aspects of cities; his more recent work on land policy deserves equal treatment.

R. W. G. Bryant. *Land: Private Property/Public Control*, Harvest House, Montreal, 1972.
Canada's leading expert on land policy reviews the alternatives from an historical perspective.

S. Budden, and J. Ernst. *The Movable Airport*, Hakkert, Toronto, 1973.
How Toronto got a tentative site for a new international airport — highlighting citizen influence and technological farce.

H. Carver. *Cities in the Suburbs*, University of Toronto Press, Toronto, (out of print), 1962.
Carver provides a strong conceptual scheme for an alternative to the suburbs which, unfortunately, was beyond Canadian planners.

H. Carver. *Compassionate Landscape*, University of Toronto Press, Toronto, 1975.
Carver's autobiography is a history of Canadian planning from inside CMHC.

J. Caulfield. *The Tiny Perfect Mayor*, James Lorimer, Toronto, 1973.
The story of the not-so-reformist "reform mayor" of Toronto, David Crombie, especially the folly of his housing policies.

D. H. Clairmont and D. W. Magill. *Africville*, McClelland & Stewart, Toronto, 1974.
An account of the life and destruction of the black community in Halifax and planned social injustice.

R. Collier. *Contemporary Cathedrals*, Harvest House, Montreal, 1975.
An account of modern major developments, such as Place Ville Marie, analogous to cathedrals, with no help for the future.

M. Daly. *The Revolution Game*, New Press, Toronto, 1970.
Canada's experiment with formalized citizen participation in the short, unhappy life of the Company of Young Canadians.

M. Dennis and S. Fish. *In Search of a Policy*, Hakkert, Toronto, 1972.
An excellent overview of Canada's housing policy documenting repeated adevice, ignored by the government, but failing to offer a complete analysis of land and development.

E. Dosman. *Indians: The Urban Dilemma*, McClelland & Stewart, Toronto, 1972.
A primer for the phenomena of urbanization of the Canadian Indian and new images of an old problem.

E. Forsey et al. (League for Social Reconstruction), *Social Planning for Canada*, University of Toronto Press, Toronto, 1975.
A reprint of the 1935 classic of Canadian socialist thought including a full discussion of national planning and an introduction and up-date by the original authors.

G. Fraser. *Fighting Back*, Hakkert, Toronto, 1972.
The classic story of Canadian urban renewal: a must for all city planners and inner-city citizens.

S. Firth. *The Urbanization of Sophia Firth*, Peter Martin Associates, Toronto, 1964.
What it is like in human terms to move from the Maritimes to Toronto.

L. O. Gertler (ed). *Planning the Canadian Environment*, Harvest House, Montreal, 1968.
Articles from the professional planning journals which highlight the evolution and background ideas of Canadian planning.

J. L. Granatstein. *Marlborough Marathon*, Hakkert, Toronto, 1971.
One street's fight against the CPR's real estate company.

D. Gutstein. *Vancouver Ltd.*, James Lorimer, Toronto, 1975.
A landmark study which shows how economic power works to run the city of Vancouver.

L. Haworth. *The Good City*, Indiana University Press, Bloomington, 1972.
An esoteric attempt to rediscover the city by a University of Waterloo professor of philosphy.

M. Hugo-Brunt. *The History of City Planning*, Harvest House, Montreal, 1972.
A history of cities with a superficial ending on Canadian planning

K. Keating. *The Power to Make it Happen*, Green Tree, Toronto, 1976.
An examination of community organizing based on a case study and a critical evaluation of "representative democracy".

H. Lithwick. *Urban Canada: Problems and Prospects*, Information Canada, Ottawa, 1970.
An analysis of Canada's urban problems from a systems perspective which misses reality as often as it hits it.

J. Lorimer. *Citizen's Guide to City Politics*, James Lorimer, Toronto, 1972.
A detailed account of who runs our cities and how, which should be required reading for all students of urban studies.

J. Lorimer. *The Real World of City Politics*, James Lorimer, Toronto, 1970.
City Politics as it happens — this should be read alongside Kaplan's *Urban Political Systems* to contrast "real" as opposed to "academic" understanding.

J. Lorimer and M. Phillips. *Working People*, James Lorimer, Toronto, 1971.
Photographic and written descriptions of the life of working people in downtown Toronto.

R. Lucas. *Minetown, Milltown, Railtown*, University of Toronto Press, Toronto, 1971.
Attitudes of small-town, urban Canada which should be understood by all planners.

S. B. McLaughlin. *100 Million Canadians*, McLaughlin Planning and Research Institute, Mississauga, 1973.
How a developer would solve all urban problems through massive growth.

J. B. Milner. *Community Planning: A Casebook of Law and Administration*, University of Toronto Press, Toronto, 1963.
The basic planning law casebook; somewhat out of date but including the "fundamentals" of planning.

D. Morton. *Mayor Howland*, Hakkert, Toronto, 1973.
Toronto's first reform mayor's efforts to make Toronto "the Good City".

Ontario Economic Council. *Subject to Approval*, Queen's Printer Province of Ontario, Toronto, 1974.
An account of the land development process in Ontario which is amazingly frank for a government document.

M. Parnell. *Rape of the Block*, Edmonton Social Planning Council, Edmonton, 1972.
A good guide to neighbourhood defence which does not turn to positive suggestions.

J. Pasternak. *The Kitchener Market Fight*, Samuel, Stevens, and Hakkert, Toronto, 1975.
Another classic urban renewal story where de-

velopers, planners, politicians and the media join forces to destroy a traditional market.

Pollution Probe. *Rules of the Game*, Pollution Probe, Toronto, 1972.
A how-to-fight-city-hall manual which outlines the development game and citizen strategies to combat it.

Pollution Probe. *The Tail of the Elephant*, Pollution Probe, Toronto, 1972.
An attempt to understand Ontario's provincial planning strategy, the Toronto Centred Region Plan, and its overwhelming effect.

A. Powell (ed). *The City: Attacking Modern Myths*, McClelland & Stewart, Toronto, 1972.
The University League for Social Reform exposes many urban myths: academic.

H. Rankin. *Rankin's Law*, November House, Toronto, 1975.
The political autobiography of a long-time radical Vancouver alderman.

B. Richardson. *The Future of Canadian Cities*, New Press, Toronto, 1972.
A journalist's scrapbook on Canadian cities which yearns for social justice but can't figure out how to achieve it.

P. Rutherford. *Saving the Canadian City*, University of Toronto Press, Toronto, 1974.
The flavour and thrusts of Canada's first urban reform phase, 1880 to 1920, including the rise of city planning and reform politics.

F. A. Schwilgin. *Town Planning Guidelines*, Department of Public Works, Ottawa, 1973.
A planning manual of the traditional variety with a Canadian flavour.

J. Sewell. *Up Against City Hall*, James Lorimer, Toronto, 1972.
Toronto's leading reform alderman tells what it is like to work for the people in city hall.

D. L. Stein. *Toronto for Sale*, New Press, Toronto, 1972.
How Toronto's city politicians are selling out the future of the city for short-run profits of developers.

L. Stinson. *Political Warriors*, Queenstron House, Winnipeg, 1975.
Recollections of a social democrat over the founding of the CCF, the rise of the NDP in Manitoba and particularly about reform politics and "Unicity" for Winnipeg.

Vancouver Urban Research Group. *Forever Deceiving You*, Vancouver, (out of print), 1972.
The first Canadian how-to-fight-city-hall manual with excellent case studies.

M. Wheeler. *The Right to Housing*, Harvest House, Montreal, 1969.
Papers from Canada's first Conference on Housing, 1968, which declared "all Canadians have the right to be adequately housed whether they can afford it or not".

J. W. Wilson. *People in the Way*, University of Toronto Press, Toronto, 1973.
The story of resettlement along the Columbia River of B.C. by the principal planner, a humanist.

J. S. Woodsworth. *My Neighbor*, University of Toronto Press, Toronto, 1972.
A reprint of Woodsworth's classic study of urban immgrants in Canada.

About the contributors

Grant Anderson graduated with a degree in urban geography from the University of British Columbia. He is currently concluding a master's degree in city planning at the University of Waterloo, specializing in planning in the inner city.

Dida Berku is a law student at McGill University and a member of CRISE.

Brian Bourns is an alderman for an inner-city ward of the City of Ottawa. He worked for the last several years as a community organizer and free-lance journalist.

Jon Caulfield is a former city hall columnist for *The Toronto Citizen* and is author of *The Tiny Perfect Mayor*.

Batya Chivers is the author of the Task Force report on the implications for Edmonton of the Commonwealth Games. She is a member of Keegano residents' organized co-op and a member of Communitas Centre for community animation and planning.

Ron Clark is a city planner who has worked for the Ministry of State for Urban Affairs and who is now director of planning for the City of Regina.

Peter Coda has for the past ten years worked as an organizer of various environmental and citizen groups.

Mike Cooper is a community planner who has extensive experience working with community groups across Canada. He is currently the Neighbourhood Improvement Program Co-ordinator for the Hillhurst-Sunnyside Community Association in Calgary.

Kent Gerecke studied planning at the University of British Columbia and the University of Waterloo. He is currently chairman of the Department of City Planning at the University of Manitoba and is a member of the editorial board of *City Magazine*.

Donald Gutstein is a graduate architect who specializes in urban research and community organizing in Vancouver. He is active in the community group in the Kitsilano area of Vancouver where he lives. He was co-author of the 1972 booklet *Forever Deceiving You*, and author of *Vancouver Ltd*. He is a member of the editorial board of *City Magazine*.

Irene Harris lives in Toronto, was director of the West End Assistance Association and a member of Pollution Probe's urban team. She was Darcy Goldrick's campaign manager and is now his assistant.

Guy LeCavalier obtained his M.A. (sociology) at Universite de Montreal and his Ph.D. at the Johns Hopkins University. A former member of the Social Research Group in Montreal and professor of sociology at the University of Ottawa, he is presently a sociologist consultant and editor of *Simgames*.

Bruce McKenna is a recent graduate of Osgoode Hall Law School, Toronto, and a former student of urban and regional planning at the University of Waterloo. He is currently articling at the Toronto law firm of Osler, Hoskin and Harcourt.

John Piper has lived in Saskatoon for ten years. A graduate of economics and geography, he has been an outspoken critic of business politics at Saskatoon City Hall.

Dave Reynolds lives in Nova Scotia and is a member of the Ecology Action Centre.

Barry Sampson and Bruce Kuwabara studied architecture at the University of Toronto from 1967 to 1972. During the last three years they have collaborated with architect George Baird on several built projects, competitions and Toronto planning studies. Bruce Kuwabara contributed to *Onbuildingdowntown* and both Kuwabara and Sampson worked on *Built Form Analysis*. Both these reports were completed for the Toronto Planning Board. Barry Sampson acted as adviser to the *Typical Block Study* for the city's St. Lawrence Housing Development.

Peter Spurr is a researcher at Central Mortage and Housing Corp. in Ottawa.

Brian Wilkes attended Western, York and Waterloo Universities and is an ecologist by training. He is presently a parks planners for the B.C. government.